Making the American Team

Sport and Society

Series Editors

Benjamin G. Rader

Randy Roberts

A list of books in the series appears at the end of this book.

★ Making the American Team
Sport, Culture, and the Olympic Experience

Mark Dyreson

University of Illinois Press

Urbana and Chicago

© 1998 by the Board of Trustees of the University of Illinois
Manufactured in the United States of America

1 2 3 4 5 C P 5 4 3 2 1

This book is printed on acid-free paper.

Library of Congress Cataloging-in-Publication Data
Dyreson, Mark, 1959–
Making the American team : sport, culture, and the Olympic
experience / Mark Dyreson.
    p.   cm. — (Sport and society)
Includes bibliographical references and index.
ISBN 0-252-02349-8 (cloth : acid-free paper).
ISBN 0-252-06654-5 (pbk. : acid-free paper)
1. Sports—Political aspects—United States. 2. Nationalism and
sports—United States. 3. Sports—Social aspects—United States.
4. Olympics—Philosophy. I. Title. II. Series.
GV706.35.D97   1998
796'.0973—dc21   97-4663
CIP

Contents

Acknowledgments

Sometimes writing is a solitary endeavor. Mostly, other people help. A great many people helped me to produce *Making the American Team*. The University of Illinois Press staff, Editor-in-Chief and Director Richard Wentworth, series editors Ben Rader and Randy Roberts, copyeditor Bruce Bethell, and the rest of the crew provided crucial editorial support. The Missouri Historical Society and the United States Olympic Committee gave me access to important archives. I would also like to thank University of Utah archivist Randy Silverman.

Friends and students somehow survived the affliction of interminable Olympic stories, especially Eleanor Duvall, Victor Eschler, Mary Bell Hill, Tom Hill, Pat Morris, Ryan Paul, and Glenn Powles. My colleagues at Weber State University, the University of Texas–Pan American, and the University of Arizona who urged me to continue to work on the project need my thanks as well: Tim Conrad, Lyall Crawford, James Dolph, Jock Glidden, Frank Guliuzza, Henry Ibarguen, Kathryn MacKay, Chris Padgett, Candadai Seshachari, Neila Seshachari, Wayne Thompson, Peter Vernezze, and Michael Wutz from Weber State; Dave Carter, Bob Frodeman, Jeffrey Mauck, Chris Miller, Hubert Miller, Sarah Neitzel, Chuck Prather, Rodolfo Rocha, Ray Welch, and Andrew Yox from the University of Texas–Pan American; and Karen Anderson, Richard Cosgrove, Harwood Hinton, Paul Hirt, John Mering, C. W. Miller, and Virginia Scharff from the University of Arizona (I express my gratitude also for the help given by the late James Donohoe, also from the University of Arizona). Each of you helped me to finish. The Weber State University Research, Scholarship, and Professional Growth Committee, including Brook Arkush, Linda Eaton, Sue Harley, and Gary Malecha, supported this book.

Many colleagues read all or portions of the manuscript and helped me to hone my arguments. I would especially like to thank Melvin Adelman, Bill Baker, Norm Baker, Bob Barney, Richard Crepeau, Andy Doyle, Gerald Gems,

Larry Gerlach, Elliot Gorn, Allen Guttmann, Stephen Hardy, Colin Howell, Peter Levine, John Lucas, Patrick Miller, John Nauright, S. W. Pope, Steve Riess, Nancy Struna, and David Wiggins for their insights and scholarly support. As it always does, the North American Society for Sport History provided a great environment for introducing the ideas that became this book.

Paul Carter, Juan Garcia, and George Brubaker were there at the beginning when this began as a master's thesis. Donald Mrozek served as an insightful reader and sage adviser throughout the book-making process. Ben Rader provided cogent reading and editing for the project.

My brothers Eric, Curtis, and Arn suffered gracefully when I inflicted chapters on them. My mother and father, Margaret and Delmar Dyreson, did the same. My wife, Jodella Kite Dyreson, took time away from her own book projects to read and critique every line.

Making the American Team

Introduction

Most Americans know more about sport and sports than they do about politics, science, religion, or their own Constitution. They discuss sports with friends, relatives, and strangers with more passion and conviction than they do any other subject. "Who won the game?" breaks more silences than any other imaginable query. Common across class, race, and sometimes even gender lines, sport talk and metaphors pervade American discourse. "If there is a common language in socially atomized, economically stressful, morally wandering America, it revolves around sports," ruminates Harrison Rainie in a late twentieth-century effort to gauge the national temper.[1]

The omnipresence of sport in American life perplexes, confounds, and irritates many critics. The sporting illiterate constitute a tribe of social outcasts more untouchable than smokers. Sport haters find themselves labeled "un-American." Still, even though sport has become the most important institution through which many Americans deliberate political, racial, ethical, and social questions, scholars too rarely take sport seriously.

That failure to consider sport seriously has hampered historical understandings of the United States, for the grand experiment in forging a working republic in this nation has become permeated with the cultural practices of modern athletics in myriad ways: politicians persistently frame their messages in athletic rhetoric; African American Olympians protest their exclusion from republican promises with black-gloved protests against racism; judges hear frequent cases about the constitutional rights of athletes, teams, and sporting leagues; and Olympic basketball and hockey contests serve as defining moments in American foreign policy.

More than two hundred years after the founding of the republic, sport provides American life its most popular forum for discussing crucial social and political questions. Athletic debates find their structure in a variety of political notions, including conceptions of race, gender, and class; theories of equity, power, and fairness; and ideas about personality, character, and ethics. This would probably have surprised the nation's founding fathers. Although the elites who constructed the American republic sought to establish institutions that would foster public virtue and to create mechanisms for citizen participation in political and social issues, they never dreamed of a future in which athletic games and contests would spark so many robust civic dialogues and define the meanings of their republic.

The title for this book, *Making the American Team*, signifies a new perspective for thinking about the relationship between sport and nationalism. It indicates that sport was made, or invented, to serve a purpose. That purpose had an intimate connection to the construction of an American team—a national identity for the United States. In making an American team, Americans invented a sporting republic. The idea of a sporting republic challenges readers to consider sport in two new ways. I use the idea of inventing something to indicate that I think of sport as a "technology." The concept of a sporting republic signals my assertion that sport is intimately related to the way in which people understand power. Sport and the political philosophy of republicanism have been directly connected in American history. In spite of some popular misconceptions, sport and politics have never been separate entities in American life. The purpose of this study is to develop these two ideas and explore the connections between them. Sport was an invention designed to meet certain political goals. Those goals are best understood in the context of ideas and beliefs about the nature of the American republic.

Reconsider Harrison Rainie's assertion that in the late twentieth-century United States, sport provides the only common language for a "socially atomized, economically stressful, morally wandering" nation. Rainie directly confronts the political sensibilities of his readers. He warns that the nation no longer shares a common sense of purpose. Indeed, his argument serves as a republican "jeremiad," a warning to a people who have lost their way, one of the most enduring political messages in American history. It offers through sport a way to rebuild a sense of community, which is one of the fundamental requirements for the survival of the republican experiment. Rainie's jeremiad acknowledges that participating in sport as players and spectators represents ways for taking part in an essentially political process.

That is precisely why a group of American intellectuals and writers more than a century ago formulated the idea that sport is a powerful public technology. In the late nineteenth and early twentieth centuries, a critical mass of American thinkers began to argue that modern sport is one of the most important tools for shaping human societies. Those thinkers created a conversation in which American ideas about sport and republics became inextricably linked.

Through an expanding national print media, much of the American public shared in those conversations. Many Americans came to see sport as a powerful reform instrument that could revitalize their rapidly modernizing nation.

These intellectuals espoused ideas that mixed sport into the struggles between classes, races, ethnic groups, and genders. They announced that sport would reconstitute popular representative government, restore equity in American society, and rejuvenate public virtue. They argued that sport would create a common set of values. In short, in the grand tradition of American political philosophy, they made universal promises about the power of sport to reinvigorate the republican experiment.

In this study the idea of a republic reflects the actual social discourses of American thinkers. It also serves to connect sport and politics. Republican ideas about representative democracy, social mores, the commonweal, and civic virtue shaped American conceptions of sport. American ideas about sport shaped the dialogue about the nature of the American republic. The idea of a sporting republic represents both the popular American fascination with sport and the intersection of political and athletic ideas in American minds.

The American thinkers who developed the idea of the sporting republic understood their creation as an invention. They believed quite literally in an athletic technology with the power to shape human environments. Of course, technologies have always influenced the sporting practices of human cultures. Some technologies have been employed as essential ingredients in athletic games, whereas other technologies have been designed to enhance athletic performance. Moreover, certain technologies have created opportunities for spectators to watch sporting contests. In addition to acknowledging such technological influences on sport, however, some cultures have considered sport to *be* a social technology designed to reconfigure social patterns. Between 1876 and 1919 many American thinkers conceived of sport as social technology. They invented a sporting republic.

The idea of sport as a technological system may seem rather startling at first glance. Remember, however, that technologies are not just machines and "made" things—inanimate objects. Technologies are also organizations of human energy designed for problem solving. Since the rise of agricultural civilizations, armies and navies have been important human social technologies. More recently public schools have been employed as social technologies. The advocates of modern sporting ideologies express their belief that sport is a social technology when they promise that sport will teach people the value of team play and cooperation, assimilate immigrants and colonized peoples, prevent crime and behavioral deviance, transmit the values of fair play and regulated competition, spark nationalism, ameliorate racial divisions, smooth over class tensions, temper gender differences, or rescue the inhabitants of technological civilization from the artificial sterility of the machine process. Whether or not they overestimated the power of sport to change society, many of the late nineteenth- and twentieth-century promoters of athletics considered sport to be the most significant social technology for shaping modern cultures.

Thinking about sport as a technology helps to explain sport's omnipresence in modern human cultures. Sport functions as a language system in regional, national, and international societies. The language of sport provides modern cultures with opportunities to communicate about a wide variety of issues. Sport gives powerful groups symbol systems for engineering social consensus. It also arms less powerful groups with symbol systems to threaten the establishment. Many promoters of sport insist that the language of sport is one of the most important educational vehicles available to modern cultures. Sport can communicate important traditions and ideas, influence public opinion, and shape politics. Sport, as an athletic technology, provides a critical force for shaping modern cultures.

The American inventors of the sporting republic were not operating in a historical vacuum. Indeed, during the nineteenth and twentieth centuries, industrializing nations around the globe have used sport as social technology. In modern technological civilizations monumental architecture devoted to sport reappeared for the first time since the coliseums and ball courts of the classical civilizations of antiquity. Giant stadiums sprang up in industrial cities. Spectators by the thousands filled those stadiums to witness amateur and professional sports. Sporting goods manufacturing and the sale of sporting events became big businesses.

Modern social processes organized, regularized, centralized, and nationalized sport. Modern transportation and communication revolutions transformed sport and radically increased its capacity as a social technology. The rise of national print media made reading the sports pages a daily habit for millions of newspaper subscribers. Sports sections crowded mass-circulation dailies. Magazines and journals published regular essays on athletics. Publishing houses produced a tremendous volume of pamphlets and books about sport. An international press corps promoted national sporting rivalries. The widespread conversations generated about sport in the United States, in the Anglo-American world, and around the globe created a climate in which the sporting republic could flourish.

The most important American discourses about sport and politics focused on the Olympic Games. The modern Olympic Games were made possible in large part by new communication and transportation technologies that allowed athletes from around the world to compete in the Olympic contests and spectators from around the world to witness the results. More than any other event or institution, the creation of the modern Olympics in 1896 produced one of modern civilization's most important national spectacles. At center stage in those spectacles, "America's athletic missionaries" performed Olympian feats. The American media lionized their deeds. American thinkers explained Olympic championships as triumphs of republican civilization. The American public devoured tales of national prowess and celebrated Olympian achievement. Within the process of inventing a sporting republic, the Olympic Games provided the most important symbols for making sport the nation's common civic language.

In the period between 1876 and 1919, a great many American thinkers and much of the public thought that sport could build a strong sense of community in a nation in which modernization threatened the commonweal on which the republican experiment depended. Sport was not the only tool they considered for constructing a national community. Various reformers promoted public schools, offered democratic political reforms, designed new economic systems, championed labor organizations, supported socialism, and floated many other schemes as the secrets to forging a modern national community. Some even proposed war. Indeed, in 1876, the centennial of the republic's founding, most Americans would have identified war as the catalyst that propelled the United States headlong toward modernity. The Civil War, concluded only eleven years earlier, had radically changed the United States. The war had wrecked antebellum America's regional political, cultural, social, and economic systems and created new national structures. It made baseball—a New England and New York game—into a national pastime. It forged national communities of commerce and industry and produced national fraternal organizations and war widows' groups. The Civil War loomed in American imaginations as the great national crusade, the most important community-building event of the nineteenth century and perhaps of all American history.

In the five decades following the Civil War, many critics decried the republic's declining communal fabric as the great plague of modernity, but although some national leaders called for "splendid little wars" to rekindle the national sense of purpose they remembered so vividly from the bloodletting between 1861 and 1865, no one seriously proposed another civil war. After all, although the Civil War had created new possibilities for a national community, it had done so at a horrendous cost. It not only created communities but also destroyed them. Any Southerner could testify to that reality. Indeed, virtually everyone in the United States knew one of the 620,000 people who perished in the war and so could testify to that reality. The Civil War very nearly destroyed the republic. War on a large scale, and especially another civil war, did not seem like a realistic technology for building a modern national community in the United States.

Was there, Americans wondered, a healthy substitute for war? Could a nation invent a social technology that would bring all war's positive benefits to the republic—robust vitality, civic engagement, grand purpose, commitment to high ideals, energetic nationalism, abundant and exciting life—without any of war's negative consequences? Responding to that seemingly impossible task, a group of American thinkers invented the sporting republic. Influenced mightily by their work, the philosopher William James in 1910 formally declared sport to be a moral equivalent for war.[2] In 1876 Bull Run, Shiloh, Antietam, Gettysburg, and the Wilderness marked the hallowed fields on which modern nationhood had been dearly purchased. The major battles of the new moral equivalence for war would be fought on Olympic playing fields at Athens, Paris, St. Louis, London, and Stockholm. In such arenas, to echo an old American cliché, winning was indeed everything.

★ 1

Inventing the Sporting Republic

Between the centennial celebration of their nation's founding and the end of World War I, Americans used sport to debate the meaning of their republic. During that period sport became one of the most important institutions in American civilization. Sport fostered discussions about questions that rested at the heart of the republican experiment. Struggles over equity, power, and fairness; issues of race, gender, and class; expositions on citizenship, character, and ethics—all those and more informed athletic discourses.

During that period a powerful group of American thinkers defined the United States as a sporting republic. They thought that sport could shape the nation's political culture. By *sport* they meant athletic events, institutions, and ideas that constituted a system of rational recreation for the nation. They thought of sport as a tool—literally an athletic technology—through which they could make a republican culture strong enough to meet the challenges of modernity. Convinced that they had invented this athletic technology, these sporting republicans were confident that they could use it to construct a viable civilization.

In fact, the sporting republic belonged not only to the intellectual and political elites. Large segments of the public found the idea to be a compelling vision. Together they generated a new American *lingua franca*.[1] That common language found its most forceful expression in discussions of American experiences at the revived Olympic Games. The re-created modern Olympics Games, revived in 1896 and thereafter held at four-year intervals until the catastrophe of world war in 1914 interrupted the cycle, sparked more discussions about the nature and purpose of sport and its relation to American civilization than did any other athletic event or institution.

The modern Olympics provided the intellectual classes and the masses with common subject matter. If at times intellectuals inhabited worlds separate from the cares and concerns of most people, during the Olympics both the public and the contemplative classes focused their attention on sport. The Olympics created a conduit for discourse across social boundaries that often inhibited communication. The ideas that underlay the sporting republic received their most explicit exposition in American conversations about the Olympic Games. Through the games sport became "a working force" in the "common consciousness" of modernizing American civilization.[2]

The Republic's Well-Being and Sport

The idea of a sporting republic functions at two levels. Formed from the Latin *res publica* ("a thing belonging to the people"), the word *republic* conjoined with the term *sport* signifies a common interest in athletic games.[3] A republic of sport, like a "republic of letters" or a "republic of science," is a community organized around certain activities.[4] Organized sport became one of the basic features of American life in the decades after the Civil War.

The idea of a republic also constitutes one of the central symbols of American political culture. During the late nineteenth and early twentieth centuries, American encyclopedias identified the United States as the world's leading republic and the nineteenth and twentieth centuries as an unparalleled epoch of republican progress. A popular history of the nation had as its title *The Great Republic.* One of the most influential journals founded during the period took the name *The New Republic.*[5] The idea of a republic, which centered on belief in popular representative government, conceptions of civic virtue, images of shared communal values, and visions of a citizenry animated by fealty to the commonweal or public good, helped to frame crucial political and cultural debates in the modernizing United States.[6]

The use of the term *sporting republic* symbolizes both the popular fascination with sport and the basic intersection of political and athletic ideas in American civilization. For turn-of-the-century American thinkers, republicanism was more than simply a form of government and a political philosophy. It provided a set of interpretive devices for understanding the world and a popular language for explaining the meaning of social life. The incorporation of sport into republican arguments indicates the intimate connections that developed between sport and politics.

In the late nineteenth- and early twentieth-century United States, debates over the nature and structure of the republic engaged American minds. Many American thinkers warned that the republic was in grave peril. Modern social, political, and economic forces threatened to destroy the United States. American republicans worried that individuals, corporations, and governments had lost the ability or desire to pursue the common good. They fretted that common values had been shredded. They lamented the decline of civic virtue. They even feared the collapse of representative government. They counseled that the nation needed to find mechanisms for restoring the republic. The quest to revitalize the republic consumed America's intellectual and middling classes. How, they wondered, could new paths toward the common good be found? How could the moral center of the nation be resurrected? How could the republic be saved?

"Few people realize how great is the part played by sport in the life of a nation," surmised Price Collier in an 1898 essay. Collier admitted that "most of us think of the hour or two spent at some form of exercise as a pastime which has little or no bearing upon the political life about us." He argued that such a perception was drastically flawed. The sporting life, he insisted, produced precisely the type of citizen needed for national and individual success in the revolutionary conditions that characterized modern life. "It was no mere epigram of the Iron Duke about the playing fields of Eton, and Waterloo," Collier proclaimed, referring to the duke of Wellington's quip that the Battle of Waterloo was won on the playing fields of Eton, a reference readily recognizable in literate Anglo-American culture. "There was a direct connection, just as there is a direct connection between that hardy, plain-living family of Deweys from Vermont, and Manila," he continued, heralding the hero of the American victory over the Spanish fleet in the 1898 war over Cuba. Thus Collier implicated athletics as a key factor in the United States' emergence onto the world stage near the beginning of the twentieth century.[7]

Collier's insistence that "hardy, plain-living" American folk committed to the sporting life made their nation great was a typical expression of the idea that sport could reinvigorate the republic. His universal claims that sport could unite all citizens in a common culture revealed the narcotic appeal of the sporting republic. American stories about the modern Olympic Games focused intently on evidences of national "well-being."

An American Olympian, James Connolly, helped to forge the connections between sport and national well-being that gave meaning to the Olympic dialogues. Connolly won the first championship the United States ever earned in Olympic competition when he hopped, stepped, and jumped farther than anyone else at the inaugural modern Olympic Games in 1896 at Athens. Connolly later earned renown as a writer of adventure stories and tales from the high seas. He covered the Olympic Games of 1908 and 1912 as a contributing reporter to several national magazines. Connolly injected powerful political ideas into his popular accounts of the Olympics.[8]

In a fictionalized account of the first modern Olympics entitled "An Olympic Victor," Connolly created a memorable scene that used discus throwing to

illustrate national character. Connolly depicted the discus competition as a ti-
tanic contest between an American challenger based on Robert Garrett, who
was the actual 1896 Olympic champion, and a Greek champion named Gouskous. In Connolly's rendition of the struggle, a partisan Athenian crowd pushed
the Greek discobulus to a prodigious effort. On his final heave the Greek athlete managed a Herculean throw that the delighted crowd celebrated as a sure
winner. The American discus thrower still had one chance left, however. He
stepped to the center of the stadium for his final toss. "In his preparation was
seen evidence of that which was making his nation so great," wrote Connolly.
"He was not to be shaken in his preparation by the cheers of the tens of thousands for the victorious Gouskous. Calmly he took position and coolly surveyed
the prospect." The American Olympian's "eye seemed to remain glued on a
point far down the centre line. At the instant of execution a panic seized the
Stadium. Suppose he should throw so accurately that the discus would sail
straight down the centre line? Which was exactly what he did."[9]

Why did the American win the discus contest? According to Connolly, he won
neither because he possessed more physical skill nor because luck determined
the outcome. He won because he was an American. He triumphed because
American civilization had created in him a spirit that could conquer the world.
He won because he was a representative of a "chosen people," a product of the
social system that promised the best future for humankind. Connolly knew how
to weave political ideology into "An Olympic Victor." He had an Athenian newspaper pay homage to the "melting pot" as the crucible of the Olympic discus
triumph. "Ah, well might the Americans say that their mixed blood was welding a nation that is to be invincible in time," trumpeted the fictional periodi-
cal. "Their vitality to-day in the games is but symbolical."[10]

"Symbolical" is certainly what the modern Olympic Games have been for
Americans. The Olympics provided public spaces for making sport a tool
in the struggles to forge a national culture for the modern United States.
The explanations that the media offered for American successes at the early modern Olympic Games illuminated American ideas about their sporting republic.

Sport and Political Philosophy

What did sport have to do with the nature and structure of the American republic? What link exists between sport and politics? The inventors of the sporting republic wanted to create a tool for making national standards out of their
ideas about republican forms of government, their beliefs in constitutionalism
and rule by law, their conceptions of civic virtue, and their definitions of com-

munity. They thought that participation in athletics, spectatorship at sporting contests, and the rapidly growing public discourse surrounding sport constituted important political behavior. They began to conceive of their nation as a sporting republic. They defined a sporting republic as a polity in which the new athletic technology and the public dialogues it spawned could shape culture. They believed that sport could inculcate public virtue. They asserted that sport could mold citizens. They argued that sport could solve troublesome social conflicts. They insisted that sport could reform American institutions. They were certain that sport could produce a nation committed to fair play and rule by law.

The nature of organized sport lent itself easily to such interpretations. In 1907 the American philosopher William James recognized that athletic games could provide a rational structure for experience. In critiquing philosophical arguments that posit a deterministic universe, James employed an illustration from the gridiron. "The aim of a football-team is not merely to get the ball to a certain goal (if that were so, they would simply get up on some dark night and place it there), but to get it there by a fixed *machinery of conditions*—the game's rules and the opposing players."[11] Sport, defined and ordered by structured rules, codes of conduct, and definite goals—what James meant by "fixed machinery of conditions"—presented people with extraordinary experiences, fraught with lessons that its advocates believed could and should be applied to the real world, particularly the political world. Sport provided important cultural analogies and allowed the creation of concrete constructions where prescriptive truths, what one ought and ought not to do, were supposed to be readily apparent and rigidly followed.[12]

Certainly the creators of the idea of a sporting republic envisioned their construction as producing adherence to those precepts. "A boy who learns to lie and cheat and to deal in subterfuge in football and baseball . . . will follow the same methods in business or professional life when he gets out into the world," admonished journalist Caspar Whitney in an 1897 codification of the athletic ideal. "On the contrary, a boy who learns by his athletic life to do everything he can honorably to win, but to submit cheerfully to defeat rather than indulge in trickery and meanness, will carry the same spirit in all his recreation and work in after life."[13] Fair play and good sportsmanship were athletic commandments. Properly conducted, thought the public moralists who were enamored of athletics, sport would provide a glimpse of what the "real" world ought to be like. Much of American political experience, as well as a great deal of Western political philosophy, has revolved around similar ideas.

The hallmark of Western political theory, from Plato and Aristotle to modern thinkers, has been an abiding interest in how to ensure justice in the polity. Even dissenters from the tradition, such as Thomas Hobbes, who preferred security to abstract notions of justice, have had to begin with the concept of a just society in their refutations of the Western tradition. The key argument for advocates of constitutionalism is that rule by law is the best political system for providing equity in the body politic because it provides a rational "machinery of conditions" for regulating the political game. No man should be judge in his own case, insisted John Locke, for that would be patently unfair. People gave up recourse to personal power to enter civil society so that their natural rights could be preserved and fairness and justice could characterize human relations. That sacrifice of individual will—sometimes partial, as in Locke's civil covenant, and sometimes total, as in the Jean-Jacques Rousseau's social contract—protects a person from the capricious tyranny that other wills might impose.

American political culture drew its fundamental structure from the same philosophic core. "No man is allowed to be a judge in his own cause, because his interest would certainly bias his judgment, and, not improbably, corrupt his integrity," wrote James Madison, echoing Locke and presaging a cardinal tenet of organized sport. Madison, as the philosopher of the Constitution and the great defender of republican principles, stands at the center of American political culture. In the "Federalist Number 10," he addressed the issues of competition, talent, and fairness. Madison knew better than Locke that although a constitution might prevent individuals from judging their own cases, groups of individuals or factions cannot be so easily regulated by an umpire, since factions might well be able to choose umpires from their own ranks.

Madison believed that factions cannot be extinguished in a human society without altering human nature or destroying human liberty. The first remedy seemed impossible, and the latter is extremely undesirable. The effects, rather than the causes, of faction had to be relieved to ensure fairness in society. Madison warned that Americans could not count on their leaders for such relief, since "enlightened statesmen will not always be at the helm." They needed to place their trust instead on "fixed machinery of conditions," the rules of the political game, on the institutions and mechanisms of the Constitution. Only a well-designed republican system could prevent the tyranny of faction from destroying liberty.

Madison argued eloquently that the rules of the game were constructed well enough to do just that. Of course, Madison thought that a fair system would preserve the differing abilities of individuals to acquire property, a stance for which he has often been condemned. Nevertheless, the important thing to remember is that in Madison's estimation such a system was the fairest.[14] That the Constitution provides equity for all citizens and factions is a central tenet of American political culture. For example, during his bid for the presidency in 1912, Woodrow Wilson proclaimed that modern society should operate by the same rules that governed sporting contests: "Give me a fair field and as much credit as I am entitled to, and let the law do what from time immemorial law has been expected to do—see fair play."[15]

The Gospel of Fair Play and the History of the American Republic

A survey of the political history of the United States indicates the centrality of the issue of fairness and the force with which the ideal of fair play motivates popular consciousness. The ratification of the Constitution turned on whether that document could order and regulate American life. The triumph of Thomas Jefferson and the repudiation of the Federalists owed much to perceptions of fairness. The slavery issue, Andrew Jackson's bank war, the Homestead Act, the rise and role of big business, the Populist crusade, Progressivism, the Square Deal, the New Freedom, the New Deal, the Fair Deal, the civil rights movement, the War on Poverty, affirmative action—each in one way or another dealt with what certain factions perceived as questions of fairness. Those incidents form the actualities of American political history. Beneath them lies the cultural pattern that propels many Americans to see issues and events in terms of whether they provide equity in economy, polity, and society.

American culture's preoccupation with legal methods for ensuring fairness makes the American fascination with organized sport more understandable. Sport re-creates the cherished values and norms of republicanism in its fervent devotion to the spirit of the rules. The good sportswoman or sportsman and the good citizen were, in different spheres, one and the same person. "Let me mould the sports of my countrymen, and who will may frame their laws," quipped John Corbin in a bit of hyperbole typical of athletic boosters at the turn of the century.[16] His outburst reflected both his faith in the power of sport to shape political culture and the belief that it could shore up the "machinery of conditions" that provided the foundation for the republican experiment.

George Hibbard seconded Corbin's proclamation and captured the essence of the sporting republic's ideology. "There are certain things that are fair and certain things that are not fair—dodges that are admissible and others that bar at once the one who practices them—and it is singular how similar these rules are to the general rules governing sport," he declared. Hibbard made sport and modern social organization inseparable. "It is not alone with national questions or with public questions that the sporting spirit concerns itself, but it enters into the very texture of our being, and is every day affecting our behavior one toward the other and directing our conduct in the ordinary incidents of life," he lectured. "The sporting spirit has entered into business, and not only has made the commercial world something of an arena, but has also imposed on the contestants a set of rules for their governments," Hibbard testified concerning his wildly optimistic understanding of the role that sport played in the production and reproduction of American culture.[17]

Seen from such a context, the fact that the cult of organized athletics and the sporting ideal arose in the same nations—Great Britain and the United States—in which the principles of constitutionalism and republicanism most completely shaped political life was more than merely coincidental.[18] Nevertheless, if the rise of modern sport was indeed associated with the political culture of republican constitutionalism, one might ask why athletics did not manifest itself in seventeenth-century England after the Glorious Revolution and the Petition of Right or in the eighteenth-century United States during the Constitutional convention. Why were John Milton, John Locke, George Washington, and James Madison not apostles of sport?

Sporting culture was not a necessary condition for the rise of a constitutional democracy; it was instead an abstraction of and ritual for the principles of rule by law. What spurred the invention of modern sport was not the existence of the English and American constitutions but rather the fundamental change in the relationship between individuals and the community in republican nations engendered by the Industrial Revolution and other processes of modernization. Republican political philosophy held that vigorous citizens were required for the maintenance of republican institutions. How could that be accomplished in the machine age, with the agrarian culture that classical republicans had identified as the source of vigor and morality moving down the path to extinction? The inventors of the sporting republic thought that the essence of republican civilization could be cultivated under modern conditions through a national commitment to sport.

Western intellectuals, and particularly American thinkers, believed that modernity threatened the foundations of republican society. Fear of republican collapse animated the construction of new ideas about sport. By the latter half of the nineteenth century, the explanations offered by traditional republicanism and classical liberalism no longer seemed to fit the realities of social practice in the corporate-industrial nation-states. Republican political philosophy and liberal society had reached a critical juncture. Many American thinkers wondered whether modern societies could be both liberal and republican. That crisis helped to generate among American thinkers the conception of a sporting republic. The sporting republic combined ideas about the power of athletics to shape human beings with the enduring theory that republics are the best of all forms of government. A grandiose vision of sport as an instrument for re-creating, adapting, or conserving republicanism emerged in American thought. The never-ending debates about the kinds of laws and customs that best balance liberty and authority, the kinds of society that best maintain virtue and equity, and the fundamental nature of the republic were enveloped in the common language of sport.

In fact, the idea of sport as a common language sprang from the political conflicts that rent the late nineteenth-century United States. The disappearance, real or imagined, of a common national culture served as a popular motif in fin de siècle critiques of American civilization. Images of disorder revealed the social cost of rapid change. The dislocations of post–Civil War industrialism distended society and destroyed the mythology of the traditional communities that had constituted the nineteenth-century American experience. Loss of personal control over economic and political mechanisms, as national systems supplanted local and regional patterns, disturbed the social fabric. Boom-and-bust cycles ravaged the business climate and seemed beyond the control of human skills. A permanent industrial working class emerged, labor unrest swelled, and violent strikes upset the comfortable assumptions of the republic's troubled bourgeoisie. A "leisure class" of industrial titans, frequently depicted as a parasitic cabal without a shred of social concern, provided the middle-class masses with a fearsome countersymbol to the horror of a permanent proletariat. Urbanization and immigration, linked in fact and perception, added to the sense of unease.

Labor wars, ruthless exploitation, and corporate oligopoly elicited a host of responses. Single-cause panaceas for social ills proved to be especially popular. Free coinage in silver, the single tax, Bellamyite National Clubs, and a variety of regulatory schemes for bringing order to chaos competed for public support. In regions that mechanized farming and the railroad had transformed into a global breadbasket, first the Grange and then the Farmer's Alliances focused discontent. Agricultural unrest exploded into the Populist Crusade by the early 1890s, coinciding with spiraling labor unrest and a devastating depression. From many perspectives, and particularly from middle-class eyes, the nation seemed to be engulfed by a maelstrom of conflict that overmatched existing institutions and threatened important values. The transition to modernity appeared to imperil the very existence of the American republic. Images of decline consumed American imaginations.

The inherited political and cultural traditions of republicanism provided a popular framework for interpreting the disruptions engendered by rapid social change. Republican ideology had long asserted the necessity of a vigorous citizenry for ensuring political liberty and guarding against the vices that made overly artificial civilizations easy prey for tyrants. In the preindustrial world republicans had insisted that vigor and independence grew from agrarian roots.

They opposed the symbol of the healthy, moral yeoman farmer to the dissipat-ed, venal city dweller. As the agrarian world began to disappear, some republi-can thinkers replaced yeoman farmers with athletes in an effort to modernize their paradigms. Those attitudes represented part of the rationale for the cre-ation of Victorian gentlemen's sporting clubs in the mid-nineteenth-century urban United States. The republicans sought a middle ground between nature and artifice, a pastoral clime that would nurture physical, political, and moral strength. They had always linked robust health, the virtues of hard work, and physical prowess to the republican tradition.

Cultural critics argued that the United States had lost its vitality. Analyses of the fallout from modernization borrowed themes and imagery from the liber-al storehouse for up-to-date versions of republican complaints. Visions of list-lessness and dissipation filled mass-media depictions of the crises. A stereotyp-ical journalistic tour through an American city revealed an environment of destructive artificiality that spawned feeble children; overstimulated and de-praved youths; legions of urbanites suffering from nervous exhaustion, wast-ed muscles, and pasty complexions; and generalized images of widespread, cancerous modern "dis-ease."[19]

The grim, gray patina of civilization in decay extended to the heartland. "Even in our small towns the social organization is too loose-jointed and spiritless to enter heartily into schemes for the thorough education of the body; and as to farm life, there is a vast deal of balderdash talked about that Arcadian mode of existence," wrote a *Harper's* correspondent in 1884.[20] Even *Outing,* an Ameri-can magazine devoted to rational recreation that promoted Arcadian (pasto-ral) mythology on many occasions, admitted that "there is no denying that the farmer needs recreation . . . and the farmer's wife is more to be pitied in this regard than he."[21] These Americans wondered whether the new machines and factories, the railroads, the reapers and harvesters, and the expanding cities would strip the vitality from their human creators.

Modernity would crush the republic, argued many, unless the nation discov-ered that sport was the key to its well-being.[22] In promoting sport, its inven-tors exhibited a zealotry that sometimes rivaled that of turn-of-the-century American millennialists. The summer picnicking meetings of farm families moved J. R. Dodge to ruminate on the general meaning of the sporting life in modern civilization. "The subject is one of vital importance to the health and vitality of the American people," insisted Dodge. "It has intimate relations with the social life and the intellectual progress of the country. It has much to do with its industrial development, its capacity for production, and with the just equalization of material blessings among the people," imagined Dodge. "If to write the songs of a people is more influential than the making of its laws, the right direction of a nation's recreations may be of more importance than we imagine."[23] Dodge's commentary underscored the growing notion that sport plays a crucial role in generating public virtue, or "culture."[24] In the relationship between making the republic's laws and making their games lay the central concept of the sporting republic.

The Origins of the Common Language of Sport and the Invention of Athletic Technology

The understanding that athletic games were human inventions animated the conceptualization of sport as a technology. The notion of sport as an instrumentality, an athletic technology, and a political entity—a sporting republic—might at first seem very odd. For more than a century, however, that combination of ideas has driven national conversations about vital cultural and political issues.

In the latter half of the nineteenth century, the social and political possibilities of sport captured American imaginations. In 1888, in the course of an essay for *Outing* magazine, an American writer explained sport as the nation's true common language. Political debates and presidential elections generated some interest, he admitted, but not as much as sport. In other arenas "the fiercest controversies in science and religion may rise and subside, the whole current of ecclesiastical thought may change, whilst the 'Tracts for the Times' will remain a mere phrase to millions who are keenly alive to the more cosmopolitan questions involved in athletism." In fact, he proclaimed, sport provided the most powerful linguistic device for "civilizing" the world. "While other forces of aggregation have welded together peoples having a common ethnological origin into a nation, such as Italy, and consolidated independent states into a system, such as Germany, it has been the function of athletics to unite in a common interest the whole (Anglo Saxon) world," he declared.[25]

The idea that sport could forge a sense of community attracted American thinkers who were concerned that modern conflicts threatened the core of their republican experiment. They hoped that a national devotion to sport might spark a common discourse among the atomized citizens wandering the socio-economic battlefields of their rapidly modernizing republic. "We get easily differentiated from each other in the struggle for bread and a living," opined an editor of *The Independent* in 1907. "In fact," continued the editor, "there is no such thing as a commonwealth of intercourse remaining. A good playground seems to be exactly what we all need."[26] That image, "a commonwealth of intercourse" generated from playgrounds and playing fields, found frequent expression in late nineteenth- and early twentieth-century American writing.

Sport, thought its most ardent advocates, could create a language of shared symbols with encoded social and political meanings. They even dreamed that sport could transcend "the struggle for bread and a living."

American promoters of sport hoped that athletics would quickly become not only a national language but even a global one.[27] The composer of "The Progress of Athletism" mused, "Remarkable as it may at first sound, it is true that no fact to-day 'flashed round the girdle of the globe' would excite so widespread a curiosity, or so much personal interest," as the news of an athletic contest.[28] In considering sport as a form of communication, American intellectuals thought that they had discovered a new system for building communities in modern environments. The energy harnessed by sporting systems seemed to offer stunning social possibilities, just as the energies harnessed by the other revolutions in communication and transportation altered modern conceptions of space and time and revolutionized cultures throughout the world.[29]

Sport became, in American imaginations, a powerful social technology.[30] The connection between sport and technology signified more than just a literary flourish. The association of sport with languages and other forms of technology explains something important about modern athletics, a link that has eluded most historians and philosophers of sport. Sport itself is a technology. Technologies are ways of organizing the world to solve problems.[31] Sport is a social technology designed to solve important political and social problems through athletic organizations of human energy.

Certainly turn-of-the-century American thinkers understood sport as a technology. "Athletism is one of the distinctive forces of the nineteenth century," declared *Outing*'s historian of sporting trends, adding sport to the list of energies that many thinkers declared were forging a "modern" world. "And of all the forces, acting upon the social, moral and physical life of the century, it is probably destined to be the most permanent in its effects."[32] Without an understanding of sport as a technological system—as "athletism"—such a commentary concerning the importance of sport in the modern nations then emerging in western Europe and North America would seem jarringly inaccurate. In such proclamations from the American popular press, "athletism" joined the other "isms"—mechanism, industrialism, corporatism, bureaucratism, rationalism, nationalism, secularism, scientism, capitalism, socialism, and so on—that characterized the modern age. Athletism was one of the dynamic new human-engineered systems forging a new world.

American intellectuals understood sport as an invention, part and parcel of the technological revolution that marked their historical experience. In one of the first scholarly looks at the "rise" of modern sports, the progressive historian Frederic L. Paxson provided a chronology for the invention of athletic technology. In a 1917 essay Paxson declared that "between the first race of the America's cup in 1851 and the first American aeroplane show of February last, the safety valve of sport was designed, built and applied."[33] Sport, Paxson asserted, was *designed, built, and applied.* Paxson, a disciple of frontier theorist Frederick Jackson Turner, understood the "safety valve of sport" as a human-engineered substitute for the safety valve of the frontier, a mechanism for channeling abundant human energy in socially productive ventures. With the frontier extinguished by the march of progress, as all good Turnerians assumed, Paxson thought that rugged individuals and republican institutions could be generated by an American devotion to sport.

In the modernizing United States, American advocates of sport designed, built, and applied a technological system that they thought could create, channel, control, and conserve human energy. They crafted athletic technology out of a variety of forms of physical culture. Anglo-American folk games shaped some of their design. They also included the ideology of Muscular Christianity and republican concepts of the relationship between vigor and public virtue in their system. The champions of sport attached their athletic technology to the emerging mass-communication, amusement, and consumption systems that characterized the new industrial order and made sport into a powerful conceptual tool for directing human energy in "progressive" directions.[34]

Defining the limits of what constituted sport presented an important part of the new athletic technology. For the sporting republicans, athletic technology comprised all forms of rational recreation and any strenuous games or contests that contributed to their schemes of progressive social reform. That made for a rather fluid set of definitions. They sometimes touted the value of sports that looked very similar to working- or leisure-class amusements, but they demanded that those games be played according to middle-class rules. Thus they often lauded boxing while they abhorred the spectacles of bare-knuckle prizefighting. They approved of sailing but condemned the yachting regattas of the "idle" rich.

The sporting republicans sought to define the entire spectrum of American physical culture under the rubric of the "amusement problem." Urban reformer and sporting promoter Richard Henry Edwards argued that properly defining sport posed the most significant social question of the era. "No one who has been at a baseball game or a picture show, at a circus or the vaudeville, at a country fair or among the children of a city street, can doubt that all America believes in amusement," he observed. "The important question is *the sort of amusement* in which she believes, for the sort of play on which her attention is focused fashions the national character."[35]

Sporting republicans designed "amusements" to provide a language for political instruction. Inventions arise from the intersections of social environment, intellectual climate, well-prepared imaginative minds—and an occasional episode of serendipity.[36] Modern forms of sports appeared as American society transformed itself through market and industrial revolutions. The decline of local communities under the pressures of modernization sparked the formation of a multitude of sporting clubs. Formed by a variety of groups, from immigrants to eastern establishment elites, the sporting clubs sought to preserve some semblance of community in the face of rapidly changing social patterns.[37] They also generated intense interest in sport, producing a fortuitous climate for using sport to transcend the traditional patterns of community and weaken local associations in favor of national organizations.

The new athletic technology was frequently employed to delineate, shape, and control the American public. *Outing*'s George Hibbard insisted that sport "is not only making a new physical America, but making a new mental one as well, and in regard to many a 'live question' and vital issue it is creating or influencing our opinion." Hibbard thought that the sporting spirit and the national conversation it sparked could forge political consensus on many of the important issues facing the American republic.[38] Questions of power infused the new literature detailing the meanings of the sporting republic. Just what kind of Americans were telling those stories, however, and what kind of agendas and perspectives did the storytellers bring to their subjects?

Who Invented the Sporting Republic?

The inventors of the sporting republic were people who read the history of the United States through republican lenses and perceived that modernization had produced a crisis. They were people who by the early twentieth century would come to define themselves as "progressives" on many political and social issues. Their very use of the word *progressive* implied that they had a sense of themselves as an inclusive and universal group. After all, who would oppose progress? Nonetheless, even the self-defined progressives could not agree on an exact set of specifications for the progressive civilization they envisioned.[39]

In their quest to shape economic, political, and social patterns, these individuals often worked at cross-purposes. Still, some general tendencies linked them. Many of them came from the elite and middle-class strata of northern industrial society, frequently from urban areas. They fit neatly into the ranks of the self-defined progressives who wanted to preserve the republican experiment.

The sporting republicans often had experiences in college athletics and the sporting clubs that guarded elite status in urban America. They touted organized athletics to further their political ambitions or their professional careers and often accomplished both simultaneously. Included among the ranks of the inventors were public moralists, scions of the Eastern establishment, social reformers, settlement house workers, municipal administrators, politicians from every level of government, scientific experts, teachers, professors, social scientists, a new class of professional athletic organizers, public health advocates, sporting goods manufacturers, athletic entrepreneurs, and significant numbers of journalists and editors.

Among the inventors were powerful and famous people whose names were readily recognizable outside of sporting arenas: Theodore Roosevelt, Jane Addams, and William James. Also playing prominent roles were famous sporting personages, such as Walter Camp, who created modern football, and the baseball magnate, sporting goods entrepreneur, and popularizer of modern athletics Albert Goodwill Spalding. Less well known people also contributed. Many of the inventors came from the new middle classes emerging in urban-industrial society.[40] James Connolly had an outstanding career as an amateur athlete, won an Olympic medal, and became a prominent writer.[41] Price Collier, a Unitarian minister who gave up the pastorate and also became a popular writer, penned odes to the strenuous life such as "Sport's Place in the Nation's Well-Being."[42] Social workers Gertrude Dudley, the director of the Women's Department of Physical Education at the University of Chicago, and Frances A. Kellor, the author of *Experimental Sociology* (1902) and *Out of Work* (1905), promoted women's inclusion in the sporting republic.[43] Kellor settled in New York City and served as the chief inspector for the federal government's Bureau of Industries and Immigration. She participated in the woman's suffrage movement, worked on projects to assimilate immigrants, and pushed for municipal reforms with her friend Lillian Wald, who had founded New York City's renowned Henry Street settlement house.[44]

Albert Shaw earned a Ph.D. from Johns Hopkins; cultivated friendships with Theodore Roosevelt, Woodrow Wilson, and progressive economist Richard T. Ely; wrote extensively on urban reform; edited *The American Review of Reviews*; and promoted American participation in the Olympics.[45] Luther Halsey Gulick, who earned an M.D. from City University of New York, held major leadership positions in the YMCA, led the Boy Scouts of America, and with his wife cofounded the Camp Fire Girls. Gulick helped James Naismith to invent basketball and promoted sport relentlessly.[46] James Edward Sullivan, the son of Irish immigrants, rose to prominence as the leader of the most important national sporting organization in the period, the Amateur Athletic Union, and helped to lead the American Olympic movement. Sullivan contributed substantially to the new ideas about sport.[47] Caspar Whitney adapted sports journalism to the middle-class press, producing athletic features for *Harper's Weekly* and *Collier's*, editing *Outing*, and serving in the first decade of the twentieth century as a member of the American and International Olympic Committees.[48]

These journalists, professional physical educators, lawyers, and urban reformers represented the important contributions of the new middle classes to creating and promoting the sporting republic. Their conceptions of sport also typified the responses of the new middle classes to rapid social change. They helped to organize American sport.

Ironically, their most vocal opponents came from the same social stratum. The new athletic technology did not appeal to the entire American intellectual class. Thorstein Veblen, an iconoclastic socialist philosopher and a scathing critic of laissez-faire political economy, rejected the "sporting craze" as an atavistic psychosis left over from a more barbarous phase of human development. Veblen declared that industrialized civilization had no need for sport.[49] In the pages of *The Nation*, editor E. L. Godkin and his staff, staunch defenders of the values of Anglo-American laissez-faire liberalism, agreed with Veblen on practically nothing except that sport had no important function in modern industrial civilization. Godkin despised the popular expressions of mass society and lumped sport together with the other popular enthusiasms that amused the common herd, such as "the greenback craze, and the silver craze, and the granger craze, and the cholera craze."[50]

The inventors of the sporting republic insisted that Godkin, Veblen, and the other opponents of modern athletics had focused on perversions of sport and failed to grasp the positive aspects of the new common language. Like any instrumentality or invention, they noted, sport could be misused. As athletic booster John Corbin observed, "The simple fact is that all good institutions, such as football and Sunday-schools, are lamentably liable to abuse."[51]

Organizing and Popularizing the Sporting Republic

The roots of the sporting republic fit neatly into the same complex of historical experiences that had given rise to America's new middle classes. The emergence of modern sport coincided with the transformation of American society by successive waves of industrialism. As early as the 1820s, during the antebellum reform movements, child guidance advisers, health experts, and Muscular Christians preached—in particular to an urban middle-class audience—that sport guaranteed self-improvement and national survival in a changing world.

The sporting republic emerged forcefully later in the nineteenth century as the processes of modernization transformed the United States. The historical properties of athletics captured the attention of the professional, technical, and managerial leaders of the corporate order as they embraced the machine process and the new business dynamic. At the same time the potential for an excessively artificial and "inauthentic" commercial civilization contained in the new order repelled them. The new conceptions of sport seemed to promise an efficient way to bridge the gulf between the idealized world of nineteenth-century small-town America and the energetic yet potentially dehumanizing society produced by corporate capitalism.[52]

By the late nineteenth century, middle-class "awareness" of shared work and social patterns had reached a critical juncture. Broadening participation in consumerism refocused class boundaries. A new middle class emerged, organized around the acceptance of a constellation of ideas and beliefs rather than on similarities in occupation and labor patterns.[53] New technologies of social production, new forms of corporate and capitalist organization, new structures of market relations, and new political realities at the local, national, and international levels required new frames of reference. Confronted with monumental changes, the American middle classes used sport to transform their culture.

The new athletic technology became enmeshed with industrialism. A thriving sports industry sold athletic goods and knowledge to consumers. A. G. Spalding presided over the development of a huge sporting "trust" that pushed into new markets and captured the ability to define "official" sporting practice.[54] The organizational revolution that characterized the late nineteenth and early twentieth centuries, highlighted by centralization, nationalization, and bureaucratization, gave athletics a distinctively modern shape as clubs, collegiate teams, and professional leagues followed the patterns typical of most modern social institutions.

The transportation and communication revolutions that spawned the new order created an atmosphere in which modern sport grew rapidly. Railroads facilitated the rise of professional baseball and college football, engendering American rivalries among cities and among colleges. It was more than a coincidence that in 1869 Americans witnessed both the completion of the transcontinental railroad and the first transcontinental tour of a baseball club, Cincinnati's famed Red Stockings.

The effective mass-communication system emerging in the late nineteenth-century United States aided the efforts to link ideas about sport and republics immensely. In fact, without the emerging mass print media, an athletic technology that promoted sport as a common national language could not have developed. Newspaper sports pages, an innovation of national scope by the 1870s, spread athletic symbolism rapidly. Sports pages crowded mass-circulation dailies, and reading them became a habit for millions of Americans. By the 1880s the call to use sport to revitalize the republic echoed ceaselessly in the national press. Magazines devoted solely to sport, such as *The Wheelman* and *Outing,* sprang up. The great chronicles of progressive politics and middle-class sentiment, *Munsey's, Harper's, Century, The North American Review, The New Republic, The World's Work, Collier's, The American Review of Reviews, The Atlantic Monthly, The Outlook, The Independent, Ladies Home Journal, Cosmopolitan, Charities and the Commons, The Survey, Popular Science Monthly,* and *Scientific American,* among many others, ran essays and editorials discussing the role of sport in modern life.

The many essays and editorials advocating sport explored the power of athletic technology for revitalizing American civilization and modernizing the republic. Promoters of progressive ideologies of sport used the press to shape and control the national conversation about sport and its relation to politics. Since they wanted to preserve both the material standards of living generated by modern industrialism and the imaginary social consensus they associated with the historical development of the American republic, they used the mass media to foster a belief that athletic technology could forge a healthy national culture. Their belief in sport as a mechanism for building community was the most important factor in their fascination with sport.

These advocates' certainty that sport could create a national community reveals a crucial facet of progressive thought. At the heart of Progressivism resided a quest for the secrets of community formation. Since the middle of the nineteenth century, sporting clubs had served as institutions for creating communities within an emerging mass society. By the late nineteenth century, hundreds of those clubs provided a sense of belonging for elite, middle-class, immigrant, and working-class groups. It was only a small and logical step to imagine that sport might build a national culture. The sporting republicans hoped that sport was the secret for transporting the imagined solidarity of the small town to the greater national community.

Promoters of sport defended it vigorously because they thought that the common language of sport offered important opportunities for republican regeneration. To support their views, they drew on classical models, just as the founding fathers of the American republic had. American proponents of sport constructed a usable history of classical athletics to bolster their claims. The theories favored by many late nineteenth- and early twentieth-century Hellenists proposed that ancient forms of sport were intimately related to the ideal of the polis, the Greek concept of the democratic community in which constitutional law rather than human whim guides society. Most intellectuals considered the polis to be the original birthplace of republicanism. Historical ideas connecting sport and the polis amplified intellectual enthusiasm for the new athletic technology. Borrowing liberally and inaccurately from Greek and particularly Athenian history, classicists enamored with athletics buttressed political arguments for sport through a lavish mythology that connected classical sport and Western political ideals by making sound minds in sound bodies the foundation of the democratic tradition.[55]

American thinkers generated a political science in which the traditional Western ideal of a harmonious republican community found expression on playgrounds and playing fields. Not only had sport energized ancient republics, argued nineteenth- and early twentieth-century American sports historians, but it had also played formative roles in the "age of democratic revolutions." Three years after the American republic celebrated its centennial in 1876, Lloyd Bryce, writing in *The North American Review,* identified sport with the historical development of republican governments and liberal societies. "Since the vast political and social convulsion of the last century, the rights of man have superseded the rights of kings, and in the larger humanitarianism of the day our rough and cruel customs are being cast aside, or at least toned down," he wrote. Bryce insisted that sport was the key to building republics.[56]

Sporting republicans sought to persuade the nation that athletics had always been an intrinsic part of the nation's well-being. In a series of articles for *Outing* in the late 1880s, John P. Foley dressed the presidents of the United States in athletic garb. He noted that "the great cities have not yet given the country a President" and indicated that chief executives sprang from the healthy moral climes of the pastoral tradition. Foley made George Washington and his successors into athletic founding fathers devoted to the gospel of fair play. He told stories of a stout-hearted Washington chastising poachers and of a young tough named Andrew Jackson who whipped the local bullies to protect the smaller boys. They might have lacked the well-developed games and sports of modern society, but Foley's heroes of the early republic clearly manifested the characteristics of a later generation's idealized sports heroes.[57]

Having transformed the icons of American history into athletes, the sporting republicans next focused on the more recent past, crafting into American folklore various tales of strenuosity from their romanticized childhoods in the still vital local communities of the mid-nineteenth century. A. G. Spalding, in his quest to make baseball a purely American form of athletics, engaged in major league historical revisionism to promote the fable that Abner Doubleday invented the game in 1839 during a bucolic boyhood in Cooperstown, New York. Endorsed by a Spalding-created "commission" designed to investigate the origins of baseball and transmitted to the public in Spalding's *America's National Game,* the Doubleday fiction became a hallowed part of baseball lore.[58]

Theodore Roosevelt was particularly artful in evoking images of vigor from the recent past and juxtaposing them against the feared "overcivilization" of the machine age. Although lamenting that the frontier had closed and its strenuous experiences were forever lost to "the American boy," Roosevelt announced that football fields provided a modern substitute for the "winning of the West."[59] Everything Americans needed to meet the challenges of the modern age could be found in athletic experience. "In short, in life, as in a foot-ball game, the principle to follow is: Hit the line hard; don't foul and don't shirk, but hit the line hard!" commanded Roosevelt.[60]

The Sporting Republic and the Challenge of Modernity

The fundamental appeal of sport for the shapers of social discourse rested in its dual nature. American thinkers connected sport both to the emerging technological systems that were rationalizing modern society and shrinking time and space and to the dream of restoring the imagined balance, order, harmony, and community of their republican histories.

Thus, although firmly embedded in nostalgia, ideas about sport also played innovative roles in programs designed to reform the modern world.[61] Sporting republicans crafted a folklore asserting that athletics had been related to public virtue since at least ancient Greek times.[62] Republican political philosophy requires a fundamentally moral citizenry, since it proposes that power ultimately rests in the hands of the people. American thinkers declared that athletic people are moral people. They proclaimed that athletic nations are virtuous nations. That made the sporting republic an invented tradition, or a custom that purports to be of greater antiquity than it is, since the idea that sport is crucial to a nation's well-being dates only to the latter half of the nineteenth century. The founding fathers would not have recognized such claims. Thomas Jefferson indicated that God had made the "breasts" of farmers, not athletes, the depository of "substantial and genuine virtue."[63]

Price Collier, in articles such as "Sport's Place in the Nation's Well-Being," celebrated the idea that sport, rather than a Jeffersonian commitment to agrarianism, could guarantee public virtue. Collier's ideas struck responsive chords. The president of Ohio State University, James H. Canfield, described Collier's work "as by all odds the most sane and convincing statement of the true value of true sport and of the true sporting spirit that I have ever seen." Canfield wanted Collier's article produced as a pamphlet and distributed throughout the nation, a call that the chancellor of the University of Nebraska, George E. MacLean, seconded.[64]

With an optimism that rivaled the extravagant claims of patent medicine peddlers, Collier tried to sell Americans on the idea that sport would steel the

United States to meet all the challenges faced by the nation as it neared the twentieth century. Commitment to the strenuous life would provide an "antidote" to "the poison of the fierce lust of money," a corrective to the "rude jostling of the self-advertising social strugglers," and a "remedy" to "the disease of political corruption." Sport would give Americans the strength "to meet and vanquish" dangerous "fads in religion and morals." Sport would inoculate the nation against modern dangers.[65] Sport, in Collier's estimation, would commit the nation to the quest for the common good and rescue the republic from any peril it might face. A legion of social commentators concurred.[66]

One of modern sport's most important theoreticians and popularizers, Luther Halsey Gulick, in an essay proposing a "new athletics," codified the ethos of the sporting republic when he described sport as a "great new social agency" spawned by "the most fundamental needs of our time." Gulick claimed that with modernization a new era in civilization had dawned, as industrialism and urbanization created a mass society in which "corporate conscience" would surpass individual accountability as the key to continued progress. "This is predominantly a social century," Gulick explained. "The present difficulties are not difficulties to be solved by physical science; they are primarily difficulties with regard to human relations." Gulick rejected the classical liberal assumption of societies composed of independent individuals and asserted that "we exist in groups." That "fact," argued Gulick, made the communal properties of sport extremely important. "Athletics are but one expression of that vast social evolution that is changing the world," he announced. "The mass, the team, the gang, the institution"—those entities were the fundamental unities of the new order. "The times demand men with higher corporate morality, and it cannot be obtained from books or from lectures," Gulick declared. Only sport, through its powerful "social effects," could create a modern republic.[67]

The sporting republic's theorists grounded their athletic ideas in the nostalgic realm of traditional American values while steadfastly asserting sport's necessity as a modern institution designed to preserve liberal culture. Their approach to sport matched the methodologies by which the self-defined progressive intellectuals sought to create a modern form of republicanism. The "new athletics" belonged to the new social world of modern mass culture, coded in the language of Progressivism. A society organized around industrial and corporate enterprise demanded a different ethic and a different relationship between the individual and the community. Individual talent needed to be directed into socially efficient action. In organized sport Americans found the perfect vehicle for welding individual accomplishment to group effort. "Unselfishness must be practised at every turn," preached athletic advocate Francis Tabor in an 1899 sermon on the social effects of "true sport." "The strong must help the weak; and the weak must be aroused, that they may not be a drag upon the strong."[68] That belief garnered enormous popularity as Theodore Roosevelt's cure-all for modern ailments, "the strenuous life." Roosevelt's modern gospel neatly merged sport with politics.[69]

The Politics of the Strenuous Life

Social atomization, economic stresses, moral wanderings—each of these maladies threatened the rapidly industrializing republic from middle-class and progressive perspectives. When Theodore Roosevelt seized on participation in sport as method for combating these maladies, he demonstrated his remarkable political acumen, for the concepts of sport appealed to large segments of the population. Roosevelt appropriated the new ideas into his formidable political arsenal, doing so more effectively than any other politician of the era. Preaching to his fellow citizens in the 1890s that the modern industrial order required "not the life of ignoble ease, but the life of strenuous endeavor" hardly represented original thinking. His claim that a restoration of national vitality would further the project of fitting the power of American industrial machinery into the traditions of American republicanism had been said before. His great hope that sport could provide a tool for achieving those goals was not unique. But his rhetorical skills and genius for linking the popular symbols of American culture to his designs quickly earned him a leadership role in the crusade to make sport an integral part of the republic.

In the popular imagination Roosevelt stood as the most powerful champion of the merger between sport and republicanism. As president he once argued for government support of sport programs as the only available republican method for making urban children "strong and law-abiding."[70] A titan in both progressive politics and athletic evangelization who cherished opportunities to testify how sports had transformed him from sickly childhood into vigorous manhood and earned him the public title the "human dynamo," a strenuous moralist who called the $10 million Chicago playground system "the greatest civic achievement the world has ever seen," Roosevelt cemented the alliance between sport and the larger universe of progressive concerns.[71]

Roosevelt believed that traditional republicanism had to be incorporated into modern culture.[72] Americans who pursued the strenuous life "must be in the future, as they have been the past, the backbone of this nation, or we have evil times ahead of us," wrote Roosevelt to playground leader Henry Curtis. "The country must restore and readjust the old-time conditions, and at the same time develop them to meet the new needs," he insisted.[73] Roosevelt imagined that sport would breathe life into his vision of progressive civilization.

Roosevelt's vision of that athletic national culture included several key concepts. Sport would generate a masculine nationalism and make his nation the world's strongest and boldest people. It would restore civic virtue to a republic in peril. It would provide authentic experiences in a world threatened by artifice. It would inculcate a sense of fair play that would shape American economic and social relations. In short, sport would serve as a crucial institution for creating Roosevelt's version of a twentieth-century American republic.

Immersed in the gospel of fair play, imagined Roosevelt, the American public and its political leaders would strip control of the new industrialism from "conscienceless stock speculators," "debauching judges" and "corrupting legislatures," "selfish" merchants and manufactors, and labor union organizers and other antiestablishmentarian elements who practiced "reckless incendiarism." Roosevelt pitched the strenuous life deftly and directly to the middle of the American polity. Neither robber barons nor labor radicals had any place in his vision of a national culture. The "people" would triumph over the "interests." Sport would multiply the common good. The strenuous life would rescue the republic from decline. The strenuous life would build an authentic new community. The strenuous life would ensure that the twentieth century would be an American century.[74]

Roosevelt's combination of sport and nationalism enchanted some Americans. The grandiose promises of the new athletic technology appealed mainly to middle-class and elite sensibilities. Steel workers, miners and day laborers, farm hands, sweatshop toilers, and children in factories did not really need a more strenuous life; they needed a better one. In fact, some historians have argued that Roosevelt's strenuous life was designed solely for training a new leadership elite. Sport for "the classes" touted the value of competition and the virtues of rugged individualism. Sport for "the masses," those historians argue, had a different and far more sinister purpose. It was designed to make them docile workers for the new industrial order.[75]

Certainly the perspectives that shaped Roosevelt's and much of the American intellectual classes' attitudes toward sport sprang in part from their locations in the American social structure. The working classes did not fear, as the elite and middle classes did, that industrial economies would produce working lives plagued by "ignoble ease." Furthermore, the new ideas about athletic technology sometimes found expression in social control programs. The sporting republic, invented by elites and the new middle classes, was designed to promote their ideas about what constituted the "good life" and to inculcate their attitudes in the working classes.

In fact, some theoreticians offered sport as a way to combat what they perceived as antirepublican ideologies, as literally "an antidote to socialism." The

English philosopher C. S. Loch thought that sport would foster "social peace" and lead the working classes to convert to middle-class standards.[76] *The American Review of Reviews* thought that "although Mr. Loch's arguments are addressed to the people of London, they are equally applicable to conditions in many of our American cities."[77]

The American athletic enthusiast Lloyd Bryce envisioned the struggle between republicanism and its enemies in even starker terms than did Loch. In the 1880s Bryce published and edited the influential political journal *The North American Review* and served as a Democratic congressperson from New York.[78] He imagined that sports "might become effectual antidotes to the subversive theories put forth by mad enthusiasts, whose disordered imaginations are only the natural result of living in a poisoned physical and moral atmosphere." Bryce, a faithful adherent to the classical republican formula, argued that "conspiracies against the commonwealth are not planned in the cottage of the peasant; they are hatched in the crowded tenements of great cities." "The true medicine" for those modern evils, revealed Bryce, was for the "state" to encourage sport. Bryce thought that a national devotion to athletics would create a republic in which "the toilers in the mines, as well as the mechanics in the cities, will daily exchange the polluted air of the scenes of their labor for the invigorating atmosphere of heaven."[79]

Clearly, the muscular republicans thought that athletics could surmount class struggles. Roosevelt and his fellow sporting republicans argued that sport would generate a universal commitment to equity that would create a just society even for the working classes. Besides, they much preferred the old republican mythology of a classless society to any comprehensive theory of class structures. Lloyd Bryce presented a typical argument concerning the power of sport to negate class interests. "Of one thing there is no doubt," Bryce declared concerning the new athletic technologies. "They are a means of bringing the different classes of society amicably together . . . and this is one of the greatest needs of the time." Bryce thought nothing could beat sport for "uniting the different classes of society in bonds of friendship, or reconciling the poor to the apparent injustice of the social order as it exists." As he saw it, sport demonstrates to all segments of society that "there is no such thing as luck or fate, and that what a man is to be depends very largely on his own strenuous industry, watchfulness, and self-control." If sport taught only that lesson to every American, concluded Bryce, it "would confer an inestimable benefit upon society."[80]

The Universal Claims of the Sporting Republic

Developed by elite and middle-class thinkers in the latter half of the nineteenth century, the idea of sport as a social technology for creating a modern form of republicanism attracted a great deal of attention. The inventors of the sporting republic designed their athletic ideology in an effort to balance individual liberty and civil authority. They wanted to explore, define, and explain the most important problem in turn-of-the century liberal political and economic philosophy: the nature of the interplay between individual will and state power in industrial culture. Such concerns had always been at the heart of republican political philosophy and the liberal tradition. The adaptation of American athletic culture represented a part of the continuing effort to reconcile liberty and authority in Western culture.

The new and widely disseminated athletic literature created majestic visions of the role of sport in rejuvenating the American republic. Elite and middle-class intellectuals saw the republic as facing grave threats. They depicted a republic divided by class warfare and economic dislocations that produced a bewildering array of factions; disenchanted by new scientific and philosophical perspectives; discombobulated by increasing cultural, ethnic, and religious pluralism; distended by the rapid pace of modernization; and discomforted even by the growing material prosperity and technological power with which they often measured progress. The rapid pace of change affected every social class, but access to power and the new mass-communication media gave the elite and middle-class intellectuals most of the public opportunities for identifying the causes of the crises of modernity and for framing solutions to them. They were certain that sport was a powerful tool for crafting their version of a modern republic.

They had invented an American *lingua franca* centered on sport. That language soon filled American newspapers and magazines and peppered conversations in saloons and barbershops, at dinner tables and fence posts. The revival of the Olympic Games in 1896 would give that language a new force and even more nationalistic cadence. Was it, as they claimed, a universal language? Was the new athletic technology universally applicable? Were there limits to the promises of the sporting republic? Could it actually solve crucial social problems? Could sport rejuvenate the republic? The re-created Olympic Games would generate a national debate on those questions.

★ 2

Athens, 1896:
"See the Conquering Heroes Come"

"Winning isn't everything, it's the only thing," reads an American axiom generally credited to football coach Vince Lombardi.[1] Lombardi's sentiments are not particularly original, especially when it comes to modern celebrations of the Olympic Games. If Americans do not win at the Olympic Games, then suspicion arises about the American way of life. After all, in the popular American folklore surrounding the Olympics, U.S. athletes do not win gold medals because of superior athletic ability or because the fates of sport smile on them. They win because they are Americans and because the American way of life has provided them with an unbeatable combination of virtues, habits, and spirit. At the Olympics Americans try to prove that their citizens are indeed made of the "right stuff." They compete as "America's athletic missionaries," the apostles of the American way of life.[2]

In the re-created Olympic Games, inaugurated in 1896 at Athens, the apostles of the sporting republic found a nearly perfect forum for exhibiting their athletic technology and communicating their strenuous ideology. The modern Olympics created an ideal location for staging American spectacles.[3] Cultural performances, or the "stories a people tell about themselves," represent the public expressions of what the human creators of cultures think and believe those cultures mean.[4]

The Olympics have provided Americans with opportunities to tell stories and ask questions about their culture. American athletes, sporting officials, media commentators, and large segments of the public have devoted themselves to patriotic celebrations of Olympic experiences. Intellectuals have used the Olympics to craft sweeping estimates of national character, glowing odes to national strengths, and bitter denunciations of national shortcomings. A great many Americans have come to see Olympic performance as indicating how the United States ranks as a global power. The United States has developed an intense athletic nationalism—the devotion of emotion and energy to the state through sport—by participating in the modern Olympics.

In fact, the re-creation of the Olympics rapidly accelerated the practice of expressing nationalism through sport. Athletic nationalism in the United States originated in the nineteenth century. During that period in the United States and Great Britain, sport evolved in the popular consciousness from the seamy amusements of the underclass and the idle pastimes of the wealthy into a cultural force that, according to the claims of its adherents, could build character, inculcate values, and provide unparalleled experiences in strengthening the will to meet the rigors of modern life.

The transition of sport from a rude sideshow into a mainstream institution coincided with the transformation of British and American society by the Industrial Revolution. In the "age of innocence" preceding the cataclysm of World War I, many Americans imagined that sport might create not only a national community but an international one as well. "As a means of bringing the family of nations into more friendly relations, international athletic contests have within a few years proved to be very effectual," surmised Lloyd Bryce in 1879. He asserted that the America's Cup yacht races "contributed in a greater degree toward inspiring both nations with mutual respect, and dissipating petty jealousies, than did the much-lauded principle of arbitration, as exemplified in the settlement of the *Alabama* claims, or in the fisheries award." Bryce hoped that international athletic competition would expand and believed that the diplomatic consequences of sport would be tremendous. "Surely our modern public games are not unworthy of their descent from the games of ancient Greece," he announced, "nor is it altogether visionary to expect that the time will come again when the successful competitor in these contests will receive honor from his fellow citizens comparable to that paid to the Olympian victor."[5]

Pierre de Coubertin and the Genesis of the Modern Olympic Games

Bryce's commentary proved prophetic. In 1896 the Olympic Games were revived. A French nobleman, the baron Pierre de Coubertin, led the movement to re-create the Olympics. Coubertin, born in Paris on January 1, 1863, resembled much of his generation in France in being thoroughly disheartened by his nation's defeat and capitulation in the Franco-Prussian War of 1871. The French intelligentsia felt that their nation's pathetic showing in the war stemmed not from Prussian might but from the decadence and disorder of French civilization. Coubertin accepted as his life's work the revitalization of French society.

When Coubertin studied the globe's most powerful nation during the late nineteenth century, as well as the nation that seemed destined to inherit that mantle—Great Britain and the United States, respectively—he was struck by the cult of sport and the role it played in the cultures that appeared to promise the shape of civilization to come. In contrast to France, Great Britain and the United States seemed to Coubertin amazingly progressive and astoundingly dynamic. Why, he wondered, did French civilization languish while Anglo-American cultures exuded power and energy?

Coubertin discovered his answers in sport. The athletic practices encouraged by educational systems in England and the United States enchanted Coubertin. He found inspiration especially in Thomas Hughes's *Tom Brown's Schooldays* (1857), a reverential depiction of English education and rugged sport. In 1886 the baron made a pilgrimage to Rugby, the elite school at which Hughes set his novel. There Coubertin had a vision. "In the twilight, alone in the great gothic chapel of Rugby, my eyes fixed on the funeral slab on which, without epitaph, the great name of Thomas Arnold was inscribed, I dreamed that I saw before me the cornerstone of the British Empire," confessed the baron.[6] He fanatically embraced the belief that athletics build character, that Waterloo had indeed been won on the playing fields of Eton. He prophesied that a France fortified by sport would never again suffer the humiliation of conquest by barbarians, German or otherwise. He fervently believed that if France would adopt Anglo-American sporting culture, it would regain its status as the leading nation of modern civilization.

Frustrated that the rest of France did not share his vision, Coubertin decided that a revival of the Olympic Games would ignite French interest in Anglo-American athletics. He was not the first to call for a renewal. As early as 1852 the German scholar Ernst Curtius voiced the idea of reviving the ancient Olympic Games to his European contemporaries. But it was Coubertin who adopted Olympism and worked unceasingly for its realization.

Coubertin's plan for modern Olympic Games was more than simply an exercise in pragmatic nationalism. His notion of Olympism included as fundamental elements a thoroughly romantic scheme for promoting international peace and assuaging the "moral disorder produced by the discoveries of industrial science." His fanciful reading of the history of the ancient Olympics encouraged utopian dreams. Coubertin imagined that "healthy democracy, wise and peaceful internationalism, will penetrate the new stadium and preserve within it the cult of disinterestedness and honor which will enable athletics to help in the tasks of moral education and social peace as well as of muscular development." He assumed that the innate morality of sport guaranteed that the Olympics would "give the youth of all the world a chance of a happy and brotherly encounter which will gradually efface the peoples' ignorance of things which concern them all, an ignorance which feeds hatreds, accumulates misunderstandings, and hurtles events along a barbarous path toward a merciless conflict."[7]

Coubertin dreamed that the Olympics would create an international language of sport. Nevertheless, he abhorred the fin de siècle notion of cosmopolitan-ism that counseled the abandonment of national cultures for the utopian dream of a unitary world society. Instead, he posited a modern league of nations tol-erant of difference and linked by athletic games and sportsmanship. He pre-ferred romantic patriotism to virulent strains of nationalism. He championed a love of country that celebrated national pride without recourse to a destruc-tive chauvinism that belittled the merits of other, different national cultures. Very quickly, however, the ideas of Coubertin and his newly formed Interna-tional Olympic Committee ran headlong into the peculiar athletic nationalism manifested by the American sporting republic.

When Americans heard that Coubertin wanted to revive the ancient Greek sporting festivals, they sensed an opportunity to prove their athletic principles in a world forum. "Should a series of international Olympian Games be orga-nized, each country and race will have an opportunity of proving what stuff its youth is made of," *The American Review of Reviews* gleefully reported in 1894 after hearing the baron's announcement of the revival. Only the fact that women were not to be included in the competition tempered the magazine's enthusi-asm for the opportunity to show off the sporting republic on the world stage. "We note with regret that M. Coubertin does not allude to the considerable part played of late by women in athletic sports," worried the editors, who wanted an opportunity to prove not only that American men were not "mollycoddles" but also that American women were not "swooning damsels."[8]

One of the late twentieth-century leaders of the Olympic movement, Inter-national Olympic Committee president Juan Antonio Samaranch, remarked on one of the innumerable occasions when political considerations had intruded on the supposedly pristine world of the Olympic Games that he "had always known that sport and politics did not live on separate planets."[9] In fact, since their creation the modern Olympics have been explicitly linked to certain po-litical movements. Coubertin meant his revivals of ancient Greek festivals to promote vigor in French culture and to forge friendly bonds between nations. Most of the American intellectuals who embraced Olympism had different agendas. They saw sport as a democratic institution that could produce good citizens and serve to unify American civilization. They were sure that the glo-bal adoption of American understandings of sport would lead the nations of the world to convert to the American political system. That particular brand of secular millennialism gave the Olympic movement an intense power in the United States.

Coubertin's fine distinctions between nationalism and patriotism escaped American sensibilities. In fact, American journalists were by the late nineteenth century already beginning to calculate national superiority based on results from international playing fields. "Genial Uncle Samuel, who loves a race perhaps better than anything else on earth, and who is by no means deficient in a fondness for coming out ahead, may be pardoned for feeling just a little complacent at present," boasted Henry Wysham Lanier in an 1895 essay for the *Review of Reviews.* Lanier then launched into a lengthy recounting of American victories in America's Cup races, international track meets, rowing competitions, and tennis matches. With athletic supremacy over mainly English rivals established, argued Lanier in a rather questionable reading of results from international playing fields, new worlds to conquer came into view. "In looking forward to the athletic prospect for 1896, by far the most important event is the wonderful international meeting to be held at Athens, which has been everywhere hailed as a revival of the Olympic Games," trumpeted Lanier, hyping Coubertin's festival of modern strenuosity.[10]

Lanier's proclamation of the Olympics as the pinnacle of athletic performance fell mainly on deaf ears. Fewer than a score of American athletes, most of them collegians from Princeton University or the Boston Athletic Association (BAA), answered Coubertin's initial call. Their deeds in the first Olympics, as American cognizance of the event grew, would be completely out of proportion to their numbers. They would set standards of achievement and patterns of participation for future American Olympians. Even more important, they and in particular their chroniclers convinced the nation that the Olympic Games were a fitting forum for the sporting republic to express its peculiar blend of political belief and muscular persuasion. In short order Lanier's estimation of the revived Olympic celebrations as the zenith of athletic spectacle became commonly accepted wisdom in the United States.

A Holiday for the "Fast Set" or a National Mission?

News of the Olympic revival "was received with the greatest enthusiasm by lovers of athletic sport the world over," announced *New England Magazine,* but not everyone in the United States agreed with that assessment.[11] Some Americans viewed the revival of the ancient games as a dubious proposition. "The sun of Homer, to be sure, still smiles upon Greece, and the vale of Olympia is still beautiful," wrote Rufus B. Richardson in *Scribner's New Monthly Magazine.* "But no magician's wand and no millionaire's money can ever charm back into material existence the setting in which the Olympic Games took place."[12] A pessimistic commentator on Princeton's Olympic adventure ridiculed the notion of an Olympic revival in a letter to the *New York Times.* "Princeton may have a heavy surplus in its treasury, and its team may be in need of an ocean voyage[;] these are purely local questions," laughed the writer. "But," the gadfly warned, "the American sportsman should know that in going to Athens he is taking an expensive journey to a third rate capital, where he will not even have a daily post from the outside world, where he will be devoured by fleas, as was the emperor Frederick; where he will suffer physical torments greater even than at Saratoga Lake, and where, if he does win all the prizes, it will be an honor requiring explanation."[13]

Some commentators thought that the games would be an exercise in frivolous nostalgia. "The Greeks knew nothing of the pitiless, unrelenting drain on the nervous forces, which the mere running of the complicated machinery of modern civilization inflicts upon us," theorized Paul Shorey in *Forum*. The revival of an antiquarian institution seemed out of place in a world where "to be ready for his opportunity when it comes, the statesman or captain of industry must slave at his desk eight hours a day," noted Shorey. "At this price are won the prizes of modern life," he admonished, "and the men whose hearts are set upon them will not consent even in youth to loiter whole days in the gymnasium like Socrates or Critias or Alcibiades." Thus, Shorey concluded, "the only classes in the modern world whose interest in athletics is wholly genuine and unfeigned are professionals, idle young amateurs of wealth, a few educators, and the least studious among our college youths."[14]

The collegians who ventured to Athens kept good standing in their classes, excepting triple-jumper James B. Connolly, who quit Harvard when he could not secure permission for the trip. Connolly ranked near the bottom of his class at Harvard. When his dean advised him against going to Athens because he might not be readmitted, he blurted, "I am not resigning and I am not making application to reenter. But I *am* going to the Olympic Games, so I am through with Harvard right now. Good day sir."[15]

Shorey's rejection of collegiate athletics typified the animosity that certain sectors of the business community directed toward athletics. A few industrial magnates, such as Andrew Carnegie, dismissed sport as a waste of time. Carnegie scoffed that American collegians who were more interested in sporting clubs than practical business knowledge "have been 'educated' as if they were destined for life upon some other planet than this."[16] Shorey and Carnegie expressed a minority viewpoint, however. Most of the business community preferred extracurricular athletic activities to the leisurely vices of the "fast set." They recognized in sport a power for preparing young men for corporate life.

Models of the Sporting Republic

The college sport boom of the 1880s and 1890s contributed immensely to the literature of the sporting republic. Supporters of the strenuous life argued that sport made colleges into model republics. Eugene L. Richards, a Yale mathematics professor and a major booster of the rapidly growing collegiate athletic establishment, proclaimed that "in athletics the college world is a little republic of young men" and rhetorically asked, "Is the system worth something as a means of preparation for the responsibilities of the larger republic?"[17] Walter Camp, Yale's pioneering football promoter and a major public figure in the cult of the strenuous life, concurred with Richards. Camp focused on the "law-making" prowess of college teams and sporting clubs and lauded the experiences in practical democracy that he felt that athletics provided for college students.[18] As Albert Shaw explained, "Educators everywhere have begun to appreciate the fact that physical culture is as truly a part of the business of schools as mental and moral culture." Athletics and physical education became increasingly professionalized and firmly integrated into the modern college curricula. "Greek, or Calculus, or Chemistry may be optional; but proper care, discipline and development of the physical man, in the judgment of the chief educators, should be uniformly required of every student," opined Shaw. He considered the revived Olympics to be one of the most "hopeful signs of the day."[19]

The new brand of higher education placed athletics at the center of college life and bred new traditions among the genteel "Eastern Establishment." The Eastern Establishment provided many key figures in American political, intellectual, and economic circles during the late nineteenth and early twentieth centuries. Perhaps because athletics had played such an important role in producing a sense of community during their formative years at prep schools and Ivy League colleges, those powerful elites were among the leaders in the fight to create a sporting republic. They served the nation as self-appointed "cultural custodians," and so their support of sport carried tremendous weight in public debates over the value of modern athletics.[20]

Admission to the powerful clique generally required an education from one of the ivy-covered institutions that dotted the eastern seaboard. Like the archetypal Ivy Leaguers characterized in Owen Johnson's *Stover at Yale,* the American Olympians were immersed in the "four glorious years, good times, [and] good fellows" of college life. The "real" world lurked after college: "only four years, and then the world with its perplexities and grinding trials."[21] The lessons of the playing field, Johnson insisted, would temper collegians for their struggles.

One American academician, Professor William A. Elliot of Allegheny College, asserted that the Olympic trip might alleviate some of the impurities that plagued the sporting republic. "Every one of our out-of-door sports has been debased to the service of the professional athlete, whose object is to develop not a symmetrical and healthy man, but a distorted animal machine fitted by long training for the performance of this or that particular feat or skill." Elliot hoped that the new Olympic Games would rescue American athletics from professionalism and set new standards for sport by replacing the scramble for the "almighty dollar" with the quest for the "simple olive branch." Elliot believed that such a change in direction was "absolutely essential to the physical salvation of a race as tensely strung and nervous as Americans."[22]

The Allegheny College professor's hopes that the Olympics would enforce a beneficent standard of amateurism on college athletics marked the beginning of a long tradition of viewing Olympism as a purifying element in the games of the sporting republic. If sport was to prepare people for the business of life, then it had to escape from the very evils that made it a necessity in a modern civil society. That sport cannot do so remains a troubling irony. In offering collegiate athletes as Olympians, Americans tried to perpetuate the illusion of the Olympics as a pure form of sport. Thus many American intellectuals and parts of the public associated Olympic sport directly with the supposed character-building features of the sporting republic. The arguments of the Shoreys and Carnegies, which did not allow athletics a function in the modern world, were significantly out of tune with the spirit of the times.

Coubertin had insisted to his critics that the Olympics would not be an exercise in antiquarianism, unconnected to modern problems and concerns. "Modern, very modern, will be these restored Olympian Games," he wrote.[23] Charles Waldstein, in *Harper's Weekly*, declared that Olympic sport "is international and democratic, and accordingly it responds to the ideas and needs of the present day."[24] Professor Elliot echoed Coubertin and Waldstein: "The new games are not to be the old ones transplanted to these modern times, but they are designed to hold the same relation to general athletics of to-day as did the Olympic festival to the athletics of its age." In American minds, accustomed to seeing the classical Greeks as Americans who just happened to live in the Bronze Age, such a statement conjured visions of an international stadium in which they could exhibit their sporting republic. Elliot certainly thought in those terms, insisting that the spectacle in Athens would make the common contemporary Greek hunger for American-style democracy. "Yesterday a serf he is to-day learning the arts of democracy," opined Elliot. Not having heard of the plans underway in Boston and Princeton, however, he lamented, "At this writing it is not certain that America will be represented at all."[25] The professor should not have worried. The sporting republic could not resist an opportunity to vie for the imaginations of the world on the fields under Coubertin's "flag of athleticism."[26]

The First American Olympic Team

On March 2, 1896, a small contingent of athletes gathered at the docks of Hoboken, New Jersey, to begin a journey to Athens. The American Olympic hopefuls had booked a transatlantic passage on the North German Lloyd Lines' steamer *Fulda*. The send-off was a raucous affair, punctuated by cheers for Princeton University and the Boston Athletic Association. The Olympians sailed first class on the *Fulda*. Sumptuous banquets, masked balls, and comfortable deck chairs beckoned, and waiters catered to the athletes' needs. The trainers kept close watch on their charges, exercising them in heavy sweaters and light, rubber-soled shoes on the second cabin deck, which the captain had ordered cleared for the team's workouts.[27]

The impetus for the trip came from a Princeton professor of history, William Milligan Sloane. While in Europe to gather data for his work on Napoléon, Sloane had taken interest in Baron de Coubertin's attempts to revive the ancient Olympics. Sloane served as the American representative to the International Olympic Committee (IOC) while it was planning the Olympic revival. In 1896 he became the chairman of the American Olympic Committee. He convinced Princeton to send a four-man team consisting of Robert Garrett Jr., Francis A. Lane, Albert Clinton Tyler, and H. B. Jamison, all members of the Tiger track squad and the junior class. The BAA sent a squad comprising Arthur Blake, Thomas E. Burke, Ellery H. Clark, Thomas P. Curtis, and William W. Hoyt, under the leadership of "athletic instructor" John Graham.[28] James B. Connolly of Boston's Suffolk Athletic Club accompanied the Boston group. Blake, Clark, Hoyt, and Connolly were Harvard men. Burke represented Boston University, and Curtis wore the colors of the Massachusetts Institute of Technology and Columbia College.[29] Brothers and U.S. Army captains Sumner and John Payne of Boston joined the track and field contingent and competed in the pistol-shooting contests. Swimmer Gardiner Williams completed the team.[30]

Princeton's Professor Sloane had noble aspirations for the first Olympics. "I am only interested in sports from a moral view," claimed Sloane. "I believe that international contests do lots of good. The more higher classes of different nations get to know one another, the less likelihood there is of their fighting." By "higher classes" Professor Sloane had in mind the new group of progressive, professionally oriented, college-educated Americans that emerged in the late nineteenth century. The professional class was moving toward new perspectives on formulating solutions to problems in American society. They had invented modern sport in the United States and sought to reform certain sectors of society through it.

Certainly the Ivy Leaguers who composed America's first Olympic team were members of the "higher classes." Robert Garrett captained the Princeton squad. Garrett's uncle and namesake had been president of the Baltimore and Ohio Railroad Company. Garrett put the shot, hurled the discus, and high-jumped. He also found time for membership in "the popular Tiger Inn Social Club" and was "one of the leaders of the social circles of the college." Princeton's Francis Lane was a sprinter from Franklin, Ohio. Lane, favored among Princeton's contingent "to win glory for his college and country at Athens," took great pride in his academic accomplishments and surrounded himself with "distinctively intellectual" friends. Albert Clinton Tyler, from the exclusive Wyoming section of Cincinnati, Ohio, and the right tackle of the Princeton varsity football eleven, went to Athens to pole-vault. Tyler had recently secured a membership in Garrett's fraternity, the Tiger Inn Club. Another member of the prestigious Tiger Inn Club, H. B. Jamison of Peoria, Illinois, completed Princeton's contingent. Jamison planned to run the 400-meter race at Athens.[31]

Princeton's Olympians outfitted themselves in "white suits with orange and black bands from shoulder to waste [*sic*], and the Stars and Stripes in miniature on the breast, thus showing the college and country" that they represented. Professor Sloane expressed his pleasure at Princeton's entry and regretted "that other institutions have failed to show a like courage." Questions of courage aside, since the Athens games had been scheduled for mid-April, which fell in the midst of spring semesters at American universities, most collegians who had gotten word of the Olympic meeting could not attend. Princeton's trainer, "Scotty" McMaster, assured the *New York Times* that the "Princeton team would bring honor to its college and its country."[32] The *Cleveland Leader* disagreed: "It is not likely that the little group of American athletes who are on their way to Athens to take part in the new Olympian games . . . can make a very good showing for this country. They are only a few men from the Boston Athletic Association and a few from Princeton College, and the party will have hardly a single athlete who would be picked out to share in an international contest which was to be held in America."[33]

Although the American Olympic Committee had been formed in 1893, it played no part in organizing or financing the 1896 team. Princeton's team found financing when a "rich, anonymous donor allowed them money to travel."[34] James Connolly later asserted that Robert Garrett had financed the Princeton contingent's trip.[35] After considerable difficulties in raising the necessary funds by a subscription from the Boston Athletic Association membership, the BAA expedition was bankrolled by stockbroker Arthur Burnham and guaranteed by the promises of Massachusetts's governor Oliver Ames.[36] The elite collegians went to the first modern Olympics with Eastern Establishment funding.

As they settled into their first-class berths, the Princetonians and the Boston Athletic Association's "fine-looking fellows" seemed to be on a European holiday rather than a crusade of athletic conquest. As a *New York Times* reporter gossiped, "The athletes will be accompanied by Mrs. T. Harrison Garrett, the mother of Captain Garrett, who will also chaperon a small party of young ladies on the trip."[37] The *Fulda* was bound for Gibraltar, where the Olympic team would board another steamer for Naples and then proceed to Brindisi by rail. At Brindisi they planned to sail on a Mediterranean steamer for the west coast of Greece, from there completing their trek to Athens by rail.[38]

Crisis Years

The baron de Coubertin's France was not the only nation struggling to come to grips with the "moral disorder" engendered by "industrial science." The year 1896 witnessed the culmination of an anxiety that had racked American society since the end of the Civil War. Ever since the conclusion of sectional conflict, the United States had been lurching along a path toward a future characterized by an industrialized, market-driven economy; an increasingly powerful central government; and an urbanized, specialized mass society. The birth of a "modern" order meant the destruction of older patterns. Americans were torn between the promises of wealth and progress that the new systems offered and the customary comforts of traditional patterns. Often Americans tried to reconcile both the imagined past and the hoped-for future during the transition to a modern order.

Albert Shaw hoped that the revival of the Olympics would usher in a new global era "binding together rival nations, and relegating the barbarism of war to an evil past." Shaw admitted that this position was "utopian," but he believed that sport might indeed produce "some ground for hope" and bring an international "programme for disarmament, with arbitration as a substitute for war."[39] Using the familiar modern rhetoric of conflict and common ground, Shaw cast sport as a tool for building national and international communities. "Experience has shown," he insisted, "that athleticism and sports can be made to minister to almost everything that is pernicious and degrading on the one hand, or can, if properly controlled and directed, minister powerfully to everything that is wholesome and ennobling."[40]

In 1896 the arbitration of social and economic disputes within the United States, let alone international conflicts, appeared to be a near impossibility. The American economy was reeling from the unregulated rush toward an industrialized system of production and a nationalized market. A decade of prosperity had come to an end in the Panic of 1893 and its corresponding financial crash. Businesses failed in record numbers. Unemployment grew to the point where one out of five American workers was idled. The depression served to stagger the old Protestant notion that poverty and unemployment result from sin. Americans found other causes for their calamities—sinister monopolies, trusts and the evil machinations of Wall Street, or other forces remote from individual control and accountability. Among laborers anxiety boiled over into activism. When labor struck, the corporations moved ruthlessly to maintain the social order. Coeur d'Alene, Idaho; Homestead, Pennsylvania; George Pullman's factory town and Chicago in Illinois; the anthracite coal fields of Kentucky, Indiana, Ohio, Pennsylvania, and West Virginia: all those locales erupted in violence during the early years of the 1890s.

Theodore Roosevelt sought to assuage the fears that the crisis years produced. Roosevelt assured the public that the economic and cultural calamities of the 1890s had not permanently marred the republic. "A nation's greatness lies in its possibility of achievement in the present," Roosevelt wrote, "and nothing helps it more than the consciousness of achievement in the past." In 1896 the past held George Washington, Abraham Lincoln, and other heroes of the American Revolution and the Civil War.[41] The present had a boatload of possibilities sailing to the inaugural modern Olympic Games.

An Athenian Spectacle

The college youths who traveled across the Atlantic on the *Fulda* were determined to add an Olympic adventure to the good times of their college days, but they were also in Greece to meet athletic challenges. On one level they resembled Baron de Coubertin's ideal Olympic amateurs, modeled on the British sporting gentleman, far more than future American Olympians would. Still, the "will to win" motivated them, particularly the triple-jumper Connolly, who gave up Harvard to compete at Athens. Coubertin insisted that the Anglo-American sporting gentleman radiated *eutrapelia,* an Aristotelian virtue comprising vitality, versatility, and most important, a sense of proportion.[42] The extreme "will to win" that agitated the BAA and Princeton's athletes would make a mockery of Coubertin's understanding of the American brand of sport, however. The American team journeyed to the mythical home of sport with a purpose. "All of us who love beauty, who have done no impiety or sacrilege, who believe in fair play, and who have stout hearts are Greeks in the highest sense," mused George Horton, the U.S. consul at Athens.[43] The American press insisted that "new" Athenians, the American branch of the family, were going to Athens to show the world the strength of their brand of civilization.

The Panatheniac Stadion in Athens had been refurbished by a wealthy Grecian merchant, George Averoff, to showcase the inaugural modern Olympics.[44] American observers marveled at the site, in spite of their discomfort at the general poverty they saw in Greece. *The Nation,* despite Godkin's dislike of American sport, covered the Olympics. Its reporter cabled that Athens "need not blush before the more stately and lavish magnificence of greater cities and wealthier nations; the immortal ruins of the Parthenon and the glorious Attic sky cannot be found or matched elsewhere."[45] Charles Waldstein claimed that the refurbished monument expressed a democratic spirit, unlike the slave-built architectural wonders of antiquity, particularly Egypt's pyramids. "The Stadium now will convey to the visitor some impression of magnitude, not in a monument erected by slaves for the glorification of one ruler, but in a structure to house a free and powerful community uniting in the peaceful delight at physical strength and skill."[46]

When the American team finally reached Athens, the emotional sight of the city that they had been taught was the birthplace of democracy and the Western tradition overwhelmed them. "All that we had ever read or heard of Greece and all that we had never read nor heard, but that was born within us, lay like white-heated strata in the hotbeds of our imaginations," recalled Connolly. No one spoke when the Parthenon came into view from the train. "But when breathing came easier—'Athens!' we cried; and the little word stood for all our years of thought, speech and subconscious reflection of the glory of things that were." The Americans felt a heavy obligation to prove themselves the heirs to the Greek tradition they imagined, a tradition that located the first stirrings of republicanism in Athens's "Golden Age."[47]

Athletes from Austria, Australia, Bulgaria, Chile, Denmark, France, Germany, Great Britain, Hungary, Sweden, Switzerland, the United States, and Greece participated in the games. Thousands of European and American tourists vacationing in the Mediterranean and the Holy Land flocked to Athens for the Olympic pageant. The heavy cruiser USS *San Francisco,* moored in Athens's harbor, provided the American team with additional fans. The Greek organizers created a festive atmosphere highlighted by constant band music, numerous concerts, nightly illuminations of Athens and Piraeus, torchlight marches, and fireworks displays. Visitors could also see the Greek royal family, the king of Serbia, Grand Duke George of Russia, and the widow of Crown Prince Rudolf of Austria with her two daughters. The pageantry and the crowds at the stadium lent "something to replace Olympia, and almost persuaded one that the old times had come around again when there was nothing more serious to do than to outrun, outleap, and outwrestle." One American tourist eagerly awaited an Olympic performance of Sophocles' *Antigone* but found the play a "disappointment to one who had seen 'Antigone' presented at Vassar College in 1893."[48]

Triple-jumper James Connolly later fictionalized his experiences at the original Olympic gala in a popular tale entitled "An Olympic Victor." He pictured
eager American tourists "rushing everywhere, with seemingly inexhaustible
supplies of energy—likewise of money." The Americans tried to buy everything
in sight. "Many of them seemed not to understand that even an unlimited purse
is not always potent." They wore "in their lapels little flags of their country, and
whenever a group of them assembled they were challenging one another to
wager on the chances of this or that competitor in the games."[49]

Hurdler Thomas Curtis remembered that the Greeks welcomed the American team by marching them through the city, to the delight of thousands of
onlookers. The organizing committee feted the Americans at the *Hôtel de Ville*,
where "speech after speech was made in Greek, presumably very flattering to
us, but of course entirely unintelligible. We were given large bumpers of the
white-rosin [resin] wine of Greece and told by our advisors that it would be a
gross breach of etiquette if we did not drain these off in response to the various toasts." Curtis recounted, "I could not help feeling that so much marching, combined with several noggins of resinous wine, would tell on us in the
contests the following day."[50]

The games began on a mild April 6, with 40,000 fans in the refurbished stadium and thousands more on the surrounding hills. That date marked the sev-
enty-fifth anniversary of the Greek declaration of independence. "The Greeks
have never forgotten the generous sympathy which the American people were
the first to display for the Greek cause in 1821; the stirring eloquence of Henry
Clay and Daniel Webster in behalf of Greek liberty, and the material aid brought
to Greek shores by Samuel G. Howe . . . are given a prominent place in modern Greek history," reported *The Nation*, playing up the American role in the
Greek struggle for political autonomy and identifying the United States as the
benefactor of all democratic-thinking peoples. The powerful journal of political opinion linked the enthusiastic welcome of the American Olympians with
the struggle for democracy.[51] As the games began, the media glibly connected
Olympic sport, American athletics, and political causes.

American Triumphs and Interpretations of the Results

New York Times reports estimated that the spectacle drew 100,000 people on
April 7.[52] *Outing*, however, warned that "while the crowds must have been enormous," American cablegrams estimating attendance were "no doubt exagger-
ated."[53] The "resinous wine" apparently had little impact on American performances, for the team dominated the track and field events as the throngs
watched. The BAA produced winners in seven events. Thomas Burke won the

100- and 400-meter races, Thomas Curtis triumphed in the 110-meter hurdles, Ellery Clark finished first in the high jump and the long jump, Connolly won the triple jump, and William Hoyt won the pole vault. Princeton's Robert Garrett won the shot put and discus competitions. Only the victories of Australian Edwin Flack (whom the Greeks insisted was "the same thing" as an American) in the 800- and 1,500-meter races and the climactic marathon victory of Greece's Spiridon Loues kept the Americans from sweeping the track and field events. One Athenian newspaper hypothesized that American success sprang from a physiology that "joined the inherited athletic training of the Anglo-Saxon to the wild impetuosity of the Redskin"—certainly an odd rendition of the "melting pot."[54]

"I think it was on the third or fourth day of the games that the Americanization of Europe began," recalled Curtis. The Americans shouted the Boston Athletic Association cheer, "B.-A.-A.—Rah-Rah-Rah!" whenever one of the Bostonians turned in a good performance. The "cheer never failed to amuse and astonish the spectators," Curtis chortled. The king even requested that the Americans perform a cheer for him. When they did, adding "a mighty '*Zito Hellas*'" to the finish, the stadium roared with approval.[55]

Charles Waldstein commended the crowds for their enthusiastic support of every nation's competitors. "Still, I venture to say that the greatest glee was shown at each successive victory that fell to our nation, the youngest of all, that carried off the palm and gained by far the greater number of prizes, namely, the Boston and Princeton boys," he noted. According to Waldstein, the Americans were well-received because of their democratic spirit. Prince George of Greece, the "chief umpire" of the games, admitted to Waldstein, "We all love the American athletes. They behaved so well, and are such good fellows. They taught our people a lesson with their true interest in sport itself. They would sit down with our men, rub their limbs after each trial, and advise them without any idea that they were rivals."[56] "America's athletic missionaries" taught every aspect of sport, from track and field techniques to spectators' manners.

The news of the collegians' victories at Athens filtered back to the United States through the American press. A few skeptics dismissed the importance of national victories. "To say that Mr. Robert Garrett's victory over the Greeks in hurling the discus was in sentiment as if nine Englishmen should thrash our champion league team, savors as strongly of anti-climax as the Georgian's evocation of Chicago as the 'Atlanta of the West,'" grumbled a *Scribner's* reporter. "One cannot help feeling that Mr. Garrett ought not to have done it."[57] Most of the press, however, celebrated the victories of Garrett and his Olympic teammates. "Who can read without a glow of patriotic pride and classical reminiscence that Robert Garrett of Princeton, N.J. has defeated the champion Greek discobulus, Paraskevopoulos, by six or seven inches?" wondered a *New York Times* correspondent.[58] "When it is considered that the Americans had little practice after their long voyage, and that Garrett was a novice at discus throwing . . . the wonderful versatility of the American athlete is apparent, and it is little wonder that, when the news of his victory was cabled to the United States, the halls of old Nassau rang with cheers," observed the *Scientific American.*[59]

Caspar Whitney became infected by the nationalism that the American Olympic victors inspired, telling *Harper's Weekly* readers that "from the oldest to youngest our athletes have taken the lion's share of honors." Whitney added a plug for Boston, observing that "six men went from the Hub, four of whom represented the Boston A.A., and they have secured seven first prizes."[60] An American eyewitness in Athens recounted in the *New York Times* that "it was hard at the very outset to see one flag go up as a signal of victory so many times in succession." He added, "One of the Princes is said to have remarked to an American: I really hope you won't sweep everything."[61] Perhaps Charles Wald-stein misread the Grecian "glee" that accompanied American wins. The *Scientific American,* nearly mimicking the *New York Times* correspondent, allowed that "it was indeed hard for the Greeks to see the American flag go up so many times in succession."[62]

But the press really worried little about Greek feelings. The *Chicago Record* imagined that the Greek athletes had entered the stadium ready to claim all the prizes, as "Greek poetry" demanded. "So they would have done had it not been for a number of bright young nineteenth-century college men who impertinently refused to consider traditions, and proceeded to beat their competitors in the most approved fashion of the college field," gloated the Chicago daily. The *Philadelphia Public Ledger* crowed that "it is an unusually fine feather in the American cap to have so many of the events . . . won by American athletes." The Philadelphia newspaper allowed that no comparisons could fairly be made between the modern American champions and the legendary Greek victors in the ancient games, but when the current American "performances were matched with those of athletes from all the leading countries of civilization, . . . the Americans came out ahead. That is honor enough for the present." The *Atlanta Constitution* added that "though America has none of the traditions and but little of the training possessed by these nations of the Old World, she has evinced her superiority over them in the games of their own choice, and from the heights of Mount Olympus she has transferred the laurel branch to her own distant borders."[63]

Despite the celebrations and headlines in the American press ("The Americans Ahead: Progress of the Olympic Games at Athens," "American Athletes Won: Princeton and Boston Boys Successful in Olympian Games," and "Honor for Americans: Sustained Their Reputations at the Olympic Games"), the American team won events only in track and field—excepting a one-two finish by Captains John and Sumner Payne in the twenty-five-meter military revolver shooting contest.[64] The United States did not field competitors in wrestling, weightlifting, cycling, gymnastics, fencing, or tennis, and Gardiner Williams found the Aegean sea much too cold for springtime swimming.[65]

The American press decided that triumph in track and field indicated victory in the Olympic Games, a tradition it continued in the reporting of later Olympics. Track and field became the focal point of American Olympic success stories. A *New York Times* commentator asserted that American dominance "in a programme of events that seemed carefully modeled on the classic pentathlon [a discus throw, a javelin throw, a standing broad-jump competition, a 200-meter footrace, and a wrestling match] indicates their success not over the Hellenes but over continental Europeans would have been yet more marked had the programme been modernized, and included for example, a football match which, if it had no prototype in Olympia, vividly recalls a Homeric battle."[66] The sporting republic, the press insisted, had proven its vigor.

Some sports authorities found the quality of competition at the first Olympics generally less than world class. Besides "the only remarkable performance of the games," Spiridon Loues' marathon run, the contestants' times fell "below the average of winners usually seen at important Anglo-Saxon track games." Caspar Whitney observed that "there seems to have been really no English entries of the first class; and outside of Burke, Hoyt, and Clark, there was no one of the Americans who could be expected to win in open games in the United States." The media blamed poor planning and organization for the lackluster quality of athletes at Athens. With "the wide world to draw upon, these Olympic Games should have had the representative athletic strength of nations—they could have—if the management had been efficient and opportune," remarked Whitney.[67] *Outing* concurred, disappointed about the level of competition and disgusted with the failure of the IOC to publicize the Olympics in the Anglo-American world.[68]

Odes to American Victors

The competition might have been less than first rate, the planning might have been less than adequate, and the American victory might have been less than complete, but the Olympic Games at Athens in 1896 laid the foundation for a mythology of American invincibility at future Olympics. Sportswriters played a central role in shaping the sporting republic. One popular story in American newspapers claimed that the American victor in the discus competition had sent a telegram home after his victory claiming, "Guskos [actually Gouskous, a former Greek champion discobulus] conquered Europe, but I conquered the world." A reporter confessed that the cable was a fraud, "but he took great pride in it: for he said it was what Garrett [the American discus thrower] ought to have sent."[69]

The American media, including newspapers, magazines, scholarly journals, novels, and popular histories, played an integral role in shaping the perception of the Olympics in the United States. They created the "explanation-forms" of the sporting republic. Paul Gallico, a leading American sportswriter in the 1920s and 1930s, argued that since the end of the Civil War, American society had used sport as a self-examining "mirror." Americans imagined themselves most clearly on playing fields. For the past century, he wrote in the 1960s, Americans had been preferring dreams of athletic heroics to those of military, political, or financial glory. Sport allowed Americans to craft an image of themselves, asserted Gallico; through heroic sporting deeds, "we are able to see clearly and judge ourselves."[70] Robert Garrett's victory did not belong just to him. It belonged to the mythmakers and culture crafters. It belonged, as would all future American Olympic feats, to those who sought to build a republic through sport.

The American athletes at the first Olympics greatly valued their victories. One competitor admitted, "I couldn't have congratulated my opponent if he had beaten me on my own ground, as a Greek fellow . . . did me."[71] In a telegram to Crown Prince Constantine, the Americans did thank the Greeks for their "great kindness and warm hospitality of which we have been continually the recipients."[72] In the pages of The Outlook, Maynard Butler sternly reminded future American Olympians that "as athletes they must look to their laurels in long distance running," but she also counseled that "as men, they must remember in 1900 and 1904 the pattern of generosity in defeat set them by the Athenians in 1896."[73]

The Americans planned to "look to their laurels in long distance running," but losing gracefully seemed almost anti-American, as Connolly illustrated in his fictional account of the marathon race. When Spiridon Loues passed his fallen American foe (Blake in reality), a remarkable scene ensued. The American runner had led the race until, overcome by exhaustion, he collapsed in a heap beside the road. The Greek police monitoring the race had rushed to aid the fallen runner when Loues strode past the American and "even smiled at him; but such was his humiliation, nevertheless, that he was motioning the guards to draw off his jersey, on the breast of which he wore the flag of his country. That flag he did not want to be seen on him, as he, a defeated man, was being driven into the city." "Truly," Connolly had Loues think, "this pride of country, it adorns like a laurel wreath. No wonder the Americans are a great nation."[74]

The Olympics generated emotions in addition to national pride. Some Americans shared Baron de Coubertin's romantic belief that the modern Olympics could be a "potent, if indirect, factor in securing universal peace."[75] Waldstein believed that the Olympics would be a catalyst in the creation of an international federation of humankind: "Is it too visionary to hope that these games may contribute to the realization of this ideal striving of the nobler citizens in our civilized communities: that they may intensify this longing for a great federation as they combine all nationalities in peaceful emulation, out of which the physical welfare of our men will ensue?"[76] The implication underlying the notion was that if such a federation came to fruition, it would take on an American shape, given the millennial promise of the sporting republic to bring progress, democracy, and justice to all who fell under the spell of the United States' brand of athletics.

Coubertin himself cheered the national pride exhibited by Olympic athletes. "The victors in the *Stadion* at Athens wished for no other recompense when they heard the people cheer the flag of their country in honor of their achievement," the baron observed.[77] Americans paid no heed to the baron's distinctions between nationalism and patriotism, however, turning Olympic sport into jingoistic spectacle. *Outing* declared that the American Olympians had so overwhelmed the world that "their victories were applauded as vociferously as if they had been Greeks instead of Americans."[78] When the *Fulda* returned to the United States, crowds gave the athletes a "royal welcome." The fans on the docks paid tribute to the champions while a band struck up "See, the Conquering Hero Comes."[79] Baron de Coubertin's Olympic maxim insisted that "the essential thing is not to have conquered but to have fought well."[80] The Americans had, in their minds, conquered. Fighting well was fine, but winning was the important thing. The results of the Athenian athletic adventure allowed Americans to judge themselves superior to the rest of the world in everything from performing Sophocles' *Antigone* to hurling discuses.

Anticipating Future Olympics

Timoleon Philemon, the Greek secretary general of the first modern Olympics, announced as the games closed that "the brilliant success which crowned the first Int. Olympic Games celebrated in Athens, and the enthusiastic interest with which these athletic contests have been regarded by the whole Hellenic race, seem to us sure proof that the blood of our glorious ancestors still flows in our veins."[81] The success of the Athens Olympics had spawned plans for the creation of the Panatheniac Games, to be held in Athens every four years, in between the Olympics. The IOC planned to continue the Olympics on the cycle begun in 1896, rotating the spectacles among the great cities of the "civilized" world. The Greeks took pride in their Olympic achievements, but the Americans had cornered the market on identifying Olympic achievement with national prowess. Breathless accounts in the American press depicted a battle to host the 1904 Olympics—the 1900 games had already been scheduled for Coubertin's Paris—between Berlin, Stockholm, and New York.[82] The sporting republic wanted to display its vigor on its home turf.

The explanations that the media offered for American successes at the inaugural modern Olympics set the pattern for future discussions of athletic achievement and political culture. In 1896 the American sense of proportion demanded victory from its athletes, contradicting Baron de Coubertin's notion of *eutrapelia*. The special providence of American civilization had been wed with Olympian achievement. The Olympians deeds had been translated into righteous affirmations of American ideals. The first volume of American Olympic mythology had been compiled.

Approaching Olympia at a different angle from Coubertin, American athletes, sporting officials, and public chroniclers turned the Olympics into evocative spectacles for the examination and celebration of American political culture. The rest of the world was often skeptical, and frequently scandalized, by the athletic stories that Americans told about themselves. For a nation conditioned by history and tradition to think of itself as a "city upon a hill" or a "chosen people," global reception of their messages mattered, paradoxically, both immensely and very little. The rejection of the American message could be read as either a failure of righteousness by "America's athletic missionaries" or the blind stupidity of other nations. Given the particular dynamics of American athletic nationalism, Coubertin's call for a special kind of patriotism and international tolerance of diversity met with little sympathy in American athletic circles. From the beginning the United States sought to turn the Olympics into an American spectacle.

In the cultural crises that accompanied modernization, the Olympics provided the United States with a secular corollary to the old Puritan doctrine of assurance, a very American trope that linked worldly success with spiritual purity. In a nation in which, although Calvinism itself may have lost its vigor, Calvinist nerves still tempered perspectives, assurance was no minor issue. The Athens Olympics provided the sporting republic with the perfect forum for proving to Americans that the powers of sport were at work reforming society. Future Olympics would pose a variety of questions about the political culture of the United States, including inquiries about the relations between classes, races, and genders. Those questions would give Americans a chance to reflect on the nature, the purpose, and the destiny of their nation. Knit together by the sports pages of the newly emerged mass media, the United States would continue to examine itself at the Olympics.

Professor William Milligan Sloane, the original prophet of the Olympic idea in the United States who supposedly adhered as closely as any American to Coubertin's vision of Olympism, constructed a theory of culture production based on his history of the ancient and modern Olympics. In his interpretation of classical antiquity, Sloane contended that "Greek civilization imposed itself upon the central world by an irresistible moral compulsion." The professor hypothesized that "no single factor so contributed to create this moral force as the Olympic Games."[83] Sloane argued that the modern Olympics had created the same moral force in the twentieth century that he imagined the classical Olympics had created in the ancient world. "The field therefore of the Olympic idea is not merely sportive and social, it is educational and sociological as well," wrote Sloane. "The intercourse of athletes and their friends makes for reciprocal good will and international peace: but in its largest aspect the idea makes for the general uplift and personal purity of untold millions."[84]

America's Olympians preached their national values in the hope that they would aid in the "general uplift and personal purity of untold millions," in the United States and around the world. American Olympic mythology taught that Olympic success sprang from the same forces that shaped the idealized portrait of the American republic: political liberty, hard work, free competition, egalitarianism, respect for and understanding of law, and innovation—the cornerstones of the democratic experiment. As Greek civilization had imposed itself on the world of antiquity "by an irresistible moral compulsion," so too might the "chosen people" shape the twentieth century. Such was the hope of the inventors of the sporting republic. Thus the modern Olympic Games would provide Americans with the same great moral forum in their world that Professor Sloane insisted the ancient Olympics had provided the Greeks. In these arenas winning was indeed everything.

3

Paris, 1900:
Exhibiting American Athletic Nationalism

One of the founders of the American sporting republicanism, Caspar Whitney, set a challenge for U.S. athletes preparing to contest for national pride at the second Olympic Games, scheduled for 1900 in Paris. Whitney had a great deal of disdain for French sporting life, which he portrayed as antithetical to the traditions and prowess of American sport. Whitney thought that in contrast to the robust republicanism that American devotion to the sport produced, French athletic practice mirrored the corruption and decay inherent in France's bankrupt version of republicanism. A host of American political critics shared Whitney's view of France's failing republican culture, pointing as Whitney did to the contrasts between French and American culture. The uniqueness of Whitney's argument stemmed from the fact that he made sport central to his republican cultural critique. His attitude presaged the nationalistic tensions that would soon surface at the Paris Olympics, particularly since Whitney was to play a leading role in organizing the American performance and explaining American conduct.

In May 1900, with the Olympic track and field competition only two months away, Whitney published a scathing essay in which he declared that "the Frenchmen is not a sport-lover as we . . . understand it." Whitney asserted that whereas Americans radiated strenuous energy, the French exhibited a "national indisposition to vigorous out-of-door play, and national prejudice against anything not of French origin." American sport fueled the construction of a wholesome and progressive modern civilization, he continued, but "whatever there has been in France of sport indigenous, has owed its life either to fashion—as, for example, stag-hunting—or to the national gambling instinct, as in the case of horse-racing." *Outing*'s editor concluded his broadside against French athletics with a fusillade against the average Frenchman, who "affects to make a pleasure of his sport, but deep in his heart I believe he really curses the Anglo-Saxon sporting wavelet which has swept over his country in recent years."[1]

Athletic Nationalism and Pierre de Coubertin's Dream of International Olympic Harmony

Whitney's attack on the French was not unique. At the beginning of the twentieth century, an intense athletic nationalism flourished in the United States. In the climate of militant expansionism that infected the country at the turn of the century, athletic nationalism took on a distinctively strident character.

"Perhaps there is no higher test of a man's all-around abilities than his power to govern wisely; at any rate, it is a truth borne in mind, in this connection, that the governing races today are races of sportsmen," mused Price Collier in a fin de siècle survey of Anglo-American sporting culture for *Outing*. "The people who play games are inheriting the earth, perhaps because it makes them meek," chuckled the Unitarian minister. He attributed what he perceived as the weaknesses of other nations to their lack of the sporting mentality. "The French do not play games," Collier reported, and as a result their birth rate had declined precipitously, threatening a dangerous depopulation and indicating their general malaise and lack of vigor. The Spaniards did not play games either, "and travelers in and students of Spain and the Spanish agree that their two most salient characteristics are overweening personal pride and cruelty." Collier noted that the Chinese despised exercise "and can scarcely be driven to fight, even for their country, and their lack of decision and their pulpy condition of dependence are now all too manifest."

Collier identified the sporting life as the key to Anglo-American world domination. "The rules of amateur sport, written and understood, are really, though in different phraseology, the rules for the making of the highest type of manhood," he insisted. Although the average inhabitant of other nations might be "quicker mentally" than Anglo-American folk—Collier exhibited a profoundly anti-intellectual bias—"they are all far inferior to the American or Englishman in the fundamental virtues that make a first rate man," he proclaimed. "Steadiness, truthfulness, loyalty, resourcefulness, endurance, gentleness—they win out against any other qualities." The practice of amateur sport nurtured and sustained those qualities, although gentleness seemed out of place. "And they win logically because even weaker races see that such virtues are more lasting," Collier insisted. "As a result in India the natives will lend their hoarded wealth to their English rulers, while they hide it from native rulers; and the Anglo-Saxon's word has come to be more valuable in the markets of the world than other men's bonds, and all because there is a man behind it."[2]

Caspar Whitney concurred with Collier's labeling of China as backward and "non-athletic"—although Whitney discovered evidence in Japan that some Asians were more forward-looking.[3] "It speaks highly of the sagacity of Japan's nineteenth century latter day sponsors that they should appreciate the peculiar need to Japan of implementing in her boys a taste for healthful and vigorous physical effort, so that when they grow to manhood there should be a fresher and a sturdier mental activity, with its corresponding elevation of ideals," observed Whitney. That Japan, "in her progressive strides, has also taken on one of the wisest features of modern civilization—athletics"—validated for Whitney the assumption that the Japanese were on the correct path to modernity.[4]

Lloyd Bryce added Germany and Russia to the list of nations plagued by ignorance of the strenuous life. "Had Bismarck guided the restless spirit of the German nation out of the path of war into the channels of competitive games, there would be less occasion for the present restrictive measures," he reported. "If the Russian student were encouraged to devote his superabundant vitality to physical exercise, he might become less of a political visionary, . . . while, if the entire people had some form of national games, they might cease to be the 'empire of the discontented.'"[5] By 1900, as the United States moved toward becoming a world power of the first rank, American commentators had decided that athletics was a necessary ingredient in the composition of modern states. Results from the playing fields confirmed American ideas of power, race, and progress.

Such was the climate in which France's Baron Pierre de Coubertin penned an open letter to Americans in 1900 detailing his conviction that the games of the Second Olympiad were destined to become the most important athletic event ever held in the history of the world. He deflected Whitney's criticisms by noting that "Anglo-Saxons have some trouble in getting used to the idea that other nations can devote themselves to athleticism." Coubertin diplomatically gave credit to the United States and Great Britain for blazing the sporting trail, while holding firmly to the conviction that "if this honor is incontestably theirs, it does not follow that young men of other races, with blood and muscles like their own, should not be worthy of walking in their footsteps." The baron wanted the Paris Olympics to serve as "a sort of athletic starting-point for the twentieth century." Coubertin thought that the Olympic movement could profoundly reshape the modern world.

In a rumination on the differences between ancient and modern Olympic spectacles, the baron clarified his vision of the Olympic movement's role in the construction of modernity. "The Olympian Games of ancient times brought the Greek world together every four years in the beautiful valley of Olympia, to contemplate a spectacle the uniformity of which seems to have constituted an additional charm in the eyes of the spectators," surmised Coubertin. The ritual sameness of ancient Greek Olympic festivities, repeated cyclically at their original site, met the needs of classical Greek civilization. Ancient routines did not match modern desires. "The inclination of the modern world is entirely different," the baron revealed. Moderns demanded that their spectacles provide both variety and novelty, he noted, because modern transportation and communication systems had intensified curiosity and created so many new experiences that people had time to see things only once.

Coubertin had taken modern sensibilities into consideration by planning to rotate the Olympics among the capitals of the world rather than re-create a permanent Olympian site. He insisted that the move to Paris in 1900, and in the future to other cities, would provide modern spectators with both novelty and variety. "We have not been drawn into the error of constructing a cardboard Stadium to reproduce Pericles, with the hill of Montmarte in the background to replace the Acropolis," he promised, noting that such an approach would have proved "ridiculous and paltry."

Instead, the games of the Second Olympiad had been attached to "a permanent festival of attractions," the massive Parisian International Exposition commemorating the beginning of the new century. According to Coubertin, those arrangements ensured that the Olympic organizers would concern themselves only "with the technical part of the sport in question."[6] What better venue for the exhibition of a modern technology such as organized sport than at the spectacle held to honor the transition from traditional society to the machine-driven universe of modernity?[7]

World's Fairs, Olympic Games, and the Control of Modern Energies

The pairing of Olympics and expositions made logistical sense, as the baron de Coubertin understood. World's fairs attracted travelers from all over the globe and served as nexuses for international events. By the latter half of the nineteenth century, the exposition had become the great Western festival for the celebration of mechanisms and material progress. "The great fairs which the energies of Europe and America have held may be regarded as the tentative efforts which civilization is making in the art of organization, grouping and harmony," wrote John Brisben Walker in the popular turn-of-the-century mass-market monthly *Cosmopolitan*.[8] Expositions dangled images of contemporary progress and utopian tomorrows in front of millions of eager spectators.

Beginning with London's fantastic Crystal Palace Exposition in 1851, world's fairs schooled the West in the gospel of progress. "Expositions accentuate the deficiencies of the past, give us a realization of our present advantages, predict the developments of the near future, and equip the arm and brain alike of the mechanic, the engineer and the philosopher for further and immediate advances into the realms of the possible," announced Walker.[9] By the early twentieth century the exposition had become a modern spectacle signifying progress, prosperity, and utopian potential.[10] The connection between expositions and Olympic Games also underscored the fact that by the beginning of the twentieth century, much of the industrialized West considered sport to be a technology and an important agent of social reform.

Coubertin's dream had been to link ancient with modern values, and although he made concessions to his contemporaries' fascination with novelty and variety, he insisted that the revived Olympics functioned in a transhistorical fashion. "To-day, as in former times, the Olympian Games respond to a natural and healthy inclination of humanity," he preached. "In all times and in all countries, if young men are active and in good health, they will be fond of manly games and competitions in which they display their strength and agility, and, incited by the instinct of emulation, they will desire to contend, in the name of their country, against young men of other lands," Coubertin theorized in an effort to link the cultic patriotism of Greek city-states with the veneration of the modern nation-state.[11]

Coubertin hoped that the Paris Olympics would counter the unnatural and unhealthy inclinations that he believed resulted from rapid modernization. Modernity and its social and cultural perils consumed his attention. He worried that elemental forces unleashed by new historical developments threatened civilization's future. The baron thought that Western civilization's overemphasis on intellectual life, particularly in the eighteenth century, had disturbed the ancient equilibrium between mind and matter, unleashing dangerous currents that were whirling the world down bleak paths. Coubertin drew some of his insights from the romantic tradition, which arose to oppose the "escapism" of the Enlightenment's tendency to abstract all experience and perception. He eschewed the arid rationalism of the Enlightenment and turned instead to a concept of primal forces that he believed motivated human behavior and shaped civilizations. He understood those primal forces as basic forms of human energy, such as war and nationalism, which could paradoxically create and destroy civilizations.[12] The nineteenth century, posited Coubertin in a summary of his theory of history, "which is nearing its close in troubled and uncertain peace and whose beginning was marked by events so sanguinary, succeeded an epoch of great intellectual activity and of marked physical inertia."

The root cause of the present epoch's trouble, according to Coubertin, was the Enlightenment's excessive adoration of mental power. He explained the conflagrations of the French Revolution and Napoléon's reign as the inevitable unleashing of primal responses to an era of excessive intellectualizing. "It is true," averred Coubertin of the Napoleonic episode, "that . . . upon the frontiers of their own land and in far distant lands—at the foot of the Pyramids,

on the Danube, in Spain, under the walls of the Muscovite Kremlin—the sol-
diers of France, during a period of twenty years, gave to the world one of the
greatest athletic spectacles which it had ever witnessed."

The awesome force of unregulated human energy, the primal aggressive
urge from which he thought war and sport originate, thrilled and astounded
the baron. Nonetheless, he recognized that the elemental forces of human
nature needed to be controlled, or they would rip the modern world asun-
der. Approaching the matter from a much different direction, he came to a
conclusion about sport very similar to the one proposed by William James.
The modern world, the baron believed, required a moral equivalent for war.
Coubertin heralded the new social technology of organized sport as the key
tool for shoring up the "uncertain peace" in which the globe awaited the
twentieth century. His revived Olympic Games, first at Athens and then at
Paris, were designed as a remedy for the excesses of the nineteenth century
and of the human condition.

Coubertin offered the Olympics as an institution for directing primal forces
in progressive directions and for channeling nationalistic vigor into productive realms. "At intervals of four years it is hoped that the twentieth century may
see its youth assembling successively at the great capitals of the world in order
to contest with force and skill for the symbolic branch," the baron ruminated.
Coubertin desperately wanted to reconstruct an energetic France, but he was
aware of the dark side of nationalism. He advocated not the denial of elemental energies but their management "upon the most pacific of all battle fields,
namely, the field of sports." In such a manner might the legacy of the French
Revolution, the militant nationalism that served as the most powerful template
in nineteenth-century French political paradigms, be transmuted into the positive virtue of Coubertin's idealized notion of patriotism.[13]

The French Republic in Crisis

Coubertin's desires become all the more intelligible when viewed in the context of the French situation at the turn of the century. France floundered toward modernization. Although the country possessed the greatest store of natural resources in Europe, population decline as well as cultural and structural
resistance to industrialism relegated the French economy to a position far behind the productive capacity of Germany, Great Britain, and the United States.
Severe political and ideological schisms rent the Third Republic. The legislative totalitarianism that characterized political life in the Third Republic prevented any coherent programs of executive action and created a deep-seated
governmental inertia and Byzantine labyrinth of parliamentary intrigue. Gov-

ernments rose and fell with dizzying rapidity, secure in the knowledge that their short tenures would absolve them of responsibility for solving France's long-term problems.

Political opposition to republican principles from the Right became particularly virulent during the last decade of the nineteenth century. The antagonisms came into sharp relief during the Dreyfus Affair. In 1894 a French army court unjustly convicted Captain Alfred Dreyfus of passing military secrets to Germany. A combination of anti-Semitism in the French high command, bumbling police work, and forged evidence led to the verdict. It quickly became clear in army intelligence circles that Dreyfus had been falsely convicted, and knowledge of the injustice slowly leaked to government officials and the press. Instead of redressing the miscarriage of justice, the French army engaged in a cover-up that spread to its highest levels. The high command and officer corps were dominated by Rightist ideologues who made the Dreyfus Affair into a litmus test for support of the army, the Church, and their vision of French patriotism. Their opponents associated the struggle to free Dreyfus with the principles of the Third Republic, the concept of rule by law, and the right to equal justice.

The Dreyfus Affair, coupled with the fundamental instability of Third Republic government, pushed France into political chaos. By 1900 the republicans triumphed over the Right, but not before enormous damage had been done to political institutions and severe schisms had formed in French political culture—schisms that would plague the nation for the next five decades.[14] Coubertin, a noble supporter of the Church and the army, became an anti-Dreyfusard during the crisis even though he feared the rabid nationalism of the far Right. The passions that the Dreyfus Affair brought to the surface further convinced the baron that a cosmopolitan movement was necessary to counterbalance the destructive power of Rightist nationalism and that France desperately needed to erect its own version of a sporting republic to direct political energies in productive directions.[15] In 1900, with France still bitterly divided by the Dreyfus Affair, the baron called the youth of the world to Paris.

American Schemes and Designs

American purveyors of athletic technology would work on three tasks at the Paris exposition. They would seek to convert the world to an American style of sport. They would endeavor to vanquish the rest of the world in the Olympic arena to demonstrate to the unenlightened the superiority of the American political and social structure. Finally, they would toil to prove that modern American civilization did indeed produce, in the words of the man who in 1901 would become their president, the "strongest and boldest people." Nationalism, scientism, and the growing power of the professionalizing middle classes would meet in the quest to field a team for the games of the Second Olympiad.

The U.S. effort drew from a much broader base of support in 1900 than it had in 1896. The American Olympic Committee (AOC) had been formed in 1893 during Baron de Coubertin's second trip to the United States to promote Olympism. At New York City's University Club Coubertin met with James Edward Sullivan, the powerful secretary of the Amateur Athletic Union (AAU), and persuaded him to charter an organization to promote the Olympics. Sullivan, the son of Irish immigrants, had worked his way into a leadership position in American athletics by championing the playground movement in New York City. He served as a leader on the Public Recreation Commission of New York and helped to establish the Public Schools Athletic League.[16] In forming a management team to oversee U.S. participation in the Olympics, Sullivan, who would dominate the American Olympic movement from the turn of the century until his death in 1914, gathered the titans of amateur sport in the United States—AAU leaders Gustavus T. Kirby and Julian W. Curtiss, athletic equipment magnates A. G. and Walter Spalding, and Caspar Whitney—onto the AAU-dominated AOC. Under the command of Sullivan, the AAU and the AOC pushed their beloved track and field athletics to center stage at the Olympic Games.[17]

The leaders of the American Olympic movement worked in prominent positions from which they could advocate their brand of athletics. Whitney edited and published *Outing,* and Sullivan compiled *Spalding's Official Athletic Almanac,* published by A. G. and Walter Spalding's sporting monopoly. Curtiss had begun his business career as an agent for the A. G. Spalding Company and quickly rose to a position as the most powerful vice president in the organization.[18] The leadership drew their power from their strategic locations in modern sporting institutions.

With connections to the organizational and economic structures through which modern sport spread into mass culture, the Olympic group represented the triumph of the "culture of professionalism" in American athletics.[19] They functioned as the middle-class managers of America's middle-class sporting ideology. Sullivan, Kirby, Curtiss, Whitney, and the brothers Spalding were firmly committed to the principles of mainstream American sporting ideology. They saw opportunities in the Olympic Games to extend their power to define American ideas about physical culture, enhance their social and economic power, and lead the crusade to make sport a central component in national self-definition.

During the first few years of the twentieth century, the AOC, "having neither constitution, by-laws nor rules of procedure," moved to secure its control over American participation in the Olympics.[20] The lack of an organizational framework made the AOC a powerful institution governed by the whims of its executives. Sullivan, Spalding, and Whitney turned it into an instrument of athletic nationalism. The group had not played any part in the 1896 games. Princeton and the Boston Athletic Association had represented the United States through their own resources. Even though they were not actively involved in the Athens games, the athletic cabal criticized the IOC's organization of those contests. Whitney harped constantly on that issue. Curiously, in 1900 the IOC tabbed him as one of its three American delegates—the others were Princeton's William Milligan Sloane and James H. Hyde.[21]

Politics and the Paris Olympics

Caspar Whitney had serious reservations not only about French sporting habits but about the quality of, and preparations for, the Paris games. "The so-called Olympian games at Paris form the one cloud above the sporting horizon," Whitney lamented. He reported that French political instability in the wake of the Dreyfus case was wreaking havoc on the preparations for the Olympics.[22] By 1900 the fallout from the Dreyfus Affair had destroyed the legitimacy of the Right in French politics. A broad coalition of moderates and Leftist forces had consolidated their control over the Third Republic and were preparing to curb the power of the Catholic church and the army. The bitterness of the struggle precluded any concept of a loyal opposition. Baron de Coubertin had been an anti-Dreyfusard during the ordeal, and that fact, coupled with his noble heritage and support of the Church and tradition, made him suspect to those who controlled the government.[23]

Coubertin himself compounded his problems with the government by loading the French delegation to the IOC and the Paris Olympic organizing committee with aristocrats who tended toward Rightist and monarchist positions. The baron appointed an old friend, Viscount Charles de La Rochefoucauld, as the president of the Olympic organizing committee, but exposition officials, who as agents of the current government were directed by the triumphant republicans, objected to Rochefoucauld's royalist political leanings and forced the viscount to resign. Coubertin attempted to stay on to protect his creation. The situation proved untenable and he, too, resigned.[24]

Whitney, with only a tenuous grasp of the complexities of French politics, was worried by the fact that such a great admirer of American athletics as the baron had been removed from controlling the Paris Olympics—a curious pose for someone who was generally one of the IOC's most ardent critics. Whitney described Coubertin as a "thorough and enthusiastic sportsman" who "by his untiring energy and tact" had put together a first-rate committee to take charge of the Olympic venue at the Paris exposition. "Then the Dreyfus case came up and the Government of France, finding some of so-called royal birth on this committee, scattered it to the four winds of heaven and turned over the management of the Exposition sports to an Exposition committee," Whitney reported. He had little faith in the reformed organization. "What this committee does not know about sports would fill volumes."

Whitney declared that the Paris games were "no longer Olympian" owing to the French government's meddling, adding, "Baron Coubertin, like the good sportsman that he is, has stuck it out, expostulating and explaining to the Government, which has had sufficient good sense to listen to him, but as he has no real power there is no guarantee of protection to amateurs." Whitney also warned that the cinder track under construction for the games, the first ever built in France, could "be in great danger of not being satisfactory." He worried that the French were dangerously close to destroying the entire Olympic movement; "A number of important details have been left to the last moment, when our Gallic neighbors will rush at them in hysterical haste with results that can hardly fail to be confusing."[25]

Actually, Coubertin's problems with the bureaucrats from the *exposition universelle* stemmed as much from the fact that Exposition Commissioner Alfred Picart considered modern athletics to be a vulgar fad as from the political backlash against anti-Dreyfusards. Although Whitney's reading of the political situation was overly simplistic, his fears about the French bureaucrats were well-founded. After Coubertin lost control of the athletic displays at the fair, the nonpurists stretched definitions of athletics by including such "sports" as auto races, chess, and fishing in the Seine in the Olympic exhibit.[26]

Nevertheless, Coubertin persevered in his promotional efforts. He promised the American sporting public that the exposition officials were wonderfully competent and that although he did not consider the "motor-car races, competitions of sappers and firemen, free balloon races, and trials of carrier pigeons" to be "pure sport," they would certainly add novelty and variety to the Olympic program. Coubertin noted that Paris was a spectacular venue for the games, with pleasures and accommodations "such as never seen in the New World." He also proclaimed that at the urging of his "American friends," he had made a special request that the track and field athletic events take place in the middle of July, when American athletes would already be in Europe competing in the English championships.[27]

Creating the American Olympic Team

The baron's appeals, enticements, and clever scheduling worked. By early summer even Whitney was reporting that the University of Pennsylvania and

Princeton University planned to send contingents. *Outing*'s editor assured athletic enthusiasts that Penn and Princeton alone could whip the rest of the world in track and field events.[28] In spite of Whitney's warnings about French disorganization, several other universities and athletic clubs joined Penn and Princeton in the Olympic field. As they had in the Athens games four years earlier, American collegians dominated the U.S. contingent to the Paris games. In addition to Penn and Princeton, Georgetown, Syracuse, the University of Michigan, and the University of Chicago sent teams to Paris. New England track clubs sent "individual stars whose records have been made under the colors of Yale and Harvard," and the New York Athletic Club (NYAC) shipped athletes from Yale, Columbia, and the New York City police department. Each club and university provided its own funding for the journey to Paris. The AAU played a large part in recruiting the teams and organizing the trip. Most of the teams planned to compete in the English Championships at London's Stamford Bridge grounds in early July before venturing to Paris for the opening of the second Olympics.[29]

The American press expected great deeds from the second group of Olympians, even though after Whitney's tale of the problems that Coubertin and the IOC had encountered with French bureaucrats, it was unclear to some Americans whether the contests were actually Olympic Games or simply an international track meet.[30] The *New York Times* forgot facts and embellished the legends of the 1896 Olympics, remembering that "Americans won every available event from a field made up of the pick of European athletes."[31] Pundits expected the same kind of performance from the 1900 squad. William B. Curtis, "the father of American athletics," proclaimed that "during the past twenty years many parties of American athletes have visited Europe, but no one of these expeditions ever approached, in dignity or strength, the American army of athletic invasion whose advance-guard is already on British soil, with other divisions following fast." Curtis bragged that "the party includes the athletic strength of the country, and if they are beaten, the United States will be beaten."[32]

The AOC controlled the American expedition, even if it had not actually selected the team. A. G. Spalding served as the director of sports for the United States at the Paris exposition, with James E. Sullivan as his lieutenant. All the athletes who made the journey to France maintained good AAU standings. The American teams, accompanied by troops of fans and schoolmates, primed themselves for the Paris games at the British Amateur championships. At Stamford Bridge on July 7, the Americans won eight out of the fourteen events. "Such a clean sweep is without parallel," marveled a *Chicago Tribune* correspondent. "More especially is it noticeable when it is remembered that they opposed the best amateurs, not only from England, Ireland, and Scotland, but the colonies as well." The star of the meet was Alvin C. Kraenzlein, a sprinter, hurdler, and long jumper from the University of Pennsylvania. Lord Alverstone, the British athletic official in charge of the championships, marveled at the Penn track star's feats, quipping, "Kraenzlein, we have not got enough medals to give you. We only hope all you Americans will come over next year and defend your cup. Then we hope to have better runners to put up against you."

Some of the American competitors complained that they were treated unfairly by officials from the British Amateur Athletic Association who disallowed two American foul claims. The Americans also criticized English management of the meet, decrying what they considered to be substandard conditions for both fans and athletes. Unsated by their conquest of the British, they crossed the Channel and headed for the games of the Second Olympiad at the Paris International Exposition. Compared with the events that would unfold in France, their problems in England would seem minuscule.[33]

Scandals, Sabbatarianism, and the Quest for Supremacy

The French organizing committee had originally scheduled the games to begin on Sunday, July 15. American protests over Sabbath competition, led by A. G. Spalding and officials from Princeton and Penn, forced the French organizers to reschedule. Caspar Whitney revealed that the American teams had gone so far as to threaten a boycott if Sunday competitions were held. Whitney's report on the U.S. officials' "victory" over French planners revealed the commitments of American Olympic boosters to middle-class American values and their efforts to force conformity on the rest of the sporting world. Whitney explained that although no "first-class" American club or team held meets on Sunday, some groups, in particular working-class clubs, did engage in athletics on the Christian Sabbath. "Sports are held on Sunday by certain classes of clubs whose members have no other leisure day; and none can take exceptions to the custom—better good wholesome sport than corner loafing," wrote Whitney, mixing athletic commentary with social criticism. Whitney and the rest of American athletic officialdom were not as flexible with the French as they were with working-class athletes, however, and they gloated over their success in moving the starting date for the Paris games to Saturday.[34]

That date soon proved to be problematic. July 14 is Bastille Day, a national holiday in France. A great military parade planned for an area near the site of the games at the Paris Racing Club in Pré Catalan forced the French to move many events back to their originally scheduled Sunday starting times. American athletes, arriving on the Continent from the English championships, discovered that the problem of Sabbath competition had not been resolved.

Teams from Princeton, Penn, and Syracuse led a threatened American boycott of Sunday athletics. The coach of the University of Chicago's contingent, Amos Alonzo Stagg, complained of the late change that "everybody here feels that it is a most contemptible trick." He declared that "not a single American university would have sent a team had it not been definitely announced that the Games would not be held on Sunday. Even at this late date, it is likely that the American teams will unitedly refuse to compete if the French officials persist in carrying out what seems to us a very nasty piece of business."[35]

American athletes were skeptical that a compromise could be arranged. George Orton, a Canadian track star competing for the University of Pennsylvania and the United States at the Paris games, believed that the cablegram assuring U.S. authorities that no contests would be held on Sundays had not been officially sanctioned by the French organizing committee. Orton thought that considering all the circumstances, the French had botched the Olympic enterprise.[36] Caspar Whitney attributed the supposed breach of faith to the "wretched management" of French exposition officials and the "none too careful . . . scrutiny of the conditions under which the games were to held" by American sporting leaders. In other words, no one had listened to Whitney's prior warnings.[37]

With a crisis looming, French and American Olympic representatives worked out an apparent compromise. The French relented and allowed American contestants in field events to compete on Saturday or Monday, with the results from the alternate days to be figured into the scores of events scheduled for Sunday. For American convenience French officials also rescheduled many Saturday races to follow the Bastille Day parade.[38]

The games began on July 14 at the Paris Racing Club, a "charmingly situated glade in the Bois de Boulogne." Fewer than a thousand spectators attended the first day's events, a marked contrast to the Athenian multitudes in 1896 or the crowds generally drawn to a major championship in the United States or Great Britain. One observer reported that because of the number of Americans rooting for their team in a stand "gayly bedecked with the Stars and Stripes," "the meeting resembled more an American college meeting than an international championship held abroad."[39] The spectators were "chiefly . . . bright, young American girls, who wore the colors of various American colleges competing and gave unstinted applause as their countrymen secured victories."[40] Notwithstanding the raucous American collegians, George Orton dismissed the crowds as "a sorry showing" in comparison to the many thousands he claimed had attended the Athens Olympics.[41]

The athletes contested for "objects of art," and the U.S. team captured the lion's share of the bounty.[42] American Olympians won seventeen of twenty-two track and field events at the Paris Olympiad.[43] A *New York Times* commentator remarked that "the feature of the meeting was not only the number of events the Americans won, but the ease with which they outstripped their competitors, often finishing first and second, laughing side by side, and in a canter."[44] The *Chicago Tribune* even complained that "the facility with which the American athletes carried off prizes finally grew monotonous."[45]

American behavior during their romps to victory annoyed the French. A sportswriter from the United States observed that the American custom of shouting college cheers appalled European spectators. "At the first yell they apparently imagined some invasion of wild Indians had occurred, but, after hearing the various cries about a hundred times, they appreciated the fact that it was simply an outburst of American enthusiasm." Frenchmen "could not become reconciled to this form of cheering and they were heard to exclaim frequently, 'What a band of savages!'" The Americans also looked different. The *Chicago Tribune* asserted that "the physique of the Americans compared extremely favorably with that of the Europeans." They dressed in "natty college costumes," which marked "a decided contrast to the home made attire of some of the best European athletes."[46]

American athletes seemed none too impressed with their rivals or with the way the track and field meet was run. George Orton complained that the starter in the sprints "would not be allowed to start school-boy sports in America" and that strange French customs and rules hampered the American effort. A marked improvement occurred when the French finally took American "advice" and restructured the starter's cadence and officiating for some of the track competitions.[47] Restructuring on the American plan, however, soon proved to be problematic.

The Sabbath Compromise Unravels

Sunday, July 15, saw the collapse of the agreement that allowed Americans to compete on Monday in field events scheduled for Sunday. The French Olympic Committee met on Saturday night and, after contestants from other nations protested that the original truce gave the Americans unfair advantages, decided that events scheduled for Sunday had to be completed on Sunday. Results from the preliminaries on Saturday would still be counted, however. The French officials failed to inform some members of the American team of their changes in policy. Two American athletes, Bascom Johnson of the NYAC and Charles Dvorack of the University of Michigan, went to the grounds early on Sunday morning and were told that they could contest their events on Monday. Dvorack, Johnson, and several other American athletes returned to their hotel rooms mistakenly believing they could take on all comers on Monday.[48]

When it became clear that the original agreement had been altered, many of the Americans refused to compete or were prevented from participating in Sunday competition by their colleges. Robert Garrett of Princeton University, the hero of the 1896 Olympics, refused to compete on Sunday, as did his Princeton teammates. Michigan and Syracuse also kept their athletes off the field. Amos Alonzo Stagg's prediction of American unity against Sunday athletics proved to be naïve, however, for not all the Americans honored the Sabbath boycott. Several members of Penn's squad competed, and four of them won first places. Irving K. Baxter captured Olympic crowns in the "running" high jump and the pole vault; Walter Tewkesbury won the 400-meter hurdles; the Canadian posing as American, George Orton, won the 2,500-meter steeplechase; and Alvin Kraenzlein won the 60-meter hurdles and the running broad jump. Two other American winners, Richard Sheldon in the shot put and Maxwell Long in the 400-meter race, competed under the banner of the NYAC.[49]

The Penn stars' participation generated a great deal of hostility among American Olympians. The manager of Princeton's team, 1896 Olympian H. B. Jamison, supported the decision by his staunchly conservative Presbyterian college to prohibit Sunday contests. He indicted the University of Pennsylvania contingent for treason. Jamison charged, "Pennsylvania protested most strongly against Sunday games, but finally entered. I think her representatives should have stood with those of the other colleges."[50] Penn's manager replied, "I have no authority to prevent the men taking part on my own responsibility, and so told them, at the same time advising them that they should not contest." Five of Penn's thirteen athletes ignored their manager. They did very well for themselves.[51]

Caspar Whitney ranted that the Americans who competed on Sunday were unscrupulous "mug hunters" and published a list of shame in the pages of *Outing*. He also commended those athletes who, "regarding principle worthier to be cherished above mere prize-winning," abstained from Sunday's contest. For Whitney the Sabbath controversy served as more evidence of foreign athletic incompetence and provided new ammunition for his rhetorical war against the IOC's elite. The whole affair, charged Whitney, was "quite as miserable as was expected."[52]

Whitney dismissed the Olympic track and field competition as a farce whose "like has not been seen outside of picnic games." Mentioning issues ranging from problems with starts to spectators wandering onto the field to the fact that no European champions of note bothered to attend, Whitney painted the Olympics as a mockery of true sport. Even the supposed "objects of art" presented to the victors disappointed *Outing*'s editor. He described the prizes as "decidedly inartistic bronze birds, silver pins and studs, walking-sticks, knives, and that sort of thing." Had it not been for the Americans, railed Whitney, "the games would have been the complete fiasco they deserved to be, considering their sponsors and the character of management."[53]

One of the American Olympians whom Whitney labeled a "mug-hunter" defended himself and his Penn teammates against the charges. George Orton claimed that Penn had been unjustly accused of bad faith, painting his team's decision as the triumph of individual conscience and the democratic tradition over peer pressure and coercion. Orton revealed that Penn's manager had allowed each athlete to make his own decision. Orton went out on Sunday and won the 2,500-meter steeplechase. He proclaimed that he "thus scored America's only win in the distance events; but he won through sheer grit rather than condition, as he was not quite up to form."[54]

One athlete who was "up to form" was gravely disappointed by the events that transpired regarding the Sabbath controversy. Syracuse University's Myer Prinstein had jumped 7 meters, 17½ centimeters, on Saturday. Barred by Syracuse from competing on Sunday—ironically, Prinstein was Jewish—he was beaten by one of the six "extra" jumps allowed to A. C. Kraenzlein on Sunday, a leap that measured 7 meters, 18½ centimeters.[55] Grace Corneau, in a special cable to the *Chicago Tribune,* reported that Prinstein was extremely upset by the turn of events and blamed Penn's Kraenzlein. The Princeton and Michigan teams were also "incensed" at Penn's behavior.[56]

In a letter to A. G. Spalding, director of sports for the United States at the Paris fair, the American team decried the changed agreement. The protest, initiated by Charles Sherrill of Yale and signed by all the American teams, proclaimed, "We, the undersigned, beg to protest against the change in the agreed arrangements whereby our clubs are now unable to compete in field events on Monday, the records to count for the championships and to be filed as events."[57] Spalding filed the protest with French officials, but to no avail.

The games continued with more American victories. The *New York Times* noted that "as the Americans were so successful some of the bad feeling disappeared, but they might have had more seconds and thirds if the change had not been made at the last minute, and scarcely without warning."[58] The United States swept the hammer throw, but the Swedish competitors drew the most attention from the predominantly American crowd. The Swedes' apparent unfamiliarity "with the hammer caused some amusement among the spectators, not unmixed with a certain amount of apprehension; and once or twice the crowd scattered as the hammer showed a tendency to eccentricity in the direction it took."[59] The track and field competition at the second Olympics concluded on July 22 with a series of handicap races. Handicap races presented an interesting method for equalizing competition. The times of each contestant in the "scratch" races, or distances in regular field events, were taken as yardsticks for the assignment of handicaps. The handicap races seemed especially attuned to the creed of fair play, but the handicap competitions at Paris held no interest for the Americans. One correspondent reported that "the Americans had received too severe treatment to tempt them to exhaust themselves in running losing races."[60] Besides, July 22 was a Sunday.

Assessing American Olympic Supremacy

The United States, according to American sources, had won the Olympic Games again, even though when the medals in all the Olympic sports were counted, France had gathered twenty-six first places to the Americans' twenty.[61] The American press elevated their athletes to the Olympic championship by virtue of the U.S. domination in track and field. Americans defined the Olympic Games in their own terms and then pronounced themselves the world's best. Whitney remarked that "even with men of lesser prowess" than the collegiate champions who starred for the United States, "America must still have proved an overwhelming victor, for the superiority of our representatives was entirely convincing of American pre-eminence in track games."[62] The athletic "bully pulpit" had been established.

Whitney used the Paris games to blast English athletes and English civilization as inferior to its American counterparts, launching a long tradition of nationalistic critiques of performances at Olympic spectacles. According to Whitney, England's poor showing at Paris stemmed from the "low ethical status" of English athletic clubs and a whining nationalistic press that made Great Britain "a very bad loser."

Whitney defended his countrymen from the English charge that U.S. victories stemmed from the American penchant to make a "business" out of athletic games. "Personal study" convinced Whitney that England's system, excepting university athletics, was corrupted by wagering and professionalism. "No; it is not that America makes a 'business' of her athletic preparation," Whitney argued, "but it is that England does not know how." He dismissed the English as "inherently slow" and "sure they 'know it all.'"

That proved to be a fatal combination when the English faced the athletic representatives of the "chosen people." Indeed, although Whitney admitted that the English had quite a few positive qualities, he still ranked Americans ahead of what he considered Europe's best sporting culture. "Strong, persistent, thorough, courageous—qualities that long have kept them the superior race across the Atlantic; but in the American they encounter an opponent who not only has all these qualities, but has also, in addition, alertness, *finesse*, mobility," theorized Whitney. "Splendid courage and dogged plugging are not of themselves sufficient to scoring on either the athletic or the battle field," continued the sporting enthusiast who had doubled as a war correspondent and an ardent jingoist during the Spanish-American War. "The national temper which puts a stiff non-revolving handle into the hands of the 16-pound hammer-thrower is the same which uselessly silhouettes its officers against the sky-line as pot-shot offerings to the enemy's sharpshooters," Whitney declared; "Both are a needless sacrifice of power and skill and material, and in neither case is the game being played adroitly or to the full of the contestants' strength." Clearly, in Whitney's mind and in American public culture, the business of sport had been linked to the business of nationalism.[63]

After the 200-meter hurdle final, Penn's A. C. Kraenzlein announced his retirement. Kraenzlein, the Olympic champion in the 110- and 200-meter hurdles, 60-meter dash, and the running broad jump, told reporters, "That was my last race," adding, "I am through with athletics, and shall devote myself to something more serious."[64] Olympic athletics was serious business, however, as Kraenzlein well knew. He had won the running broad jump on the first Sunday of competition, snatching the gold medal away from American champion Myer Prinstein of Syracuse, who had been barred by his college from competing on the Christian Sabbath. Prinstein and Kraenzlein had been intense rivals in American collegiate circles, and when Prinstein learned of Kraenzlein's victory, he challenged the Penn star to a Monday jump-off.[65] Kraenzlein refused, and Prinstein's teammates had to restrain the enraged Syracuse athlete from assaulting the Olympic hero.[66] Prinstein angrily alleged that Kraenzlein had promised him not to compete on Sunday.[67]

The Olympics were serious business for Myer Prinstein and for America's sense of nationhood. The novelist Hjalmar Hjorth Boyesen discovered that American Olympic victories had made Americans comfortably sure of their "physical superiority."[68] The American Olympians had tried to impose their sense of sporting ethics onto the world, turning an athletic meeting into a religious crusade. The attempted Sunday ban of competition indicated the degree to which Americans identified athletic practice with cultural, religious, and political principles. Sport, in the American mind, functioned as a tool for imposing a culture on the world and on their own nation. Nonetheless, a principle separate from preserving the sanctity of the Sabbath called to many of the American athletes. That principle—that their victory would confirm the special status of their nation as the boldest and strongest people in the world—motivated their quest for Olympic glory.

Ironically George Orton, the Canadian who had adopted the creed of the American sporting republic, had revealed the conflicts inherent in American athletic nationalism by choosing a chance at victory over strict adherence to

Sabbatarianism. Orton certainly believed in converting the world to the tenets of American sport. He understood that one had to win in order to crow about national superiority. Prohibitions concerning competing on Sunday conflicted with nationalistic interests. Orton clearly linked American victory, including his own, to the superiority of his adopted civilization. He attributed Olympic victory to the superiority of the American style and the scientific approach of American technique. He also gave credit to the inherent "nervous force, grit, courage, or whatever it may be called" of his American teammates, "which so often wins races." Orton found that quality almost wholly lacking in European athletes.[69]

The urge for a nationalistic display surpassed other desires, such as need for religious orthodoxy on Sabbatarianism. Significantly, the fracas over Sunday competition raged more bitterly between U.S. athletes who had been denied a chance at Olympic victory and those who had won on Sunday than it did between French and American Olympic officials. The Americans who participated in Sunday competitions knew their actions would spark criticism in the United States. The frustrations of the various U.S. collegiate and athletic club teams at not being able to present a united front to the world boiled over into public recriminations. For the American press the ethics of the religious stand seemed important, but for most reporters victory appeared more worthy, for it indicated principle in action. The media chastised the athletes who had competed on Sunday, but it also lionized them as victors.

Americans equated Olympic championships with national superiority. That equation ensured that the conception of an Olympian amateur that took hold in the United States differed significantly from the baron de Coubertin's public definition of the ideal Olympian. The baron's sporting gentleman possessed an Aristotelian sense of proportion that commanded an emphasis not on "conquering" but on "fighting well." American Olympians, seeking to confirm the special providence of their national mission, had a different sense of proportion, one that violated the spirit of Coubertin's maxim.[70] For the champions of national aspirations, fighting well counted only if they also conquered. Americans knew that winning was not everything in the Olympic arena. It was the only thing. Such conceptions made the American sporting republic a very jingoistic institution. In the United States the ethos of athletic nationalism, personified by Orton, Kraenzlein, and Whitney, had triumphed over the chivalrous romantic aesthetic of Coubertin. Very soon Coubertin would lose more Olympic ground to the American insurgency.

During the IOC meeting at the 1900 Olympics, Baron de Coubertin announced that the games of the Third Olympiad had been awarded to the United States. According to one American sports authority, Charles J. P. Lucas, the IOC had decided that "in view of the two victories of American athletes and the lively interest America had shown in the games, . . . it would be eminently just and proper to award to America the third revival of the games."[71] The games were coming to the "new Athens," and the Americans planned an ode to the strength of their conception of sport.

"When one compares the abuses which sport causes with those to which it puts an end, one cannot refrain from singing its praises and laboring for its propagation," wrote Coubertin. "It is for this very purpose that I have revived the Olympian Games." Although the baron warned that Olympism had "enemies, like every other free and living work," he was nevertheless optimistic: "But it has stanch [sic] friends who are of great assistance. It is to these that I appeal to prepare from this time onwards the celebration in America of the Olympian Games of 1904." He urged his friends to help make the first Olympics held in the United States a "great success," hoping that they would "draw across the ocean qualified representatives of all the sporting societies of the world, for a manifestation which will be both worthy of the noble and ancient Olympian past and of the glorious future of the great American republic."[72] The baron would be surprised by his American friends.

★ 4

St. Louis, 1904:
An "All-American" Olympics

In 1904 the Olympic Games once again found a home at a world's fair. At the Louisiana Purchase Exposition, in the midst of dynamos, locomotives, automobiles, dirigibles, airplanes, and other evidence of human control over the energies of nature, athletic technology would be hailed as the real key to building a progressive civilization. The third Olympic Games would inculcate the idea that physical culture produced a special American "race" and defined the national identity. They would encourage a common belief that levels of civilization and rates of cultural progress could be measured through sport. They would dramatically magnify the power and scope of American athletic nationalism. The Olympics would be held up as an accurate portrait of American realities, even though it realistically represented an idealized picture of middle-class assumptions.

In 1900 Baron de Coubertin and the IOC had awarded the third Olympics to the United States. The exact site for the games had not been determined, however. A complicated and contentious battle over controlling the location and content of the Olympics ensued between the IOC and American athletic officials, among various branches of the American sporting bureaucracy, and among several American cities.[1] By 1900 a powerful team of athletic leaders worked to solidify their control over the American Olympic movement. The Olympic Games Committee, charged with overseeing the third Olympics, was dominated by American IOC representatives and AAU officials James Edward Sullivan and Caspar Whitney—the editors, respectively, of *Spalding's Official Athletic Almanac* and *Outing*. Princeton's William Milligan Sloane was also a member of the IOC, but Sullivan and Whitney considered him to be an ivory tower academician who knew nothing about the realities of Olympic athletics or politics. Sporting and professional rivalries in the United States shaped a site selection process during which Philadelphia, New York, Buffalo, Chicago, and St. Louis emerged as contenders for the Olympic venue.

The Fight to Host the Olympics

On July 28, 1900, shortly after the U.S. team finished crushing the rest of the world's athletes in track and field contests at the Paris Olympics, the *New York Times* reported that the AOC and the University of Pennsylvania had decided that the third Olympics would be held in Philadelphia.[2] Coubertin and the IOC politely entertained Philadelphia's offer while quietly pushing officials from Chicago to bid for the games. Philadelphia's bid quickly evaporated. In the autumn of 1900, after the conclusion of the Paris Olympics, Coubertin decided without consulting the rest of the IOC that either New York or Chicago would get the games. Privately, both Coubertin and William Sloane leaned toward Chicago.[3]

While the IOC struggled to select a host city, AAU boss James Sullivan declared that Coubertin and his international comrades had no power over sport in the United States and that the Olympic bids needed to be sanctioned by the AAU. Sullivan abruptly announced that the third Olympic Games would be held by the AAU in conjunction with the Buffalo Pan American Exposition—in 1901. The AAU leader wanted to scrap the four-year Olympic cycle and classical symbolism so dear to the baron and secure the Olympic movement in American hands.

Sullivan and Coubertin, perhaps the two most powerful figures of their time in world sport, disliked each other intensely. The American ruler of amateur athletics wanted to strip aristocratic influence and foreign control from the Olympic movement. He detested Coubertin's power, blasting the Frenchman as inept and misguided. He desired an American-engineered Olympics highlighted by track and field and run according to the rules and rituals of the sporting republic. Sullivan staged his athletic extravaganza at Buffalo's 1901 Pan American Exposition, although he did not attach an Olympic label to it. He did insist that it was the greatest sporting spectacle ever held, however, far surpassing the 1900 Olympics at the Paris International Exposition.[4]

Coubertin and the IOC forestalled Sullivan's assault by insisting that the Olympics maintain their quadrennial cycle. The games would have to be held in 1904. With Buffalo's challenge thwarted, Chicago emerged as the leading contender. The baron had visited the 1893 Columbian Exposition and come away much impressed with Chicago's civic spirit. University of Chicago president William Rainey Harper and athletic leader Amos Alonzo Stagg had determinedly lobbied the IOC for the games. Chicago's Olympian Games Association, headed by Henry J. Furber Jr., raised a $1 million war chest to make European trips boosting Chicago's image at IOC meetings. Furber, a prominent Chicago business leader with a corporate law practice, extensive holdings in real

estate and insurance, a doctorate from a German university, a scholarly publishing career in economic journals, and membership in the Chicago Athletic
Club, served as the key player in Chicago's successful bid.[5]

In May 1901 the IOC met in Paris to name a host city. New York, Buffalo, and
Philadelphia had already fallen from contention. Nevertheless, Chicago's boosters worried that St. Louis, then planning a world's fair to commemorate the
centennial of the Louisiana Purchase, might divert the Olympics. Construction
delays had postponed the St. Louis fair from 1903 until 1904, and fair officials
sent word that they were interested in securing the Olympics. They asked the
IOC to delay its decision until 1902 to allow the Louisiana Purchase Exposition
to organize a proposal for staging the Olympics. The IOC refused and unani-
mously awarded the games of the Third Olympiad to Chicago.[6]

When word of the selection reached Chicagoans that May, the city erupted
with joy. University of Chicago students celebrated with a week-long party.
Henry Furber quickly moved to marshal national support for the Chicago
Olympics. He proclaimed that the games "should make a universal appeal to
the pride and patriotism of every American." He promised that the American
version of the Olympics would be an egalitarian enterprise aimed at "the masses" and designed "for the scientific and ethical advancement of the race—and
especially of this nation." He also predicted an Olympic championship for the
United States, a forecast that he realized would not surprise the "average American," since American athletic success "seems to him natural, if not inevitable,
so accustomed has he grown to the conquests which have been won by 'Yankee push.'"[7]

Furber's rivals for national attention, Sullivan and the AAU, knew all about
"Yankee push." They planned to yank the Olympic games away from Chicago.
Sullivan, an original member of the AAU, had by 1904 served for fifteen years
as the secretary of the most powerful amateur athletic body in the United States.
He had been the assistant director, under A. G. Spalding, of the American Olympic delegation and of the Physical Culture Department at the Paris world's fair
and second Olympic Games, as well as the director of athletics at Buffalo's 1901
Pan American Exposition. The dominant personality in the early twentieth-
century administration of amateur sport in the United States, Sullivan had the
power to impose his will on the third Olympics.[8]

Furber and the Chicago Olympic organizing committee immediately ran into
a series of problems. As funding and planning lagged, the Chicago Olympics
encountered competition for national attention in the form of the elaborate
athletic spectacles planned for St. Louis's Louisiana Purchase Exposition. Fair
officials arranged for the national AAU championships to be held in St. Louis
during the same month that the Olympics had been scheduled in Chicago.

To avoid competition with the St. Louis festivities, Furber and the Chicago-ans asked the IOC to delay the Olympics until 1905. St. Louis asked for a transfer of the Olympics and pressured Furber's team. As early as July 11, 1902, the *St. Louis Republic* argued that St. Louis should get the Olympics and proposed the appointment of Chicago's A. G. Spalding as chief of athletics to facilitate the switch.[9] By November 1902 American newspapers were offering the nation extensive speculation on the Olympic rift between Chicago and St. Louis while Coubertin pondered the crisis.[10]

The baron preferred Chicago to St. Louis, remembering the latter from his 1893 United States tour as a parochial backwater. However, Sullivan and the Louisiana Purchase Exposition officials wielded considerable power over am-ateur sporting events held in the United States. When exposition authorities named Sullivan the chief of the Physical Culture Department, the Chicago organizing committee lost the support of much of the American athletic es-tablishment. Coubertin waffled while civic leaders from the two midwestern cities battled for position. Negotiations by two "Chicago men"—A. G. Spalding and the director of exhibits at the St. Louis world's fair, Frederick J. V. Skiff (who was also a member of the AAU's national organizing committee)—pushed Chicago to yield to St. Louis.[11]

On February 10, 1903, Coubertin, without much consultation from the IOC, unilaterally announced that the IOC had shifted the Olympics to St. Louis.[12] The March 1903 edition of the *World's Fair Bulletin,* putting the best face on the struggle, announced St. Louis's victory and praised Chicago for the amica-ble fashion in which the transfer had been handled.[13] With the Louisiana Pur-chase Exposition running the show, Coubertin and the IOC relinquished com-plete control of the third revival of the Olympic Games to Sullivan and the AAU.[14]

St. Louis was an ironic choice for the celebration of the grandest symbol of the "new safety-valve," as the progressive historian Frederick L. Paxson had la-beled sport. After all, it had very recently been the "gateway to the West," the jumping-off point for that older safety valve, the American frontier. The world's fair itself celebrated the Louisiana Purchase, Thomas Jefferson's $15 million procurement of an imagined agrarian safety valve. The frontier loomed as an enormously powerful symbol in American minds at the turn of the century. Frederick Jackson Turner's thesis concerning the availability of free land, the dynamics that allowed for an escape from social tensions, and the evolution of American civilization profoundly influenced American perspectives.

President Theodore Roosevelt, a thinker quite familiar with questions of ath-letics, energy, expansion, and frontiers, opened the Louisiana Purchase Expo-sition by reiterating his understanding of the connections between the strenu-osity produced by frontier expansion and the public virtue generated by

American political culture. Roosevelt agreed with Turner that the frontier had made the United States the leading civilization on the globe, but he dissented from the historian's pessimistic conclusion that the end of a continental frontier portended dire consequences. The president contended that new frontiers beckoned, opening the prospect for national revitalization.

Roosevelt theorized that the Louisiana Purchase had launched the United States on the path toward world domination, sparking the dynamic energy flow that directed the nation by 1904 to the threshold of an American century. The world's fair, noted the president, symbolized that history. "We have met here today to commemorate the hundredth anniversary of the event which more than any other, after the foundation of the Government, and always excepting its preservation, determined the character of our national life—determined that we should be a great expanding nation instead of a relatively small and stationary one."[15] The Louisiana Purchase Exposition was dedicated to educating the American public in such Rooseveltian truisms and shaping the national identity.

The erosion of the trans-Mississippi frontier had rapidly altered St. Louis, and city leaders worried that what had once been an expanding metropolis faced an uncertain future. During the first half of the nineteenth century, the city had been the focus of westward expansion and the largest urban center on the Mississippi River. The post–Civil War industrial boom transformed St. Louis, which had long been a transportation hub, from a commercial capital into a factory town as the railroad replaced the river as the dominant mode of trade. At the beginning of the twentieth century, the city suffered acutely from common urban maladies—overcrowding, ethnic tensions, pollution, political corruption—and earned a prominent spot on American lists of "shameful" cities.[16]

St. Louis had also lost its position as mid-America's leading metropolis. Boosters had made a futile bid to host the 1893 Columbian Exposition, but that honor went to Chicago, a younger urban center whose fortunes seemed to have surpassed its rival's. The world's fair of 1904 offered St. Louis a second chance. The gateway city's civic leaders designed the Louisiana Purchase Exposition to inaugurate a "new St. Louis." They labored to best the marvels of Chicago's world's fair in every venue. Their skillful maneuver of wresting the 1904 Olympics away from rival Chicago bolstered the effort to revamp their city's image.[17]

Designing Exhibits of the Science of Sport

At the third Olympics the U.S. sporting experts wanted to promote athletic nationalism, educate Americans about the potential reform power of the strenuous life, and demonstrate that sport could serve as an instrument for realizing the promises of a republican ideology that pledged status based on achievement and celebrated social mobility.[18] Commentators at the St. Louis games would explain American victories as proof that the New World republic was far superior to Old World social systems and credit the superiority of the United States to the "common people" who became great achievers in a "free" society. Athletic experts would also undertake several experiments in sporting science. They would turn the human body into a mechanism and study the effects of stress on long distance runners. They would also seek to discover whether industrial civilization could produce athletes who could match the vigor of so-called primitive peoples. A fashionable myth at the turn of the century held that "primitive" peoples were far more physical, living as they did in "natural" states, than were the artificial products of more advanced cultures. In conducting the experiments, these experts were fundamentally motivated by a desire to convince the nation that a scientific understanding of athletic technology could guarantee the progress of American civilization.

The strenuous life's champions insisted that the athletic exhibits were more important than any of the other scientific and technological marvels exhibited at the fair.[19] When observers compared the progress of civilization between the Chicago fair and the St. Louis exposition, they found that the greatest leap forward had been made in the growth and spread of the sporting life. "The difference between the year 1893 at Chicago and 1904 at St. Louis is perhaps more marked in the Department of Physical Culture than anywhere else," noted John Brisben Walker. He told the readers of *Cosmopolitan* that the magnificent athletic preparations were designed to produce "strong-bodied, sane-minded citizens."[20] A host of newspaper articles promoted the idea that the St. Louis fair was the first exposition in history to include athletics among its exhibits— ignoring the Paris Olympics at the 1900 Universal Exposition and the games held at Buffalo's 1901 Pan-American Exposition.[21]

In a series of public speeches, James Edward Sullivan, the Department of Physical Culture's chief, stressed the political and social implications of the athletic exhibits. He concentrated his message on the idea that modern existence, with its physique-withering routines and artificial environments, required the application of the new technology of sport to social problems if civilization were to continue to progress. Sullivan explained that the study of "scientific Physical Culture" and the rapid spread of sport marked a response to "a basic force of life" and signaled a return to "a wholesome civilization." He repeated the familiar litany of middle-class sporting ideas: strong bodies build vital minds and moral nations. "The sound body is the safest guardian of morality and of civilization—so agree teachers and philosophers as well as physicians," declared Sullivan. "The first decade of the new century finds the world ready to actively support the movement toward intelligent physical training, the principal avenue to which is sane competitive athletics," he concluded.[22] Sullivan planned to demonstrate his patriotically American version of "sane competitive athletics" to the world in St. Louis.

Sullivan and the Department of Physical Culture stressed the scientific component of the Louisiana Purchase Exposition's athletics by placing presentations on the social meanings of the strenuous life in the official Olympic program. The presenters list for the workshops included the leading theorists in American sporting science, among them Luther Halsey Gulick, G. Stanley Hall, and Henry S. Curtis. The "World's Olympic Lecture Course," organized by Gulick, included popular addresses such as "The Influence of Manly Sports on Peoples," "The Moral Phase of Athletics," "The Development of the City as Related to the Health of Children," and "New Conditions of Civilization Which Make Physical Training Necessary." Under the Olympic banner the St. Louis fair sponsored professional meetings, including the inaugural convention of the American Physical Education Association. Sullivan even arranged for the presentation of seven Olympic gold medals for the best articles presented at the sport science meetings.[23]

Exposition organizers augmented the scientific proceedings with "Olympic" demonstrations of athletic technology. They invited sporting exhibits from European nations with government-directed athletic programs and from American cities in which school systems had responsibility for physical training. The Department of Physical Culture erected an enormous display for the athletic festival. In one division the dominant U.S. manufacturer of sporting goods, A. G. Spalding and Brothers—a virtual Standard Oil of athletic implements—housed their wares. Exhibits of anthropometric devices; scientific studies of human motion; plans for regulated playgrounds, gymnasiums, and athletic fields; textbooks on physical education; and training charts and devices filled part of the athletic pavilion.[24]

The highlight of the physical plant was a granite-and-steel gymnasium equipped with the latest technical devices and an adjoining stadium with a seating capacity of 15,000. Olympic organizers boasted that the stadium contained "the greatest track ever built for athletic sports in America."[25] Constructed on the campus of Washington University, the buildings would serve as a site for collegiate sport after the 1904 games. The exposition also had a "model" playground and gymnasium, manufactured by playground movement experts, in the fair's Department of Social Economy.[26]

Consolidating American Control

Largely because of the close ties between the media and athletic nationalism's champions, the American press lauded the sport scientists' efforts to make the

Louisiana Purchase Exposition a showcase for the ideals and institutions of the sporting republic.[27] "For the first time in the history of Physical Culture, this great factor in the welfare of society is officially recognized as a special department by the Exposition," crowed *Spalding's Official Athletic Almanac,* which served as the quasi-official voice of the AAU and the American Olympic movement under Sullivan's editorship. Sullivan cast the Olympics as the centerpiece of the physical culture exhibit and promised the grandest Olympian Games in history. *Spalding's Almanac* bragged about American successes in the first two Olympics and pledged that "the representatives of athletics in America propose that nothing shall be left undone to make this first American Olympiad a phenomenal success."[28]

The AAU pushed the patriotic angle and managed to garner the support of most of the national sports organizations for the St. Louis enterprise. Caspar Whitney convinced President Theodore Roosevelt to serve as the honorary president of the Olympics. According to Sullivan, Roosevelt's acceptance of the honor "proved conclusively that he approved of the organization, had given the subject a great deal of thought and believed that the successful carrying out of the program meant much to the future success of this country as a strong nation."[29] The Olympic Games became an American exhibition of the gospel of the strenuous life. The AAU tabbed David R. Francis, the head of the Louisiana Purchase Exposition, successful grain merchant, former mayor of St. Louis, governor of Missouri, secretary of interior in the Grover Cleveland administration, and later ambassador to Russia, as the official president of the Olympics and named the stadium after him.[30] Sullivan and the AAU actually controlled the games, however.

The AAU had grabbed complete authority over the third Olympics from the IOC, and American sporting officials pushed their power to the limit. They designated as Olympic sports not only the international competitions included in the first modern Olympics at Athens in 1896 but a whole host of scholastic, collegiate, and even professional contests. Under Olympic auspices the Louisiana Purchase Exposition put on track meets for Missouri schoolboys; a national championship for YMCAs; sectional and national collegiate championships in track and field; college football, basketball, and baseball games; the first-ever meeting in football between Indian school powers Carlisle and Haskell; golf, archery, wrestling, boxing, fencing, lacrosse, swimming, bicycling, rowing, roque (croquet), and tennis tournaments; a Turner meet; and a jamboree of "Irish" games. They even proposed a meeting of the National and American League baseball champions for an Olympic championship, a series that never materialized.[31]

The entire series of events began on May 14 with an interscholastic meeting featuring St. Louis area high schools and continued through September. In mid-August, with the Olympic national cycling championships just completed and an Olympian struggle ready to commence between American YMCAs, the fair's Department of Physical Culture, in conjunction with the Department of Anthropology, decided to conduct a "scientific" experiment designed to uncover which races and cultures had the most athletic energy. Many sporting experts theorized that cultural patterns and environmental conditions represented the key determinants of national vigor. Which cultures and what kind of environments, they wondered, produce superior human specimens?

Testing the Myth of the Natural Athlete: The "Savage Olympics"

To test their hypotheses, the fair's athletic officials proposed a novel experiment. They planned to borrow "natural athletes" from one of the St. Louis fair's other venues. The managers of the fair's Department of Anthropology, under the leadership of Professor William J. McGee (who used "WJ" as a first name), demonstrated how various environments affect the human organism. McGee, one of the foremost anthropologists in the United States, designed his exhibits so that visitors could see "significant evidences of the slow, tedious evolution of civilization." McGee and his colleagues constructed their exhibition using pioneering anthropologist Lewis Henry Morgan's classification system, which categorizes stages of social evolution mainly on the basis of technological development. Curious visitors to the Anthropology Department displays saw a variety of cultures, including Ainus from Japan, Tehuelche Indians from Patagonia in South America, Pygmies from central Africa, a variety of Filipino groups, and many representatives from American Indian tribes. The anthropologists had erected, in effect, a human "zoo" with over two thousand occupants where the curious throngs could see what the experts promised were "realistic" scenes of aboriginal life. Exposition officials had even managed to secure the notorious Geronimo to appear in the exhibit.

In addition to providing the "native" exhibits, the anthropologists constructed a model Indian school designed to show how "primitive" peoples could be reconstructed as citizens of modern nations. Professor McGee declared "progressive acculturation" to be the prime mover in the evolution of human societies. "Long an accident of intertribal enmity, acculturation becomes under the principles of constitutional government an intentional and purposeful means of promoting the common weal," he argued, contending that the U.S. government had done a great service to American aborigines by practicing "progressive acculturation" in Indian schools. As McGee described it, the schools worked like a scientific melting pot, recasting "primitive" types into the citizens of a modern nation. The anthropologist considered the melting pot to be a rational device for constructing a national culture in which even "primitive" peoples could be included. Through that mechanism "the once bloody warrior Geronimo completed his own mental transformation from savage to citizen and for the first time sought to assume both the rights and responsibilities of the higher stage," announced McGee. The anthropologist insisted that through Indian schools and similar mechanisms, social engineers could transform people "from dull-minded and self-centered tribal existence into the active and constructive and broadminded life of modern humanity."[32]

When it came to questions of physical culture, McGee reversed his position in the nature versus nurture controversy. He and Dr. S. C. Simms, the head of the University of Chicago's Field Museum of Anthropology, spread word around the fairgrounds about the marvelous athletic ability of the "savages." Many of the Department of Physical Culture's sporting experts were quite skeptical of the anthropologists' claims. To resolve the controversy, the exposition staff, under the direction of McGee and physiologist Luther Gulick, constructed "Anthropology Days," an "Olympic Games" for the exposition's "primitives." Common wisdom, reported Sullivan, had for years taught "that the average savage was fleet of foot, strong of limb, accurate with the bow and arrow and expert in throwing the stone." Anthropology Days would test those claims.[33]

St. Louis journalists confirmed common assumptions in articles previewing the "Tribal Games." One report announced that the Moros from the Philippines had taken to athletic training "like ducks to water" and with a little more practice might soon worry "the more civilized white men" competing in the regular Olympics later that month.[34] Another article reported that a Moro had very nearly broken the world's record in the standing broad jump. Barefooted and leaping "native style," the Moro bested the mark that won the event at the 1900 Olympics. Sullivan revealed that the Department of Physical Culture was grooming the Moro for the standard Olympics.[35] Were the "primitives" the globe's great natural athletes? Held on August 12 and 13, Anthropology Days put the myths to a "scientific" test.

American sports fans eagerly awaited the spectacle. They "had heard of the marvelous qualities of the Indian as a runner and of his splendid power of endurance." They "had read much of the stamina of the Kaffir, of the remarkable athletic feats of the Filipinos, and of the great agility and muscular strength of the giant Patagonians."[36] Preliminaries for the "athletic meet of the aborigines" proved both exciting and dangerous. An African Pygmy practicing the running broad jump became incensed at photographers covering the proceedings and threatened to dispatch one of them with a spear. Luther Gulick ran across the track and stopped the picture-taking session, threatening to destroy the offender's camera. Gulick, who was photographing the Pygmies for "scientific purposes," then put away his own camera, while WJ McGee warned the rest of the spectators to take pictures at their own peril. The *St. Louis Globe-Democrat* reported that in spite of the Pygmies' quirks, the aboriginal contests would draw "a big crowd."[37]

The crowds attending the "Tribal Games" saw a spectacle that the *St. Louis Star* claimed offered "more real fun, if not bona-fide sport," than any of the Olympic-designated events held previously.[38] Aborigines clad in "native costumes" competed in "events suited to the nature of the contestants." Geronimo attended the contest with bow and arrow in hand, silently watching the spectacle. St. Louis newspapers described the aboriginal Olympics as a great success and noted that McGee, Gulick, and Sullivan had been "astounded" at the tribal athletes' performances. Some reporters expressed disappointment that American Indian tribes had been allowed to compete, since their previous exposure to Anglo-American athletics gave them a tremendous advantage. The desire to quantify performance shaped even the aboriginal Olympics. Native Americans won the meet with 34 points; the Filipinos, Moros, and "Negritos" placed second with 16½ points; the Patagonians won third with 10; the Cocopas (a Native American tribe from central Arizona) placed fourth with 5; and the Syrians came in last with 1 point.[39] The winners received cash prizes: $3 for firsts or seconds and $1 for thirds. Given amateur rules in 1904, the awards precluded future Olympic eligibility.[40]

According to expert opinion, however, future eligibility was not really a problem for these Olympians, since they had proved themselves vastly inferior athletes. Contrary to reports in some St. Louis newspapers, American athletic scientists were not "astounded" by Anthropology Days in any positive fashion. McGee, Gulick, and especially Sullivan declared that the experiments proved to be a great disappointment for believers in the myth of the natural athlete. The athletic events pitting the primitives against each other, in Sullivan's estimation, "were only successful in that they were destructive of the common belief that the greatest natural athletes were to be found among the uncivilized tribes in various parts of the world."[41]

The official report of the Louisiana Purchase Exposition on Anthropology Days noted that "the representatives of the savage and uncivilized tribes proved themselves inferior athletes, greatly overrated." A Pygmy ran the 100-yard dash in a time "that can be beaten by any twelve-year-old American school boy." Spectators who watched the "giant Patagonians" put the shot found their "best performance was so ridiculously poor that it astonished all who witnessed it." John Flanagan's toss, the second-place heave in the regular Olympic fifty-six-pound throw, surpassed the combined throws of the best three Patagonian competitors hurling sixteen-pound weights. The Sioux Indian who won the 100-yard dash did it "in a remarkably slow time." The Sioux who won the running broad jump could not equal Olympic victor Ray Ewry's *standing* broad jump record.[42]

Sullivan insisted that the results from the aboriginal athletic contests proved "conclusively that the savage is not the natural athlete we have been led to believe." All the "civilized" sporting contests—the runs, jumps, and throws of the American sporting tradition—were won by "Americanized" Indians. On the final day of the anthropological Olympics, the organizers set up some "native" games. An Igorotte from the Philippines won a pole-climbing contest with a "marvelous performance" that much impressed Sullivan. An archery contest saw a "little Cocopa boy named Shake" win by piercing the target one time. Sullivan found the bow-and-arrow games a ridiculously incompetent display of native ability, refusing to swallow Dr. Simms's explanation that most of the tribes did their shooting from horseback. The Pygmies engaged in a spectacular mud fight, which Sullivan found very amusing. But a display of a "shinny" game by the Pygmies and the Cocopa Indians, "which required team work . . . , showed conclusively the lack of the necessary brain to make the team and its work a success, for they absolutely gave no assistance to each other, and so far as team work was concerned, it was a case of purely individual attempt on the part of the players."

Sullivan judged the Anthropology Days to have been an extremely enlightening event. "Dr. McGee attributes this utter lack of athletic ability on the part of the savages to the fact that they have not been shown or educated," chuckled the director of the 1904 Olympics. "He thinks perhaps if they could have the use of a professional trainer for a short time that they would become as proficient as many Americans. This writer doubts it." Still, the "savage" games "were most successful and interesting, and ones that scientific men will refer to for many years to come. It taught a great lesson," Sullivan added with irony. "Lecturers and authors will in the future please omit all reference to the natural athletic ability of the savage, unless they can substantiate their alleged feats."[43] McGee tried to save face. "I am very much pleased with the results of the meet," he announced, adding that he wanted to repeat the experiment in a few weeks—after his natives had a chance to train. McGee testified that while he still thought "primitive peoples" were experts in certain native sports, in "all-around development no primitive people can rank in the same class with the Missouri boy."[44]

Baron de Coubertin, who did not attend the St. Louis Olympics, regretfully pardoned the Americans for Anthropology Days, remarking that "in no place but America would one have dared to place such events on a program, but to

Americans everything is permissible, their youthful exuberance calling certainly for the indulgence of the Ancient Greek ancestors, if, by chance, they found themselves among the amused spectators."[45] In the context of the exposition, Anthropology Days was not really an aberration. It reaffirmed, like the other scientific and technical displays, the basic belief in the superiority of the industrial civilization that lay at the core of the exposition's appeal. Anthropology Days indicated that civilized environments shaped superior human organisms. For American social scientists and athletic leaders, the results of Anthropology Days confirmed that the best place to build their national culture was on the ethnocentric bedrock of Western civilization. Even Professor McGee, for all his touting the prowess of "primitives," admitted that Americans had developed more fully than any other peoples because of their affinity for sport. Athletics build "mind, muscle and morality," McGee agreed. The American love of the strenuous life confirmed his nation's role as the leader of evolutionary progress.[46]

The "Civilized" Olympics Commence

While the scientists argued about the data from Anthropology Days, most popular pundits associated evolutionary progress in sport with assaults on the record books. The commencement of the "regular" Olympics—the international competitions—a little more than two weeks after the "savage" Olympics concluded provided a venue for challenging global athletic standards. "The world's records tremble on the eve of the Olympic games . . . at the World's Fair," crowed the *St. Louis Post-Dispatch*. Sullivan, recovered from his feigned astonishment at the failure of natural athletes, predicted "that old heroes of the sod and cinder track will be vanquished and that new world's marks are destined to be established." The vanquishers would probably be "a new school of athletes, the rank and file of strong young American manhood," gushed the *Post-Dispatch*. The 1904 games would be not only greater than any previous Olympics, declared the hometown daily, "but doubtless the greatest to be held for years to come," surpassing the future Olympics that had been awarded to Rome in 1908 and Stockholm in 1912 and not likely to be topped until "the middle of the twentieth century," when "the Olympian games come back to America."[47] Most of the American press took the same tone. Even the usually staid *New York Times* prophesied that the 1904 games would "undoubtedly prove to be the greatest athletic meeting of modern times."[48]

The St. Louis games marked a watershed in popular consciousness of the Olympics. Intensive newspaper coverage of the 1896 Olympics had been mainly restricted to the New England and New York papers that covered the doings of local athletes in Athens. Reporting in American dailies expanded during the 1900 Olympics, but the great majority of stories appeared in the eastern and middle western newspapers that generally covered intercollegiate and international contests. Press coverage of the 1904 Olympics, sparked by the transfer controversy between Chicago and St. Louis, achieved a truly national scope. The expanded Olympics captured imaginations in hinterlands and local enclaves. The Ft. Shaw Indian School in Montana announced that its basketball teams were bound for the Olympics. Beloit College thought it had a good chance to capture an Olympic baseball crown. YMCAs throughout the nation planned Olympic fund-raising strategies to send teams to St. Louis.[49]

Newspapers provided the public with histories of the ancient and modern Olympics. Invariably the articles described convincing American victories at Athens and Paris by focusing on track and field competitions while conveniently ignoring events in which the United States had performed poorly. Americans prepared for another Olympic conquest and wondered what challenges the rest of the world might mount to their claim of Olympic supremacy. The press regaled the nation with tales of athletic hordes from every nation on earth descending on St. Louis to wrest the laurels of Olympian supremacy from American heads.[50] The *St. Louis Globe-Democrat* told its readers that Greece, Germany, Hungary, Australia, New Zealand, and Canada would mount strong challenges to American athletic supremacy.[51] The *St. Louis Post-Dispatch* headlined its Sunday magazine supplement with Olympic material that promised that the world's greatest athletes would be at David R. Francis Stadium to contest for Olympian glory.[52]

The international track and field contests, what the *Post-Dispatch* called the "Olympian games proper," were open to the "amateurs of the world"—as sanctioned by the AAU—who could afford the $2 per event entry fee.[53] Sullivan even tried to recruit female collegians to his Olympic extravaganza.[54] The guarantees of a grand "international" meet proved hollow, however, as few of the "amateurs of the world" bothered to attend the St. Louis Olympics. Only small, unrepresentative contingents from Austria, Canada, Cuba, Germany, the British Empire, Greece, Hungary, and Switzerland made the journey to the heart of the North American continent. The lack of foreign entries produced an Olympics that was principally an American track meet dominated by U.S. athletes.

Americans had little sympathy for those nations that did not bother to attend the extravaganza. "England and France did not send a single competitor to America, and the French people showed their ingratitude by an entire absence of representation," complained one of the most comprehensive eyewitness chroniclers of the 1904 Olympics, Charles J. P. Lucas, noting that Great Britain's athletes in St. Louis were from Ireland, Australia, and New Zealand. Lucas alleged that without American entries the 1900 Olympics would have degenerated into a "farce" and blasted Europeans for failing to enter the St. Louis sporting festival. His rancor led him to jest that England and France were not really missed at the 1904 Olympics, considering that "it is doubtful, indeed, if a single Frenchmen could have finished even fourth in any of the events. In fact only one Englishman would have stood a chance of winning any event whatever."[55]

When significant foreign competition failed to materialize, American newspapers hyped the Olympics as a contest between pioneer vigor and urban vitality. "The principal feature of the Olympic games will be the dual meet, practically speaking, between the East and West," crowed the *St. Louis Globe-Democrat*. The St. Louis daily predicted that the East would be "compelled to drain the bitter dregs of defeat."[56] The *Louisville Courier-Journal* concurred, urging western athletes—those who resided "between the Ohio and Mississippi rivers"—to defeat the champions from "the staid old East and Europe."[57] Those sentiments underscored the American assumption that the republican vigor cultivated on the playing field made "common" citizens superior to the aristocratic classes of the Europe and their imitators on the Atlantic seaboard. A special Olympic cup awarded to the best club team at the Olympics complicated the East versus West rivalry. The *Chicago Tribune* agreed that the West had the best athletes but lamented the division of western stars into teams from Chicago, Milwaukee, St. Louis, Kentucky, and California, while the athletic power of the East was concentrated in the New York Athletic Club (NYAC).[58] The East was not quite as united as the western press claimed, however. The Greater New York Irish American Athletic Club also sent a team to St. Louis, led by former NYAC shot putter John J. Flanagan.[59]

The "real" Olympics—in American minds, the international track and field competition—began on August 29 and ran until September 3. Opening day, a clear and warm Missouri summer afternoon, brought five thousand spectators to the new stadium.[60] At the conclusion of the first day's events the United States had scored eighty points. Ireland was in second place with four points, followed by Germany with three and Hungary with two. American athletes totally overwhelmed the foreign competitors who had bothered to attend. The crowd demonstrated their appreciation of the few non-American participants by cheering foreign athletes. American Olympic officials even refused to penalize an Hungarian hurdler who had false-started when he misunderstood the "American method." Americans fans could afford to be good sports with inferior opponents. The Hungarian hurdler proved too slow to make the final.[61]

The first day's pattern of scoring continued throughout the Olympics. The *Chicago Tribune*'s prediction of "an all American struggle" proved accurate.[62] The press ignored national rivalries and reported heavily on the scores of the sectional contest between the American East and the American West, world's records set by Americans, and the competition between urban athletic clubs.[63] The American organizers of the third Olympics originated the custom of giving gold, silver, and bronze medals for first, second, and third places, respectively.[64] The United States won seventy gold, seventy-five silver, and sixty-four bronze medals in the third Olympic Games. The next closest nations in the medal hunt were Cuba, with five gold, two silver, and three bronze medals, and Germany, with four gold, four silver, and five bronze medals.[65] The United States dominated its beloved track and field competition, winning twenty-one of the twenty-two events and placing second in twenty-one and third in twenty-one.[66]

A "Scientific" Marathon

An American won the marathon for the first time in a strange race conducted under the "scientific" scrutiny of the staff from the Department of Physical Culture. The race demonstrated the desire among sport experts to use medical science to turn the human body into a dynamo. Their experiments on Olympic runners provided a bizarre commentary on their understanding of how to increase energy and improve athletic performance. Dr. Gulick had the runners measured, weighed, and tested before and after the race to study the effect of marathon "strain" on the human heart. Twenty automobiles followed the runners around the course, each car occupied by a physician in charge of monitoring the racers' conditions.[67] Charles Lucas, who traveled the course in the vehicle attending to the eventual winner of the race, Thomas J. Hicks of Cambridgeport, Massachusetts, claimed that "the Marathon race furnished information the like of which will be of more value to scientists in the study of humanity than any event contested in the stadium or in America for some years to come."

The marathon provided an enlightening commentary on the early twentieth-century combination of medical, automotive, and athletic technologies. The field for the race included seventeen Americans, eleven Greeks (who were living in the United States), one Cuban, one South African, and two "Kaffirs from Zululand" on loan from the fair's Department of Anthropology. The race began on a hot Missouri day, "90 degrees in the shade" according to Lucas, over a course laid out through extremely dusty, hilly Missouri roads. The twenty autos raised so much dirt on the backcountry roads that runners had to stop periodically "to choke and cough until they cleared their throats." William Garcia of San Francisco swallowed enough dust to cause a nearly fatal hemorrhaging of his stomach lining. Two more near-fatalities occurred when one of the automobiles assisting the runners rolled down an embankment. Stones and other debris littered the route, making the course, in Lucas's estimation, "the most difficult a human being was ever asked to run over." Judging from the accident, apparently it was fairly difficult for the cars, too.[68]

Other hazards intruded as well. The two "Kaffirs" (the use of that pejorative term by Olympic officials, fair organizers, and the American press indicates the depth of contemporary American racism) were chased off the course by dogs. One of them, a mail carrier named Lentauw (the name means "lion"), became the butt of a *St. Louis Globe-Democrat* wit. "The last view that was obtained of the 'Lion' was from the aforesaid lonely road," quipped the columnist; "The 'Lion' was cavorting wildly across a stubblefield after the manner of the original African cakewalker, with a plain yellow cur of an American watchdog running a close second, with prospects of a speedy union between the cavernous display of canine molars and the rearmost portion of the 'Lion's' garments."[69] Lentauw escaped the mutt and finished ninth in the race.

American commentators marveled at another foreign competitor in the marathon, tiny Felix Carvajal of Cuba. Another mail carrier, Carvajal had supposedly run from one end of Cuba to the other. During the race he reportedly took only one drink of water. "He was clad in a cheap negligee shirt," remembered Lucas, "wore heavy street shoes, and, having no running trousers, had cut off the legs of his street trousers to make himself look like a runner." Carvajal frequently stopped to chat with spectators in "broken English" and ate some green peaches that caused him a great deal of discomfort. Despite those distractions he finished fourth. "Had Carvajal had anyone with him—he was totally unattended—he would not only have won the race, but would have lowered the Olympic record," theorized Lucas.[70]

Lucas himself, along with Hugh C. McGrath from the Charlesbank Gymnasium in Boston, attended to Hicks. Lucas declared that "the Marathon race, from a medical standpoint, demonstrated that drugs are of much benefit to athletes." Lucas and McGrath administered sulfate of strychnine and egg whites to Hicks twice during the race. When the runner asked for water, they refused and instead sponged his mouth out. After the twenty-mile mark they bathed him in water that had been kept warm in the boiler of a steam automobile and gave him a dose of strychnine and some brandy. Lucas observed that "over the last two miles of the road, Hicks was running mechanically . . . , like a well-oiled piece of machinery. . . . The brain was fairly normal, but there was more or less hallucination, the most natural being that the finish was twenty miles from where he was running." In spite of the torture he received from his trainers, Hicks appeared to be in the lead as he neared the stadium for the finish of the race.[71]

An excited crowd awaited the runners at the finish line in Francis Stadium, but the first athlete to enter the stadium was not Hicks but Fred Lorz of New York City's Mohawk Athletic Club. "An American wins!" shouted the partisans. "Pandemonium reigned for a few moments" recounted the *Globe-Democrat*. Lorz, however, had ridden part of the way in an automobile after tiring and dropping out of the race. When the race officials and the spectators discovered that Lorz had used a car to complete the marathon, "every one felt very cheap."[72]

Lucas condemned Lorz as a cheat who had "robbed a man who, four miles out on the road, was running the last ounces of strength out of his body, kept in mechanical action by the use of drugs, that he might bring America the Marathon honors, which American athletes had failed to win both at Athens and at Paris." Lucas impugned the patriotism of the "native-born" Lorz and glorified the Americanism of Hicks, an emigrant from England who "chose to carry the Stars and Stripes in the race and represent America." Lorz freely admitted that he had contested part of the marathon in a car and claimed that he had not intended to deceive spectators and officials. The distance of Lorz's auto trip became a point of contention, however. At first he claimed that he had ridden in the car for only one mile and, since he had finished two miles ahead of Hicks, that he still deserved the victory. Some reports claimed that Lorz had traveled at least twelve miles by automobile. After the Olympics the AAU banned him from competition for life. Hicks finally arrived to claim the victory, too exhausted to carry off the trophy signifying his triumph.[73]

The controversy over the marathon did not end when Hicks was awarded the victory. Everett Brown, the chairman of the Chicago Athletic Association (CAA), protested Hicks's victory on the grounds that the runner had been paced by an automobile driven by the officials who were overseeing the marathon.[74] Dr. Gulick and the judge of the course, Charles Senter, who were riding in the lead car, rejected the Chicagoan's contention. Olympic director James Sullivan refused to hear the protest, and Hicks remained the official winner.[75]

Sullivan, upset about the problems that had occurred during the race and the conditions of the runners at the finish, proposed the abolition of the marathon from Olympic competition. Sullivan found few allies. "True it is," opined the *St. Louis Globe-Democrat*, "the Marathon race does test the strength, running ability and grit of a man, yet it is the best race of its nature in the world."[76] Dr. Gulick and his staff found no medical evidence to support Sullivan's contentions of the dangers of marathoning—although everyone was certainly aware of the legend of Pheidippides and his fatal run, which had inspired the Olympic event. The race would remain a part of the Olympic program. Hicks's achievement made him the hero of the 1904 games.

The War for the "Spalding Cup" and an Orgy of American Self-Congratulation

The CAA's protest had been a calculated effort to have their own Albert J. Corey, the runner-up in the marathon, declared the victor. The points from a marathon win would have aided the Chicago association's attempt to win the Spalding trophy, a "magnificent loving-cup emblematic of the Olympic championship."[77] The Spalding trophy bestowed the title of "Olympic champions" on the club team that won the track and field portion of the 1904 games. "The chivalry of amateur sport was in all the struggles," insisted the *St. Louis Post-Dispatch* of the Olympic temper, "and not an unsportsmanlike act marred the cleanliness of the games."[78] The *Post-Dispatch* must not have been watching the bitter battle for the Olympic "amateur championship" that raged among the CAA, the NYAC, the Milwaukee Athletic Club (MAC), and the Greater New York Irish American Athletic Club.

The rancor over the Spalding trophy threatened to create serious rifts in the athletic establishment. Lucas described it as "the most bitter fight in the history of American athletics." The AAU clubs contested for the championship throughout the Olympic Games. After the final day of competition, with the NYAC leading sixty-three points to fifty-nine, CAA officials filed a protest against four of the New York team's points. Olympic officials disallowed the three points won by John Dewitt for the NYAC in the hammer throw when it was discovered that Dewitt did not live in the metropolitan New York area. The CAA had also protested the single point awarded to the NYAC for a fourth place finish in the tug-of-war, claiming that since the New York team withdrew from the four-team competition, it did not deserve any points.[79]

Particularly galling to the CAA was the fact that the Milwaukee Athletic Club had won the tug-of-war with a team recruited from Chicago by MAC president Walter Liginger, who just happened to also be the president of the AAU as well as the head of the Olympic organizing committee.[80] Exposition officials put off a final decision on the protest over the tug-of-war point until a November 1904 AAU board of governors meeting.[81] The executive conference, held in New York City, disallowed the CAA's protest. Two months after the Olympics had concluded, the NYAC won the Spalding trophy. The AAU placed the CAA second, the MAC third, and the Greater New York Irish Athletic Club fourth in the "international" standings of the third Olympics.[82]

The dispute over the Spalding cup enraged James Sullivan, who felt that the arguments sullied his Olympic presentation. In his public reports of events at St. Louis, however, Director Sullivan ignored the controversies. He declared that the 1904 games "were without question the greatest athletic games ever held in the world." Over 9,000 participants competed in some form of "Olympic" activity in St. Louis. "The entry list indicated conclusively the great and universal interest that was taken in the different athletic competitions, and it is confidently stated by those who ought to know that it contained the largest series of entries recorded by any one organization or corporation that has held an athletic meeting or a series of athletic meetings," bragged Sullivan. According to the AAU the Olympic track and field meet attracted the "most noted athletes" in the world.[83] Sullivan condemned the IOC for its failure to encourage European participation in the St. Louis games, but he would not allow the lack of international competition to tarnish his Olympics. "When one looks over the list of Olympic winners and then over the list of eligible men in the world, there are perhaps two men living to-day who were not in the stadium who could have won Olympic honors," he conjectured, implying that all the best athletes in the world were Americans.[84]

The confirmation of national athletic supremacy complemented what Sullivan insisted was the central purpose of the St. Louis Olympics—educating the world in the doctrines of American athletics.[85] Several members of the IOC who witnessed the Olympics came away with positive images of the sporting republic. "This is the grandest athletic meet I ever witnessed," gushed Hungarian IOC member Father Ferenc Kemeny. Dr. Jiri Guth of Bohemia and Dr. Willibald Gebhardt of Germany, also IOC representatives, concurred.[86] Many Americans thought that Sullivan had put on the greatest showing of the strenuous life ever seen. "If the study of mankind is man," wrote the president of the Louisiana Purchase Exposition, David R. Francis, seriously misreading Alexander Pope, "the study of the body that holds and sustains and is the man can not be properly left out of the curriculum." Sullivan boasted that his athletic displays at the fair had placed sport firmly into the modern curriculum. He opined that visitors to St. Louis had "beheld the birth of modern Physical Culture as a science." The nation had learned, to Sullivan's satisfaction, to consider "Physical Culture in co-ordinate position with the other principal divisions of human and social need and activity—in formally placing it in its proper relationship to human welfare and progress before the world."[87]

Sullivan had a lot of help in touting the St. Louis Olympics as scientific confirmation of sport's contribution to "human welfare and progress," as well as compelling evidence for the superiority of American styles of physical culture. The *World's Fair Bulletin* asserted that Sullivan's show would not be surpassed for at least a generation, listing thirteen new Olympic records made in the twenty-six "official" Olympic events contested at St. Louis. The records had been set before crowds that the *Bulletin* described as "gratifying."[88] The St. Louis and national presses disputed official claims about attendance and profit making but concurred with Sullivan and the Louisiana Purchase Exposition staff that the Olympics showcased the prowess of the sporting republic.[89] "Modern Sprinters Strive to Break the Records of the Ancients" read a *St. Louis Republic* headline.[90] American commentators read the results of St. Louis as proof that their nation had surpassed the standards set by both antiquity and modernity in sport, politics, and public virtue.

American purveyors of athletic technology, administrators and athletes alike, had accomplished the tasks that they had set for themselves. They had defined the Olympic Games according to their preferences, sporting contests centered on track and field games. They had proved to their own satisfaction that they were bolder and stronger than even nature's athletes. They believed that they had vanquished the rest of the world. Finally, they had explicitly connected Olympic achievement to American political culture.

The third Olympic Games helped to cement the sporting republic more firmly to progressive reform agendas and created the now widely held perception that success in international athletic meets somehow correlates with national power and social progress. The St. Louis games whetted the public appetite for sportive conquest. In the Olympic Games that followed, Americans increasingly demanded spectacular performances from the teams, reading victory as a sign that providence still favored their nation while worrying that defeat meant that serious maladies afflicted the republic.

Victories for the "Best Men"?

The reading of Olympic sport into political philosophy nevertheless created some conflicts in the sporting republic's ideologies. What factors, wondered many Olympic observers, contributed to the power of the sporting republic and propelled American civilization toward global dominion? "Let the best man win, whoever he is," was best-selling western novelist Owen Wister's shorthand for the American formula.[91] Such sentiments could be found at the core of American political culture and motivated progressive attempts to create a society free from special privilege or unfair advantage.

The same language shaped the ideology of the sporting republic. "A fair field and no favor, was the spirit that moved all the contestants who entered and they lived up to it with exemplary exactness," wrote J. W. McConaughy of America's Olympians at the games of the Third Olympiad.[92] The press idealized the U.S. Olympian as an American everyman who confirmed Wister's words as being very close to the realities of American life. Nevertheless, those media images did not necessarily square with the facts. In 1896 and 1900 American Olympians had come overwhelmingly from colleges and universities, a rather elite group of Americans. In 1904 the collegiate complexion of the team began to change, and some observers rushed to associate Olympic achievement with their beliefs in egalitarianism and the role of the "common man" in American society.

While James Sullivan held to the notion that champions were mainly trained in college, he did note that increasing numbers of working-class athletes had won distinction in St. Louis. By the Department of Physical Culture chief's count, out of ninety-four athletes placed in the "official" Olympic program, fifty were collegiate stars and forty-four never had college training.[93] Charles Lucas dissented from Sullivan's support of collegians. He denounced American colleges for failing to support the games properly, chastising Harvard, Yale, Pennsylvania, Columbia, Dartmouth, Georgetown, Amherst, Michigan, Wisconsin, Minnesota, and "Western minor colleges" for failing to send teams to St. Louis. Lucas decried, with a few exceptions, the "poor sportsmanship" of universities in their lack of support for the Olympics and insisted that "the American colleges are not to be thanked in the least for the clean-cut victory of America in the Olympic Games of 1904." He overstated his case somewhat. Athletes from the colleges that had failed to send teams to the Olympics had actually participated in the St. Louis games as members of various club teams. Even Lucas admitted as much. "True it is, American collegians competed in several events, but their care, training and expenses were undertaken by members of the Amateur Athletic Union of the United States, and not by the colleges."[94]

Still, Lucas gave most of the credit for America's victory in the Olympics to the "American workingman." He asserted that the St. Louis games showed "that the college boy is not solely the acme of American athletics" and pointed to the performances of New York City policemen John Flanagan and Martin Sheridan, hurdler Harry Hillman, and marathon champion Thomas Hicks. Lucas called Hicks a heroic "American workingman."[95] An orphan and a "buffer by trade," Hicks symbolized the American belief in social mobility and individual power. In fact, Albert Corey, the runner-up in the marathon, had been born in France and worked, albeit less heroically, as a laborer and "professional strikebreaker." Corey had moved to Chicago to take advantage of a butchers' strike.[96] The descriptions of the two long-distance runners epitomized turn-of-the-century American conceptions of immigrants pursuing happiness in a land of opportunity and of old ethnic nationalities giving way to a common national type. Although such conceptions might have been at odds with much of American experience, they were nevertheless commonplace fictions.

Obviously American ideals do not always match American realities. In many places in early twentieth-century America, letting the best person win also meant excluding from the game everyone who was not white, of northern

European descent, Protestant, male, and American-born. The southern and eastern European immigrants arriving in the United States in large numbers during the early 1900s filled the lowest ranks in the American labor structure. Slavs, Czechs, Poles, and Hungarians joined the Irish in mines and mills. Eastern European Jews labored in the garment industry. Italians worked in labor gangs, dug ditches, and maintained railroads. African Americans, ninety percent of whom still lived in the South, were even more oppressed than immigrants. They worked in agriculture mainly, or in turpentine camps, or on the docks and wharves of southern ports. When industry recruited them, it was often as strikebreakers—an experience they shared with Albert Corey. About 30 percent of African Americans worked as personal or domestic servants.[97]

Against an American backdrop of ethnic tension, racism, and segregation, sport was occasionally depicted as an arena in which race or ethnicity should not matter. Such a position seemed hopelessly wishful, given the exclusionary policies that characterized so much of American sport. Nonetheless, the belief that the cliché "let the best man win" actually characterized American society remained attractive. In St. Louis the focus was on ideals rather than certain troublesome realities, such as the place of African Americans in the United States. Images of the superiority of American civilization and its white, Anglo-Saxon, Protestant, bourgeois mainstream culture dominated the world's fair. One had only to purchase a ticket to the Anthropology Department's human zoo to indulge in the ethnocentric productions that characterized the fair.

Still, in some small ways, the Olympics offered fleeting glimpses of different possibilities. The St. Louis games witnessed the first African American medalist in Olympic history. The University of Wisconsin's George Poage finished third in both the 200- and 400-meter hurdles.[98] The great Myer Prinstein, the Jewish long jumper who had been barred from competing on the Christian Sabbath by Syracuse University at the Paris Olympics, finally won his specialty at St. Louis.[99] Jewish, Irish, and other immigrant names dotted the American roster in 1904. Then there was Hicks, the English-born "workingman" who "chose" to wear American colors.

The athlete served political commentators in constructing a middle-class vision of a civilization in which class distinctions were transcended by abundant opportunities. "They come from all walks in life, differing in birth and vocation as much as they differ physically and mentally," wrote Thomas I. Lee of the American "record breakers." American athletes were transformed into icons who represented the ideal of social mobility. "Clergymen and bookmakers, millionaires and stablemen, doctors of philosophy and district messenger boys, army officers and privates, bankers and day laborers, all these have raced and broken one another's records," declared Lee.[100]

Scientific Proof of Superiority

The St. Louis Games served as a "scientific" template for measuring the progress of the American "race" against other civilizations and cultures. After the third Olympics Arthur Ruhl imagined that "if we could send a team back to that ancient stadium in the Peloponnesus—with their spiked shoes and crouching-starts and American nerves—I suppose there is not the slightest doubt that man for man, leaving out beauty and sentiment and, also, the more brutal semi-glad-iatorial contests, they would win as surely as that first funny little team won at Athens when the Olympic games were revived twelve years ago."[101] American Olympic folklore held that at Athens, Paris, and St. Louis the Americans had vanquished challengers from every other modern nation. In Arthur Ruhl's mind "America's athletic missionaries" had even surpassed the ancient Greeks, the in-ventors of the adage that sound bodies build sound minds and superior civili-zations. In the eyes of many athletic experts, the American "race," which qua-drennially garnered most of the modern Olympic laurels, had been forged by a union of all European ethnicities.

"Scientific data" from another clash of cultures—not Ruhl's imaginary con-test between the modern United States and ancient Greece but the results from Anthropology Days—indicated that the inventors of the sporting republic were more confused about the relations between race and sport than their pro-nouncements about the openness of American playing fields revealed. At the national level they tried to maintain a conception of sport as a "melting pot." When it came to questions of empire, however, they drew different conclusions from the experiments run at St. Louis's human zoo. James Sullivan asserted that the "savage" Olympics had from the "scientific standpoint" proven "conclusively that the average savage or foreigner is not equal to the white man." Even the cultural anthropologist WJ McGee shared similar racist sentiments. Anthropol-ogy Days, he proclaimed, demonstrated "what anthropologists have long known, that the white man leads the races of the world, both physically and mentally, and in the coordination of the two which goes to make up the best specimen of manhood, they have the 'spirit and the sand.'"[102]

Contemporary American folklore has tried to maintain that race matters less in sport than in any other segment of American society, yet racism and ethno-centrism dogged the foundations of the sporting republic. Sullivan, the son of Irish immigrants who had risen to the pinnacle of the American athletic hier-archy, consistently rejected the idea that Anglo-Saxons were the world's great-est athletes. He also championed the cause of immigrant sporting stars. His attitudes did not extend over the "color line" in American sport, however, regardless of George Poage's speed. He endorsed the theory that the "white man" marked a superior type.

In St. Louis Americans had learned that sport symbolized their national identity and that their genius for athletics set them apart from the rest of the world. Devotion to the strenuous life characterized the American "race." But what race were the citizens of the sporting republic, the vigorous people who had proven themselves more fit than nature's champions, foreign rivals from modern nations, and even the imaginary athletic legends of antiquity? How color-blind were American playing fields and gymnasiums? How open to immigrants and excluded groups were American Olympic teams? What powers did athletic technology have for revising or reproducing the categories of race and ethnicity? Would women find places in the sporting republic? Those questions would confront the sporting republic as it attempted to conquer an empire and convert the globe with its legions of "America's athletic missionaries."

★ 5

The Limits of Universal Claims: How Class, Gender, Race, and Ethnicity Shaped the Sporting Republic

The 1904 St. Louis games made the Olympics a permanent part of American culture. The St. Louis Olympics reached a massive audience throughout the United States and guaranteed that American ideas about the sporting republic would be inextricably bound with Olympic performances. Sporting republicans made universal promises about creating representative democracy through athletic games. They pledged themselves to an athletic restoration of civic virtue. They vowed to make sport multiply the public good. They insisted sport shored up the very foundations of the republican experiment.

In St. Louis American Olympians had been canonized as "everymen" whose world-beating prowess originated from the opportunities provided by republican society. At the same time, the realities of the St. Louis games demonstrated that, just as in the larger republic, there were limits to universal claims. Class, gender, race, and ethnicity each affected the dialogues surrounding American Olympic performances. Women did not play significant roles in the St. Louis games, and they were seriously underrepresented in the sporting republic. Class distinctions shaped American ideas about sport, engendering rivalries between "workingmen" and "college boys" and arguments over the nature and purpose of athletic competition. Although an African American had won a medal in St. Louis, the interpretations of athletic prowess offered by the media from both the "regular" and "savage" Olympics indicated that race and ethnicity still mattered very much in American sport—as they did in all other aspects of American life. The identification of "native" versus immigrant Olympians revealed the ethnic tensions that divided even European American groups.

The St. Louis Olympics marked a critical juncture not only for the growing popularity of the Olympic Games in the United States but for the crusade to transform the United States into a sporting republic. By the end of 1904 the nation's leading sporting republican, Theodore Roosevelt, had been elected to the presidency. The sporting republic had gained tremendous power in American imaginations. The nation had hosted the Olympics. The national media published the work of a legion of confirmed sporting republicans who produced glowing accounts of sport as a mechanism for revitalizing American civilization. The popularity of organized sport had grown dramatically. American educational institutions increasingly incorporated sport into their curricula. Participation in sport as well as spectatorship at amateur and professional contests had become a basic feature of American life. Social reformers believed that sport provided a technology for remaking the national culture. A major park- and playground-building movement designed to republicanize American cities was underway. The athletic principles of the gospel of the strenuous life had captured American imaginations.

The champions of the strenuous life promised that sport would create a society in which the "best man" could win. Advocates of progressive reform, many of whom were also staunch supporters of sport, made the same promises about the political, economic, and social changes they insisted were necessary to reinvigorate the republican experiment. Were any of the promises being fulfilled? Was American society changing? Could the "best men" win? Would the "best women" even be allowed in an Olympic race or near a ballot box? Class, gender, race, and ethnicity each set limits to promises of the sporting republic.

Republican Claims of Universalism and Olympian Icons of Democratic Ideals

American republicans have historically made all-encompassing claims about their political systems. "All men are created equal," trumpeted Thomas Jefferson in 1776. Rule by law, written constitutions, and representative democracy have been touted as universally beneficent institutions. In practice, the new republic of the United States that emerged at the end of the eighteenth century did not treat men of all colors or classes as equals. Women were not explicitly included in Jefferson's universal claim.

Republics, according to their supporters, always provide schemes of representation for "the people." But both the quality and the equality of that representation have been exclusive properties throughout most of American history. Many groups have been denied full partnership. Exclusions based on race, ethnicity, class, and gender have deep roots in American political culture. Representation belonged first only to property-holding European American men and then more inclusively to all European American men. One hundred and forty-three years after the United States declared itself an independent republic, women finally garnered the franchise. African Americans received constitutional promises for voting rights eighty-nine years after independence, but even then those promises proved mostly hollow. Significant enjoyment of African American voting rights required another century of struggles. Battles over inclusion and exclusion continue to rage in contemporary American politics.

Just as the founding fathers proclaimed that their political system manifested a universal nature, so too did the American thinkers who imagined that they could revitalize the republic through sport. Who could obtain citizenship in the great republic of American sport? Anyone could, according to the rhetoric of most defenders of the strenuous life. They maintained that as the linchpin of their effort to build a national community and revitalize the republic, sport stood as the most democratic of all American institutions. "The sporting spirit is about the most democratic, unstellar thing I know," wrote Robert Haven Schauffler, an American tennis player. "In the eyes of the law all men are *supposed* to be equal. But in the eyes of the law of sport all men are actually equal," Schauffler announced, translating Jefferson's dictum into the language of sport.[1]

Sporting republicans announced that Jefferson's self-evident truth that all men are created equal manifested itself most clearly in the composition of American Olympic teams. They portrayed American athletes at Olympic Games as democratic icons, painting pictures of teams comprising "Anglo-Saxon, Teuton, Slav, Celt, Black Ethiopian and red Indian."[2] American Olympians supposedly stood above race, caste, or class distinctions. *The Independent* celebrated teams chosen "without regard to class, wealth, race, color or previous condition of servitude."[3] Athletic official Robert M. Thompson insisted that American Olympic teams were "thoroughly democratic, representative of all sorts and conditions of men—except bad men."[4] Thompson insisted that "neither color of skin nor texture of clothing counted" on American Olympic teams. Sportswriter Edward Bayard Moss proclaimed that "there was no class or color distinction" on American teams. "Each man and youth was an integral part of the team, bearing the American shield, with his work to do."[5] Journalist Carl Crow added that "in this democratic country, athletic competition is confined neither to the rich nor to the poor, but is shared by all alike. We honor the men who set the marks with little or no regard for who or what they are off the athletic field."[6]

In spite of the hyperbolic claims, the idealized portraits of modern athletics offered by sporting republicans did not always reflect actual social practice. Just as the larger republic did not always live up to the promises of its rhetoric, so too did the sporting republic fall short of its ideals. Class, gender, race, and ethnicity shaped American sport. Those realities configured American conceptions of the sporting republic. Universal claims had limits.

How inclusive was the sporting republic? Who could participate, and to what extent? Sporting republicans sought to make their version of sport a universal feature of American culture. They wanted everyone to play their games and thus to learn their values and join their ranks. Nevertheless, they failed to win universal acceptance for their new ideology of sport. Some groups wanted to continue to use athletics to mark off class, gender, and ethnic boundaries. Other groups were excluded or marginalized. Not everyone was welcome in the sporting republic.

The Dynamics of Sport and Class

The champions of the sporting republic promised that sport could offer level playing fields for Americans of all social classes. In fact, they insisted that sport transcends class. The literature explaining the prowess of American Olympians celebrated the image of American teams composed of men from every stratum of society. In St. Louis in 1904 some commentators had gone so far as to credit the "workingman" with leading the United States to victory. American rhetoric touted Olympic stadiums as level playing fields where class distinctions did not matter. Indeed, many advocates of sport imagined that a national devotion to athletics would make the old republican dream of a classless society into reality.

Yet class distinctions and class consciousness shaped the sporting republic. The middle and elite classes believed that sport could create a national culture. They demanded that the national culture embody their visions of progress. They sought to control the processes of industrialization and urbanization, mold other social classes, and win the struggle to define modernity. Their efforts to construct a national culture followed a dynamic, if not always consistent, logic that they defined as universal and progressive. They came to believe that sport could help them to reestablish commitments to the common good. They championed sport as an integral part of a modern republic. In doing so, they tried to set limits on what values sport ought to teach, what sorts of athletic games constituted sport, and the manner in which those games could be played.

Sporting republicans crafted an ideology that matched middle-class views of the modern world. They insisted that sport would teach a new work ethic, one that would preserve the traditional values of diligence, discipline, and perseverance. At the same time, they tied those virtues to the communal enterprise of the team. Athletics stresses egalitarianism. Participants succeed or fail in accordance with their abilities, yet they also depend on the talents of their teammates. The corporate structure helps players to win. Athletic abilities include more than simply physical skill.

According to progressive formulations, sporting contests produced a healthy modern social order by providing space for liberty. Edward Ross, a University of Wisconsin sociologist and one the pioneers of the new social sciences, located an escape route from class struggle in sport. In Ross's estimation, considerations of labor and living conditions were hopelessly mired in the realm of class. Recreation transcends class, however. "The disposition of leisure time is preeminently a conscience matter," insisted Ross. "A youth submits perforce to the conditions of his work, but he chooses his recreations in freedom." Ross believed that through sport Americans could rebuild a sense of community that would surmount class divisions—a national culture of shared values.[7]

That same social vision could be discovered in Lester Ward's sociology or Herbert Croly's political science.[8] Progressives thought sport could create social consensus and control class conflict. Fear of conflict blurred for them the lines between social control and social justice.[9] They believed that in sport they had found a way to legitimize competition between individuals. The rigorous competition on the playing field was not, in the progressive conception, the brutal combat of the struggle for survival but the socially accepted striving for common goals. John Corbin described sport as an antidote to Darwinian forces. "The bare struggle for existence exacts strength and masterhood," he wrote, "but to live in the fair name of a sportsman it is necessary to rise to spiritual heights."[10]

Sporting republicans declared that they had discovered the answer to the class conflicts of the industrial epoch. They maintained that sport would repair the social cleavages created by corporate capitalism. Recreation provided a new arena for shaping the masculine, middle-class ideal of citizenship. "The things we do, when we do what we please, are vitally related not only to health, but also to morality, and the whole development of the finer self," proclaimed pioneering play theorist Luther Halsey Gulick to the members of the American Academy of Political and Social Science.[11]

In the formulations of Gulick, Ross, and like-minded boosters of sport, the mere winning of one's daily bread, the drudgery of labor, had been rendered insufficient for making the complete person. Work became a restricted realm required by modern conditions.[12] "When released from the daily work, the mill we have to tread in order to live, then we strive to become what we would be if we could," surmised Gulick. Gulick believed that athletics liberate people. In modern society, asserted Gulick, leisure had become a mass, rather than an aristocratic, reality. That fact, he claimed, was the truly revolutionary consequence of the Industrial Revolution: "The world has never before seen such equality of opportunity and the possibilities latent in this fact are stupendous."[13] The ideology of the sporting republic reordered the political understandings of leisure and work in important ways. No longer did the "chosen people" labor in the earth; now they played in green fields. The older virtues of middle-class work habits found new powers in sport.

Middle-Class Attacks on Competing Ideologies of Sport: Defining Acceptable Forms of Amusement

Certainly the sporting republic was not the only ideology of physical culture that existed in the industrializing United States. The "manly art" of bare-knuckle boxing offered working-class males dramatic depictions of a social reality that differed greatly from the realities expressed through middle-class ideas of sport. Prizefighting symbolized the triumph of masculine skill in a brutal, primal world. The rowdy bouts in saloons, dance halls, and mining camps underscored a working-class ethos that rejected the middle-class creed of genteel sport.[14]

Richard Kyle Fox, an Irish immigrant who settled in New York City, made a fortune promoting boxing and other working-class amusements in his *National Police Gazette*. A scandal sheet in Victorian eyes, Fox's *Gazette* represented everything the sporting republic was not—blood sports, tantalizing sexual pleasures, and illicit activities. It sought to lure middle- and working-class men away from the prudish conception that sport promotes public virtue and seduce them into accepting idea that sport belongs to the world of masculine pleasure.[15]

Advocates of social reform through athletics also found enemies among financiers, whom they accused of "commercializing" sport. The intriguing possibilities of new amusement and entertainment technologies, such as the great "playground" constructed at Coney Island in the 1890s for the residents of New York City, attracted the attention of both the middle and working classes. Condemned by true believers in sporting republicanism as false idols that sucked energies from more constructive and uplifting pursuits, the amusement parks nevertheless drew many customers and encouraged revolts against genteel standards.[16]

The contest to define the role of sport and recreation in the social life and political culture of the United States spawned a host of attacks on what progressives defined as the unhealthy and immoral "amusements" created by working-class countercultures and the new commercial enterprises that sold leisure-time diversions. Of course, the companies that manufactured bicycles, canoes, and other athletic implements for the sporting republic profited from their commerce in equipping the nation for the strenuous life.[17] Also profiting were the physical educators and amateur athletic officials who staffed the new national organizations, lobbied governments to build playgrounds and organize athletic leagues, and found jobs as "experts" in schools and colleges. Sporting republicans sanctioned the sale of "legitimate" sport in much the same fashion as Theodore Roosevelt drew lines between "good trusts" and "bad trusts."

Recreation professionals who pushed middle-class versions of sport sometimes railed against "leisure-class" sporting styles. Playground movement leader Joseph Lee launched an attack on the "grotesque expenditures of our millionaires" for "the futile steam yacht."[18] Nonetheless, most of the campaigns against the sporting republic's competitor ideologies were directed against working-class pastimes. Middle-class champions of the strenuous life had one tremendous advantage in their quest to limit sporting practices and ideas. They had far greater access to the national media.[19] Athletic reformer Richard Henry Edwards blasted the amusements favored by "the masses," particularly the "unrestrained commercialism" of recreations he defined as "vices": saloons, dance halls, amusement parks, vaudeville, pool rooms and "similar 'hang-outs' for men," prizefighting, racetracks, gambling, working-class holiday celebrations, and other "immoral" forms of play.

Through "restrictive" political and social action, such as lobbying for laws to close saloons and regulate amusement parks, and "constructive" actions, such as replacing the "glaring evils" of commercialized amusement with wholesome alternatives, particularly amateur sport, Edwards hoped to engineer a national community founded in middle-class conceptions of public virtue. He envisioned an America knit together by professional city recreation departments that would "take the lead in the high art of social education—the stimulation of common action and community consciousness." Edwards was a true believer in the sporting republic, imagining "the unifying power of organized recreation" leading the way to "the commonwealth of the future in which the uses of leisure shall be no less effective than the uses of labor in the service of the common good."[20]

The historian Frederick L. Paxson agreed with Edwards that sport served the nation as the most powerful agency for promoting "common good." Paxson identified sport as a crucial factor in restoring the nation's well-being from the horror of Civil War, the corruption and ethical decline of the Gilded Age, and extinction of the frontier and abundant space for expansion. "Moral indifference," wrote Paxson, had given "way to a real concern for honest methods; and those who would not of themselves reform are being squeezed by sheer force of public disapproval into a reluctant degree of compliance with the rules." He saw sport as a key factor in "squeezing" people into reforming. "We know that we shall live to see a dry America, and one of equal rights for all," Paxson prophesied. "And who shall say that when our women took up tennis and the bicycle they did not as well make the great stride towards real emancipation; or that the quickened pulse, the healthy glow, the honest self-respect of honest sport have not served in part to steady and inspire a new Americanism for a new century."[21] Paxson's "new Americanism" had significant roles for women. He thought that sport could empower women and might even help them in their struggles to win the vote.

Women and the Sporting Republic: Control and Liberation

Women played complex roles in ideas about the sporting republic. Although not fully excluded, they were not granted complete and unquestioned citizenship. Women had long been important figures in republican discussions of public virtue. From elite and middle-class perspectives, sport was seen to influence public virtue directly, making it impossible to ignore the gender issues surrounding sport.

Progressives seeking to design a "new woman" for American middle-class and elite cultures hoped to replace "creatures of the kitchen and fireside" with healthy recreationists "of the great outdoors."[22] Their quest to transform "swooning damsels" into athletic women raised a host of questions about gender, politics, and social formation. Those questions created problems for a patriarchal culture committed to a vision of women as not only the fairer but the weaker gender. Some critics declared that sport would only make women masculine and condemned the "new women" who adopted the strenuous life for their "disorderly conduct."[23] Others argued that feminine versions of athletics should be created as methods for regulating and directing feminine energy. Some progressive social theorists, including Paxson, conceived of sport as an agent of feminine emancipation. The twin motifs of liberation and control animated the discussions of the impact of women's sport on health, self-control, marriage, motherhood, sexual attractiveness, moral bearing, athletic etiquette and demeanor, political participation, and social equality. Republics were supposed to guarantee liberty, yet American women at the turn of the century still could not vote. What could sport do for women? Would tennis racquets and bicycles help women win "real emancipation"? Would women find places on American Olympic teams? Would sport liberate or control American women?

Charlotte Perkins Gilman, one of the leading progressive fighters for new conceptions of womanhood, insisted that athletic behavior and feminine autonomy were directly linked.[24] Her sociology of the evolution of gender roles within human societies started with a "free" primal woman who was "as nimble and ferocious" as her male counterpart. Gilman's ancestral female archetype "ran about in the forest, and helped herself to what there was to eat as freely as he did." When men enslaved her, however, she lost her freedom, her contact with the environment, and her natural physicality.[25] Some proponents of women's sports theorized that Gilman's free and independent woman could be resurrected if modern women were to rediscover their "nimble and ferocious" natures on American playing fields.

Paxson shared Gilman's vision of athletically liberated women, and other voices besides Paxson's sang the praises of women's sport. In fact, some commentators thought that the appearances of women on American playing fields were more significant than their struggles to gain access to political power. "To whomsoever the athletic woman owes her existence, to him or her the whole world of women owes a debt incomparably great," announced Anne O'Hagan in a 1901 essay for *Munsey's Magazine.* "Absolutely no other social achievement in the behalf of women is so important and so far reaching in its results," continued O'Hagan in a tone quite familiar to those who had read the apostles of manly athletics. "With the single exception of the improvement in the legal status of women, their entrance into the realm of sports is the most cheering thing that has happened to them in the century just past," she proclaimed, ranking the right of women to participate in athletics above even "the half winning of the ballot."[26]

Some of the strenuous life's champions dismissed feminist assertions. Price Collier trumpeted the power of sport for training a male leadership class. "If our more manly citizens could rule us, then, no doubt, we should be better off," read Collier's maxim.[27] Collier restricted his athletic ideology to the regeneration of middle-class American manhood. For Collier and like-minded compatriots, sport provided a way to cut what they perceived as the apron strings of a thoroughly feminized civilization. Certainly some of Theodore Roosevelt's athletic rhetoric should be read as attack on the perceived feminization of American society. The focus on sport as a rejuvenator of Victorian masculinity might seem to rule out any positive feminine role in American athletics. However, while a few committed chauvinists articulated such a position, it did not really fit the logic of the sporting republic's ideology.

Since they understood that the energies of the age threatened the entire social structure and that modernization affected women's lives as well as men's, many supporters of the strenuous life demanded the incorporation of both genders into a rigorous sporting program. A complex ideology of feminine strenuosity, directed by and at the elite and middle classes, emerged in the United States in the late nineteenth and early twentieth centuries. Nevertheless, whether athletics for women led to Paxson's "real emancipation" or toward the reinscription of Victorian gender roles in the new national culture proved to be an extremely contentious issue. Those debates often centered on political understandings of the roles of women in American society.

Sport, Republican Motherhood, and Feminine Citizenship

Since progressive theories of sport stressed the relationship of athletics to republican political culture, they often proposed significant places for women's sport. In debates over gender roles, the rhetoric and ideology of republicanism had tremendous power. Since the birth of the republic during the War for Independence, American political philosophy had connected the idea of a virtuous citizenry to virtuous mothers. The concept of "republican motherhood" demanded that as the moral guardians of civilization, women be responsible for inculcating republican values in their families, their communities, and the nation. Women, in republican formulas, were responsible for the commonweal.[28]

The ideal of vigorous womanhood had deep roots in middle-class American culture. Antebellum "feminists" such as Catharine Beecher prescribed air and exercise for republican mothers. They offered literate and fit women as the solution for the crudities of American life and as partners for the intelligent male citizens of a genteel republic.[29] Dr. Mary Taylor Bissell, a public health advocate, urban reformer, and stalwart champion of sport for women, updated that idea for the 1890s. Bissell envisioned a new version of the "American girl, clever, versatile, accomplished," who would overcome the "emotional strains" of modern life through an athletic discipline that would ensure "a stable character."[30]

Bissell and her colleagues promoted physically cultured women to a generation that distrusted contemplation and preferred action. "The general adoption of athletic sports by women meant the gradual disappearance of the swooning damsel of old romance, and of that very real creature, the lady who delighted, a decade or so ago, to describe herself as 'highstrung,' which, being properly interpreted, meant uncontrolled and difficult to live with," smirked Anne O'Hagan.[31] The advocates of the new national culture believed that sport would smooth the relations between the genders and help to channel women's sexual energies into "proper" activities. Both women's and men's magazines encouraged women to participate in bicycling, tennis, tour walking, canoeing, polo, horseback riding, auto touring, golf, swimming, and most of the other games and sports sanctioned by bourgeois sensibilities. "Swooning damsels" were out of style.[32]

According to masculine athletic ideology, the social changes created by modern industrialism had changed the republic and altered male roles. A conversion by American men to the strenuous life would help to adapt republican values to modern conditions. Physical educators and urban reformers Gertrude Dudley and Frances Kellor made precisely the same argument in building their case to justify women's sport. Dudley and Kellor noted that the rise of "the industrial world" had created a situation in which "the most significant change in society's demand upon women to-day is the substitution of co-operative effort for individualistic effort and the development of group consciousness beyond the family circle."[33]

In promoting women's sport, Dudley and Kellor duplicated the logic used by boosters of men's sport.[34] They asserted that sport would spark a new ethical sensibility in women that would match the increasing scope of their participation in public affairs. Possessing a keen understanding of the way in which Theodore Roosevelt and others had linked sport and politics, they declared that expanded roles for women in modern society necessitated a thorough familiarity among American women for "the rules of the game." Dudley and Kellor claimed that athletic training for both women and men could help to clarify the rules of the social game. "The welfare of society depends upon the rules being upheld or changed only with the full knowledge of all," they argued; "This being true, is there any reason why women, in their respective fields of activity and thought, should not abide by the rules of the game or contribute to their enforcement and improvement?"[35] Dr. Thomas Wood, physical education director at Barnard College, concurred with Dudley and Kellor. He argued that sport gives "to young women, as well as to young men, a part of the best preparation for the more serious work of later life." Wood stressed that "women, as well as men, need to learn through practical experience the rules of fair play, generous treatment of rivals and opponents, merging self into co-operative effort, concentration of power, and the blending of all energies toward an impersonal goal," all of which Wood believed that sport could provide.[36]

Sporting republicans insisted that modern athletics had as much power for shaping women as it did for shaping men. Dudley and Kellor listed the qualities that athletics provided for women, citing virtues strikingly similar to those that progressive social theorists identified as the key ingredients in using sport to make a manly America: a sense of fair play, reason, self-control, efficiency, cooperation, loyalty, courage, responsibility, and citizenship. Dudley and Kellor noted that those qualities are "not essentially masculine" but "human qualities needed for human fellowship." Proponents of women's sport maintained that the lessons women learned on playing fields carried over into other avenues of life. "Other things being equal," the athletic woman "is ordinarily a fairer competitor and better citizen," they insisted. "The responsible, reliable player becomes the same kind of citizen, for in games moral energy is stored up and habits established which govern the activities in later life," they concluded. Dudley and Kellor believed that athletic women would raise standards in American homes and communities. "Modern civilization is complex, strenuous and often artificial and our system of education needs organized games to prepare the girls for organized life and activities," they reasoned.[37]

Dudley and Kellor championed an athletic version of republican motherhood. Their ideas held a strong appeal among social workers who accepted the responsibility for the moral revitalization of American life. From her bastion at Hull House, Jane Addams and her settlement workers set out to regenerate urban America by using sport and other social technologies to incorporate into the republic the groups that the middle-class most feared, immigrants and the urban working-class poor.[38]

Addams and the settlement movement staunchly supported the belief that sport energizes public virtue. "This stupid experiment of organizing work and failing to organize play" had ended in disaster, insisted Addams.[39] Addams, like her fellow Chicago social workers Dudley and Kellor, thought that playgrounds could also bring women together. The social workers envisioned a crusade for women's recreation that would rescue women in factories and on farms from the drudgery of modern existence.[40] As Dudley and Kellor concluded in their study *Athletic Games in the Education of Women,* if women were "defective in the qualities which make for rapid adjustment" to modern conditions, then athletic training was precisely what was needed to "increase their social understanding and efficiency." Dudley and Kellor promoted the idea that sport could train women for roles in a modern republic—the same prescription that their male counterparts offered to American men.[41]

The medicine that the reformers prescribed, however, was supposed to have somewhat different effects on men and women. In many ways the progressive theories of sport sought to preserve the traditional Victorian construction of womanhood by proposing that "wholesome" sport creates moral women and stable families.[42] Progressive promoters of sport pitched the notion that athletics prepares both men and women for life, but they generally insisted that it prepares them for different kinds of life. Sport prepares men to win the competitive struggle of the marketplace, to apply the lessons of "fair play" to society, and to understand regulation, power, and conflict. Sport prepares women to win men and live harmoniously with them, and it breeds the physical and mental strength required for American women to mother a "strenuous" race.

The strenuous life had roles for women, places defined and animated by the cultural assumptions that Americans held about the nature of femininity. One of the traditional roles for women that sport was supposed to serve was the cultivation of sexual attractiveness.[43] Athletic experts constantly reassured the public that women's sports would not develop any masculine traits among American women. They stressed that femininity, grace, and beauty could be cultivated on the playing field, in the gymnasium, or among the splendors of nature.

Christine Terhune Herrick told the readers of *Outing* that "experience and observation justify me in saying that the woman who can tramp roads or the golf links, climb fences, scale cliffs, and endure material hardships side by side with a man is far more likely to be sought for by him as a companion than the girl who takes care of her complexion in a hammock on a veranda." Herrick asserted that athletics not only could garner women husbands but could make them into better mothers and homemakers. She even intimated that sport could help those women who were so inclined to carve out successful niches in arenas that had formerly been male provinces.[44]

An emphasis on maintaining feminine moral purity indicated one of the boundaries between sport for men and women. Many of the protectors of public virtue, both male and female, demanded that women's sport be kept "pure" from the guiding principles of men's sport—in particular, from the spirit of competition and the quest for victory that infused male athletics. Keeping women's sport pure often meant in practice keeping it separate.

Dudley and Kellor, while agreeing that an emphasis on victory and domination is not healthy, declared that "separate games for girls" made little sense. "While good citizenship requires varying forms of expression, does it demand different moral qualities of men and women, considered as citizens?" they queried. "Are not unfairness, selfishness, lack of honor, failure to co-operate, the spirit of gain overshadowing the spirit of service, disastrous to the group irrespective of which sex practises them?" They concluded that games and clean competition produce strong values in both men and women.[45]

Competition on Whose Terms? The Limits of Women's Citizenship in the Sporting Republic

Whether women were to play separately or with men, the focus of women's sports was on moral purity. Moral purity required that women refrain from the zealous pursuit of athletic victory. The new attitudes toward sport afforded middle-class women some of the same opportunities as men, with one extremely significant exception. Women played sports to increase their health, improve their figures, share common interests with men, channel dangerous energies, and learn the value of cooperation. Women were prohibited from playing to win.

An occasional voice dissented. In the pages of one mass-circulation women's magazine, *Good Housekeeping,* Anna de Koven blasted the "eminent authorities" who claimed that femininity and strenuous competition could not be reconciled and proclaimed that "no sport is too reckless, too daring, or too strenuous for the more experienced among athletic American women."[46] Most of the advocates of the strenuous life rejected De Koven's claims.

Competition, strife, the battle for supremacy—the sporting lessons in the gaining and maintaining of power—were considered to be strictly male preserves. "The ladies—bless them!—can't go into a thing of this sort in the rough and ready way that men do," wrote journalist Robert Tyson. "They are too much hampered with conventionality."[47]

The determination and devotion that victory requires could not be reconciled with the cultural stereotype of feminine moderation demanded of women athletes. "It seems that the keynote of woman's place in sport is moderation," posited F. G. Aflalo. "It is fine to see her getting health and enjoyment from her outdoor exercise, but not to devote herself to it with the same passion as the stronger sex. She should swim, but need not attempt the Channel. She should scull a boat, but not compete at Henley. She should fence—there are few more healthy exercises for young women—but not fight duels."[48]

That sport should train women to fulfill their culturally prescribed roles became acutely clear when discussions turned to the quintessential realm of power and supremacy in sport, record breaking. "The aim of athletics among women has been the establishment and maintenance of a high general standard of health and vigor, rather than some single brilliant achievement," proclaimed Anne O'Hagan. "So far . . . women have made freedom and fun their objects in athletics; and there are certain indications that this temperate view of the subject is gaining ground even in the ranks of the record breaking sex itself."[49]

A small segment of the sporting elite condemned the excessive focus on winning and record breaking in American sport in both men's and women's athletics. Dudley and Kellor decried the drive to make "championship teams" and develop "record-breakers and pennant winners."[50] One of the foremost physical educators in the United States, Harvard's Dudley Sargent, concurred.[51] Nonetheless, most progressives heartily endorsed the masculine will to victory as an indication of American exceptionalism and the providential nature of their history. For women, they demanded that sport meet the parameters of what they perceived as proper feminine behavior. Record breaking and the spirit of conquest stood beyond the pale in the Progressive Era. Occasionally American women entered some of the Olympic contests dotting the peripheries of the world's fair games of 1900 and 1904, but they lacked official support or public status as Olympians, competing instead as individuals. Margaret Abbott won a gold medal in the Olympic golf tournament at Paris in 1900. She later married Finley Peter Dunne, the American humorist whose "Mr. Dooley" became a frequent commentator on Olympic politics. By the 1908 and 1912 Olympics the IOC began officially to sanction women's competition in a few sports such as tennis, archery, figure skating, swimming, and diving. The United States failed to field a women's Olympic team, however. Before 1920 American women were officially excluded from the ranks of "America's athletic missionaries."

According to athletic boosters such as Anna de Koven, Frederic Paxson, Gertrude Dudley, and Frances Kellor, sport created an "athletic woman" who broke old stereotypes and demonstrated that she had the strength to ride bicycles, play basketball, and mark ballots. Charlotte Perkins Gilman dreamed of the return of nimble and ferocious women who would run freely through modern society. Sometimes women's sports opened up new dialogues and broke through gender stereotypes.

Sometimes, however, the progressive advocates of the strenuous life rejected the idea of fierce, nimble women. Instead, American athletic ideology frequently reinforced the tightly gendered patterns of Victorian culture. Mary Taylor Bissell understood both the separateness and the underlying similarities of men's and women's sporting practices. "So long as baseball and football and the boat race stand for the national expression of athletics," she noted, "the experiences of girls in any similar department will seem like comparing moonlight unto sunlight, and water unto wine."[52]

A century later those words seem prophetic. Women's sport still languishes compared with the public adoration heaped on men's games. Women, as Bissell knew, had a place in modern American sporting practice, but it was generally designed to be a separate place. That separation kept women out of the most important of the sporting republic's games, the Olympics.

Drawing a "Color Line" in the Sporting Republic

If middle-class and elite women's places in the sporting republic were often segregated, other people found themselves nearly completely excluded. In spite of the performance of George Poage, who at the St. Louis Olympics became the first African American athlete to win a medal, and of universal promises made by the sporting republic, certain groups of Americans found themselves outside its boundaries. As in the larger republic, the sporting republic had few places for people of color. African Americans, Asian Americans, Native Americans, and others had thriving sport cultures of their own, although they remained invisible to most European Americans. For example, Native American groups practiced traditional sports such as lacrosse and footracing. A few Native Americans and African Americans played major league baseball in the late 1800s. Jim Crow policies prohibited blacks after 1900, however, and the African American players responded by creating professional touring teams that competed on a circuit linking black communities. Those teams laid the foundation for the 1920 creation of the Negro National League. In addition, professional prizefighting had a small and important African American constituency. People of color appeared occasionally in the sporting republic as Olympians or college athletes. Generally, however, the American sports establishment effectively excluded African Americans, Native Americans, and Asian Americans.

Many people in the African American community nevertheless hoped that sport could help to integrate American society. William Henry Lewis, the son of manumitted slaves, used sport to achieve an impressive number of "firsts" for African Americans. He became the first African American to captain an Ivy League football team when he starred at Amherst College. In an era of different eligibility standards, he also played at Harvard while attending law school, winning All-American honors in 1892 and 1893—the first African American on the All-American squad. He coached for a time at Harvard and wrote a book entitled *A Primer of College Football.* He turned down a head coaching position at Cornell and went on to work as a pioneering civil rights attorney. Lewis challenged the color barrier at the American Bar Association. He fought discrimination first as a "radical" allied with W. E. B. Du Bois and then as a "conservative" aligned with Booker T. Washington. In 1911 Lewis became the first African American assistant attorney general of the United States.[53]

The achievements of Lewis and a few other pioneering African American athletes in integrated competition and in their postplaying careers sparked a series of debates over racial issues. George Poage's hurdling exploits at the Olympic Games of 1904 signaled the first in a long and distinguished history of African American Olympic performances. The successes during the later nineteenth and early twentieth centuries of African American and Native American athletes in open competition sometimes forced a reconsideration of the color barriers in American society. The *New York Evening Post* satirically noted that Native American Jim Thorpe's victory in the Olympic pentathlon trials, along with African American standouts Theodore Cable's and Howard Drew's triumphs at prestigious track meets, all on the same Saturday in 1912, indicated that "it is plainly time to draw the color line in athletics." The *Evening Post* sarcastically remarked that "colored athletes have a bad habit of becoming prominent in later life" and recommended that barring them from American playing fields would preserve the "safety of the white race" from encroachment by non-Europeans who might translate athletic success into prominent careers in law or politics.[54]

Most progressive commentators offered much different interpretations. So-called experts mixed pseudoscience, stereotype, and racism into strange brews. Some sportswriters, ignoring the so-called evidence from the "savage Olympics" at St. Louis, speculated that African Americans might prove to be better athletes than European Americans since scientific opinion identified blacks as belonging to a more "primitive" niche on evolutionary charts. In those sorts of theories, such "backward peoples" enjoy a primal physicality that more "civilized" people have lost.[55] Critics dusted off the familiar myth of the natural athlete to support their suppositions about race and physical superiority—especially when it came to explaining the dominance of black boxers such as the Australian Peter Jackson and the American Jack Johnson. Sometimes sport was used to reinforce racism.[56]

Sport and African American Intellectuals

Sometimes sport was used to combat racism. African American intellectuals used the exploits of black athletes in integrated competitions as arguments for racial justice and equality. Edwin Henderson told the readers of *The Crisis,* W. E. B. Du Bois's pioneering integrationist journal and the official voice of the National Association for the Advancement of Colored People, that the black college athlete destroyed racist stereotypes. "It is impossible to estimate the effect of his career upon the minds of thousands of Americans who have seen him perform or have read of his doings," asserted Henderson. The head of physical education at M Street and Armstrong High Schools in Washington, D.C., Henderson lauded the moral courage of African American sportsmen such as Lewis in proving the equality of their race. Fighting intense prejudice and discrimination with calm nobility, the African American stars were breaking down racial barriers. Indeed, Henderson argued that "when competent physical directors and equal training facilities are afforded the colored youth the white athlete will find an equal or superior in nearly every line of athletic endeavor."

Henderson thought that an application of American athletic technology to the African American community would produce sporting performances that would illustrate racial equality and bolster the fight against "the prejudiced attacks of Negro-haters." He hypothesized that slavery had created a natural reservoir of strenuosity in African Americans and called on black leaders to nurture "the native muscular development and vitality of the Negro of the South" in order to assault European American conceptions of racial superiority. (Ironically, his assertion that African Americans had "natural" athletic advantages would later be used by white commentators to reinforce racial stereotypes.) Henderson urged black colleges and universities to modernize their physical education departments so that black athletes could challenge world records. "Let our leaders encourage development in this field and no race will show to better advantage in fair and clean competition," he proclaimed.[57]

Henderson's insistence that African American performances on collegiate playing fields contributed to the cause of racial justice found corroboration in a short story entitled "Breaking the Color-Line," by Annie McCary. McCary's tale of racism and fair play at fictional elite universities "Starvard" and "Gale" melodramatically recounts the trials and tribulations of a young African American runner. Chosen for a relay team by his white but progressive northern team captain and then ostracized by racist southern athletes, the hero's gritty performances in the face of hatred from his own teammates win him the admiration of all right-thinking "Starvard" men. As he breasts the tape to win the big track meet against "Gale," the protagonist is portrayed as breaking not only the worsted (ribbon) marking the finish but also the "color line" that divided American society.[58]

The Crisis endorsed the sporting republic's ideology. The editors of the magazine pictured African American athletes on its cover. They encouraged faith in sport as an arena for racial progress. They demanded equal citizenship in both the sporting republic and the larger American republic. Segregation and intransigent "color lines" nonetheless represented the lived experience for most of the early twentieth century's African American athletes.[59] Du Bois and his correspondents certainly understood that they were fighting for an ideal that the reality of racism often tarnished. "Fair and clean" competition frequently proved illusory to people barred from athletic opportunities in many amateur and professional sporting arenas.

African American social critics were not always as optimistic as Henderson and McCary. John Henry Adams, *The Crisis*'s penetrating cartoonist, depicted lynching as the real "national pastime."[60] In fact, despite republican promises, in the decades between the end of slavery and World War I, most American playing fields and gymnasiums offered only limited access to people who were not of European descent.

African Americans were never completely excluded from every aspect of American sport, although white racism severely limited their access. When people of color participated in nationalistic athletic spectacles, particularly in the Olympic Games, the intense patriotism of American political and athletic ideology sometimes clouded racist sentiment. International stadiums became one of the few arenas in which the mass public cheered America's "invisible" peoples.

The Race Question and European Ethnic Groups

Whereas racism toward peoples from non-European ethnic groups generally excluded the vast majority of people of color from the promises of the sporting republic, responses toward various European ethnic groups revealed a much more complex pattern of American ideas about race. In an era in which massive European immigration to the United States generated increasing ethnic pluralism, advocates of the sporting republic insisted that athletic games and pastimes could produce a homogeneous national culture. The question that Crèvecoeur had posed during the beginnings of European settlements in the so-called New World reemerged in the new theories of sport. What, then, made an American? Given a new urgency at the turn of the century by the tremendous immigration fueled by industrial capitalism, that question served as the focal point for an intense battle over the issue of an American national identity.

Sport, insisted athletic boosters, would unite a multiethnic nation inundated by millions of immigrants into a community with common interests and values. Price Collier had asserted that "the governing races today are races of sportsmen,"[61] yet a great deal of confusion existed in American intellectual circles and in popular understanding of what precisely the term *race* meant. Was race a biological category, or did it express national tendencies? Was it a nationalistic invention or a scientific reality? American intellectuals used race in efforts to mark biological, sociological, and political boundaries. They even used race to delineate technological differences, distinguishing peoples by their machines and methods for organizing the world for problem solving. The imprecision reflected the complicated and often confused understanding of the connections between sport and race.

Anglo-Saxonism, the idea that English ethnic groups are the world's "favoured races," enjoyed popularity in certain circles and shaped some American outlooks. Price Collier's conception of "governing races" had a strong Anglo-Saxonist component. The historian John Fiske's doctrine of manifest destiny argued that Anglo-Saxons were destined to conquer the globe. Novelist Jack London, an ardent proponent of the strenuous life, concurred with Fiske. Theodore Roosevelt and Secretary of State John Hay embraced Anglo-Saxonism.

Anglo-Saxonism did not command a consensus of opinion on racial theories, however. Many progressive thinkers insisted that although the "American race" owed much of its structure to the traditions of an ethnically northern European, Protestant middle class, race was not defined by a particular color or caste. When Americans contrasted their social system to those of other nations, they consistently asserted that they offered opportunities to every ethnic group in the United States. The fact that the ideal of equality of opportunity paled next to the reality of ethnic discrimination did not diminish the fervor with which they promoted the belief in a realizable ideal of social equity—at least for Americans of European descent. "Those who have not faltered in the faith that the highest development of humanity will come through the evolution of a really democratic republic, and that America will be its home, see in this commingling of the bloods and restless spirits of all European lands, with much that is evil, an overwhelming preponderance of good," proclaimed Columbia University sociologist Franklin H. Giddings in a typical progressive description of the American race.[62]

Political activists and social reformers who rejected Anglo-Saxonism and narrow theories of race based on heredity did so for a variety of complex reasons. In part, the great numbers of immigrants who came to the United States between 1880 and 1914 and their importance in the American work force made a broadly based nativist movement difficult to sustain. Equally as important, many American thinkers were suspicious about simplistic biological models of society. Reading Darwin differently than American apostles of classical laissez-faire political economy did, self-styled progressives created a social philosophy that defined the concept of a "governing race" in national rather than genetic terms. Many Americans began to conceive of an American race composed of European "mixed bloods." The image of the melting pot, a term popularized by dramatist Israel Zangwill's 1908 play, arose as the United States attempted to cope with the massive immigration of southern and eastern Europeans. Sport played an important role in the push toward the creation of a new ideology celebrating an American race.

Many progressive republicans argued that, even though American civilization owed much of its distinctive character to Anglo-Saxon experience, it should not be closed to the members of any ethnic race or class. Lester Frank Ward, a pioneering sociologist and one of the intellectual fathers of progressive thought, discounted biological definitions of race as primary factors in evolutionary progress. Ward rejected the notion of varying degrees of racial intelligence and argued, in typically progressive fashion, "that there is no race and no class of human beings who are incapable of assimilating the social achievement of mankind and of profitably employing the social heritage" of the progressive Western world.[63]

Sport, the Melting Pot, and Americanization

Through sport, and particularly Olympic contests, Americans sought to confirm the idea that the United States was indeed a land of opportunity for anyone willing to clamber into the melting pot. According to the popular culture's pundits, the success of the United States in international athletic competition stemmed from efficient republicanism, effective assimilation, and the essential fairness of American society. In practice such idealistic blueprints for the melting pot proved nearly impossible to implement. American playgrounds, like American society as a whole, erected daunting racial and ethnic barriers. Still, some reformers thought that sport could break down even the most resilient strains of American racism.

Robert Haven Schauffler thought that sport could create a national identity in the United States that would transcend ethnicity. An American expatriate who played tennis for Italy in the 1906 "interim" Olympic Games in Athens, Schauffler also offered explanations for the composition of national identities. Although he swung a racket for the Italians, his sentiments were wholly American. In Schauffler's description of the Olympic engagements at Athens, only the Americans and an occasional Englishman comprehended the true nature of sport.[64] Schauffler did not restrict the understanding of those concepts to Anglo-Saxons, however. He fully subscribed to that popular American version of racial consciousness, perhaps best enunciated by Josiah Strong in *Our Country* (1885), in which anyone could become an Anglo-Saxon.[65] Schauffler argued that American athletics served to unite a multiethnic nation into a common civilization. "All in all I believe that the sporting spirit is about the most precious thing the New World has to offer the immigrant," he proclaimed. "For do not we Americans owe in great part to this spirit all that we are to-day?"[66]

In the fierce debates surrounding late nineteenth- and early twentieth-century conceptions of a common civilization, juxtapositions such as Schauffler's of modern athletics and the prospect of the "Americanization" of immigrants frequently found sympathetic editors and publication in the new mass media. "Every alien that crosses the sea is looking to us as exemplars of the grand old ideal of playing the game with a fair field and no favor," declared Schauffler. "Our chief duty is to train the newcomers . . . by letting our 'sporting blood' flow freely and equally through every vein of the body politic," he concluded.[67] In using the imagery of blood, immigrants, and the composition of the body politic, Schauffler employed some of the central republican tropes of his era.

The "politics of culture," as historian Alan Trachtenberg has perceptively called one of the key arenas of ideological conflict in modernizing America, involved the emerging institutions of modern sport in the war over which factors constituted national identity.[68] Schauffler had insisted that a true "sporting spirit consists in being fonder of fair play for its own sake than of power."[69] He, like many of the athletic reformers inspired by definitions of modernity conditioned by Progressivism, saw the question of national identity from ideological rather than biological perspectives—but his definition of the sporting spirit disguised the real relation between athletics and social order. Despite Schauffler's protestations, sport had as much to do with power as with fair play. In constructing a particular ideology of athletics, a politically charged cultural pattern presented to the public as normal and "American," bourgeois and elite advocates of athletic reform admitted that their version of sport related directly to power relations. By providing a political philosophy for sport and marking the boundaries of acceptable athletic practice, the inventors of the sporting republic garnered the power to define the concept "American."

American thinkers cheered sport as the perfect tool for assimilating immigrants. The YMCA helped to lead the crusade for athletic Americanization. Clayton Sedgewick Cooper, a YMCA leader and author of the *American Ideals* title in the Library of Good Citizenship series, urged Americans to look at immigrants as unformed beings of great potential. He lauded the social machinery that professional reformers had marshaled to meet the immigration challenge, such as settlement houses, immigration leagues and councils, educational programs and other benevolent enterprises, and, most important, sport.[70]

Jane Addams, one of the leaders of the campaign to Americanize immigrants, led the charge for athletic assimilation. She offered a compelling vision of sport as a community-building tool. Addams declared that sport would make the huge immigrant populations in American cities into stalwart republican citizens.[71] Addams's support for sport underscored the widespread commitment to the strenuous life in late nineteenth- and early twentieth-century American reform circles. As the 1908 edition of *The Encyclopedia of Social Reform* claimed, "Public provision of recreation for adults as well as children is increasingly recognized as essential, especially in the modern city."[72]

For reformers committed to the rational control of social evolution, it was precisely the problems of the city and the immigrant that sparked their efforts to produce a national sporting culture that would preserve the "Americanness" of the republic. Joseph Lee, one of the leading recreation scientists in the United States, conjectured that Crèvecoeur's old haunt, "the village community," had in the past been "the crucible of the race, the soil in which it grew, its nest, its natural habitat, its second home to which the social mind has reference." Lee noted that modernization had thinned farm populations and spurred urbanization, crimping the "American play tradition." According to Lee, modernization was combined with "the curiously sterilizing effect" that immigration brought to "our recreational life."

Lee complained that "the immigrant has not brought his own games with him, and except for baseball, crap shooting and marbles, seems to absorb very little of our American tradition." Lee contended that crowded cities, depopulated farms, and "unlimited alien immigration" threatened the United States with cataclysmic consequences. "The loss of a nation's play tradition would be almost as serious as the loss of the tradition of oral speech or of the great legal and constitutional methods which the ages have gradually evolved," he warned, "for life can no more go on without play than it can without language or without laws." Lee proposed sport as a tool for rescuing the republic from a grim fate.[73]

Athletic Technology and Republican Cities

Urban reformers wanted to construct parks and playgrounds to secure a new "crucible of the race." They offered organized sport as a remedy for ethnic conflict. "The American city, which has mixed up Jews and Greeks and Italians and Slavs in a single community," warned American Playground Association leader Henry S. Curtis, "has worked strongly against the development of that sense of trust and affection which is essential to highly organized and frequent play." He declared that the growing ethnic character of American urban life meant the destruction of "community feeling" and "social leadership." He proposed rational recreation as a solution.[74] His colleagues concurred. Philadelphia Playground Commissioner Otto T. Mallery opined that "under the living conditions which the mass of our people are surrounded, the playground is an important factor in race development."[75]

Of course, the masses often had their own ideas about what constituted sport. Certainly the ideology of a sporting republic faced challenges from alternative sporting cultures that immigrants brought from their homelands. In fact, various ethnic groups, especially "old immigrants" such as the Irish and Germans, used European sports to preserve traditional patterns of ethnic identification and mark their distinctiveness from the national culture pushed by the elites and nativist middle classes.[76]

Athletic reformers nevertheless insisted that the new conditions of life prevented immigrants from continuing their folk customs and necessitated that ethnic variety conform to a standard version of athletic physical culture.[77] They demanded that the new athletic technology incorporate immigrants into a thoroughly Americanized national culture. Sporting practices identified as foreign, from German *Turnerverein* gymnastics to British cricket, were excluded from the sporting republic.[78] As Olympic leader and New York City recreation specialist Gustavus T. Kirby testified, sporting republicans wanted the nation to understand that the games and practices of the sporting republic transmitted American values to immigrants more effectively than any other institution did.[79]

The champions of the sporting republic enthusiastically fed the flames under the melting pot with athletic fuel. Playground leaders offered numerous testimonials to the assimilative power of rational recreation. "The playground deals with race cleavage by Americanizing immigrants," maintained Ohio State

University social worker and director of women's physical education Dorothy Bocker. She exulted that an immigrant youth had written a play based on Israel Zangwill's book *Melting Pot* and staged it at one of Seattle's playgrounds.[80]

Amalie Hofer Jerome, one of the founders of both the Playground Association of America and the Playground Association of Chicago, recalled that on a "recent visit to a playground which assembles many nationalities, including blacks and whites, I was told by the policeman who has been on that beat since the ground opened, that it was all hopeless; that there never would be any good come out of it; that 'they fight and pester as much as they did in the beginning.'" Jerome refuted that vision by presenting the perspective of the playground supervisor, who testified to the "great human passion for social organization and social communion" engendered on the playground.[81]

Ernest Poole admired Chicago's public playground system, which provided spaces for "all . . . races—Irish, German, Swedish, Polish, Bohemian, Jew, Italian." Poole marveled that in such conditions "play has become a deep wholesome Americanizing force."[82] Poole's analysis mirrored a later study by Otto Mallery, who told exactly the same anecdote as Poole had concerning a Chicago basketball team composed of a variety of ethnicities on which "play has become a deep, wholesome Americanizing force."[83] In Poole's version, written three years earlier, he related the story of a basketball team made up of a hodgepodge of nationalities fighting together to win games. Poole's team had a German, a Jew, a Swede, a Pole, and an Irishman as its starting five. Mallery had the same nationalities on his team, except he left out the Swede. "On inquiring I found that the Irishman was leader," noted Poole.[84]

Richly ironic symbolism clothed Poole's (and Mallery's—or was it the same team?) ritualized description of the basketball team as melting pot. The Irish leader of the basketball squad whom Poole pictured in such positive terms provided the countersymbol to the typical middle-class rendition of the evil Irish "boss" running a political machine fueled by ignorant immigrant voters.[85] Athletics Americanized the relationship, argued Poole, and rendered it wholesome and republican. "From a park to a ballot-box the distance is not half so far as it seems," Poole insisted.[86]

Sporting republicans proclaimed that athletics would assimilate immigrants, build communities, and infuse the nation with a republican spirit. The cover of an issue of *The Playground,* one of the official journals of the recreation movement, symbolized that vision. It showed a group of well-behaved former rowdies in an organized play house. "The Club vs. the Gang in the Republic of Play," read the caption.[87]

Social reformers expressed an incredible optimism concerning the powers of the new athletic technology. Not only did they believe that it would recast immigrants into American shapes, but they held that it would also remold the urban environments that ethnic diversity had supposedly forged into menacing shapes. The American bourgeois could not give up the city, as Thomas Jefferson once counseled them to do. The metropolises spawned by the national market now stood as the middle-class location for success. Through the new athletics the middle-class moralists planned to retake the cities.

Among the popularizers of the crusade to use sport to retake American cities, no one enjoyed a greater reputation than New Yorker Jacob Riis, the Danish immigrant who chronicled the underside of urban life in America with devastating power. Riis promoted athletics as the most important tool available to Americanizers. He endorsed the adage "rather a playground without a school than a school without a playground."[88] Before the invention of the sporting republic had encouraged strenuous activity, Riis related, the children of tenement districts faced a choice between the street, the dance hall, or the saloon. Crime and vice, street gangs, and moral degradation were the only logical outcomes of such an environment. "Young people do not deliberately choose evil," surmised Riis with the transcendent optimism of a progressive moralist. The "rational recreation" offered by organized sport provided a healthy environment for immigrant youths. Riis warned against any forms of sport or play that were not inspired by the creeds of sporting republicanism. "As well might we abolish all law and hand the Republic over to rank anarchy," he warned.[89]

In Chicago Jane Addams and her allies echoed Riis's call for using sport to create a common civic culture. One of her associates at Hull-House, Victor Von Borosini, penned an essay for the American Academy of Political and Social Science touting the virtue of sport for assimilating immigrants into a national culture. "American-style" sport for the immigrants, announced Von Borosini, could save the republic from problems spawned by immigration and urbanization.[90] Addams concurred with her settlement house colleague. She contended that the best place to construct an American national culture was in parks, in gymnasiums, and on playing fields. She announced that "public recreation centers" and the "athletic field" offered "the basis of a new citizenship."[91]

The Dream of a National Culture and the American Gospel of Fair Play

Imagining immigrants transformed into athletic Americans led Addams, Von Borosini, and Riis to link sport with culture. The idea of culture in late nineteenth- and early twentieth-century American thought matched the concept of public virtue in earlier republican theorizing. Culture represented the repository of values that gave strength to modern republicanism. American promoters of culture, middle-class and elite intellectuals such as Jane Addams, defined the term as a lifestyle dedicated to high ideals and civic engagement. Culture served as an antidote to destructive modern forces—the harsh grind of work in the industrial system, the anonymity of life in urban mass society, and the greedy society spawned by corporate capitalism.

The champions of culture promoted it as the cure for the republic's evils, a cure of which all Americans should partake. They specified the groups that were particularly in need of culture: recent immigrants, African Americans and other non-European ethnic groups, middle-class men and women tempted by modern desires to forsake traditional ideals, and selfish plutocrats. Promoters of culture also believed that it would provide a common set of values to bind together an increasingly diverse nation. Culture could be acquired by reading great books or pursuing a liberal arts education. It could be captured by imbibing the social gospel or working in social reform movements.[92] Culture could also be obtained through sport.

Dudley Allen Sargent, Harvard's pioneering physical educator, believed that the cultural power of sport could transform American civilization.[93] According to Sargent and like-minded thinkers, sport provided a route to the production of a republican national culture. In this context the contention of many historians of immigration, such as Alan Kraut, that baseball and other sports gave new arrivals to the United States "vigorous ties to their fellow countrymen without demanding a sacrifice of . . . tradition" needs some revision.[94] In fact, the games and exercises advocated by athletic reformers sought to exclude other forms of ethnic identification. Sporting republicans insisted that athletic technology create an entirely American identity.

Their demands grafted sport onto older patterns of American self-identification. The athletic contrast of a vigorous and open United States to a decadent and class-bound European civilization marked one of the central motifs of American sporting commentary in an age in which international competition—typified by the revived Olympic Games—was in its booming infancy. Deeply embedded in the cultural mythology that grew up around modern American athletic practice lay the politically charged concept of fair play. Hugo Munsterberg's interpretive essays on the civilization of the United States claimed that "the demand for 'fair play' dominates the whole American people, and shapes public opinion in all matters whether large or small."[95] American commentators produced a myriad of versions of the American faith in fair play, echoing Munsterberg's insight.

American thinkers used the gospel of fair play to reinforce the old American belief that their nation was a "city on a hill." In their imagined athletic land of opportunity, talent would win regardless of race, creed, or color. They told those stories to mark a contrast with their visions of the decayed Old World. Their sense of mission stretched back into the mythical fabric of American history. Even though it frequently failed to jibe with American realities, it nevertheless formed one of the primary lenses of American perception. The social institutions spawned by the rise of a corporate order threatened the traditional versions of American exceptionalism as the universe of Jefferson's independent agrarians disappeared into the maws of the machine process. The myth was reborn, transferred from frontier, family farm, and forest democracy onto another green landscape—the manicured, carefully chalked confines of the playing field.

Drawing creativity from the Olympic playing fields, the new historians of national identity translated the cultural symbolism of "Young America" into a modern form. In the revived Olympic Games Americans searched for their own "cement of racial and national feeling," as *The Nation* so aptly described American athletic nationalism.[96] For the working press and athletic reformers, the Olympic teams served as models of their vision of the republic transformed from multiethnic and class-divided reality into a cohesive national culture. They hostilely rejected European contentions that their Olympians represented an athletic army of immigrant mercenaries. After the 1912 Olympic Games at Stockholm, an indignant editor at *The Independent* responded to the charges that no "American race" existed by proclaiming that the "United States owes its supremacy over all other nations to the fact that it is a union of all races." The editor proudly maintained, "We rightfully lay claim to all those sheltered under our flag, many of them despised and rejected of their native lands. When an Italian from Paterson, N.J., kills a king we get the blame. Shall we not get the praise when an Italian from Paterson, N.J., wins a race?"[97]

The proclamation that the United States was a "union of all races" shaped Olympic reporting in the decade after the 1904 games at St. Louis and underscored the connections between the political understandings of athletics and the creation of a common civilization. In the progressive constructions of a sporting republic, the playing field served as the civic forum in the drive to construct a national culture. Their ideology of sport fit into a broader tradition of American nationalism, a pattern asserting that, as the historian Arthur Mann posited, "nationalities are changeable rather than irrevocable."[98]

The Limits of Sporting Republicanism

European nationalities might have been changeable on American playing fields, but the direction of change indicated the limits of the sporting republic. Sport was supposed to transform immigrants into citizens of a national community that was heavily influenced by northern and western European—particularly English—patterns of culture. European immigrants found opportunities in the sporting republic, albeit frequently as fodder for the melting pot. They were generally required to lose their European ethnic identities to become sporting republicans.

Most of the power for defining the political concepts inherent in the sporting republic rested in the hands of intellectuals who spoke for the middle classes. Middle- and upper-class men were always included in theories for promoting athletic technology. Their values and standards shaped American attitudes about what constituted "legitimate" forms of sport.

Working-class and immigrant Americans found their places in the sporting republic proscribed by the thrust to inspire middle-class standards of public virtue through "legitimate" sport. Their traditional athletic games and pastimes were dismissed as barbaric, destructive, or commercialized. They were invited to adopt new ideas about sport. Sporting republicans made it clear that they wanted to do more than just promote their own ideology of sport; they also wanted to stamp out athletic practices that they considered unwholesome—whether those sports were "foreign" or "socialistic."

Middle- and upper-class women were also included in the new theories concerning sport, although their roles were constrained by patriarchal definitions of femininity. Still, they sometimes found opportunities for defining an athletic "new woman" who challenged Victorian gender boundaries. Middle- and upper-class women enjoyed a substantial, if subordinate, citizenship in the sporting republic—except on American Olympic teams. They were excluded from Olympic arenas.

African Americans, Native Americans, and other groups rarely made appearances in the sporting republic. African American intellectuals sought inclusion, arguing that success in sport would force whites to recognize the inherent equality between the races. The new ideas of sport included many references to athletics as a color-blind institution. In actual practice, however, American sport was rigidly segregated. For the vast majority of people of color, citizenship in the sporting republic, like citizenship in the larger republic, remained a hollow promise.

The universal claims of the sporting republic were limited by the ways in which attitudes toward class, gender, race, and ethnicity shaped social practice in the late nineteenth and early twentieth centuries. Those universal claims and the issues of class, gender, race, and ethnicity were revealed in American writings on the re-created Olympic Games in 1906, 1908, and 1912. When an Italian from Paterson, New Jersey, or a Native American who grew up in the "Indian Territory," or an African American from Springfield, Massachusetts, distinguished himself on Olympic fields, would the nation lay claim to his feats? Would his Olympic achievements ameliorate the divisions of class, gender, race, and ethnicity that plagued the republic? Would his athletic victories serve to push the limits of the sporting republic toward more inclusive boundaries?

Robert Haven Schauffler, the American tennis player who would compete for the Italians at the 1906 "interim" Olympics in Athens, remained firmly committed to a universal ideal. "It was a merry sight to see the picked youth of the globe gravitating toward a common type," he recalled of his Olympic experience in Athens. "For the American that sight was a proud one as well, because the boys with the shields on their running shirts seemed, somehow or other, to have a little less gravitating to do than the others."[99] When Americans played, they conceived of their recreations not simply as a respite from toil but as a forum for creating a national identity. Crèvecoeur's vision had found its way into the heart of American physical and political culture.

Athens, 1906, and London, 1908:
Uncle Sam Was All Right

The Olympic Games encouraged national discussions of political, social, and scientific concepts between the public and the intellectual classes. Theories about sport abounded in interpretations of American performances. The public fascination with Olympic sport encouraged thoughtful analyses of the relationship between athletic practices and political culture. The St. Louis games of 1904 had captivated a mass audience in the United States. Olympic festivals at Athens in 1906 and London in 1908 would feed the public fascination and fuel intellectual speculation about American Olympic experiences.

The issues of national identity, immigration, and ethnic character played a major role in the 1906 and 1908 Olympics. In popular dialogues the national press encouraged the idea that American teams represented a "union of all races." Commentators promoted the notion that Americans victories at the Olympics indicated the superiority of American society. The press asserted that the United States led the world in the production and application of athletic technology. Intellectuals contended that scientific understandings of sport had reached their apogee in the American theories and practices.

By 1906 the Olympic Games constituted a major component of the common language of sport. Publicizers of the strenuous life who depicted the United States as a sporting republic frequently employed Olympic evidence. Promoters of athletic technology often used Olympic proofs.

In 1906 Vincent Van Marter Beede advised the nation that American boys should not spend all their time studying. "If a boy is 'on the team,' and plays fair, all the better for him," wrote Beede, for "the lad who is without athletics is in peril of his soul." In Beede's estimation, the Olympic Games represented the ideal athletic contests. He praised "the beneficent influences which the old Greek games are exerting today in our preparatory schools and colleges, in business and professional life . . . , among women, in the institutional church, and, best of all, at home." Beede proclaimed that the Olympics were creating a stronger civilization in the United States.[1]

The Troubled International Olympic Movement Returns to Athens

Creating a stronger civilization was, after all, what the inventors of the sporting republic thought that athletic technology was all about. Progressive athletic reformers had convinced the nation that social advance and modern athletic endeavor were inextricably linked. One troubling reality intruded on their successes, however. The rest of the world had not been paying attention. American Olympic prowess drew little international notice, and the Olympic movement itself had foundered. The second Olympics had been relegated to a sideshow at Paris's fin de siècle International Exposition. From an international perspective the third Olympics, held at St. Louis in conjunction with the Louisiana Purchase Exposition of 1904, suffered a similar fate. In spite of the American fascination with the Olympics, much of the rest of the world paid little heed to the games. Lost amid the myriads of exhibits and events at world's fairs, the Olympic flame flickered and nearly died. Only a return to Athens for an "interim" Olympics in 1906 would rekindle worldwide interest in Baron de Coubertin's spectacular athletic struggle of nations.

To ensure that the Olympic Games would remain forums for American athletic nationalism, the AAU and the AOC continued to consolidate their control over the American Olympic movement. The AOC was dominated by a small corps of like-minded men and prominent sporting figures led by James Sullivan, Caspar Whitney, Julian W. Curtiss, Joseph B. Maccabe, Bartow S. Weeks, Frederick T. Rubien, Gustavus T. Kirby, Luther Gulick, and Frederick Skiff. They each had ties to the AAU, and many of them were prominent in the sporting life of metropolitan New York City. The Olympic managers turned the American teams into crusaders for the national aspirations. They resisted regulation by the government, officials in American higher education, or other national organizations. They cultivated good relations with the media, and they sought to finance their ambitious projects through voluntary public subscriptions.

After the nasty fight between American clubs at the 1904 games, these men moved to end the division of American entries into college and athletic club squads, creating the first truly national Olympic team. With their selection, financing, training, travel, and participation completely under the control of the AAU cabal, America's newly nationalized athletic missionaries received their first calling in 1906.[2]

After the original revival of the Olympic Games in 1896, Greek representatives to the IOC had argued that the games should reside permanently at Athens. Baron de Coubertin opposed a permanent site. He had always planned to celebrate the Olympics in the great cities of the Western world. The baron escaped a confrontation over the issue when the spirit of Greek nationalism, kindled by the first modern Olympics, sent Greece off on an ill-advised 1897 campaign to liberate the Greek provinces that were still a part of the Ottoman Empire. War with the Ottomans so devastated Greece that an Athenian home for the Olympics became impossible. By 1904, however, after St. Louis's "all-American" Olympics, a recovering Greece renewed its Olympic bid. Under the leadership of the Greek royal family and Crown Prince Constantine in particular, the Greek parliament "legalized the Olympic Games as a national institution" to be held permanently in Athens.[3]

Coubertin was not pleased by Greece's obstinacy, but he recognized the powerful influences that joined Athens and the Olympics in Western minds. The baron and the IOC compromised with the Greek initiative, acceding to a Panatheniac Olympics to be held on a four-year cycle between the regular Olympic schedule. In the spring of 1906, a decade after the first modern revival, the Olympic festival returned to Athens. James Connolly, the original American athletic missionary, applauded the restoration of the games to Athens. Connolly condemned the 1900 and 1904 Olympics for permitting "the glorification of this or that association, the scoring of points for the club or college, and the cabling of the same across the ocean," adding that the result was an "athletic meeting that reminded one of a brewery picnic in Jones' Wood." Connolly thought that an Athenian sojourn would help to purify the American Olympic spirit. "We have good men interested in athletics here in America. Some of them are on the American Committee, and, not using athletics for business or social purposes, men who will go to any expenditure of time and energy to advance a great cause. And if they would but make the journey to the coming games it would mean much, for no matter how much inborn enthusiasm they may have for clean athletics, they will need to see its expression in Greece to experience it in full tide."[4]

Organizing the American Entry for the 1906 Games

The "good men" of the AOC, led by James Edward Sullivan and Caspar Whitney, planned to go to Athens. For the first time they worked to take a national team with them. No longer would contingents from American colleges and athletic clubs constitute the U.S. entries in the Olympics. Under the auspices of the AAU, Olympic organizers conducted a series of local fund drives that raised $15,000, which they used to send "the pick of American brawn and muscle" to do battle in Athens. The AOC received substantial funding from athletic organizations, including the New York Athletic Club, the Intercollegiate Athletic Association, the AAU, and the Greater New York Irish American Athletic Association. Financial magnates S. R. Guggenheim, August Belmont, J. P.

Morgan, and George Pratt contributed heavily. Former Olympians Robert Garrett (the discus champion in 1896) and George Orton (winner of the steeplechase in 1900) and athletic leaders F. B. Pratt, A. L. Shapleigh, Frederick Skiff, and Charles Dodge also pitched in.[5] James Sullivan, tabbed as the "commissioner" of the American Olympic delegation, once again headed the U.S. Olympic effort. President Theodore Roosevelt substantiated Sullivan's control over American Olympic sport by publicly confirming the AAU chief as the head of the U.S. Olympic effort. Roosevelt's confirmation of Sullivan, even though the president had no official power in the AOC, highlighted the esteem with which Roosevelt was held in the athletic world rather than any federal control over Olympic sport.[6]

American officials made minor protests over the scheduling of the 1906 games. The Greeks planned an April 22 opening, a time when many of the best American collegiate stars would be busy with school. The AOC pleas for a change to accommodate university students fell on deaf ears. Nevertheless, in spite of the collegiate "handicap" placed on the American entry, the AOC gathered a team made up of the finest American track and field athletes, including stars from the 1900 and 1904 games, such as sprinter Archie Hahn, middle distance runner J. D. Lightbody, jumpers Myer Prinstein and Ray Ewry, and all-around champion Martin Sheridan. The team, buffeted by high seas during a journey from Naples to Athens on the *Barbarossa,* arrived in Athens in a "crippled condition." The Americans recuperated quickly when they realized that they faced the best Olympic field yet assembled.[7]

The interim games drew 901 entries from twenty-four countries. Austria, Belgium, Bohemia, the British Empire (England, Ireland, Scotland, Canada, Australia, and South Africa), Denmark, Egypt, Finland, France, Germany, Holland, Hungary, Italy, Norway, Russia, Sweden, Switzerland, Turkey, the United States, and host Greece participated in the spectacle attended by "all the nations that regard athletics and gymnastics as the progress and inducement of civilization." For the first time in Olympic history Great Britain sent a significant contingent to the games.[8] "Never before, in the history of the world had there been such a gathering, and nowhere else, do I believe, is it possible to duplicate the Olympic Games in the manner in which those of 1906 were conducted," proclaimed Sullivan, who admitted that even the Olympics he had organized two years earlier in St. Louis suffered by comparison.[9]

The Greeks staged a marvelous interim Olympics. The Panatheniac Stadium, partially refurbished by George Averoff for the 1896 games, had finally been completely refinished. Its Pentelic marble façade and huge capacity—80,000 seats—won it accolades as the world's greatest stadium. "It is safe to say that he who has not seen the Stadium at Athens in all its magnificence of white

Pentelic marble, with the glorious Attic sky for a canopy, has no idea of what such an amphitheatre can be at its best," announced D. Karopothakes, a Greek correspondent who reported on the Olympics to the readers of *The Nation*.[10] The Americans agreed that the stadium was indeed beautiful but complained that the track was not up to American standards because of tight turns and an odd shape.[11]

Despite the misgivings about the quality of the track, the AOC had nothing but praise for the way the Greeks ran the games. Sullivan, in a veiled attack on the IOC, declared that the Olympic atmosphere and the job turned in by the managing committee would lead any reasonable observer to conclude that the Olympics had found a permanent home in Greece.[12] Athenians scrubbed their thoroughfares and bedecked their city in Olympic finery. Much of Europe's royalty showed up for the Olympic party, led by Edward VII and Alexandra of England. Baron de Coubertin, beset by financial and political problems, could not attend. The spectacle attracted visitors from around the world. "Every language of Europe could be heard in the happy crowds that streamed daily into the Stadium, or surged along the brilliantly-illuminated streets every evening," related Karopothakes.

Fervent Greek patriotism, even more intense than in 1896, added an urgency to the proceedings. The large numbers of Greeks who had made the Olympic pilgrimage from provinces of the Turkish Empire struck Karopothakes as particularly significant. "To these children of 'enslaved Greece,' as they call themselves, it was all like a beautiful dream, fraught with patriotic emotion, after the repression and tyranny under which they live ordinarily."[13] Greece wanted to use the Olympics to display their national spirit. They felt that they had to do well in the athletic events to demonstrate that they were a modern nation.

William N. Bates, the director of the American School at Athens, witnessed a particularly intense pressure on Greeks regarding the marathon. Spiridon Loues' victory in 1896 and the legendary traditions surrounding the race had convinced the Greeks that the marathon was their race. "They seemed to think that the reputation of their country was at stake and that as a matter of national pride they must win it," observed Bates. On the day during which the marathon was contested, over 200,000 people lined the race route and filled the stadium. When a Canadian runner triumphed, with the hosts finishing only as high as fifth, Greece plunged into an afternoon of national mourning.[14]

Celebrating American Triumphs in Athens

The Greeks had certainly not cornered the market on the Olympic exhibitions of patriotism. The United States was in Athens to demonstrate its national superiority. As the games opened before a reported 100,000 spectators (20,000 more than the stadium supposedly held), the U.S. team marched into the stadium to defend its self-proclaimed title of three-time Olympic champion. Once again the American athletes dominated the track and field competition, which the Greeks, following the American lead, had made the centerpiece of the games. The United States won eleven first places, with four for the British Empire, three for Greece, two for Sweden, and one each for Russia, Austria, and Germany. Sullivan cheered that the Americans had "'spread-eagled' the field" and "upheld American supremacy . . . against all comers." AOC scoring supported Sullivan's contention, calculating the final results as 75⅙ points for the United States, 41 for the British Empire, 28 for Sweden, 27½ for Greece, 13 for Hungary, 8 for Austria, 7⅔ for Germany, 6 for Finland, 3 for Italy, and 1⅓ for Belgium.[15]

"These figures give to the reader the general standing of the world, athletically, with America far in the lead," gushed Sullivan. The AOC leader theorized that the United States dominated athletics because Americans led the world in the understanding of sporting technology. "Our men were trained scientifically," he revealed. "We go into athletic sport with an earnestness that the other countries cannot understand; and our methods of training and practicing were simply revelations to the foreigners." Scientific training and an environment that produced "American pluck" made the United States unbeatable. Sullivan related the tale of George Bonhag's victory in the 1,500-meter walk to illustrate his assertions. Bonhag's triumph was significant because race walking was not a popular pastime in the United States. The AOC chief insisted that despite Bonhag's inexperience in the event, the lessons ingrained by American social patterns pushed Bonhag across the finish line first. "He showed the natural ability of an American when placed in a position with responsibility on his shoulders," asserted the AOC leader.[16]

The special American environment bred athletes who could meet challenges. Olympic victory confirmed national superiority. "Pretty work," telegraphed A. G. Spalding, thanking the American squad for its "glorious victory" in Athens. "Hearty congratulations to you and the American contestants," President Roosevelt cabled to the team; "Uncle Sam is all right." Sullivan recalled that when the message was read to the athletes in an Athenian hotel, "three long cheers were given for our athletic president." Athens's leading paper, *Estia,* wondered "who is this 'Uncle Sam' who deigned at last to be pleased after the tearing up by the roots of the olive tree of Altis [the mythic sacred tree that grew on the plain of Olympia] by the unrivalled athletes of the New World and its transportation to the United States?" After defining *Uncle Sam* for its Greek readers, *Estia* concluded that "the American athletes . . . could not have dreamed of anything better, of anything greater, than to have the first American citizen [President Roosevelt] interpret by right the thoughts and desires of 'Uncle Sam.'"[17]

For many Americans, following the lead of their president, Olympic victories confirmed American vigor and promised the fulfillment of national aspirations. When the *Republic* bore the team into New York harbor on its triumphal return voyage, a large crowd welcomed the American champions to the strains of the "Star Spangled Banner." The U.S. claims of Olympic domination rankled many Europeans, however, particularly the English and French. Sullivan tried to respond to the critics and put the American "Olympic championships" of 1896, 1900, 1904, and 1906 into the proper perspective. Sullivan acknowledged that the United States had not won canoe, revolver, gymnastic, or boating championships. In fact, he noted, they had not entered in those events, holding out the possibility that Americans would have won if they had participated in those "non-athletic" sports: "America entered its team for athletics, and all claims made by Americans have been for the athletic events, as the word is understood, and these events took place in the Stadium. In other words, America excelled the world athletically, just the same as France excelled in swordsmanship, the Swiss in shooting, Italy in boating and bicycling, the Danes in foot ball, and the French are certainly entitled to a great deal of credit for their all-round showing in all other than the track and field events."

But, warned Sullivan, if Americans did start entering the "non-athletic" contests, the rest of the world would not stand much of a chance. The AOC leader noted that the St. Louis games furnished data indicating that the United States was far ahead of the world in every type of physical culture. Of the 390 events contested in 1904, encompassing all manner of leisure activities, foreigners had won but 14. "America scored close to 3,500 points in these Olympic events at St. Louis; in other words, more points by many hundreds than was scored by all other nations at Athens in 1896, and Athens in 1906," blustered Sullivan. He ignored the fact that hardly any foreign athletes had bothered to make the long journey to compete in St. Louis—Olympic Games that he had designed.[18] Sullivan's message was clear. The United States ruled the world in the "real" Olympic Games, track and field events. If they wanted to do so, Americans could also start dominating the contests that they heretofore had "allowed" their European rivals to win by not bothering to enter.

Karopothakes shared Sullivan's convictions. He declared that the "Anglo-Saxon conception of athletics . . . was also that of the ancient Greek world; and in this conception such sports as swordsmanship and marksmanship have no place, though bicycling may fairly enough be offset against the chariot race." His linkage of classical Greek and modern American athletics indicated the degree to which he had been converted to the gospel of the sporting republic.

"Nor can weight-lifting be considered a very noble sport," added Karopothakes; "Although a Greek won this event, more than one Greek was heard to speak of it as a 'porters' match,' and to wish that Greece might have won any other prize instead." Karopothakes went so far as to call "non-athletic" sports "un-Olympian." He did concede that they were needed on the Olympic program to keep Europeans from giving up in the face of American supremacy. Still, the "un-Olympian" activities had opened a dangerous door. "Let us only hope that the day will never come when automobile races will be admitted to the Olympic programme," he pleaded—apparently unaware of the Olympic program in 1900 at Paris.[19]

The structure of the 1906 interim games indicated that American ideas about the content of the Olympic Games had taken over the Olympic movement. Track and field dominated the proceedings. Even more important, much of the world accepted track and field as the true measure of national vigor. Given those standards, Uncle Sam was indeed all right.

Uncle Sam was also on the attack. Sullivan not only righteously pushed the American conception of track and field–dominated Olympics, but he tried to whittle away at the power of Baron de Coubertin and the IOC. His reports from Athens consistently praised the organization of the 1906 games in comparison with previous Olympics. The Greeks "taught us that an athletic meeting between foreign countries may be conducted fairly and honestly, with a feeling of goodwill toward one another," he announced in a not very well hidden jab at the Paris Olympics. Sullivan, Whitney, and the rest of the AOC still distrusted the IOC. They wanted to create a new international body, one that would expand American control over the Olympic movement. Sullivan, worried about how Americans would be treated at 1908 Olympics, questioned the IOC's policy of rotating the games between cities. "All admit that Olympic Games, in order to amount to anything, must be held at Athens," he proclaimed.[20]

Selecting an Olympic Site and an American Team

The next celebration of the Olympics would not be held in Athens. The fourth Olympic Games had originally been scheduled for Rome. Coubertin wanted a new "classical" site for the games, but the 1906 eruption of Mount Vesuvius made the Roman venue untenable. Seeking to incorporate Britain more firmly in the Olympic movement, Coubertin looked across the English Channel for Rome's replacement. England had not played a significant role in any of the previous three Olympics, although it did send a large contingent to the interim games. The IOC sought to remedy British apathy. Selecting London as a site brought the homeland of Baron de Coubertin's athletic philosophy firmly into the Olympic movement. The organizers of the London Olympics, remembering the ill-managed Paris games and the parochial St. Louis games, planned a magnificent international gathering in London. The 1908 Olympics also provided an opportunity for the United States to put the sporting republic to a test against the progenitor of modern athletics, England. The battle for world supremacy in athletics, and symbolic supremacy as the globe's most vigorous nation, would take place on English turf at London's Shepherd's Bush Stadium.[21]

American Olympic officials chose their 1908 Olympic contingent in a tryout held in Philadelphia.[22] The AOC and AAU provided funding for the team, collecting money through public subscription.[23] During the financial drive Sullivan stressed that the team symbolized the United States. In his discussions with the British Olympic Council, which managed the games, Sullivan claimed that he and the AOC "represented President Roosevelt and the American nation."[24] The press supported Sullivan's position. They pictured a team comprising "Anglo-Saxon, Teuton, Slav, Celt, Black Ethiopian and red Indian," an athletic representation of the melting pot and its egalitarian ideology.[25]

The press anticipated an orgy of American successes. *Collier's* advised Americans that the 1908 Olympic tryouts indicated that the team would be as strong as any of the previous Olympic "champions."[26] Caspar Whitney added that the "quality" of the American entry was highlighted by the eight records broken in the Philadelphia trials.[27] Edward G. Hawke revealed that "Englishmen are curious to see whether America will sweep the board of trophies as they did at the four other Olympic festivals."[28] The media joked that the Olympics had completely captured the attention of the American public. The *Brooklyn Daily Eagle* published a cartoon portraying Uncle Sam on a telephone labeled "Direct Wire to Olympic Games" while he tried to quiet the strident posturing of the two Lilliputian presidential candidates, William Howard Taft and William Jennings Bryan. The cartoon was captioned "Just a Moment, Please!"[29]

The Olympic movement's idealism still found voices amid American boosterism. *The Living Age* reprinted an essay from the English *Outlook* that boasted, "We have reasonable grounds for believing that the London games will help to dissipate causes of war, on the ground urged by the old class of schoolmaster that a round with the gloves was the best foundation of friendship."[30] *Blackwood's* replied that "to attempt to check warfare by an athletic meeting is like trying to dam a waterfall with a spider's web."[31] An American idealist retorted that the Olympics did indeed act as a counterweight to militarism and served as "part of the new movement to promote the friendship of nations."[32] As it turned out, the voices of idealism paled beside the clamor for Olympic gold.

The British spent $250,000 constructing the 85,000-seat Shepherd's Bush Stadium for the games. *The American Review of Reviews*'s London correspondent marveled that "no such building has ever been seen in modern Europe; in size, indeed, it appears to surpass the most famous amphitheaters of antiquity; and if it has not their romantic associations or their architectural grandeur, it testifies to the incomparable skill of the modern engineer."[33] Edward VII, thrilled by his visit to the interim games, wanted the London Olympics to serve as the "final glory" of his reign. Although the Franco-British Exposition was taking place right across the street from the Olympics, the British organizing committee managed to keep the fair from seizing control of the athletic exhibitions. A powerful group of elite British sportsmen made up the organizing committee, headed by IOC member Lord Desborough and including another IOC delegate, the Reverend R. S. de Courcy Laffan, as well as Lord Montagu of Beaulieu, Lord Cheylesmere, Sir Lee Knowles, and Major Egerton Green. The organizers incorporated an even wider variety of sports than had been on the program at Athens, including both association and rugby football, polo, yachting, and billiards.[34]

Opening Ceremonies and International Incidents

The "real" Olympics—track and field—opened on July 13. Two thousand Olympians representing mainly Western nations marched past King Edward VII of England "in a most impressive column."[35] The English *Outlook* believed that the greatest achievement of the London Olympics had been accomplished before the actual competition had even begun. "There has been drawn up a code of rules for every sport, translated into three languages and accepted by every foreign nation that has competed," asserted the English monthly. The British editor proclaimed that the British-crafted regulations were the first international code of sport to enjoy the "unanimous sanction of the world's sporting representatives" and credited the British Olympic council "with an invaluable contribution to the common language and friendship of humanity."[36] Unfortunately, the new code proved to be of little value in the intense struggle for Olympic supremacy that followed.

The battle began at the opening ceremonies. The United States contingent had been angered before they passed the royal box when they discovered their flag missing from the many banners of the competitor nations on display at the stadium. English explanations—the officials claimed that a suitable American flag could not be found—failed to appease American wrath. The U.S. team ignored international protocol, keeping their colors aloft when they passed the king. Ralph Rose, the Irish American shot-putter carrying the stars and stripes, growled, "This flag dips for no earthly king." Rose's exclamation gave birth to an American Olympic legend and set the tone for the London games.[37]

The fourth Olympics quickly turned into a battle between English and American athletes, officials, and spectators. Both nations believed that certain Olympic incidents revealed their national characters and the vices of their enemies. The Americans had come expecting a contest that would underscore the political superiority of their institutions. The British obliged American desires for a battle both ideological and athletic. "The champions of each nation seem to believe that they are upholding their nation's honour as well as proving their strength and suppleness," worried *Blackwood's*. "Facile arguments concerning the decadence of this people or that are established on insufficient premises," charged the magazine, lamenting the fact that more and more nations, and in particular the United States, seemed to transform sport into a "strenuous business."[38] *Blackwood's* sentiments were a lonely dissent. Americans had long considered sport to be a strenuous business and engaged in vigorous displays of athletic nationalism. With the flag incident on opening day, the Olympic referendum on national character and vigor began in earnest.

Much of the American press congratulated Rose for his "patriotic" gesture, calling it a manifestation of the "Spirit of 1776." Gustavus J. Kirby, an AOC member and the chairman of the Intercollegiate Association of the AAU, voiced the AOC's opinions on the controversies. Kirby related that the British officials told the AOC that a careless decorator caused the absence of the American flag at the opening ceremonies. "If it were mere carelessness, certainly the carelessness was gross; for not only was there no American flag among those of the other nations of the world flying from the stands in the Stadium, but there was none even on the grounds," responded the American official.[39]

Kirby's justifications did not satisfy all the American commentators. *The Bookman* criticized the choice of Rose as flag bearer. "Now Ralph Rose is unquestionably an athlete of considerably ability, but beyond that one cannot truthfully go," wrote the editor, recalling Rose's indiscreet challenge to fight world heavyweight boxing champion James J. Jeffries after the 1904 Olympics and the rowdy behavior that ended his scholastic career at the University of Michigan. "All this was perfectly well known to those in charge of the American team," observed *The Bookman*, "yet this young man was selected to carry the American flag in the march of competing athletes past the Royal Box. . . . He deliberately chose to insult the English people by his failure to salute King Edward." *The Bookman* castigated those who had supported Rose's defiant gesture. " 'Boyish patriotism!' 'The Spirit of 1776!' Nonsense. Sheer, caddish, boorish manners," lectured the editor. "It was an incident of which Americans should be heartily ashamed."[40]

Relations between the English and Americans did not improve after opening day. In fact, they descended into what *The Bookman* called "the Olympic muddle."[41] The American team dominated its beloved track and field events and announced its victories as evidence of the coming American hegemony in both sport and world affairs. The British vigorously dissented. The English press blasted American behavior and character. The London *Times* editorialized that the U.S. team boasted "better athletes than sportsmen."[42] The usually stolid English magazine *Academy* barked that "the Americans behaved 'odiously' from first to last." The *Academy* correspondent complained that the American fans sat in great masses emitting "disgusting noises and cries" that threatened to turn the Olympic spectacle into "a revolting pandemonium." The source also complained that American athletes cheated with great regularity. "We sincerely hope that this is the last time we shall see American amateur athletes in this country, and we can get on very well without a great many other Americans who are not athletes," charged *Academy*. "Of course it would be absurd not to admit that among Americans there are some good sportsmen and agreeable people, but they are in such a small minority that it is almost impossible to trace them."[43]

Anglo-American hostilities reached beyond the editorial columns and the incidents in the stands, leaping onto the playing field itself. Convinced by the AOC that they represented President Roosevelt and the American nation, U.S. athletes strove to prove their nation superior to the decadent denizens of the Old World. American high jump gold medalist H. F. Porter complained that "in nearly every event the boys had to compete not only against their competitors but against prejudiced judges." Porter admitted that "the judges may not have been intentionally unfair, but they could not control their feelings, which were antagonistic to the Americans." He groused that "the officials were discourteous to our men, and, further, by their encouragement of the other men, tried to beat us."[44] England's athletes responded, defending the honor of the empire against the Yankee assault. The biggest controversies erupted over the 400-meter race, the marathon, and the tug-of-war.

The Americans considered the tug-of-war an inconsequential sport, but they pointed to British tactics in the minor event as proof of a general conspiracy on the part of the English to cheat their way to an Olympic "championship." The Americans denounced the British teams for wearing hobnail boots, which gave them a tremendous advantage in the tug-of-war. The British Olympic Council admitted that their teams had used "heel-tips" but insisted that they were within the rules that the council had drawn up before the games. The AOC vehemently disagreed. But the tug-of-war tussle paled in comparison to the incidents on the Olympic track.[45]

In the 400-meter final three Americans, W. C. Robbins of Harvard, J. C. Carpenter of Cornell, and J. B. Taylor of the Irish American Athletic Club, went to the starting line to battle Lieutenant Wyndam Halswelle of Great Britain. The four ran an intensely competitive race. Near the finish Carpenter passed Robbins and Halswelle to win the race, but he found no tape to breast at the finish line. The English judges had cut it in anger, claiming that Carpenter fouled Halswelle on the last turn. The referees declared the race void and disqualified Carpenter. They rescheduled the race, but the two remaining American runners, Robbins and Taylor, refused to compete. Halswelle ran to victory in the makeup race, the only "walk-over" in Olympic track history.[46]

The American press howled that the English judges imagined Carpenter's interference. "It was the pace which killed him [Halswelle]—not any suppositious or real interference from Carpenter," wrote James B. Connolly, the original American gold medalist who covered the 1908 games for *Collier's*.[47] Gustavus Kirby revealed that a "Cambridge athlete" described Halswelle as having run with "characteristic dumbness."[48] In an interview with England's *Sporting Life* after the Olympics, Halswelle insisted that Carpenter had impeded his progress, although the lieutenant admitted that the American runner had not struck him with any "vigorous blows."[49]

The AOC angrily asserted that at the end of the race the British officials compounded an already delicate situation. "Some grabbed up megaphones and shouted into the stand, 'No race,' 'Foul work on the part of the Americans,' 'Halswell [*sic*] fouled,' etc.," recalled Kirby. An angry crowd demanded the disqualification of the "dirty" American runners—a sentiment that the British judges encouraged. One official "actually came outside the track and stood amidst a mob of excited Englishmen and started to harangue them as to the race being a good example of how the damned Yankees always tried to win," reported the disgusted AOC official.[50]

Caspar Whitney sympathized with the AOC's version of the events that transpired. Still, he chastised the American runners and officials for pulling out of the 400-meter race after the disastrous first final. "No matter how incensed they may have been; no matter how sure they may have felt of the injustice of the decision, when they entered the Games they subscribed to its rules and agreed to abide by the decisions of the judges; the decision of the judges in this case was final, and the Americans should have kept their mouths shut and abided by that decision," he scolded. "Play or pay," lectured Whitney, "that means, young gentlemen, play the game, take your medicine; be generous in victory, take defeat gallantly." Whitney scoffed that "trying to bulldoze umpires and judges out of making decisions unfavorable to you, or sulking when an unfavorable decision is made against you, is not losing like a man; and, above all things it is best to be a MAN."[51] Clearly Whitney understood that winning, not whining, was everything in the struggle to assert the sporting republicans' claims of special providence.

The Marathon Controversy

With the 400-meter race concluded, if not forgotten, public attention turned to the marathon race. The marathon provided spectators with one of the most astonishing competitions at the London games. The popular conception of American athletic prowess regarded long distance running as the province of more "sluggish peoples." Arthur Ruhl believed that events requiring powerful bursts of strength, such as sprints and jumps, fit the American character better than endurance events did. He asserted that the sluggishness required for distance runs was "rather characteristically British."[52] The Americans had monopolized the distance events in St. Louis, where Boston's Thomas Hicks had won the marathon, but that seemed to have been an aberration of the "all-American" 1904 games. After all, Hicks had immigrated from England. So the Americans "conceded in advance that England would do very well in the marathon," remembered Connolly, "and English experts themselves modestly stated that it would all be English."[53]

The marathon began on a hot July morning at Shepherd's Bush Stadium. Dorando Pietri of Italy set a blistering pace early in the race. English runners "melted into the horizon of the dusty landscape in trying to hold the flying Italian." The night before the race Pietri had announced, "I will win to-morrow—or die."[54] He very nearly fulfilled both predictions. Pietri entered Shepherd's Bush in the lead and began his final lap. Exhausted by the pace, he collapsed short of the finish line. "Dorando had fought with might and main to win the race of his life, and there he lay, a human mass," reported the *London Standard*.[55] Some British officials gave him a shot of strychnine, but he collapsed again. When the United States' John J. Hayes entered the stadium, British officials quickly carried the semicomatose Italian runner across the finish so that an American would not win.[56]

Olympic judges disqualified Pietri a few hours later and declared Hayes the victor. The ruling meant that Americans swept the top three places in the revised marathon standings. Connolly praised the winner: "Hayes, the unfaltering, won the race because he had the American athletic spirit, which tempers the hot impulse of action with the saving air of careful preparation and intelligent execution."[57] *Current Literature* described Hayes as a twenty-four-year-old New York City clerk of Irish descent, "a bright-eyed little fellow, hard as nails."[58] Finley Peter Dunne's Mr. Dooley sarcastically congratulated the Italian. "He ran a superb race, doin' th' last mile in an autymobile in two minyits." But, "owin' to some stupid misconstruction iv th' rules, th' race was given to a Yankee who resorted to what we must call th' very unsportsmanlike device iv *runnin'* th' entire distance."[59] In the minds of many Americans, Hayes's triumph signified that Americans knew how to control dynamic energies better than the athletes of any other nation did.

The AOC was incensed that it had required an official protest to get Hayes installed as the victor. "The American Committee were forced into the unbecoming position of having to protest against the awarding of the race to a runner as courageous as any the world has ever seen," complained Kirby. He admitted that no rule specifically stated that a runner had to finish under his own power. "To state such a rule would be as absurd as to say that in a 100-yard dash the runner must not use an automobile," grumbled Kirby. "The English judges asked me to find a rule covering the point and were disgusted when I suggested that they might award the race to Longboat [a Canadian runner whom Americans accused of professionalism] who had finished ahead of them all—in an automobile."[60]

The English took a somewhat different view of the situation. *Academy* thought it unfortunate that an American came into the stadium behind Pietri, musing, "If he had been an Englishman it may be safely assumed that he would have brought no objection against Dorando." *Academy* claimed that by making a protest, Hayes lost the chance of a lifetime. "If he had been a sufficiently good sportsman to allow Dorando to retain the prize he would have been the most popular man in England, and he would have done much to wipe out the feeling of disgust which had been generated by the conduct of the American athletes and their rowdy supporters."

Academy accused Americans of taking literally "the old professional maxim . . . 'Win, tie, or wrangle.'" Whitney characterized the English "balderdash" surrounding the marathon as "ludicrous."[61] Whitney's vehement nationalism and strident condemnations of English sportsmanship were somewhat surprising since he had long been a defender of an English-inspired conception of gentlemanly amateurism. His defenses of sport as a mechanism for training a leadership elite had earned him a reputation as something of an Anglophile.[62] Yet Whitney even took a potshot at the special cup that the British queen presented to Pietri to commemorate the Italian runner's effort. "It was a sweet, womanly thought that prompted the Queen's gracious donation of a consolation cup to the Italian who had so nearly won the marathon, but the subsequent lionizing of the man was a maudlin, not to say amusing exhibit of Cockney England gone daft," blustered Whitney. "They had the poor man receiving bracelets stripped from the arms of women, and exhibiting himself on the stage of a music hall, within twenty hours of his collapse on the Stadium. And yet we refer to English phlegm!"[63] The United States, however, also honored Pietri. The AOC sent him a special medal through the U.S. ambassador in Rome. Pietri himself complained that he could have finished under his own power, and the Italians were enraged at the "technical" claims made by American officials.[64]

Whitney responded to the criticisms by proclaiming American sportsmanship as far superior to English behavior. He paid homage to American marksmen, who won even though the Europeans had unfairly used special equipment. Handicapped by their British opponents' "specially made match rifles" with "hair-triggers" and longer barrels, the American riflemen stoically whipped their rivals. That was "playing the game," congratulated Whitney.[65] He admitted that a few Americans may have bragged too loudly about their triumphs, but he attributed it to the emotional victories that had once again given the United States an Olympic "championship."[66]

A Contested Championship

Claims and counterclaims about the Olympic "championship" and commentary on the ways in which the athletic contests had revealed national identity filled media accounts of the games on both sides of the Atlantic. The head of the Irish American Athletic Club, Patrick J. Conway, told a newspaper reporter that American athletes should cancel other appearances that they had scheduled in Europe and return to the United States for a national celebration. Conway wanted "American prowess" demonstrated to the world, wrote the reporter, "but there was no need to exhibit in European countries after their doings of the past two weeks in the London Stadium."[67] On the American side of the Atlantic a consensus held that the United States was clearly the Olympic victor—for the fifth straight time.

The English took a different view of the matter. In article after article the British press castigated America's win-at-any-cost attitude. Certain American observers agreed that the "Americans . . . behaved like muckers." A *Collier's* editorial echoed the sentiments of English critic and essayist G. K. Chesterton's indictment of American athletic behavior. Chesterton had long regarded America as a nation of religious zealots, and Olympic events had confirmed his suspicions. Chesterton asserted that one should look in the American sportsman "not for the light vices of vain or sensual loungers, but for the solid vices of statesmen and fanatics, for the sins of men inflamed by patriotism or religion. He can not shake hands after the fight. He feels toward his conqueror as a man toward the invader who has robbed him of his God." Chesterton clearly realized the intensely politicized nature of modern sport, even if he saw it only among Americans. *Collier's* agreed with Chesterton's sentiments, calling them "somewhat overexpressed, . . . but acute."[68] An editorial in *The Outlook* concurred with *Collier's* tone. "The manager of the American team cannot be justified for the sneering, quarrelsome, and unsportsmanlike assertions" the U.S. officials made, reprimanded *The Outlook*. "We wish we could say that the American athletes have shown themselves good losers as well as winners," jabbed the magazine.[69]

Collier's and *The Outlook*, however, were minority voices in the United States. Caspar Whitney rushed to the defense of his old friends in the American athletic establishment for they way in which they handled events in London. "Had it not been for the indefatigable efforts, the technical knowledge, and the experience of James E. Sullivan, there would have been no such winning team for America at the Olympic Games," wrote Whitney. "Put that in your pipes and smoke it all ye little Americans with petty spites who seized every opportunity to say something unkind and unjust about the A.A.U. or its president."[70]

Even the British press was not entirely hostile to the American performances at London, both in and out of the stadium. *The Bookman* commended the *Times, The Spectator,* the English *Outlook,* "and even the usually Americanophobic" *Saturday Review* for paying a "generous tribute to the prowess of the American team of athletes." On the other hand, the overwhelming majority of the American media made very little positive commentary on English performances. "There is no person on earth who talks so much about fair play as a Briton," claimed *The Bookman,* ignoring the reams of American verbiage about that hallowed principle. "But he values it so much that he sees to it that it is kept exclusively for Britons and is not lavishly wasted on the 'outlander.' " *The Bookman* recalled the famous anecdote about the time a French horse won the English Derby. "Waterloo is avenged," shouted a delirious French fan. "Yes, you ran well on both occasions," retorted an English duke. "Unfortunately, the spirit which animated His Grace has been rather too characteristic of Englishmen, regardless of social rank, whenever British athletic prestige was threatened," concluded the literary journal.[71]

Escalating the Anglo-American Athletic War

The AOC groused loudly about British boorishness. "The greatest tribute to the team," proclaimed Kirby, "is not the points and places won, but the greater moral victory in its forbearance and gentlemanly behavior under circumstances and conditions which made it hard for any self-respecting man to hold his peace and keep his temper."[72] Kirby penned the AOC's official report on the 1908 games, a long list of grievances against British officials, athletes, and fans. He accused the British officials of insulting the American flag, allowing a professional Canadian runner to participate, openly coaching British athletes, barring American trainers from caring for injured team members, stealing the 400-

meter race from Americans, making a shambles of the marathon, and generally mucking up the proceedings. He charged English athletes with unfair and unsportsmanlike behavior. Moreover, he indicted English spectators for bad manners.[73]

Kirby roundly condemned the organization of the Olympic program of events. He pointed in particular to an incident in which an American broad jumper was struck from the list of eligible competitors for missing roll call. At the time roll was called, the American was running in the 200-meter final. "Such an arrangement was to the advantage of the home team," complained Kirby. The AOC also decried the English method of drawing places for heats blindly rather than seeding the runners. The American officials felt that they lost out on several places when their fastest runners all faced one another in a single heat, with only the winner advancing.[74] Whitney cautioned Americans not to complain of "underhanded work" or "highway robbery" by the English officials. He felt that they had simply been incompetent rather than dishonest: "It was indeed dire misfortune that, in addition to being incapable, the officials were also stupid, losing their heads so completely as to establish a record for incompetency which is not likely to be surpassed in many years to come."[75]

The AOC report blasted English preparations for field events. The British had failed to provide a "plant box" for the pole vault or a landing pit for either the pole vault or the high jump. Kirby was scandalized. "It can only be understood on the ground that it was made to place the American competitors at a disadvantage," he wrote. A barrage of AOC complaints about the considerable risk of injury finally led to the implementation of landing pits, but the British refused requests for a plant box.

Kirby saved his most savage criticisms for English spectators. "One would have pardoned those Englishmen who hooted at you to 'Sit down' when you stood during the playing of 'The Star-Spangled Banner,' and forgiven the others of the same breed who endeavored to take away a small American flag from a boy in the 'American section' of the grand stand on the ground that these acts were not characteristic of the British, but committed by a few who lacked manners," related Kirby. The AOC chief insisted, however, that such behavior was not at all uncharacteristic.[76]

The British Olympic Council made a point-by-point reply to the AOC's accusations, refuting American indictments on each issue. The British report called the American contingent "a splendid team, and quite good enough to stand on their own merits; yet they will go down to history as the team on whose behalf more complaints were made than was the case with any other in the whole series of these Games, and as the only team which went away without a single acknowledgement of the hospitality which the British Olympic

Council did its best to show them in this country." The British report pointed to the international Olympic code that it had drawn up before the games and sent to each nation, and the fact that Sullivan and the AOC had previously approved British regulation of the entire affair, as evidence that the American outcry was simply sour grapes. "The Americans were treated in every respect exactly as every other nation, and as our own athletes were treated," concluded the council.[77] The British insisted that they had obeyed the rules.

The arguments between British and American athletes, officials, and commentators over which nation properly understood how to conduct itself in Olympic contests stemmed in part from radically different perceptions of the meaning of rules for both sport and society. In "American Sport from an English Point of View," the Scottish amateur golfer H. J. Whigham explored the cultural misunderstandings that led to an "open rumpus" after nearly every international contest between the United States and Great Britain. Whigham had won the American golf championship in 1896 and claimed a thorough familiarity with both English and American sport. He explained that the English perceived sporting rules as reflections of immutable social principles. Gentlemen played amateur sports according to certain social codes. Those who were not gentlemen played professional sports and followed a different canon. An athlete's status was "simply a fact which exists and cannot be altered." Whigham revealed that social customs rather than the actual rules of the sporting contests determined English athletic behavior.

Gentlemen athletes were not permitted to approach sports in a "scientific" fashion, which Whigham claimed that Americans did. They wanted to win as desperately as their American counterparts, but they could not train efficiently or specialize. They subordinated their goal of victory to the task of maintaining social tradition. Whigham's essay indicated that the English saw rules as indicators of a traditional social order shaping every aspect of human behavior. Whigham admitted that the "rise of the new democracy" had blurred some of the distinctions between classes, but it had not changed English ideas about what the rules meant.

Whigham knew that American athletes defined sporting rules in a very different fashion. Rules were instruments for achieving goals. Americans scientifically scrutinized the rules to discover the most efficient methods for achieving their goals. The goal was victory in accordance with the rules. Whigham realized that Americans understood rules in a very modern sense. Americans viewed rules as components of athletic technology rather than reflections of athletic tradition. Rules helped to organize the world for problem solving.

Whigham noted that in the United States, "whatever we may think privately, it is heresy to admit in public that such a thing as social standing exists."

Professional athletes received money for their performances. Amateur athletes did not. Class was not supposed to enter into the equation. Whigham praised the American idea of rules for inculcating national vigor by promoting sport as "the pastime of the masses as well as the classes." Yet he preferred the English tradition of rules for nurturing—at least among the classes—a well-rounded human character. Whigham concluded that in the long run, instrumental definitions of rules that sought out the most efficient athletic strategies turned the American athlete into a "mere automaton."[78]

The Arithmetic of Olympic Triumph and the Art of Explaining American Prowess

Turning from acrimonious debate over interpreting the rules to the question of Olympic superiority, the American press vociferously asserted that the U.S. team had won the London Olympics on the strength of its victories in track and field. *Harper's Weekly* crowed that "the American flag was the first pennant to be hoisted as the signal of victory, and the final contest in the Stadium also resulted in the waving of the Stars and Stripes."[79] The overall standings in all the sports contested nonetheless showed the British hosts far ahead of second-place United States, fifty-six gold medals to twenty-three.[80] Nevertheless, Walter Camp—the American sportswriter, companion of Theodore Roosevelt, and creator of the "all-American" football team—felt that the U.S. claim to an overall Olympic title was based on the "very tangible facts" that Americans were "far and away superior to the athletes of all other nations" in the track and field competition.[81] Whitney agreed, dubbing the Olympics "the most important international contest in the history of track and field athletics, for here were gathered the cream of the world's athletes; the champions of champions." The United Kingdom had entered more than five hundred athletes, and the United States entered only eighty. "Yet America captured 15 firsts, 9 seconds, and 6 thirds, to the United Kingdom's 8 firsts, 6 seconds, and 3 thirds," marveled Whitney.[82]

The Outlook concurred with Whitney and Camp. "The American athletes were chiefly concerned in field and track athletics (which may be said most closely to stand as the modern successors of the Greek games) and will base their claim on what is called international scoring," reported the magazine.[83] International scoring had the United States winning the track and field competition at Shepherd's Bush Stadium, 114⅔ points to runner-up England's 66⅓. With those figures in mind, Walter Camp declared that "it is pardonable, then, that the 'Eagle should scream.'"[84] President Roosevelt cabled his sentiments to Sullivan and the team. "Heartiest congratulation to you and team," read the telegram. "Wish I could shake hands with each man."[85]

The American press transformed the track and field championship into Olympic victory. "The supremacy of the American athletes in the games most severely testing muscle, skill and endurance is clearly established," announced the *New York Times*.[86] Why had the Americans won? Explanations focused on the preeminence of American political culture, the efficacy of the melting pot, and the virtuosity with which the United States practiced the science of play. "No marvel that, here in America, with our mixed bloods in competition and almost everybody living under pressure, we produce great sprinters, leapers, and weight-throwers," surmised Connolly. American "form," personified by Hayes and the other victors, had prevailed.[87]

Connolly praised America's 1908 Olympic champions, assuring readers that they were "typically American, of the Americans who are shaping the future rather than living in the past, and only America just now seems to be producing these remarkable athletes in any numbers." Foremost among the American victors was Forrest Smithson, a Pacific Coast divinity student and hurdler. Connolly thought Smithson would do "if you were looking for a slashing half-back."[88] In London Smithson slashed over the 110-meter hurdles in world record time. A famous photograph showed Smithson running with a Bible clutched in his hand, symbolizing his protest of Olympic events contested on Sundays.[89] Accounts of the race made no mention of Smithson's unlikely cargo, however. Indeed, a photograph of the event in *Spalding*'s "official" account of the 1908 Olympics depicted an empty-handed Smithson clearing the last hurdle.[90] The picture of Smithson with the Bible had been staged to make a political protest against Sabbath competitions. Smithson understood the powerful forum for social criticism that Olympic victories allowed. He had made a political statement.

The American team made a nationalistic statement. Throughout the games the European press had accused the United States of hiring foreign athletic mercenaries to win Olympic gold. The British media focused in particular on the Irish American members of the U.S. team. For American athletes, sportswriters, and managers, the melting pot character of the team indicated that Wister's American axiom—"Let the best man win, whoever he is"—really worked. Connolly, a proud son of the Emerald Isle himself, laughed that the United States had proved its mettle before the assembled athletic might of a decadent, aristocratic Europe. "An impressive host," he wrote, "and from the front ranks emerged triumphant the shining figure of Young America, who may be personified as a youth rather under than over twenty-five, of good height and not too great weight, of almost any racial extraction—Teuton, Saxon, Scandinavian, Latin, but mostly Irish, and always of the exuberant spirit of the nation yet in its youth."[91]

The Bookman hinted that if the British point of view were considered, some of the protest against the "composition" of the American team might be validated. The editor noted that John Flanagan, the great American weight thrower, although an American citizen, had emigrated from Ireland as a young man and according to British tradition was still a British subject. Indeed, noted the essayist, he was an accomplished athlete before he ever crossed the Atlantic. "We know that it was entirely the American system that brought him to his highest point of achievement," confided *The Bookman,* paying homage to American ideology, "but we cannot expect the English to concede that fact. In their eyes he cannot seem anything else than an importation for athletic purposes."

The Bookman noted that the Americans were so deep in the weight throws that they probably could have sent athletes who did not rankle the English as much as Flanagan, champions such as DeWitt or Shevlin. At that point the editor sprung his trap. Even if the United States had sent the native-born DeWitt or Shevlin, chuckled the editor, "English newspapers would have printed the names and vowed that one was either a Dutchman or a Boer, and the other an Irishman."[92] Whitney tried to correct the impression that the American team was composed mainly of Irishmen, while recognizing the melting pot flavor of the squad. "Of the twenty-four point winners on America's team, one is Irish-born and American by adoption; five are American-born of Irish parents; one is American-born of German parents; the balance are of American-born parents." *Outing*'s editor rejected the English accusations that the American team comprised mostly foreign mercenaries.[93]

Connolly went a step further. He ridiculed the myth of the Anglo-Saxon athletic supremacy. The improved showing of southern European athletes had raised questions in the press about the supposed superiority of Anglo-Saxon sportsmen. Connolly noted "the failure of the Saxon to live up to his reputation" and wondered, "Is the Saxon degenerating or is the Latin in a renascence?" In fact, the supreme Anglo-Saxon athlete "has nearly always had a strong strain of Irish blood," wrote Connolly, taking a swipe at the English team under whose flag many Irish athletes had refused to compete.[94]

One observer of Olympic sport was not convinced of the melting pot theory of American athletic success. Dr. Charles E. Woodruff, a member of the U.S. Army medical corps, studied the racial characteristics of the winners in the 1906 and 1908 games. He insisted that Nordic types supplied the majority of victories in Olympic competition. In explaining the preponderance of immigrants and first-generation Americans among the winners, he pointed to the effect of climate on strenuosity. The "light" of American skies gave an enormous stimulus to the nervous system of Nordic immigrants during their first few generations in the New World, claimed Woodruff. That fact explained the American dominance in events that required a great deal of nervous energy—sprints, jumps, and other field events.

Unfortunately, the excessive stimulation of American "light" soon burned out the Nordic stock, rendering families that had resided in the New World for any length of time incapable of producing champion athletes and unable to continue functioning in their "natural" roles as the governors of society. In Woodruff's slanted version of history, "the big brawny northmen" had "been the world's rulers from time immemorial." Woodruff suggested that "if America is to be at the front of civilization with the other advanced nations, its blood must be constantly recruited from Northern Europe" to replace the constantly degenerating American Nordic stock. Woodruff's conclusions and his data were not necessarily consistent. Despite his belief in Nordic supremacy, he noted that many of the American winners were not of the "blonde type." His Nordic interpretation of American athletic success was a lonely, and flawed, dissent to the exaltations of the champions of the melting pot.[95]

"Mr. Dooley" Assesses the Games

As was often the case in turn-of-the-century American popular culture, Finley Peter Dunne got the last word on the Olympic muddle. Dunne had his prototypical "average American," Mr. Dooley, recount the London games for the fictional barkeep Mr. Hennessy in a parody for *American Magazine*. Mr. Dooley quickly dismissed Woodruff's scientifically racist arguments, telling Mr. Hennessy that "on'y men iv pure Anglo-Saxon blood were allowed to compete, an th' names iv th' American team alone were enough to thrill th' heart iv th' Saxon who knows th' proud histhry iv his race—such names as Sheridan, Flannagan, O'Brien, Casey, O'Halloran, an' so on."[96]

Mr. Dooley quickly moved from the ethnic composition of the American team to other observations. He conceded that "th' English appear to have won be th' handsome margin iv three hundherd an' eighty claims iv foul to two hundherd an' siventy complaints again th' judges." The Olympics "must've been a fine lesson to th' excitable Latins present to see with what good nature th' Anglo-Saxon race fought out their sthrenuse battle." In France or Italy such a contest would have degenerated into violence, laughed Dooley. But the British and Americans were "long schooled in friendly contest iv skill an' stren'th." The Anglo-Americans kept better control of their passions than "do th' emotional nations." The games were fierce while they lasted. "But whin th' contest is over all animosity disappears. Th' vanquished extends his manly fist to th' nose iv th' victor an' writes a short letter to th' pa-apers tellin' how he was jobbed."

Dooley thought that the differences between races was clear at Shepherd's

Bush Stadium. When a Latin won, his compatriots were unable to contain themselves. "They furiously waved their handkerchiefs or puffed on cigars with straws in thim, while th' Anglo-Saxons looked on with good-natured contimpt at this display of almost feminine weakness." On the other hand, "th' Briton, long accustomed to resthrain himself in public, accepted defeat or victhry with equal serenity, in one case merely yellin' 'Foul!' or 'Kill th' bloomink Yankees!' an' in th' other dancing on his hat."

Mr. Dooley described the games themselves as "truly a gloryous spectacle, waiters rushin' in with buckets iv tea f'r th' English athletes, English officials lodgin' preliminary claims iv foul again th' American team, an so forth." The Americans "succeeded in rollin' up a score iv eight pints an' iliven disqualifications in more or less obsolete forms iv spoort known as field an' thrack athletics, such as jumpin', runnin', pole-vaulting, hurdling, et cethery." But the English, chuckled Dooley, had claimed the Olympic championship by winning such events as "wheelin' th' p'rambulator," "th' tea-dhrinkin' contest," and "th' Long Stand-up While th' Band Plays Gawd Save th' King." "Do you think th' English are good losers?" Mr. Hennessy finally asked Dooley. "Good losers, says ye? Good losers? I'll back thim to lose anny time they start," Dooley replied.[97]

Mr. Dooley spoke for his nation. In American minds the London games symbolized the new order in world affairs. The United States, embodying the spirit of Athens, had supplanted a Romanized British Empire. Olympic dominance signified that Americans best controlled the awesome energies of modernity. British antagonism concealed English fears of the sporting republic's superiority. A *New York Times* cartoon epitomized the vision of the fourth Olympics as proof of American superiority over a decadent England. It pictured a robust, vigorous-looking Teddy Roosevelt facing a skinny, effete-looking Englishman in a monocle and top hat. The two stood in front of a placard announcing the "Olympic Games" in a sketch entitled "When Greek Meets Greek."[98]

The Politics of Olympic Celebration and Proposals for American Control of the Olympics

The president himself congratulated the team "upon their splendid work in worthily upholding the athletic traditions of the country."[99] When the team returned to the United States, Roosevelt received them at his Oyster Bay retreat. The *New York Times* thought that the president was "wholly sincere in his admiration of the men of large muscular skill and endurance, and we do not doubt that he has honestly rejoiced in the American victories at Shepherd's Bush much more than countless thousands of his fellow-citizens who have vociferously cheered the athletes since their return." The president identified them as typical Americans, instructing the athletic stars to "drop the hero business and go to work." Roosevelt admonished the Olympians to cease speaking of British unfairness. "We don't need to talk," the president gloated; "we've won."[100]

A parade and an honors ceremony greeted the winners on their return to New York City. The Olympians, accompanied by military detachments, rode a motorcade to city hall while "great crowds thronged the streets, admired the military, and cheered the men of skill and muscle vociferously." A *New York Times* reporter related that the demonstrative crowd "fitly represented the feeling of the public toward the victorious athletes" and "denoted, in some measure, their fellow-countrymen's sympathy with them for the disagreeable part of their experience abroad."[101]

On the evening of the celebration, New York City's elite invited several of the Olympic champions to a lavish public dinner at the Waldorf-Astoria Hotel. Caspar Whitney could not resist a final chance to squeeze public opinion for more financial support for the American Olympic movement. He rebuked the Americans who had jumped on the bandwagon and saluted the returning victors with "hurrahing and ostentatious caperings," even though they had conspicuously failed to lend a hand in sending the team to London. Whitney groused, "When I review the experiences of our American Olympic Committee, I recall that no Vanderbilt offered a dollar's worth of help, nor an Astor."[102]

Whitney and Sullivan had molded an American Olympic team to fit the contours of the sporting republic's ideology. They had succeeded to a remarkable degree in creating a cultural pattern through which the public associated Olympic standing with national strength. Athletics were seen as building, and revealing, national identity. Athletics could even reveal flaws in the American character.

Whitney identified two habits that discredited American athletes, a "disposition to 'kick' at decisions" and "training to beat the rules." Those habits caused enough problems in the United States, but they were giving Americans particularly bad reputations in Olympic competitions. "We know that this 'kicking' and his endeavors to be too smart for the rule makers are by no means evidence of dishonest intent, but an expression of his frenzy to win," conceded Whitney. He recognized that if sport was not properly channeled, the tremendous energies unleashed by athletic exercise could be destructive. "Now there is nothing the matter with the 'get there' spirit, *per se;* it is the spirit of the land that has made us what we are—a spirit which, let us hope, will never be quenched; but it needs direction. It requires control in our sport as it does in our business." Whitney linked sport and its problems to the powerful forces that were corrupting American life. "We do things in Wall Street that would put a man behind bars if he was not ranked as being smart," wrote Whitney. "The slickness which enters into high finance has a tendency to creep into our athletics. The mad passion for money-making—anything to make money—and the placing of money-making as the highest expression of one's endeavors, one's brain, one's skill, is reflected in athletics by the passion for victory which ignores sport for sport's sake," he warned.[103]

Whitney remained an optimist. He believed that more and more Americans were comprehending the "sporting spirit" and condemning the mad passion for winning. Perhaps America had flaws. Whitney found them to be tolerable, however, particularly when compared to the incompetencies of the Europeans who led the Olympic movement. Whitney blasted the IOC for mismanaging the Olympic movement. He dismissed the current IOC as "a clumsy affair, composed largely of inexperienced men, chosen quite after the fashion that obtains in nominating patronesses to smart garden parties—by well-meaning if capricious gentlemen who appear to view the 'Comité Athlétique' as a kind of social board-walk." Whitney insisted that the Olympic movement needed a more competent international bureaucracy "to handle such a big business as these Olympic Games have become." He hoped to restrict the IOC's membership to the nations that actually participated in the games, grousing that Turkey, Spain, Russia, and Peru were represented in the council but that Canada was not. He also demanded that the new IOC appoint international managers to run the games and select the referees, rather than leave all the details of constructing Olympic Games to the host country's "partisan" organizing committee. An international institution as important as the Olympics, counseled Whitney, should be controlled by "experts," not amateurs.[104]

Whitney wanted an AOC-led purge to purify the games. England was not solely to blame, he insisted. "The responsibility must be divided among all of us who have tolerated the casual Olympic organization which provided so incompetent an international committee," he asserted; "My suggestion is dismissal of the present so-called International Olympic Committee." He proposed that the presidency of the revamped IOC be offered to Lord Desborough—a curious suggestion considering that Desborough was the British aristocrat who organized the London games, which Whitney found to be incompetently executed.[105]

Blackwood's simply could not understand why Whitney and others considered the Olympic Games so important. "Even in their golden age the Olympic Games brought but a truce to Greece," the editor reflected. "The great issues of peace and war are not decided upon accidents so trivial" as Olympic performances. "Germany is not likely to stay her hand because the English champions are superior to her own on the running path. England will not look upon American diplomacy with a kinder eye because an American has thrown the hammer farther than any athlete that came before him."[106]

The editor's attempt to disconnect Olympic athletics from the great issues of national policy indicated the degree to which sport and political life had merged in the Western world. Although a few intellectuals, such as the editors of *Blackwood's* in England and E. L. Godkin's crew at *The Nation* in the United States, tried to attack the linkage between sport and national power, it had become a truism in popular culture and intellectual discourse. The images fit together too easily. In Western minds energy had transformed the medieval world into the modern. The English worried that their nation seemed to be slipping in many of the categories through which moderns measured national vitality. British industrial production could not match the explosive growth curves of German and American manufacturing. Athletic production, in the very track and field games that the English had invented, seemed to be slipping, too. Perhaps a strong Olympic showing would make Germany stay its hand and return the United States to its proper orbit. For a people whose mythology taught them that an empire had been launched from the playing fields of Eton, perhaps it was time to "play up."

Anticipating the Next Olympics

The next celebration of the Olympics had been scheduled for Stockholm. The British, troubled by the comparisons of English and American athletic prowess, would mount a strong effort to assuage the nagging fear that the empire might indeed be on the decline. What would another British failure on the Olympic green indicate?

The Americans dreamed of more glory. The AOC had grand plans. They wanted more money, bigger and better tryouts, and a training ship to carry their champions to Sweden. They wanted Uncle Sam to whip John Bull. The second round in the battle for strenuous superiority would be fought in 1912. America's original athletic missionary, James B. Connolly, hoped that his nation would absorb the Olympic spirit: "For no country can find greater use for it than our own, which is standing now, awake and eager, where old Greece once slept— on the threshold of the world's leadership."[107] The new Athenians looked to Stockholm to stake their claim.

★ 7

Stockholm, 1912:
The Sporting Republic's Zenith

In the summer of 1912 Theodore Roosevelt, William Howard Taft, and Woodrow Wilson were engaged in a competitive and entertaining contest for the presidency. Simultaneously American athletes prepared for a midsummer rendezvous to defend national honor at the games of the Fifth Olympiad, to be held in Stockholm. Olympic hyperbole reached feverish proportions as the national political conventions set the field for the race to the White House.

Races for the White House sometimes placed second behind accounts of Olympian struggles. *Current Literature* even suggested that the nation should ignore the major political conventions selecting presidential candidates. "If you want a real world contest, turn your eyes away from Chicago, Baltimore and Washington, and fasten them upon the city of Stockholm," counseled the compendium of news and novellas. "Let us cease to talk about the initiative, the referendum, and such like things, and discuss the discus, the pentathlon, the javelin throw, and the Marathon race."[1]

Current Literature made its jibe at the election only partly in jest. Athletic nationalism demanded equal billing with presidential politics. As the American team readied itself for the voyage to Stockholm, William Milligan Sloane, the original American member of the IOC, reminisced that more than thirty years earlier Baron Pierre de Coubertin had first advocated the Olympic idea to the modern world. "The motto of M. de Coubertin was 'Ludus pro Patria'" (playing to build a dynamic nation), recalled Professor Sloane. Certainly the United States had taken Coubertin's motto to heart.[2] Playing the game for the homeland had become the central tenet of American Olympic enterprises. Social commentators, popular essayists, athletic scientists, and progressive moralists considered sport and political life to be inseparable. Lifted from the ideology of the modern Olympics, Americans made "Ludus pro Patria" the maxim for their sporting republic.

Sporting republicans worked to cement the links between sport and American political culture. "History repeats itself even though centuries intervene between repetitions," began Edward Bayard Moss's tale of the fifth Olympics. "Greek mythology records the voyage of the Argonauts to recover the Golden Fleece of the winged ram Chrysomallus, nailed to the oak tree in the Garden of Ares. Ages later," Moss fantasized, "the expedition, modernized by American business methods, is duplicated in the sailing of the United States Olympic team for the international carnival of sports to be held at Stockholm next month."[3]

The United States had created its own mythology. The American team, selected and financed by the bureaucracy of the AOC, sallied forth from its vigorous republic to defend American pride and honor in Stockholm. Victories at the Olympic Games had come to symbolize the strength and character of the nation, and the American press assured readers that the team would continue its winning tradition.

Organizing an Expedition of American Icons

The AOC moved to ensure that the team would win. William Milligan Sloane, who had changed his academic address from Princeton to Columbia, declared that American Olympic power was "brilliant" in two arenas. First, Americans led the world in raising funds to send their teams to the Olympics. Second, American athletes dominated Olympic competition.[4] By 1912 the American Olympic movement, under the leadership of James Edward Sullivan, enjoyed an enormous prestige.

The AOC included among its "vice-presidents" such American notables as New York State Supreme Court justice Victor J. Dowling; titans of American industry and finance August Belmont, Andrew Carnegie, Samuel R. Guggenheim, Harold F. McCormick, J. P. Morgan, and Rodman Wanamaker; and athletic experts Gustavus T. Kirby, A. G. and J. W. Spalding, and Bartow S. Weeks. General George W. Wingate, who along with Luther Gulick, James Edward Sullivan, and others founded New York City's Public Schools Athletic League, was also on the roster. President Taft stood as the honorary president of the AOC, while Colonel Robert M. Thompson served in the official presidency.

Sullivan continued his tenure as AOC secretary and as the powerbroker who dominated amateur sport. Sullivan and the executive committee of the AOC controlled the American Olympic enterprise, which included the most powerful leaders of the AAU and the champions of the strenuous life: Sullivan, Thompson, Kirby, Weeks, Sloane, Gulick, Julian W. Curtiss, and Joseph B. Maccabe. The executive committee chose 1906 and 1908 Olympic veterans Matthew P. Halpin and Michael C. Murphy as manager and trainer, respectively, of the Stockholm expedition. The AOC scheduled Olympic tryouts for Harvard Stadium in Cambridge, Massachusetts; Marshall Field in Chicago; and Stanford University in Palo Alto, California. AOC officials announced that they planned to select Olympians with help from the AAU, the YMCA, and the Intercollegiate Athletic Association.[5]

With the sites for team selection set, the executive committee turned its attention to fund-raising. AOC treasurer Julian Curtiss coordinated the effort while Gustavus Kirby, then the president of the AAU as well as the AOC, crisscrossed the nation to drum up support for the Olympic team.[6] The AOC proclaimed that the Stockholm expedition would be a public undertaking and enlisted the press to open the public's pocketbooks. "Shall the American records at the fifth Olympic Games, to be held this Summer at Stockholm, fail simply from lack of money?" wondered the New York Times in a fund-raising editorial.[7]

The AOC bragged that all its funds were "collected by voluntary contributions, without a subsidy in any shape or form from the Government or from any State or municipality."[8] Marshaling "American business methods" to meet the financial challenge, the AOC undertook a "patriotic" public relations campaign to garner funding for the Olympic crusade. Olympic organizers cultivated the rich and powerful, publishing lists of prominent contributors in major newspapers. John D. Rockefeller Sr., Andrew Carnegie, George Gould (son of the robber baron's robber baron, Jay Gould), Allison V. Armour, J. P. Morgan, T. C. DuPont, and Cyrus McCormick contributed $500 each to send "a team that will be truly representative of this country" to Sweden. Samuel R. Guggenheim gave $250 and August Belmont added $100.[9]

Major athletic clubs, particularly the New York Athletic Club, the Chicago Athletic Association, and the Olympic Club of San Francisco, and American colleges, especially Dartmouth, Yale, Brown, Penn, and the University of Chicago, made large contributions. Local and regional associations of the AAU, many other national athletic organizations, and businesses and corporations raised generous amounts of money. The champions of the strenuous life and former Olympic stars also contributed. Caspar Whitney gave $20, and A. G. Spalding and Brothers gave $500. Two breweries, Lembeck and Betz and Anheuser-Busch, donated $100 apiece. Through contributions and selling space on the ship that they had chartered to make the voyage to Stockholm, the finance committee managed to bring in a little more than $125,000 for the trip. They would have only $1,800 left after the festivities.[10]

The AOC campaign adopted the successful bureaucratic style employed by professional organizations that were increasingly ordering American life. Loyal voluntarism, organizational efficiency, control of media messages, access to political and economic power, and the association of their corporate efforts with popular understandings of progress and modernity made the AOC a powerful institution. It needed Olympic victories for continued success.

The press soon sounded the athletic nationalist's call demanding new victories. Edward Bayard Moss predicted that the American Olympians would receive a triumphant homecoming "if they return with the fleece of the fifth Olympiad to add to the four already hung in our trophy halls." Given history and tradition, no one expected anything less than a championship "fleece" from the American team. Moss spun the American Olympic legend in the pages of *Harper's Weekly.* "Each revival of the Olympic Games has drawn larger entry lists, and each struggle has been more severe than its predecessor, but never have the United States representatives faltered or failed to emerge from the conflict victorious," he testified. He predicted that Stockholm would see a repeat performance. "Never in the history of amateur sport has such an athletic combination gone forth to do battle on cinder track and greensward," boasted Moss of America's 1912 Olympic squad. Moss was not alone in his admiration. Olympic veteran James Sullivan marveled at the team, gushing, "Never in my long experience have I seen its equal."[11]

Media coverage of the team resonated with the imagery of the sporting republic. Class, race, and ethnic distinctions disappeared—at least in newspaper stories—on athletic common ground. Republican values and civic virtue animated the athletes. The press described a team consisting of "typical" Americans, "more than ninety per-cent native born, and composed of all classes and conditions of men and youths." The "heterogeneous gathering" included "lawyers, physicians, policemen, Indians, negroes, Hawaiians, college men, school boys, clerks, mechanics, and in fact, entrants from every walk of life."[12] *The Independent* celebrated a team chosen "without regard to class, wealth, race, color or previous condition of servitude."[13] Moss argued that the representative nature of the team cut across all economic lines. "Sons of wealthy men fraternized with youths of their own age so poor that public subscriptions by citizens of their home towns were necessary in order that they might make the trip to Stockholm." He marveled that "there was no class or color distinction on board the training ship or in the Stadium. Each man and youth was an integral part of the team, bearing the American shield, with his work to do."[14]

The American squad, according to the press, was a curious mixture of American types. It included a Christian Scientist distance runner, George V. Bonhag, whose "mind will say to his weary body" near the finish line, "You are not tired. *You must win.*" Another distance runner, a Hopi Indian from Arizona named Lewis Tewanima, could run "Marathons under the most discouraging conditions and never change the stoicism of his face."[15] Tewanima was one of the two

Native American distance runners at Stockholm. The other was Alfred Sockal-exis, an Onondaga from Old Town, Maine. The team also featured several Hawaiian swimmers, including the great Duke Kahanamoku. Edward Moss believed, however, that Howard P. Drew and James Thorpe best illustrated "the result of the countrywide search for the 1912 team." Drew was a twenty-two-year-old African American student from a Springfield, Massachusetts, high school who worked after school as a bellboy and summers in a Springfield hotel. He began his track career wearing shoes he had made "out of an old pair of ties [tires?] and a dozen wire nails."[16] By 1912 he was an Olympian and a gold medal threat heralded as a symbol of African American pride by *The Crisis,* the leading African American journal in the United States and the official organ of the National Association for the Advancement of Colored People.[17] Jim Thorpe, the Sac and Fox Indian from the Carlisle Indian School, represented American hopes in the pentathlon and decathlon.[18] In media portraits the sporting republic appeared color-blind.

Class distinctions also disappeared in Olympic hyperbole. The *New Orleans Times-Picayune*'s Martin Durkin pointed to discus thrower and long jumper Russell Byrd of Adrian College (Michigan) as proof that hard work could make an American everyman into an Olympian. Byrd was an average athlete who had originally been chosen to make the journey to Stockholm at his own expense. "As he was the son of a superannuated minister and had been working his way through college, this was out of the question," revealed Durkin. Through grit and determination, practice and "prayer," Byrd won a spot on the "paid" roster. Durkin offered Byrd's tale as lesson for American youth.[19]

The bellboys, clerks, and mechanics; the doctors, lawyers, and policemen; the Anglo-Saxons, Irish, African Americans, Slavs, Scandinavians, Native Americans, and Hawaiians; the Jews, Catholics, Protestants, and Christian Scientists of the American squad—together they faced the assembled might of the athletic world. "To dethrone America in the battle for first place is a feat that would ring around the hemisphere, and is consequently the object of every athlete and team entered for the games," Moss warned the nation.[20] Could the Americans meet the challenge? In his survey of Olympic prospects, Edward Fox found the American team so tough that one of the U.S. hammer throwers might crush the rest of the sporting world's ambitions. "With one of these terrific throws, Stockholm may see the hopes of all Europe's athletic teams, tied to the swirling wire, go splashing out into the North Sea," joked Fox.[21]

Even *The Nation,* which had long resisted a conversion to the doctrine of the strenuous life, understood that American sporting ideology was sweeping the world. "The strenuous American idea of physical culture is winning its way against the older and quieter methods," observed one of *The Nation*'s editors.

"German moralists of the new school of efficiency who have learned to cite America as the great exemplar of success, are uttering their dissatisfaction with the flabby athletic ideas of the university student as expressed in the ceremonious sword-contests of the Mensur and the elaborate beer-drinking competition." They preferred that the "new Germany" adopt the football, baseball, and track and field contests that German progressives believed created American-style social "efficiency."

The Nation also reported that France, consumed by a primitivist fad, had "gone quite mad over pugilism." *The Nation* thought it "safe to infer that on the part of the ordinary Frenchman this newly awakened fondness for fisticuffs belongs to the present renaissance of the French spirit, away from feminine decadencies and self-scarifications and lotus-eating, towards masculine self-confidence and the reassertion of those simple, healthy, primitive appetites which help a nation to make a firm stand when some other nation wants to deprive it of Morocco." *The Nation,* which in the past had often criticized the American linkage of athletics and national vigor, had connected the European fascination with American athletics to a firmer commitment to progress and national pride in those nations that imitated the American example.[22]

At the celebration of the games of the Fifth Olympiad, American Olympians would continue to try to convert Europe to American athletic nationalism. When the team gathered in New York City for the voyage to Stockholm, thousands of fans crowded onto the docks and gave the athletes a send-off "with the utmost enthusiasm and high spirits." Julian Curtiss, the chairman of the committee that financed the expedition, told the team, "We must win in such a manner that we shall gain the respect of those we defeat."[23] The specter of an American defeat did not trouble the chairman. The American boys would win and, he hoped, behave decorously.

"Eagle Screams" and American Athletic Hegemony

The American team crossed the Atlantic on the *Finland,* a Red Star Line cruise ship specially altered to allow the Olympians to train during the journey. According to one reporter, the converted steamer marked a "new epoch in Olympic history." Athletic experts reworked the *Finland* so that the team could continue training during the voyage, building running tracks, jumping and weight throwing pits, swimming tanks, and a gymnasium.[24] After ten days on the Atlantic, the team landed at Antwerp, Belgium, where manager Matt Halpin secured a practice field to get rid of the Olympians' "sea legs." After two days in Belgium the *Finland,* with its "cargo of American speed and muscle," sailed for Sweden, arriving in Stockholm four days later.[25]

Apparently the melting pot character of the American team not only captured the attention of the press but also animated the ethnic and ethical sensibilities of the athletes. Abel Kiviat, a Jewish middle distance runner, recalled how
he began a friendship with Howard Drew, a black sprinter, on board the *Finland*. "Howard and I got together almost by instinct," he remembered. Kiviat
related that one of the discus throwers had called him a "little 'sheeny.'" The
rest of the team would not stand for the slur. "Pat McDowell, a 325 pound shot
putter, and one of the other big weight men grabbed the discus thrower, who
looked like an ugly gorilla, and told him next time you say anything to little
Abel we're going to squeeze you through the little porthole and that will be the
end of you," chuckled Kiviat. "There was no repeat incident."[26] The athletes
understood their tasks. They had to win, and they had to symbolize the sporting republic's ideals.

The portion of the Olympic program that Americans considered to be the
only "real" marker of national status—track and field events—opened on July
6 and continued until July 15. The Swedes had constructed a 27,000-seat gran-
ite and gray brick stadium for the Olympics. As usual the Americans groused
about the layout of the track, but Sullivan politely identified the complaints as
minor and thanked the Swedish Olympic Committee for its efforts.[27] American spectators in the stands greeted the U.S. contingent with a hearty cheer of
"Rah, rah, ray! U.S.A.! A-M-E-R-I-C-A!" The cacophony of American college
cheers "blended with general cheering due a champion when the front ranks
of the American athletes swung through the gates," reported Will T. Irwin,
writing for *Collier's*.

The American team wore blue coats with white trousers and shoes and straw
hats. "As they came down the line, section after section rising to greet them,
the Americans in the grandstand experienced a momentary disappointment,"
Irwin observed. "The men of the martial nations which preceded them, con-
scripts all, had marched with the formal carriage of European military tactics,"
he stated. "Ours, though they kept good step and alignment, glided along in
any fashion, their arms and shoulders keeping swing with their walk. It took a
second thought to convince us that we were right and Europe wrong," remembered Irwin. "This free-and-easy gait, when performed by a six-foot youth in
perfect condition, is after all, more natural and beautiful than the protruding
chest, the stiff hands, and the unnatural step of German tactics and I leave it
to any sculptor or painter."[28]

Irwin recalled that the American procession had moved with the "loose,
springy, natural step of men in perfect control of their bodies and in perfect
condition." He imagined it as "the gait of the plainsmen who tamed our wilderness, of Jackson's 'foot cavalry,' of Sherman's army of athletes. Human be-

ings were made to walk that way." Irwin's juxtaposition of images provided an ironic counterpoint to his accusations concerning the overly soldierly bearing of the "martial nations."[29] When the team passed by Gustav V and the royal box, the flag bearer dipped the Stars and Stripes—so much for a hallowed American Olympic legend.[30]

Irwin found symbols of a new world order in the national teams assembled before cheering multitudes at Stockholm. The small Japanese delegation stood next to the Greek ancestors of the original Olympians. "Here, beside the little squad representing that most significant race which lost its domination twenty years ago," he wrote, "stood the other little squad from the race which made its offer of domination only yesterday." The American press would find many more indications of national primacy in the world hierarchy at Stockholm. They would proclaim that the points scored in track and field events especially, and to some degree in other sports, revealed national character. The opening festivities culminated with the Scandinavians, Germans, Englishmen, and "unmusical Americans" rendering a version of "A Mighty Fortress Is Our God," which conveyed a "solemn thrill" to the Olympic assembly.[31]

The Americans found conditions much more satisfactory than at the London Olympics. Nevertheless, Swedish preparations were not up to American standards. Although Swedish officials furnished the track with an electrical timing apparatus and "instantaneous photography at the finish," the AOC pronounced the technology "far behind" that employed at AAU meets. In his official report Sullivan labeled Swedes as "sportsmen of the true type" and admitted that there were no incidents with judges or officials at Stockholm. Nonetheless, his compliments were a preface to his continued attack on the IOC's handling of Olympic organization. Sullivan persisted in his campaign for the application of American standards to Olympic competition.[32]

The Swedish organizing committee, under the sway of American definitions of sport, made track and field the focus of the festivities.[33] Sullivan arrogantly declared that without track and field events the Olympics "would be a dismal failure." Americans had always considered these events to be the central feature of the Olympics, and the nation was not disappointed by its track and field stars. "As in all previous Olympic Games, the athletes from the United States showed their superiority," trumpeted Sullivan. The United States won sixteen of the thirty-one track and field events at Stockholm, also garnering twelve second places and thirteen third places. The AOC tabulated eighty-five points in the meet for the United States, twenty-nine for Finland, twenty-seven for Sweden, and fifteen for Great Britain. If Canada and South Africa's totals were added to Great Britain's, the empire still finished with only twenty-seven points in the "Anglo-Saxon" track and field competition.

In the overall standings for the 1912 Olympics, the AOC asserted that the United States had captured twenty-five gold, seventeen silver, and twenty bronze medals. Sweden had twenty-three gold, twenty-four silver, and sixteen bronze medals; Great Britain had ten gold, fifteen silver, and sixteen bronze medals; and Finland had nine gold, eight silver, and nine bronze medallions. The AOC's arithmetic gave Sweden a slight edge in the overall standings, with 133 points to the United States' 129. Great Britain scored 76 points. With the rest of the empire included, the British total rose to 118.[34] The official Swedish report showed a similar distribution of athletic power. In their calculations Sweden finished with 136 points, the United States with 124, Great Britain with 76, and Finland with 53.[35]

Americans congratulated the Finns and Swedes on their showings in Olympic track and field. Sullivan thought that Sweden and Finland were following the American example. Their victories stemmed from the fact "that America was able to point the way in international contests to the nations of the world." The AOC chief admired the patriotism of the Swedish and Finnish contingents. He remarked that an "impossible to describe" national feeling swept over the stadium whenever a Swedish performance caused their flag to be raised to the top of the stadium as a signal of victory. When the Finns swept the javelin throw, "an encouraging and sympathetic thrill rose from all," recalled Sullivan. That response indicated the understanding that the crowd and the athletes felt as the Finnish victors were forced to watch the Russian flag—"with a pennant attached on which 'Finland' was printed in bold relief"—signal Finnish victory. The rest of the world had begun to appropriate the athletic nationalism that had colored the American approach to international sport since the Athens Olympics in 1896.[36]

The results from Stockholm precipitated an orgy of athletic nationalism in the American press. *The Outlook* cheered that "in track and field events the American athletes scored only two points less than the athletes of all other countries combined, and more than three times as many as their nearest competitors."[37] Edward Bayard Moss lauded the "caliber" of an American team that had won a "sweeping victory under conditions and against competition never equalled heretofore."[38] *Current Literature* allowed that by focusing on the Olympic track and field events, which U.S. athletes dominated, "the American eagle has been enabled in past years to emit a much louder scream than would otherwise be warranted." According to the magazine, the 1912 games proved that "however you look at it, the eagle seems fairly entitled to yell her bald head off. Our athletes have eclipsed those of all other nations." The magazine added that Sweden's showing was a direct result of American coaching.[39]

The Literary Digest remarked, "So sweeping was the victory of American athletes at the Olympic Games that our press give [*sic*] more space to explanation than to jubilation." The media soon remedied that oversight. A *Brooklyn Eagle* reporter mused that "once again the climate, environments, and enthusiasm of a new-world country have produced a team of its young men which has been able to meet the combined athletic strength of the entire world and proven more than a match for it."[40]

In explaining their victories, Americans once again identified the unique social structure of the United States and the American tradition of scientific sport as the wellsprings of American domination. "If the truth be told," confided Sullivan, "the American team entered the games anything but confident of a great victory." The AOC commissioner conceded that his admission might "sound strange to you who remember the sweeping confidence displayed before leaving this country," but he pointed out that the long ocean voyage could have destroyed the team's great potential. Fortunately American athletic science had invented and constructed the training ship.

American victories did not owe to science alone, however. A New World grit stirred the champions to supremacy. Sullivan found a remarkable example of American "pluck" in the U.S. army officers' performances at the equestrian riding competition. "Mounted on nags that cost $150 each, our officers won points against riders from the armies of Continental Europe whose mounts were specially bred and cost anywhere from $1,500 to $4,000," Sullivan divulged, adding, "One of the horses we used is over eighteen years of age and a veteran of the Cuban campaign in the Spanish-American War." The American military placed third. They symbolized for Sullivan the superiority of American rugged individualism over European aristocracy.[41]

The Outlook asserted that "the wonderful record of American representatives at Stockholm cannot but be gratifying to the American people, not only from a patriotic point of view, but as an evidence of American appreciation of the value of outdoor life and physical development."[42] A devotion to the strenuous life had moved the United States to the head of the parade of nations. And of course, sport not only built character; it revealed it. "The Democracy of sport is illustrated by the almost equal division of Olympic honors between student and non-student contestants," claimed one observer of the American athletic triumphs. "There is no occasion to fear corrupting influences in American sport when a Y.M.C.A. youth and a boy from a country academy can win athletic honors in a world competition."[43]

British Debates about "America's Athletic Missionaries"

While Americans found symbols of their national virility and celebrated their exploits at the 1912 Olympics, many foreign commentators castigated America's sporting morals. They disliked American methods of financing teams, accused American athletes of being victory-programmed automatons who twisted the true meaning of sport, and condemned the team as a menagerie of immigrant mercenaries.

The complaining about the American style of Olympic athletics reached its highest pitch in the English press.[44] After the United States had won the track and field competition in London's 1908 Olympics, British athletic officials had promised that their team would show itself in a better light at Stockholm. When the British placed only fourth at Stockholm, behind Sweden and tiny Finland, Americans were hardly sympathetic. "The modern Olympic meet is chiefly regarded as a contest between nations," surmised *The Independent.* "Here the disappointment of the English is especially humiliating, because they were the first to insist that success in sports is a measure of national greatness."[45] "The defeat of the English athletes at Stockholm and the manifest proof that they were outclassed created a good deal of astonishment in Europe," noted *The Literary Digest.*[46]

The British press was not amused by American self-congratulation. *Blackwood's* opined, "For our part, we can not deplore the failure of our English athletes, concerning which so much has been said by exultant Americans." The magazine congratulated England for avoiding the "pit of professionalism" and discounted the perspectives of "the noisy press of New York" that "henceforth England is a back number in the world's history." *Blackwood's* insisted that "the fact that the Americans led in the Olympic games proves neither the decadence of English courage nor the supremacy of American wisdom. It is a triumph of professionalism, and of professionalism alone." The magazine's writer admitted that Americans had trained "more efficient athletes than any other part of the globe" but detested the American style. He complained that "the team which represented the United States at Stockholm was 'run on business lines.' It was, to use its own lingo, 'out to win.'" For Americans the "business of their heroes is not to amuse themselves, but to win; not to delight in their strength and prowess, but to show that these United States can whip the universe."[47] *The Spectator* claimed that the British saw sport differently. They had "no use for the athlete who has specialized himself into a highly efficient piece of machinery for a single purpose; we admire neither the freak-jumper nor the strongman who has exchanged elasticity for mighty strength, and the muscles of whose legs, as Stevenson says in 'The Wrong Box,' 'Stand out like penny buns.'"[48]

While certain segments of the English press launched scathing attacks on American athletic nationalism, the British were debating the meaning of their poor showings in the sports they had invented and the future course of Olympic action they should pursue. Two positions sharply divided British opinion. One group, which found a voice in Rudolph Lehman, demanded that England with-

draw from the Olympic movement. The other faction, headed by Lord Desborough, who was the chief English representative to the IOC and the leader of the
British Olympic movement, and by Lord Grey and Sir Arthur Conan Doyle, proposed a complete overhaul of English methods and huge expenditures to ensure
British victories in future Olympiads. England's athletic nationalists wanted to
build a "British Empire team" composed of sports stars from Great Britain, Australia, Canada, South Africa, and the other British provinces. In addition, they
wanted to set up a series of Olympic tryouts "at which large prizes should be
offered, in order to attract and discover possible Olympic winners."[49]

The Times of London published an appeal signed by "patriotic men of emi-
nence in war and statesmanship" demanding that the English public raise
£100,000—half a million dollars—"to train and provide for a band of men fit
to represent the country's athletic power." The Times's editors considered Lord
Grey's plea to be "a national duty. Not because we should look like sulky children who will not play in a game in which they have been beaten, but because
we are in honor bound to send to Berlin the best team that we can get together, we commend the fund to the generosity and public spirit of our readers."[50]

The Newcastle Daily Chronicle sarcastically remarked that the £100,000 in-
vestment would be money well spent. "It will, at any rate, be just as good fun
as backing horses in obscure alleyways," chuckled the editor. "And it will per-
mit the genuine amateur to proceed on his way in peace." In the London Standard "An Old Rugby Forward" reminded his countrymen that England lost only
to the "spurious amateurism of the foreign competitor." He decried the "im-
mense sums . . . now being spent to buy men and to turn them into professional
record-breakers." He blustered that "the great public" would have nothing to
do with Lord Grey's plan to "adopt American methods."[51] That, of course, was
the crux of the opposition. British critics claimed that American "professionals" had won the Olympic championship and that it was beneath English dignity to adopt the American strategy.[52] By English standards the label professional
meant that American athletes were not members of the leisure class. The London Daily News declared that "it is really more sportsmanlike to do our best in
such events, and where inevitable, accept defeat, than to try and purchase with
a great price an altogether unrepresentative victory. The lavish expenditure of
the United States on its selected athletes has no doubt resulted in their securing a considerable number of trophies."[53]

American Responses to European Criticism

James Edward Sullivan replied to the charges. He assailed the English for making "a wicked attempt to defend the crushing defeat administered to them by

the American athletes at Stockholm."[54] Sullivan maintained that the American amateur standards were the most stringent in the world. He dismissed the clamor in England as the whining of losers. Sullivan called the European assertion that Americans were "specialists" an especially "mistaken impression." The term *specialist* implied that Americans sacrificed an all-around vigor to produce grotesque athletic specimens who could do nothing else in life save sprint, jump, or throw weights. Such an implication directly attacked the basic principles of the sporting republic, which defined athletics as training for life, a key component of modern physical, mental, and moral life. "The average American amateur athlete can probably perform meritoriously in many more athletic events, outside of his specialty, than any other athlete in the world," barked Sullivan.

As proof Sullivan touted American performances in two new events that the IOC had placed on the Stockholm program to test all-around athletic ability. Sullivan reported that an IOC member told him that Europe had conceded the standard track and field events to the United States. Sullivan's source predicted that the two new events, the decathlon and pentathlon, could not possibly be won by American "specialists." "What a shock it was when James Thorpe, that wonderful all-around athlete from the Carlisle Indian School, demolished all theories and calculations," gloated the AOC boss.[55]

Thorpe captured the world's attention in Stockholm. At the closing ceremony Gustav V addressed the American star as "the most wonderful athlete in the world."[56] The czar of Russia gave Thorpe a sculptured Viking ship, and the Swedish king presented Thorpe with a bronze bust of his majesty himself.[57] Sullivan declared that Thorpe's exploits had put to rest the charge that Americans were "specialists." He then listed as confirmation Thorpe's other accomplishments—Thorpe was a member of Walter Camp's All-American football team, a lacrosse star, and a "splendid" baseball player. Unfortunately Thorpe's splendor on the baseball diamond would soon produce a major scandal.[58]

Americans charged that the Europeans, and particularly the British, did not really understand modern athletic technology. The uproar over specialization indicated European ignorance concerning the nature of sport. Other nations, complained Americans, did not grasp that the control of human and social energies requires scientific knowledge and rational planning. Sports are not games. They are devices for building healthy nations, for channeling competition in socially acceptable directions, and for erecting a national culture of shared values and ethics. "Applied science counts here, as in everything else," announced *The Independent*, "and the penalty for neglecting it is failure."[59]

American commentators made Olympic sport a part of their history of national character. In *The World's Work* Carl Crow described the genesis of the sporting republic. Although the United States had inherited a sporting tradition from England, the Americans had not been content with the aristocratic games and pastimes of their former colonial overlords. According to Crow, as industrialism and urbanization altered U.S. civilization, "the efficiency engineer began to reconstruct the whole system of American athletics." "America demanded superiority and American athletes developed with the idea that it was worth while to be the best sprinter in the game. It was the same spirit that made George Washington the best broad jumper and Lincoln the best rail splitter of their neighborhoods." Crow and many other Americans believed that the scientific training methods and the thirst for victory merely underscored the spirit that produced American greatness.[60]

The athletic nationalists believed that a less than passionate devotion to the strenuous life would produce a nation of "mollycoddles" and "swooning damsels." Americans insisted that strenuosity was a fundamental requirement of twentieth-century life. A New York Times editorial entitled "The Moral of the Games" preached the necessity of the win-at-any-cost philosophy for successful undertakings in the modern world. "It is not ourselves who say it," cried the editor. "It is those who are suffering the result of our taking our sports seriously, or some think even fiercely, as we take our business, our politics, and indeed everything. It may not be the best spirit in which to play, but the victory is accustomed to go to those who insist upon the rigor of the game."[61]

Olympic sport had become a metaphor for American life.[62] Americans claimed that Olympic victories flowed from their social institutions—in particular, from the egalitarian spaces of American playgrounds. In contrast, many foreign commentators condemned the American team as a collection of immigrant mercenaries. Georges Rozet, a French sportswriter, criticized U.S. athletic behavior in L'Information while recognizing the nationalistic significance of the Olympic Games. "The great nations seem to have agreed that their athletic success has become a patriotic question," Rozet admitted. He claimed that the French would "remain always and in everything national moralists" and insisted that "an American race does not exist." He ranted that "the hundred million individuals who live under the Stars and Stripes belong to all the races of the earth. The triumphant 'Americans' whose victories are claimed by the United States are German, Italian, Nigger, Polynesian and Sioux." He felt that "the redskin who won the pentathlon [Thorpe] was the only real representative of America. France, if she wished," declared Rozet, "could also find in her empire athletic wonders of every race and color to uphold the honor of the French flag—swimmers from Oceania, Arab runners, black boxers, yellow wrestlers—but the Frenchmen of France will be sufficient for the purpose when we employ the same training methods and spend as much money as the Yankees."[63]

The American media answered the charges that no "American race" existed and that American Olympic victories were the work of immigrant mercenaries by proudly boasting that the "United States owes its supremacy over all other nations to the fact that it is a union of all races." In the hands of the American press corps covering the Olympics, American Olympians became the personifications of the national culture's power to unite diverse ethnicities into a superior "type." An editor at *The Independent* proclaimed that all the credit for victories by immigrants should go to the United States. The editor argued that the United States took in refugees from nations that did not want them. When those refugees misbehaved, such as when in 1900 an Italian American anarchist from New Jersey assassinated the king of Italy, the United States received the blame for their deeds. The editor demanded that the United States receive the credit for Italian American Olympic victories.[64]

Journalist Carl Crow joked that "Europe's stock explanation" of American victories as belonging to those of "transplanted European blood . . . reminds one of the comforting reflection of the British commander who said that the American colonists could never have whipped the British troops had they not been of British extraction." Although Crow maintained that most of the American victors were not immigrants themselves, he insisted that all the victors—both immigrant and native-born—benefited from the American democratic tradition and the national ideals, which espoused opening competition to anyone, especially immigrants.[65]

Much of the press celebrated the contributions that America's heterogeneous ethnic groups made to the American Olympic dominance. *The Crisis,* lamenting the fact that an injured Howard Drew had failed to place in the sprints, noted how American Olympic officials took care of the African American star after his unfortunate experience and insisted that more glory would have come to the United States had Drew been able to run.[66] *The Independent* declared, "The men in whom we take pride have not only English, Scotch, Welsh and Irish blood in their veins, but Scandinavian, Russian, German, Italian, Hawaiian, Indian and other blood as well." According to the editors, the melting pot and social mobility won Olympic championships for America: "In both England and America the athletic champions mostly come from the colleges, but in England the universities and 'public schools' which devote most attention to sports are so hedged about by social and pecuniary restrictions as sometimes to shut out the best of the nation."[67]

One English athlete agreed with *The Independent*'s editorial. "A Suburban Athlete" wrote the *London Standard* to blame the British defeat at the Olympics on the class-bound structures of English society. "Caste rules the world of athletics and all is snobbery," he howled. "I think more attention ought to be paid to the humbler members of the community, and our position at the games might improve accordingly," the "Suburban Athlete" theorized. "In America a man has all the chances that his running talents entitle him to, even if he is the son of a dust-man," insisted the bitter British critic.[68]

Lieutenant von Reichnau, a German athletic observer in the United States to study the sporting republic in preparation for the sixth Olympic Games, echoed the "Suburban Athlete's" sentiments. Reichnau credited American athletic dominance to "the wide social range from which you can muster your record breakers and your prize winners." Carl Crow added that "in this democratic country, athletic competition is confined neither to the rich nor to the poor, but is shared by all alike. We honor the men who set the marks with little or no regard for who or what they are off the athletic field."[69]

Paying Homage to American Olympic Champions

Finley Peter Dunne's Mr. Dooley, as usual, offered his opinions on the "race questions." In a conversation with Mr. Hennesy, the barkeep who served as Dooley's fictional foil, Dooley satirically attacked British complaints and cleverly promoted the "melting-pot" character of the American team:

"I wish," said Mr. Dooley, "that we cud bate th' English fairly at some game or another." "Didn't we do it at Stockholm?" asked Mr. Hennessy. "We did not," said Mr. Dooley. . . . "Here it is, an exthract fr'm th' *London Daily Groan*. It was not th' supeeryort'y iv th' American team that give it th' victhry but the thranin' methods iv these barbaryans fr'm across th' water. It turns out that many iv these pretinded amachoors stopped smokin' cigareets an' afin pie weeks befure goin' to Sweden, an' while our athletics were livin' their ordhinry amachoor lives an' takin' no exercise beyant fightin' with th' wasps f'r possession iv th' breakfast marmylade their opponents were practicin' runnin', jumpin' and puttin' th' shot, so as to have an onfair advantage whin they entered th' races. Iv coorse they bate us, but we thank hiven that Englishmen have not adopted these neefaryous methods, but whin they win, though it be sildom, do so entirely on their merits. . . . But that ain't all. A cillybrated author comes out an' says it wasn't an American team that won at all. They were al' foreigners. Th' American comitymen wint to th' extint iv ringin' in a Cherokee Indyan as an American. What d'ye think iv that? Cud bad spoortsmanship go further thin that to pretind that an assisted immigrant whose people haven't been in this counthry f'r more thin tin thosan' years was an American? No wondher we won."

Mr. Dooley predicted that England would have to alter its conceptions of class and ethnicity if Britain planned to compete against the United States at the next Olympic Games, scheduled for Berlin in 1916. Dooley told Hennessy that the English planned to recruit their next Olympic team from all over the British

Empire. "Twud be a grand way iv spreadin' dimycracy all over th' wurruld. 'Gunga Din,' says wan iv th' English lords, goin' up to a British atheleet who is hittin' th' pipe undher a bamboo three an' givin' him a light kick, 'I want ye to go to Berlin an' run a thosan' yards f'r th' honor iv Ol' England.' 'Divil a fut will I put in front iv another till ye give me a vote,' says th' atheleet. An' if th' English ar-re thrue spoortsmen he'll get it."[70]

The U.S. Olympic team returned to New York City on August 23, 1912. The three presidential candidates had telegraphed the team with their congratulations and regrets that they could not be in New York to meet the returning conquerors.[71] The Olympians rode a motorcade from Fifth Avenue and Forty-first Street to city hall. Along the parade route great crowds cheered. Thousands paid homage to the American athletes "who, by their speed, strength and stamina for the fifth consecutive series, gave ample testimony to the ability of young America." American flags adorned the businesses along Waverly Place and Broadway, the thoroughfares through which the parade proceeded. Everywhere along the route "schoolchildren vied with each other in giving vent to the concerted cheer, 'U.S.A. A-m-e-r-i-c-a,' which had so often rung through the stadium upon the occasion of a victory of one of the boys who were honored yesterday." Mayor William J. Gaynor addressed the athletes at city hall. "The prowess which you have displayed has been the medium of comment for the people of the world, and particularly Europe," he noted. "You have shown that you possessed American stomachs, hearts, muscles and heads."[72]

That evening at a Terrace Gardens dinner honoring the athletes, the Olympic team filled its American stomachs. New York State Supreme Court justice Victor J. Dowling presided over the gathering. He made a "stirring speech" praising American conceptions of amateurism and athletic success. AOC president Colonel Robert M. Thompson argued "that America had gained more through the games than could be obtained through a dozen other mediums which might argue for the continuance of good-will between the nations of the world." The dinner menu was sprinkled with references to the Olympic champions, such as "*Jim Thorpe* Spring chicken."[73]

The Rise and Fall of the "World's Greatest Athlete"

Just when it seemed that the United States had forged its way to the front of the athletic world and forced England to adopt the American pattern or give up the Olympic Games, the charges that American athletes were indeed professionals gained some merit. During the winter of 1913 the AAU discovered that Jim Thorpe, the "world's greatest athlete," had received payment for playing on a minor league club in a North Carolina baseball league during the summers of 1909 and 1910. The leaders of the AAU, James Sullivan and Gus Kirby, along with legal adviser Bartow Weeks, promptly stripped Thorpe of his amateur standing and demanded that the IOC take away his gold medals. Thorpe, in a letter purportedly penned by his Carlisle football coach, Glenn "Pop" Warner, pled ignorance.[74] He claimed that he played not for the money but for the competition. "I was not very wise to the ways of the world and did not realize that this was wrong," moaned Thorpe. "I hope I will be partly excused by the fact that I was simply an Indian school-boy and did not know all about such things." The Carlisle star implicated other amateurs in the scandal: "In fact, I did not know that I was doing wrong because I was doing what I knew several other college men had done: except that they did not use their own names."[75]

Thorpe apologized for letting the nation down: "I am very sorry, Mr. Sullivan, to have it all spoiled in this way, and I hope the Amateur Athletic Union and the people will not be too hard in judging me." Sullivan, Kirby, and Weeks responded with an official communication. "It should be noted that Mr. Thorpe is an Indian of limited experience and education in the ways of other than his own people," the AAU admitted. That did not excuse his act in the eyes of the athletic leaders, however. They vigorously condemned Thorpe's actions, and they came down even more harshly on minor league baseball, insisting "that those who knew of his professional acts are deserving of still greater censure for their silence." Behind the histrionic condemnations, the AAU sought desperately to distance itself from the scandal, claiming that it had no prior knowledge of Thorpe's professionalism and no control over professional baseball.[76]

The Thorpe incident divided the American press. *The Outlook* supported the AAU's quick and firm administration of justice and held Thorpe up as an object lesson to all the nation's collegiate athletes.[77] The *Philadelphia Telegraph* sided with *The Outlook* and warned "that intercollegiate baseball to-day is honeycombed with semi-professionalism."[78] Will Irwin wrote a column in *Collier's* in which he, too, added his voice to the warnings that Thorpe was just the tip of the "semi-pro" iceberg. Irwin claimed that many of the American athletes with whom he had traveled to Stockholm had known that Thorpe had played summer baseball. Even more shocking, revealed Irwin, "not more than one Olympic winner in four, American or European, would stand the same close scrutiny which our committee has given to the record of Thorpe." Irwin drew "no morals from all this": "I state but the facts. General athletics all the world over seem to tend toward semi-professionalism, and will, I suspect, so long as athletic meets draw gate money."[79] The IOC and the American athletic establishment ignored Irwin's coldly realistic outlook.

A number of media opinions supported Thorpe. The *Columbia* [South Carolina] *State* made a somewhat tortured defense of the Indian athlete on racial grounds: "That Thorpe, being an Indian, may hardly be held with strict justice to so high a degree of moral accountability as his white competitors . . . is obviously a consideration to be pleaded in his defense at this juncture." Obviously the editors of the *State* put little stock in the melting pot theory of athletic integration. The *Washington Herald* argued that "Thorpe did not become a great runner, jumper, and weight-thrower through participation in professional baseball. His professionalism endowed him with no advantage over the college amateurs against whom he won his place on the American team."

The *Buffalo Express* agreed with the Washington daily, insisting that baseball had nothing to do with the Olympics and that Thorpe's amateur status in track and field should not have been connected to his baseball career.[80] William B. Clemence, a sportswriter with the *New York Morning Telegraph,* lamented that "while there is no wish to condone Thorpe's offense, the writer has met the Indian a half dozen times in the last three years and each time has been more imprest [*sic*] with his stolidness. . . . But yet put this Indian in a contest of any sort, whether it was on the track, over the hurdles, or throwing the hammer, and Thorpe's stolidness leaves him and he is the athlete, striving with brawn and muscle to outdo his competitor. Love of games—sports—was Thorpe's fetich and it had been his undoing. But he has been more sinned against than sinning."[81]

A few commentators thought that the entire incident smacked of hypocrisy, given the general level of corruption in American sport. They condemned the AAU for espousing what appeared to be an English standard of amateurism, one that restricted athletic participation to the leisure class. The *Philadelphia Times* cynically remarked that Thorpe had been made the scapegoat for the widespread failure to adhere to the letter of amateur athletic principles. "The sacred rules of the American Athletic Union must be observed," wrote the *Times.* "The pound of flesh must be demanded. Thorpe must be humiliated. He must give up the trophies and titles that he honestly won because of his perfect physical condition and prowess, and in the winning of which the pin-money he got for playing fourth-rate ball two years ago cut no figure whatever."[82]

The Independent thought that the Thorpe incident highlighted the "artificial and pedantic" code of sport that made amateur athletics a rich man's occupation. "Lo the poor Indian has been exposed and all his trophies shipt back to Sweden to be awarded to the next highest bidder," it gibed. Did Thorpe cheat or foul his opponents? Was the king of Sweden wrong when he hailed Thorpe as the world's greatest athlete? "No, nothing of that kind," insisted *The Independent.* "The conduct of the Carlisle Indian at Stockholm was irreproachable and he deserved all the honors he received, but it appears that he played ball one vacation and took money for it." The Christian weekly satirically announced that the fact that Thorpe was "a poor boy is no excuse. Poor boys are not supposed to take part in sport, that is to be reserved for gentlemen of leisure such as all college students are supposed to be and many of them are." *The Independent* condemned the basic principle of traditional amateurism. "Essentially it is based upon the idea that it is all right to take money if you don't need it, but wrong if you do."[83]

Generally the major concern of editorials was not whether Thorpe had been treated unfairly or whether the AAU had acted equitably. Americans were mostly worried about how the Thorpe incident would affect their international image. The *Washington Herald* anxiously remarked that the affair was "detrimental to the prestige of the United States the world around." The *Herald* scolded Thorpe for sacrificing "the reputation of American athletics."[84] *The Outlook* cried that "the humiliation is not confined to him; it extends to all who value their country's reputation for fairness in sport as in all other matters." The magazine worried that "every such incident lends aid and comfort to those who are constantly looking for proof of their assertions that Americans are constitutionally devoted to the doctrine that nothing should stand in the way of winning."[85]

The attacks on the American reputation did come, but the avalanche of criticism that Americans expected did not really materialize. The people who had pronounced Thorpe the world's greatest athlete wanted desperately to preserve his victories. Reports from Sweden indicated "a unanimous feeling of sympathy . . . for the great athlete." The Swedes thought that Thorpe should keep his medals and trophies since "the rules . . . clearly prescribe that protests against the amateur standing of participants must be made within thirty days after the distribution of the prizes." The Swedish athletic officials felt that the only way in which Thorpe could be excommunicated was if the AAU were to demand that punishment at the next meeting of the IOC. American officials did exactly that.[86]

A portion of the British press proved surprisingly tolerant in their assessments of the Thorpe debacle. The *London Globe,* while bemused that the AOC discovered the facts "very late," congratulated Sullivan, Weeks, and Kirby on their handling of the situation. Captain F. W. Jones of the British Olympic Association commended the Americans for "behaving handsomely in a trying situation." The London *Pall Mall Gazette* asserted that "excommunication is too severe a punishment for Thorpe," and the *London Daily News* politely averred that "Great Britain thinks none the worse of the Indian for his crime."[87]

Nonetheless, much of the English media turned Thorpe's fall from grace into opportunities to continue their assaults on the American sporting tradition. The *London Daily News* editor hooted, "Our patience is exhausted when we are asked to believe that Thorpe is the biggest sinner against amateurism simply because of his baseball indiscretion." A *London Daily Mirror* writer sputtered, "If Thorpe was the only shady amateur who competed at the Olympic meet, I know nothing about athletics and in my opinion foreign athletes are reformed beyond recognition." Other critics were more direct. "It seems as though the world of sport in the United States should undertake a purging process in its own interests," advised the *London Globe*.[88]

American newspapers fired insults back across the Atlantic. The *Baltimore Evening Sun* claimed that British athletes could easily be "tarred with the same stick." The *Evening Sun* hostilely suggested that "while we are cleaning house, it might be well for the British and French to make an investigation of their own athletes."[89] Robert Edgren of the *New York Evening World* summed up the entire affair: "The disqualification of Thorpe makes a slight difference in the standing of the nations at the Olympic meet. However, it isn't big enough to cause America to lose the credit of winning first place."[90]

The "Real Representative" Americans

Winning, in the final analysis, was indeed the only thing that really counted for athletic nationalists. True, the AAU had punished Thorpe. As Robert Edgren pointed out, however, Thorpe's disqualification did not mean an American loss at the Olympics. One wonders how vigorously American officials would have pursued Thorpe had his victories in the decathlon and pentathlon been the margin of U.S. victory.

Americans christened their 1912 Olympians "America's Athletic Missionaries," emissaries to the world from the sporting republic. The nation saw in sport, especially the Olympic variety, confirmation for their self-proclaimed historical role as the "city on a hill." Once again, Mr. Dooley captured the national infatuation Americans felt for their athletic missionaries:

> I don't know why I get so inthrested in these things—me that cudden't roll, let along run, a hundherd yards an' wud be sure to dhrop th' hammer on me toes if I thryed to throw it. But I do. Why is it? I ain't anything like as stirred up be our intellechool conquests as I am be a New York poliseman peggin' th' hammer th' lenth iv th' stajum. Ye don't see anny hadlines in th' pa-apers, "American Profissor Grabs First Money at Sourbun." No, Sir. I don't care whether he did or not. I wudden't mind if he was disqualified f'r spikin' his opponent or speakin' Latin through his nose. But whin an American goes over to punch a foreigner's eye or row against him or run him off his feet I set back in me rockin' chair, read ivery line iv th' reports an' give three cheers f'r him. I'm proud to be riprisinted abroad be these young fellows.
>
> Europeens usually get their idees iv America fr'm th' Americans they see trudgin'

around th' churches readin' little red books an' steppin' on th' heels iv old ladies saying' their pather an' aves, or cursin' th' hotels iv Rome because they can't get with-
ered bran f'r breakfast, or tellin' a Cardinal how much St. Peter's is like th' new co-
orthouse at Wanskaloosa. I'd like to say: "These boys that ye see hoppin' around the
th' thrack ar-re th' rile riprisintive Americans. They are our ambassadures, no th' la-
ads ye see makin' a ginuflixion befure th' king." An' th' foreigners wud look thim over
an' say: "What's th' use iv makin war again such a tur'ible people?"[91]

Mr. Dooley had certainly earned his citizenship in the sporting republic. He
and much of the nation believed that the strenuous life had shored up their
institutions, promoted democracy and republican political culture, preserved
the cherished ideals of individual competition and achievement, and increased
their nation's prestige in the eyes of the world. Who indeed would want to make
war against the Olympic champions? Had they not heeded Roosevelt's warnings and made themselves into the globe's strongest and boldest people? The
image of the athlete, directing physical and mental energies in efficient combination toward a clearly defined goal, merged perfectly with progressive visions of an efficient nation channeling the dynamic powers of industrialism,
economic growth, modern science, and the volatile democratic system. Athlete
and nation became one. American civilization pulsated with a new vigor.

Surveying the world from an American perspective in 1912, it seemed as if
athletic technology was indeed helping to create a new national culture. The
intellectual attack on the optimistic faith in a rational, progressive universe—
which would greatly alter Western life after the first decade of the twentieth
century—had not yet gathered steam.[92] Civilization appeared to be evolving
in a uniform direction. Sport furthered the process of cultural assimilation,
binding the nation together in an important set of assumptions about political culture. Athletic technology adapted Americans to the rigors of modern
existence.

Olympic experience confirmed the basic assumptions that Americans held
about the power of sport. "Of course," wrote American athletic leader James
E. Sullivan of the Olympic expeditions, "the Americans went on a mission. This
mission was to create a good feeling; to show the type of man this great country of ours produces; to bring to them the type of sportsman that comes from
this glorious nation of ours, and to show the world that we play the game fairly."[93] The sporting republic's true believers thought that athletics provided a
lever to move the world in American directions.

Elwood S. Brown, a YMCA leader in the Philippines, reported in 1913 that
the Far Eastern Olympic Association was making great strides in converting the
Asian world to the American way of life. Brown considered the Far Eastern
Olympic Association to be an adjunct to the international Olympic movement

and took pains to explain that his organization was not usurping the IOC's power. In fact, two American members of the IOC, William Milligan Sloane and Evert J. Wendell, had endorsed the Far Eastern Olympic Association and offered suggestions for its organization. The baron de Coubertin also approved of the Asian Olympic movement. Brown promised that when the athletic spirit had been developed beyond a rudimentary level in Asia, the Far Eastern Olympic Association would act as the IOC's agent in that region.

The first Far Eastern Olympic Games were held in Manila in February 1913. China and Japan sent athletes to compete with the Philippines. Brown happily reported that the Americanized Filipinos trounced their Asiatic rivals. The results inspired Frank L. Crone, the acting director of education in the Philippines, to declare that "when the history of the modern Orient comes to be written, but few events will be found of deeper significance than the Far Eastern games." He insisted that "nothing previous to this meeting has shown so clearly the departure of Oriental nations from the old conservative standards."[94]

Forging an "Invincible Compound"

The makers of popular culture depicted American athletics remaking the world. That was not surprising. After all, many Americans thought that the strenuous life had remade the United States. In an interview with the *New York Times,* Colonel Robert M. Thompson, the president of the AOC, explained how athletics was revitalizing the nation. Thompson had been converted to sporting republicanism during his years at the U.S. Naval Academy and had played an active role in the movement to build playgrounds and provide athletic leagues for New York City's youth. "I had begun to see things in America which were discouraging," remembered Thompson, "and when I found there was a movement under way to encourage sports in New York's schools I joined it very gladly." The contacts Thompson made in the playground movement led to his involvement in the Olympic enterprise. In 1912, besides serving as the president of the AOC, he donated $13,500 to help send the Olympians to Stockholm.[95]

Thompson recited the familiar litany about the team being recruited from every American social class, ethnic group, and geographical region. Considering the representative character of the American athletes, theorized Thompson, "I feel that we may use them as a fair criterion in speculation as to what sort of a race we now are building in America." The colonel claimed that through his Olympic experience, "I have now become enthusiastic in the strong conviction that out of the mixed blood of this country has arisen a compound which is invincible, or may be made invincible." Thompson offered several proofs to support his conversion to a panethnic cosmopolitanism. He posited that a list of American competitors would indicate that their veins flowed with "the Americanized blood of most of those races against which we competed—English, Scotch, Irish, Welch [*sic*], French, German, Spanish, Italian, Austrian, Bohemian, Swedes, Finlanders, Danes, Jews, Persians, Indians, and Sandwich Islanders." It awed Thompson that "these men, meeting the men of their own race, won against them, through that something which is added to their original blood by their Americanism."

What was that "something"? Thompson's commitment to the ideology of the sporting republic provided his answer. "Americanism" had produced an "invincible compound" that energized U.S. Olympians. "This team was thoroughly democratic, representative of all sorts and conditions of men—except bad men," he asserted. "Race prejudice" might have become an issue, since a "colored boy" made the Olympic squad, "but on that team neither color of the skin nor texture of the clothing counted," declared the colonel. "The question was: 'What can he do?' Any man who made good was good." Rarely had a clearer sketch of the sporting republic's creed been rendered.[96]

Thompson presented his readers with an idealized picture of class and race relations that differed considerably from the social realities. Class and economic status often limited opportunities to pursue athletic and recreational activities. In the late nineteenth century a bicycle cost about one-third of a worker's *annual* salary. In 1912 only about one out of every twenty Americans attended colleges or universities. Chances at becoming a collegiate sporting star were exceedingly rare for most Americans. They were even rarer for African Americans and Native Americans. Jim Thorpe and a few other Native Americans played in the major leagues, but African Americans had been segregated into "Negro leagues" in professional baseball. Jim Crow policies would have prevented Howard Drew from running in AAU track meets in the South. If the AOC had held an Olympic qualifying meet in the South, he could not have participated.

Irish, Jewish, Italian, eastern European, and other immigrant athletes were not always welcome on American playing fields. Discrimination based on class, race, and ethnicity remained a pervasive fact of American life. Class and ethnic tensions plagued society. Even Thompson's idealized picture touting the "invincible compound" forged in the melting pot manifested those tensions.

Thompson carefully dispensed with the notion that the American contingent was composed solely of recent immigrants. "The team, in general, was of foreign blood, Americanized," he wrote. The colonel stressed that the most of the Olympians were second- or third-generation Americans, although he admitted that his study had not been thorough enough to indicate whether the second or third generation predominated. He left that question for the sociologists. He offered those insights to support his contention that immigration was still enriching the United States and that assimilation was proceeding effectively. He knew that "in the future of our immigration . . . we are surely face to face with a serious problem, but the team has made me an optimist." Thompson worried that "many of us have thought the Nation, as a whole, was approaching that point at which assimilation must cease." He noted that statistical analyses indicated that "after the elimination of the negro vote only about 43 per cent of the men who cast their ballots in this country have been born in the United States of parents born here." Those figures, he admitted, inspired a great deal of "pessimism" in much of the nation.

The colonel confessed that in the past the only thing that kept him from embarking on the "road to pessimism" was the knowledge that the academies at West Point and Annapolis were turning increasingly "foreign" classes into "gallant young Americans, not foreigners veneered": "I had believed this to be due to the fine machinery of the institutions, but our Olympian team convinced me that this is not the case. . . . The team . . . was made up of Americans, not foreigners veneered," he added. American institutions in general, not just the special environments of West Point and Annapolis, produced "men to be proud of, young men who, to use an old-time Western phrase, 'would certainly be good to tie to,'" he declared. "Plainly the team showed that we have not as yet crossed the danger line in immigration. We are still assimilating those whom we receive. As long as we continue to do that there is no peril."

Thompson counseled the nation to hold off on preparations for the next Olympics. "To select and especially train men now would be to prepare a set of gladiators who would not be truly representative," he warned; "If our interest in athletics broadens there will be found no difficulty in getting together for the games at Berlin a team which will surpass the splendid record which we made at Stockholm." "If our interest weakens, there would be no virtue, there would be no honor in hiring gladiators for the fight," he added. Thompson was not worried about athletic interest weakening, however. He saw the athletic spirit intensifying in American life, thanks in no small part to the Olympic team. "The development of athletic sports will increase our National efficiency, and this Nation sadly needs exactly that," he declared.

Thompson adhered to the canon of sporting republicanism. He believed that athletic technology controlled energy and fostered civilized progress. "The athlete utilizes all the powers of his body, and by so doing trains his mind and keeps his morals clean, thereby approaching the ideal of the old Greeks—a sound mind in a sound body. That comes as near to perfection as humanity can well approach," preached the AOC president.

The new Athenians, those vigorous Americans of all classes and races, served national interests as beacons to the world. Thompson urged the nation to follow the Olympians down the path that they had illuminated. The "perseverance, self-denial, and discipline" that the Olympians voluntarily submitted themselves to encouraged Thompson's athletic faith. He called for more playgrounds, more sports programs in the public schools, and a greater commitment to the strenuous life. Athletic technology would allow American civilization to meet any challenge the modern world had to offer. In 1912 such a creed seemed pragmatic. In a few short years it would seem naïve.[97]

American athletic technology, which incorporated the "spirit of athletics" and the "practical form of training," as Sullivan put it, had conquered the athletic universe in 1912.[98] The AOC continued to work at creating a more effective organizational system to further American conceptions of the "Olympic Idea."[99] The Thorpe scandal appeared to be only a momentary setback to the goal of Americanizing Olympic athletics. With Europe's athletes again vanquished, Americans looked forward to "a still greater triumph at Berlin in 1916."[100]

Two years after the 1912 games, on the eve of Armageddon, Mack Whelan predicted that the Olympics would lead Prussian military minds to substitute football for war.[101] Would American-engineered moral equivalents for war lead the globe toward a new era in the history of civilizations? "As for Stockholm," remembered Will Irwin decades later, "that Olympiad seemed to me afterward like the funeral games of an epoch—perhaps on the whole the happiest one humanity ever knew."[102]

★ 8

The Idea of a Sporting Republic: Athletic Technology, American Political Culture, and Progressive Visions of Civilization

American thinkers used the Olympic Games to promote the idea that sport represented one of the most important institutions in the modernizing United States. According to commentators as different as "Mr. Dooley" and Theodore Roosevelt, Olympic victories signaled the superiority of American society over other social arrangements. Olympians stood as the "real representative Americans." Sport unified the nation. "America's athletic missionaries" served as witnesses for the republic. They also promised that through engagement in sport the republic could surmount the challenges presented by the modern world.

Olympic stories had become powerful tools for making the nation's political culture. The behavior of American athletes and Olympic officials, reporters and Olympic critics, politicians and the crowds who greeted the returns of American Olympic teams, and public moralists and progressive intellectuals who celebrated American Olympic achievements indicates the existence of an influential constellation of ideas about sport and politics in turn-of-the-century American culture.

The Olympics provided an influential symbolic vocabulary for American dialogues about sport and politics. American intellectuals and much of the public invested Olympic sport with powerful political meanings. When *Current Literature,* anticipating American Olympic victories at Stockholm in 1912, counseled its readers to turn away for a moment from the presidential campaigns of William Howard Taft, Theodore Roosevelt, and Woodrow Wilson, it was not advocating that citizens ignore politics in favor of sport. Instead, *Current Literature* wanted Americans to refrain for a short time from the partisan strife of the presidential race and take advantage of the community-building political possibilities of Olympic sport.[1] Indeed, Taft, Roosevelt, and Wilson each took advantage of the opportunity and cabled their congratulations to the returning Olympians.[2]

The idea of a sporting republic celebrated those community-building possibilities by linking athletic practices to the continued vitality of the republican experiment. By the first two decades of the twentieth century, many American thinkers were touting sport as a reliable compass for charting routes toward the creation of a progressive civilization. Some intellectuals even declared sport to be the most reliable direction finder for leading their nation in progressive directions.

Sport played a powerful role in shaping public perceptions of the world. In the later twentieth century, insightful observers have revealed the power of sport in the social organization of particular segments of American communities. Rick Telander's *Heaven Is a Playground* locates basketball at the center of underclass African American male cultures in New York City.[3] H. G. Bissinger's *Friday Night Lights* explains that life in small Texas cities and towns revolves around the public drama generated by high school football.[4] Sport played the central role in organizing the worldviews of those communities.

Early twentieth-century sporting republicans made even grander claims. They wanted sport to serve as a basic cultural organizing principle for an entire nation. Did ideas about sport have any real impact on American politics or society? In fact, they did. Sport had a tremendous influence on American culture. The public images of Theodore Roosevelt, William Howard Taft, and Woodrow Wilson indicated the extent to which sport had become a force shaping American political culture.

The Strenuous Life and New Images of the Presidency

Among American politicians, Theodore Roosevelt most clearly understood that sport represented a new common language. He spoke the language fluently. "I preach to you, then, my countrymen," thundered Roosevelt, "that our country calls not for the life of ease but for the life of strenuous endeavor. The twentieth century looms before us big with the fate of many nations." Roosevelt warned that "if we stand idly by, if we seek merely swollen, slothful ease where men must win at hazard of their lives and at risk of all they hold dear, then the bolder and stronger peoples will pass us by, and will win for themselves the domination of the world."[5]

By fusing sport and politics Roosevelt capitalized on the contemporary American convictions of an intimate link between public virtue and sport. Roosevelt frequently organized his political ideas around the imagery of sport. He also presented himself as a gigantic symbol of the sporting republic. His transformation from sickly childhood to strapping manhood through a devotion to the strenuous life became the stuff of American legend. Following that

Rooseveltian tradition, so many American athletes, from the mythological Charles Atlas to the real Glenn Cunningham, were celebrated for overcoming their physical disabilities that *Time* magazine once remarked with apparent sincerity that "one of the commonest forms of preparation for a career as a champion athlete is a sickly childhood."[6]

By the time he became president in 1901, Roosevelt had become the archetype of the fusion of American athletic culture and political culture. A *New York Times* reporter once remarked, "ANDREW JACKSON could shoot as well and ride as well as Mr. ROOSEVELT but we doubt if he could have safely faced him with a tennis net between them." Tennis, when Roosevelt played, was not for "mollycoddles" or "swooning damsels." The reporter elevated Roosevelt to the pinnacle of the list of vigorous presidents in American history.[7] Olympic supporter, consummate woodsman, big game hunter, amateur pugilist, frontier cowboy, football lover, and all-around athletic champion, the "human dynamo" personified the American sporting republican. His athletic doctrine informed his understanding of the world. Sporting metaphors peppered his political sermons from the "bully pulpit." His success in public life stemmed in large part from his ability to merge political and popular culture through athletic imagery. In a society that demanded sports pages from high-brow as well as "yellow" newspapers, Theodore Roosevelt's messages found friendly receptions.

In one cogent anecdote the *Ladies Home Journal* captured the citizen-making, community-building, culture-shaping essence of Roosevelt's mainstream sporting ideology. The popular magazine related a tale of a lad "divided between the love of books and love of sports" who got a chance to meet President Roosevelt. The president, in spite of the fact that he had urgent business with his cabinet, took the time to ask the boy to identify his favorite sport. When the boy replied that he preferred baseball, the president lamented that he himself had never been proficient in that game owing to his miserable eyesight. "What an awful pity, Mr. President," replied the lad, while a roomful of anxious power brokers restlessly waited for the pleasantries to end so that the business of the nation could be taken up. The president smiled and revealed that although baseball was not his forte, when "it comes to riding or shooting or tennis, I can hold my own, I think; and do you know jiu-jitsu?" The boy related that he did indeed. In the midst of a meeting of the nation's leadership elite, the president and the American youth shared their knowledge of the finer points of that strenuous activity.

A few months later the lad undertook, at considerable risk to himself, a mission to save a valuable government launch befouled by its own anchor. Emerging with a few bumps and bruises, he was confronted by his mother. " 'Why did you do it?' his horrified mother asked. 'What did I learn to dive for?' he asked.

'The President made me feel, when I saw him, that sports were intended to make men.'" The *Ladies Home Journal* averred that "the President's ideas of sports were fitly expressed in these words of the boy."[8]

The claim that sport could make men into productive citizens stood as an almost unchallenged truism. A significant number of athletic boosters insisted that sport also could make women into productive citizens—although that assumption was assailed more frequently and fervently than were similar assumptions about sport for men.[9] The idea that sport also could make possible a progressive national culture grew increasingly popular in the first decades of the twentieth century.

When he called Americans to join him in the strenuous life, Roosevelt united sport and nationalism into a potent combination. In late nineteenth- and early twentieth-century American politics, Theodore Roosevelt captured the coveted role of captaining the national team. If sport builds character, why would the nation look to soft leaders? Roosevelt stood as proof of that political reality. Roosevelt, although from an elite background himself, became the quintessential leader in both the political and cultural realms of the middle-class rise to power.

After Roosevelt's election in 1904 to the presidency, Caspar Whitney blustered to *Outing*'s readers that Roosevelt had won the presidency not because Republicans elected him but because "the clean-blooded, wholesome-minded, right-intended people of the country . . . sought the man rather than the elevation of the party." *Outing*, the foremost chronicle of the strenuous life in the United States, commended the nation for choosing a chief executive who was "honest, and courageous, and virile" and committed to the visions of fair play that filled its pages.[10]

Symbols of the power of sport in shaping political images and attitudes came from unlikely as well as likely sources. With the election of 1908 looming and the dynamic Roosevelt forsworn to abdicate his office, voters found in the person of 350-pound William Howard Taft an unlikely new figurehead for the sporting republic.

Taft managed a public persona that combined several critical political themes into a winning combination. William Allen White's campaign tract portrayed Taft as the archetype of the new middle class. Well off but not wealthy and a respected professional in the legal field, he became in White's rendition of his public career the typical American antiaristocrat. "The independence of America is in that class," surmised White, "for the man who does not need a valet is not much awed by a king." White also revealed that Taft was an important transitional figure between the old middle class and the new: "If Taft should be made President of this Republic he would never cease to be in the heart of him a strap-hanger, a commuter, not of the city, with its crass wealth and biting poverty, nor of the country—but a suburban president, the first of his type." White thought that Taft's suburban devotion to the strenuous life was the key to his appeal. Taft represented the "new type of American from the suburban community, who as a boy knew both swimminghole and pavement, who roamed the woods and fought the north-end gang, who was afraid of neither cows nor cars—that is a new type of man in American politics—a type that must become more and more prevalent as the country grows less and less rural and more and more urban."[11]

Taft became in White's hands "a hewer of wood," a sturdy and active replacement for Rooseveltian strenuosity. It was not only the Grand Old Party's vocal propagandist William Allen White who thought that Taft would make a good leader for the sporting republic. On the eve of the election, *Outing* published a major essay implicitly endorsing Taft as Roosevelt's successor. Entitled "Taft at Yale," Ralph D. Paine's article glorified the presidential candidate's character-building experiences at New Haven. "The Taft who ruled the Philippines, who made Cuba put her house in order, who said the right word at Panama, who was placed at the head of the War Department, who twice refused a seat on the bench of the Supreme Court of the United States, owes somewhat of his genius for doing the day's work with clear-sighted fairness to all men to the old Yale Fence and the democracy it inspired in all who lingered there," believed Paine.

The Yale Fence, a campus landmark held sacred by students, symbolized the spirit of the playing field rather than the classroom at the ancient—by American standards—college. Paine recalled that the portly candidate had entered Yale as a strapping 225-pound freshman and immediately earned the moniker "Solid Bill Taft." His cohort at Yale included football popularizer Walter Camp, future AOC treasurer Julian W. Curtiss, and the legendary rower Robert Cook. Although collegiate sport, as it was known in 1908, did not really exist at the Yale of the late 1870s, in Paine's account Taft nevertheless excelled in the vigorous activities that enriched student life: the freshman "rush" against the sophomore class, the ritualized wrestling matches, and all the horseplay around the fence.

Paine reveled in a tale from the days just after the young Taft had graduated from Yale. A Cincinnati newspaper reporter named Lester A. Rose had sullied the reputation of Taft's father, Judge Alphonso Taft, in a "sensation sheet." The *Cincinnati Commercial* for April 20, 1879, reported that Will Taft—"a tall, powerful, athletic young man"—and his brother Charles searched for Rose in downtown Cincinnati. Rose, a notorious "bruiser," had a reputation for "considerable physical courage and great endurance," related the *Commercial.* Taft and his brother, who came along to keep bystanders from intervening, quickly found Rose. When the "scandal-monger" answered to his name, the future president of the United States responded, "'You're my man,' and a blow in the face revealed to Mr. Rose the object of the call. Mr. Taft followed up the attack vigorously," reported the *Commercial,* adding that "the rules of the ring were not observed." A bystander finally got past Charles and stopped William's assault, "because the head of the under man [Rose] was being used as a hammer on the pavement." Paine and *Outing* felt that "Solid Bill" Taft, grown far beyond his freshman weight, would be an excellent replacement for Theodore Roosevelt.

An advertisement touting the vigor of William Jennings Bryan, Taft's opponent in the election of 1908, was conspicuous by its absence from the pages of *Outing.* The press never painted Bryan in athletic terms. A different energy crackled through the "great commoner," the circuit-riding revivalist of American politics. He symbolized an America different from Solid Bill Taft's. His attacks on trusts and monopolies resonated not with language of sport but with the fire-and-brimstone colors of the pulpit and the gospel of the biblical tradition. In the eyes of many Americans, he and his constituency seemed to be an uncontrolled force that if unleashed from the White House would disrupt the fiber of American society. Opponents condemned Bryan as lacking the very qualities that they claimed Taft had gained at the Yale Fence. Taft and Roosevelt shared a commitment to the strenuous life. In Taft, counseled Paine, Americans had a political leader who had imbibed deeply in the gospel of fair play.[12]

It was in relation to the concept of fair play that the ideology of the sporting republic most clearly showed its relationship to the political doctrines of progressive republicanism. The progressives hoped, in their naïve fashion, that fair play would be transmitted from American playing fields to society at large. They mistook their historical and cultural values for universal ethical principles.[13] They believed that the spirit of playing by the rules would apply not simply to sporting contests but to the entire range of economic, social, and political processes that composed their historical environment.

Woodrow Wilson thought that sport could create a society committed to fair play. In a 1911 speech to the first National Conference on Civic and Social Center Development, a group committed to creating sites where progressive values could be inculcated through athletics, Wilson portrayed the progressive state as a team committed to common purpose. Liberty he saw in typically republican fashion as the adjustment of various interests into a community. Wilson asserted that the community would be organized not by the classical method of an invisible hand or a self-regulating natural principle but by a modern conception of team spirit. In Wilson's estimation progress flowed from the adjustment of civilization to the new rules of the game.[14]

The American fascination with the political manifestations of sport reflected the analogical reasoning that related regulation of the body with regulation
of the body politic, the rules and structures of the modern athletic contests with
the constitutionalism that underlay the American republican tradition. That the
Constitution enshrined the principle of rule by law and provided equity for all
citizens and factions stood as a fundamental truth in early twentieth-century
American political culture, in spite of Charles Beard's broadside into the myths
that shrouded the American democratic faith.[15] As a young professor at Wesleyan College in 1889, Woodrow Wilson helped to coach the football team to
its most successful season in history. Wesleyan defeated the University of Pennsylvania, Amherst, Williams, Rutgers, and Trinity. Only a loss to Princeton and
a tie against Lehigh marred Wilson's record.[16] As a political candidate, Wilson
described the Constitution as a set of rules for the game of politics. The former
football coach declared during his 1912 presidential candidacy that the purpose
of American law was to "see fair play."[17]

The idea of the national life as a game—or of games as representations of
life—marked one of the central organizing principles of American thought in
the late nineteenth and early twentieth centuries. From western novelist Owen
Wister's plea to "let the best man win" to sociologist Edward A. Ross's shorthand for the "scientific" understanding of social practice as "the rules of the
social game," American thinkers used the language of sport to describe the
workings of civil societies.[18] Analogies such as laws and rules, judges and referees, and justice and fair play indicated the structural levels at which sport and
politics were intertwined.

Woodrow Wilson was an especially deft weaver of athletic and political symbols. "America was created to break every kind of monopoly and to set men
free, upon a footing of equality, upon a footing of opportunity, to match their
brains and their energies," he argued while running for president in 1912. His
language translated the republican experiment into a sporting contest. "I know,
and every man in his heart knows, that the only way to enrich America is to
make it possible for any man who has the brains to get into the game," he insisted, transforming economic theory into sporting metaphor. "I am perfectly
willing that they should beat any competitor by fair means; but I know the foul
means they have adopted, and I know that they can be stopped by law," he asserted, transforming antitrust legislation into athletic jargon. He promised the
American electorate "all the fair competition you chose, but no unfair competition of any kind." "America stands for a free field and no favor" he shouted,
determined to wed his political fortunes to the gospel of fair play.[19]

The new corporate order forced Wilson to abandon the Jeffersonian world
of free individual competition for which he nostalgically longed during the

election of 1912 and to come to grips with the new bureaucratic innovations. He came to understand "regulated competition"—the guiding principle of the emerging consumer-based corporate economy—as "fair competition."

Wilson, Taft, and Roosevelt understood that the electorate spoke the common language of sport. They knew that the Olympics provided important opportunities for political discourses. They understood that the Olympic Games offered unique opportunities in the myriad of American dialogues about sport and social issues. No other athletic event focused attention on national issues in the way that the Olympics did. No other sporting spectacle created as many possibilities for national self-congratulation or self-criticism. The Olympic Games exposed to public debate the assumptions that animated the idea of a sporting republic. That was why Wilson, Taft, and Roosevelt served as honorary AOC presidents and cabled their congratulations to American Olympic victors. That was why they used sport to communicate political messages. Wilson, Taft, and Roosevelt, each in his own way, linked sport to progressive political agendas.

Sport and Progressivism

Progressivism represented the sometimes contradictory effort to transform eighteenth- and nineteenth-century republicanism into an intellectual force that addressed modern realities. Inheriting the language and concepts of the republican tradition, progressive thinkers shifted their focus. Progressives constructed new stories out of the old scripts of classical republicanism. They paid homage to the republican ideals of public virtue and social consensus. Confronted with powerful new economic and social realities, they sublimated classical republicanism's concern with stringent restrictions on governmental power and elaborated new ideas about using the state to build a moral civilization.[20] They encouraged the belief that the government was no longer the old liberal threat to liberty but instead the instrument of the people, to be used to promote virtue and consensus. They wanted to make a national culture that matched their stories about the nature of sociopolitical reality. Many of them thought that sport could serve their political goals.

What political agendas undergirded the crusades to build parks and start athletic leagues? Did organized play increase liberty or bolster order? The liberty-order dialectic, which historians of Progressivism have translated as a conflict between desires for social justice and desires for social control, served as the starting point for republican philosophy. Since athletic technology had been designed to conserve human resources and control modern energies, sport found a place in nearly all the political programs advanced to further both social justice and social control. For reformers who thought of themselves as progressives, the distinction between justice and control was often far from clear. Athletic ideas found homes in every wing of Progressivism, from the social gospel and humanitarian crusades to the coercive programs of nativists, technocrats, and elitists.

Many intellectuals incorporated sport into social control programs. Sociologist Edward Ross illustrated the appeal of sport to thinkers concerned with regulation. Ross's influential *Social Control* sought to unravel the secrets of orderly human interaction. Ross thought that the voluntary devotion to common purpose produced by sport could replace the authoritarian patterns of social force that controlled society in premodern times.[21] University of Nebraska sociologist George Edward Howard used Ross's theory of sport as a positive instrument for social control to write glowing accounts of athletic technology as a regulatory device. Howard predicted that sport would serve the interests of progressive "social education" by controlling undesirable tendencies and producing a unified society.[22]

The most ardent American social controllers endorsed the regulatory features of the sporting life. Psychologist and philosopher G. Stanley Hall's recapitulation theory of human development required the active management of adolescent energy to prevent social anarchy.[23] Indeed, the words of the *Ladies' Home Journal*'s boy who had met President Roosevelt—that sport "was intended to make men"—took on a prophetic ring from the perspective of Hall and his influential disciples. His students played central roles in creating modern American ideas about sport. One of Hall's followers, Henry S. Curtis, laid out detailed plans for urban recreation centers housed in neighborhood schools. Curtis wanted to cluster several progressive "utilities" (libraries, baths, gymnasiums, "people's theatres," playgrounds, public gardens, and small parks) in and around the school-based recreation centers to control and direct human energy.[24] Such a plan would serve, according to Edward Mero, as "an insurance policy of good citizenship."[25]

The ideas that animated the sporting republic did not belong solely to the social controllers. Progressives who sought to liberate rather than control also thought that sport could help their campaigns. The editors of *The Crisis* thought that sport could help to liberate African Americans from the shackles of racism and segregation. Prominent reformers who identified themselves with various social justice crusades borrowed ideas and programs from the sporting republic's storehouse. W. D. P. Bliss, the Christian socialist editor of *The Encyclopedia of Social Reform,* devoted significant attention to athletic technology. Jane Addams's progressive proposals regularly included athletic elements. Her allies in the settlement house crusade—Lillian Wald, Frances Kellor, Florence

Kelley, Jacob Riis, former New York City mayor and philanthropist Abram S. Hewitt, and others—included sport in their reform packages. Riis wrote glowing accounts of sport as a liberating force. "We wrote into our national life a new bill of rights, the right of the children, of the tomorrow of the republic, to life, liberty and the pursuit of happiness," trumpeted Riis. He declared that the chance to participate in sports marked the surest path for urban youth to pursue happiness, learn the blessings of liberty and enjoy abundant life.[26]

Sport found supporters in other progressive quarters. Many academic and intellectual leaders promoted the sporting republic. Philosophers found many uses for sport. William James insisted that the practice of a strenuous life would encourage a pragmatic temper, that athletics could foster a strenuous life of the mind.[27] James's friend and philosophical foe Josiah Royce used athletic metaphors to explain the complexity of human motivation and the relation of fair play to idealism.[28] James's teammate in the revolt against philosophical formalism, John Dewey, appropriated organized athletics into his blueprint for creative democracy.[29]

Sport permeated intellectual venues beyond the provinces of professional philosophy. Indeed, many self-proclaimed social scientists considered the problems of leisure and strenuosity in modern society. Practitioners of the "new economics"—the stream of the dismal science fostered by the American Economic Association that demanded intelligent regulation of socioeconomic processes—were particularly enamored of the sporting republic's reform potential. Two of the founders of the new economics, Richard T. Ely and Simon Patten, conceived of athletic technology as a component of both regulatory policy and national vitality.[30] As Ely put it, "competition, suitably regulated, gives us a brave strong race of men."[31]

Athletic technology meshed easily with progressive methodology. Progressives roamed the distended social fabric of modern culture investigating problems and collecting reams of data. They interpreted their findings through the lenses of the new social sciences and offered solutions through campaigns of public education and moral persuasion. The campaigns to promote sport followed the same format. An emerging science of sport generated a legion of "facts" that pointed to athletic solutions for social ruptures.

The mass and elite media faithfully reported the findings of sporting reformers. American newspapers contributed heavily to the public dialogue. They showered athletic versions of Progressivism with accolades. The *Louisville Courier-Journal* declared "a foot of playground . . . worth an acre of penal institutions." The *Cincinnati Times-Star* opined that of all the urban reform plans offered by progressives, "not one is more deserving of popular support" than was the effort to remake American cities with athletic technology. A Jacksonville, Florida, reporter warned that "if the city in its progressiveness thinks that an expenditure of money for play is a luxury, we will have a sad awakening when the boy of Jacksonville becomes a voter." The *Kansas City Star* held that "there is no truer democracy than that of fair play in games where only skill, which all have a chance to acquire, counts." Newspaper editors throughout the United States regularly supported the acquisition and maintenance of recreation spaces, the supervision of athletic leagues, and the encouragement of the strenuous life.[32]

Progressives generally started their political forays through voluntary organizations and then lobbied for local, state, and national governments to make their programs permanent public policies. Richard Henry Edwards's *Popular Amusements* offered athletic progressives a blueprint for restructuring American leisure to conform to the ideals of the sporting republic. Edwards's work provided progressives with scientific arguments. Edwards created listings of organizations that could serve reformers as mentors and allies. He developed a moral theology of play to build "constructive public opinion." He also outlined a program of legislative regulation designed to enforce "restrictive public opinion." Edwards ended his compendium with a demand that governments create public recreation departments.[33]

Progressives typically identified problems that they perceived as threatening the foundations of the republic. A characteristic example occurred when a group of New York City progressives led by Luther Gulick, Frederic Howe, Henry Moskowitz, Belle Israels, and John Collier warned that Manhattan was imperiled by the fact that only 5 percent of the population enjoyed "wholesome recreation."[34] Using the press to illuminate the perils of that social evil, the reformers assumed that public opinion would quickly force solutions. They rallied various groups to the cause, including business interests. Indeed, New York real estate magnate William Harmon told his colleagues that parks, playgrounds, and athletic leagues provided "one of those rare cases where philanthropy is good business."[35]

By sharing the same languages and political scripts, the champions of Progressivism and the sporting republic's ideologues made common cause. Beulah Kennard's *Survey* essay on Pittsburgh's public recreation program stood as a masterpiece of the progressive vision of an athletic republic. Kennard employed all the standard progressive tropes in her Pittsburgh tale. Consumed by the quest for material wealth, the population of Pittsburgh ignored the nobler aspects of civilization and fell into a grimy urban malaise. The city decayed while the children of immigrants, workers, the middle-class, and the elite drifted aimlessly. In Pittsburgh's most defiled neighborhood, an infamous section of the city known as the "Hill District," Kennard claimed, "Children literally did not know how to play." She testified that the organization of athletic leagues and sports programs had saved the city.

If sport could save Pittsburgh, could it save the rest of the republic? Athletic technology was designed to attack many of the urban evils identified by progressives, such as taming gangs, lowering crime, reducing child labor, assimilating immigrants, supporting public health, cleaning tenement districts, and training all classes in the duties of citizenship. "The recreation center is one of the great agencies in counteracting the forces which tend to disintegrate and desocialize our modern industrial cities," announced Kennard. She envisioned recreation centers as outposts of the sporting republic where the republican political culture so dear to the progressive mentality could be resurrected. Kennard argued that recreation centers would serve a modern nation as town meeting halls had served the republicans of "old New England," as the centers of community life.

She concluded her progressive account with an appeal to the middle-class public on which Progressivism depended, employing a strategy perfected by Jane Addams. Having shined a light on urban evils and suggested a panacea, she tossed some middle-class guilt into the mixture. "We have piled money upon money in our safety deposit vaults, but we have wasted our riches in a way that is even more stupid than it is cruel," she warned her comfortable readers. All progressive-minded people should join her in her crusade, she insisted: "The city must re-create the bond of fellowship that shall make the common human interests of the poor, the rich, the wage earners paramount to the competitive war which sets them in opposing and jealous camps." Thus "civic unity" depended on the application of athletic technology to social problems.[36]

The calls to revitalize the republic through sport fit the basic parameters of progressive crusades. Campaigns animated by moral persuasion needed identifiable enemies. The champions of the strenuous life conjured some powerful dragons for slaying. Athletic reformers argued that arrayed against the forces of progressive recreation were vast armies of amusement profiteers who spread "social disease." Experts depicted almost every "commercial" form of amusement as immoral, from vaudeville, burlesque, and motion pictures to race tracks, automobile races, and prizefighting matches. Pool rooms, dance halls, saloons, horse racing, and amusement parks wasted human energy. Progressives insisted that the nation had to provide positive recreation to conserve that precious commodity and rebuild a national sense of community. They struggled to awaken public opinion and lead a crusade for a republican athletic culture. They insisted that sport inoculated society against disease, crime, vice, intemperance, delinquency, and class conflict.[37]

Sporting republicans asserted that their versions of athletics would counter commercial or materialistic values. Such claims represented an omnipresent motif in many spectrums of progressive thought. "The Recreation Movement is one of the greatest hopes or opportunities we have to make sure that materialism does not overwhelm our civilization," argued Charles Weller.[38] Progressive scripts invariably re-created the classical republican distaste for the values of commerce, painting pejorative scenes of greedy people who devoted their lives to avaricious self-interest for contrast with their portraits of stalwart republicans whose frank appreciation of public spirit and social duty animated the good society. In such a context the progressive condemnations of the "commercial spirit" in sport fit into a larger cultural critique. From Coney Island to prizefighting to the liquor trust, progressive sporting republicans railed against any connection of "true" sport with pecuniary interests.

The sporting republic itself had become big business, however. Arthur Reeve calculated that by the second decade of the twentieth century, Americans had invested $105 million in creating a sporting infrastructure and were expending $73 million annually to keep the system running.[39] Indeed, many of the leading proponents of athletic technology as an agent of social reform owed their livelihoods and, in cases such as the corporate empire of A. G. Spalding, their fortunes to the commercial value of sport.[40]

Through the cultivation of friendships and professional ties with every institutional branch of the sporting republic, A. G. Spalding and Brothers became the official supplier of wholesome leisure equipment—a commerce in athletics that not even the most ardent opponents of commercialized amusement opposed. "Accept no substitute," read Spalding advertisements, for "the Spalding Trade-Mark guarantees quality." The Spalding brothers compared their trademark to the government guarantee of the "gold dollar," asserting that their corporate label had "become known throughout the world as a Guarantee of Quality as dependable in their field as the U.S. currency is in its field." Stealing a line from his friend and strenuous ally Theodore Roosevelt, A. G. Spalding proclaimed that his athletic inventory provided "a 'square deal' for everybody."[41]

Spalding manufactured and marketed every conceivable sporting device, from "official" Olympic discuses to "official sacks for sack races." The company played up its connection to Olympic events, publishing AOC reports on the Olympic Games and bragging that in St. Louis during the 1904 Olympics Louisiana Purchase Exposition, officials and Olympic athletes had made exclusive use of Spalding equipment in their successful quest for a new standard in setting world and Olympic records. Numerous advertisements mentioned that Spalding had won a "gold medal" for besting the efforts of the "world's makers of Athletic Goods" in St. Louis. Spalding added its 1904 award to its "Grand Prize" from the 1900 Universal Exposition and Olympic Games in Paris.

A. G. Spalding and Brothers engaged in an even more lucrative and significant business than designing and selling sporting goods. They profited directly from defining and shaping American ideas about sport. A legion of "official
guides" to sports flowed out of the Spalding-owned American Sport Publishing Company. Spalding's Athletic Library contained the works of a veritable
who's who of American athletic ideology. The authors of Spalding's guidebooks
included James Edward Sullivan, Walter Camp, and Dr. Luther Halsey Gulick,
as well as Olympic trainers and athletes Michael C. Murphy and Dr. George
Orton and a host of other athletic legends and sport scientists. Senda Beren-
son's pamphlet on women's basketball, Jessie H. Bancroft's pamphlet on "girls'
athletics," James Sullivan's *Schoolyard Athletics,* and his annual *Spalding's Official Athletic Almanac* sold copiously.[42]

Selling the sporting republic would in the long run radically alter the relationship between athletics and American culture. The commodification of sport
would eventually lead most American intellectuals and reformers to abandon
physical culture as an instrument of political and social change. Although it had
its roots in the era marked by the invention of the sporting republic, the triumph of sport as commercialized spectacle would have to wait until the 1920s.[43]

Sporting Republicanism's Parameters

By the first two decades of the twentieth century, the ideology and institutions
of the sporting republic were exerting tremendous influence on American
political culture. Progressives of every stripe borrowed athletic technology for
their reform schemes. Athletic scientists touted the political ramifications of
their theories. Athletic concepts invaded public dialogues on every aspect of
national life. The strenuous life served as both motive and metaphor for a powerful and popular vision of civilization. Athletic technology adjusted frames of
reference to the new realities of corporate capitalism and helped to give currency to the concept of government regulation of the economy by linking political activism to the gospel of fair play and by explaining social and economic
theories through athletic rhetoric. Ideas about sport shaped political dialogues
and expectations, reinvigorated the idea of public virtue, and placed sport in a
central position in modern American culture.

A wide variety of athletic activities and contests sparked the discussions about
sport between intellectual and mass cultures. Football, track and field, baseball,
basketball, playground games, gymnastics, bicycling, walking for fitness, golf,
tennis, and a host of other sports provided stories and experiences. Outdoor
activities from hunting, fishing, horseback riding, canoeing, and sailing to the
fascination among urbanites with wilderness camping and hiking added dif-

ferent dimensions to the dialogue. Campaigns to build playgrounds, parks, and gymnasiums provoked conversations about the benefits of athletics. Crusades to organize athletic leagues, recreational activities, and physical education encouraged the debates about sport. Athletic notions found homes in American schools and colleges, urban settings, rural areas, clubs, amateur associations, and professional leagues, with each of those venues helping to create the idea of a sporting republic. The ideas that underlay the sporting republic received their most explicit exposition in American conversations about the Olympic Games. Olympic performances provided the richest environments for showcasing American attitudes about sport and politics. The Olympics had become an important force in shaping the patterns of modern American culture.

In many ways American approaches to sport mirrored developments in another area where science and technology reoriented popular understandings of energy, particularly in the movement to conserve natural resources.[44] Many American thinkers clearly understood sport as a social technology, an organization of human energy designed for specific ends—a problem-solving design. Like military science, the conservation movement, mass education, and other public technologies, sport enjoyed tremendous popularity in progressive thought. Indeed, sport gained a unique legitimacy through its transmutation into a technology. It could then serve, as so many American thinkers have always hoped technics would, as a technological solution to the problems that were nearly universally defined as the consequences of technological progress: the sterile artificiality associated with modern industrial society, the social and moral decline of the republic, urban alienation, and all the rest of the clichéd litany of modern problems. Sport had come to play a central role in American discussions about the nature and meaning of their civilization. From conversations in saloons and barbershops to debates in the mass media to the scholarly musings of philosophers, sport fascinated American thinkers.

The Moral Equivalent of War

In 1910 the American philosopher and pragmatic muse of progressive thought William James published an influential essay entitled "The Moral Equivalent of War." James's treatise provided American culture with a historical and evolutionary framework for political understandings of sport. James began his argument by defining the energy produced by the strenuosity of mortal combat as "the gory nurse that trained societies to cohesiveness." War repelled James, yet he assigned it an indispensable role in the evolution of civilization. War represents the essential form of the state, the most important technique for organizing human energy. War creates the moral bonds necessary for the progressive growth of culture. But war, and the constant preparation for armed conflict required by modern conditions, threatened to destroy civilization. How could modern people rationally escape that paradox?

James rejected the sterile technocratic solutions offered by utopian "molly-coddles" or "swooning damsels" who would remove all aggression and strife, and hence all energy, from human societies. "Fie on such a cattleyard of a plan-et," cursed James, dismissing schemes for the domestication of human nature. Instead he counseled a quest for moral equivalents of war, human-inspired technologies "analogous, as one might say, to the mechanical equivalent of heat," to power the United States and the world toward new vistas. "We must make new energies and hardihoods continue the manliness to which the military mind so faithfully clings," commanded James. Only when animated by the spark of the strenuous life, he declared, could human progress continue: "It is only a question of blowing on the spark till the whole population gets incandescent, and on the ruins of the old morals of military honor, a stable system of morals and civic honor builds itself up."[45]

James's essay marked one of the more erudite contributions to what the his-torian Donald Mrozek has defined as fin de siècle "strategies of regeneration." Mrozek has argued forcefully that late nineteenth- and early twentieth-centu-ry Americans used organized sport as a strategy of regeneration. Mrozek rec-ognized that sport played powerful roles in efforts at political and social regen-eration while focusing mainly on theories that connected athletics to personal renewal.[46]

Certainly James's "Moral Equivalent of War" argued for individual regener-ation, but James did not draw his imagery solely from the storehouse of "self-reliant" motifs. James's aesthetic and ethical concern stressed civic over indi-vidual renewal. In fact, the symbols of the republican political tradition served as his main source of inspiration.[47] Warnings of decline and calls for regener-ation had characterized republicanism since its classical conception. In con-sciously constructing a republic as a challenge to the patterns of history (no republic, as the founders knew, had ever been more than a fleeting polity), American political elites placed the regeneration motif squarely, and probably permanently, at the center of American political culture.[48]

James lamented that from a historical perspective only war had served as consistent renewer of community discipline, "and until an equivalent discipline is organized, I believe that war must have its way."[49] During James's era a cho-rus of voices proclaimed that sport could provide that discipline and regener-ate a republic under siege from modernity. Loosely interpreting James's con-cept in an issue devoted to the athletic question, the editors of *The Atlantic Monthly* proclaimed that "athletics is the only systematic training for the sterner

life, the only organized 'moral equivalent of war.'. . . No other artificial discipline is so efficient, no vent so wholesome, for the turbulent energies of
youth."[50] These sentiments were widely shared by educators, social reformers,
and politicians who thought that the "artificial discipline"—the technology—
fostered by athletics directed human energy in progressive directions. The *Atlantic's* call also matched James's desire to find a better technique than war for
organizing social power.

Calls for moral equivalents of war filled the sporting press. James had meant
moral equivalent as *superior alternative.* He thought that sport renders the
source of war—the aggressiveness of human nature and the need to dominate—"moral" by regulating and tempering warlike energies.[51]

Other thinkers interpreted the concept of a moral equivalent of war in a different fashion. Although sport might lessen the chances for civil conflict and
control the warlike impulses of the masses, it also, to those who saw some wars
as necessary, could keep the martial flame kindled and prepare the nation for
what the global interventionists and jingoes insisted would be inevitable out-
breaks of hostilities. During the late nineteenth century the American armed
services adopted athletic programs to raise fitness levels, boost morale, and
nurture the "will to win."[52] Theodore Roosevelt interpreted the concept as indicating that sport and war provided equivalent experiences for shaping moral capacity.

A Sporting Republic

Although there was a consensus that sport served as a source of social energy
providing the nation with moral equivalents of war, there was less agreement
on how to direct that energy. Still, if sport is indeed the moral equivalent of
war, as William James, Theodore Roosevelt, and the growing army of athletic
promoters declared it to be, then a role for the positive state in directing those
energies seemed only logical.

A growing chorus of voices demanded that the government fund and extend
the sporting republic. Sport scientist Henry Curtis's *Education through Play*
endorsed a state-sponsored strenuous life at the municipal and national levels.[53] Sociologist George Howard wanted a federal bureau or department of
"popular recreations."[54] Ohio State University's advocate of feminine vigor,
Dorothy Bocker, declared that the government was the most "comprehensive"
American "directive agency" and charged the state with the responsibility for
inculcating athletic ideals.[55] Playground progressive Howard Braucher demanded that local governments plan comprehensive programs for public recreatioñ.[56]
The Reverend George McNutt argued that private philanthropic and religious

organizations such as the YMCA had done such a good job of "social redemption" through the strenuous life that the national government had been blinded to its true obligations. McNutt preached that "only the State" was wealthy enough to guarantee civic virtue through the gospel of play.[57]

Even *The Nation* believed that "under ordinary circumstances, a nation of athletes will easily overcome a nation of mollycoddles." *The Nation,* which normally detested the American fascination with sport as much as it disliked government intervention in the economy, cheered the Olympics for "cementing racial and national feeling."[58]

To further that effort, by 1912 American apostles of the strenuous life had spent nearly four decades filling the discourses of popular and elite cultures with the language of the sporting republic. They hammered out the idea that sport had a crucial place in the nation's well-being. It is no wonder, then, that by the early twentieth century American political culture began to add another layer to the language of sport. If sport could shore up the foundations of republicanism and produce public virtue, should not the structure of the republic itself conform to the ideals of the playing field? Should not a nation committed to sporting equivalents of war convert itself into not only a society of athletes but, indeed, an athletic society? Had not sport become synonymous with republican life?

Many American thinkers answered those questions affirmatively. Not only did they celebrate a civilization energized by the social practices of sport, but they began to conceive of their nation as a playing field. Politicians, pundits, and the public crafted an athletic political science that used analogies, images, and symbols from sport to explain political and social realities. Terms such as *race, game,* and *contest* stood for the realities of social life. Races, games, and contests, as every patron of athletics knew, needed rules. Rules produced fair play, the fundamental virtue of civic life. In the sporting republic fair play stood as the highest ideal. The republic, noted athletic thinkers, was founded on a set of rules, the Constitution.

Americans not only came to understand sport as an element of political action and an item on progressive platforms, but they increasingly began to perceive politics itself through athletic lenses. Having drawn a broad sketch of political life as a regulated contest, social critics warned their audiences about behavior that violated the canons of fair play and good sportsmanship. Depending on the analyst's perspective, the labels of *poor sport* or *slacker* could be attached to any person, group, or institution that seemed to threaten the nation. Robber baron or striker, selfish plutocrat or radical syndicalist, trust or union, urban machine or aristocratic elite—all earned the enmity of stewards who judged fair play. The analogic descriptions of American realities pushed deeper. Competition in any realm of life was seen to be a positive feature if designated as fair. Unfair competition of any sort brought condemnation.

Advocacy groups that championed sport depicted the democratic process as a fair game open to public scrutiny and governed by regulations and ethical behavior, an honest contest of ideas and opinions in which the public interest was invariably served. The public, comprising both rivals and teammates depending on the "game" being played, needed a political system that guaranteed fair play.

Public policy was described as good rules that encouraged an equitable contest. Initiative, referendum, and recall were portrayed as methods for giving the game back to the players. Progressive calls for various types of referees and regulation—experts, regulatory laws and agencies, and other equity mechanisms—were justified in the interest of fairness. Centralized economic planning was defended as a method for ensuring competitive fairness. Public service and social reform were touted as the epitome of team spirit.

Clean games require umpires. Progressive political philosophy touted positive government as the consummate umpire and rule maker. The dean of the "new economists," Richard Ely, summed things up. He announced that the state "acts as an umpire for fair play."[59] The neorepublican theory of the state required vigorous leadership. Activity, energy, close attention to the public's sense of fair play, and a commitment to structuring social life as an equitable race represented athletic virtues that also stood as the hallmarks of the ideal government. Such a perspective demanded vigorous leadership. American leaders needed to boost the team's morale. They had to stand up to the playground's bullies. They had to glorify fair play. They had to lead the nation to victory. American stories about the Olympic Games confirmed those concepts.

★ 9

The Decline of the Sporting Republic

In the late nineteenth and early twentieth centuries, American ideas about sport and republics became intertwined. In the estimates of both the intellectual classes and the public, the practice of sport had real political consequences. Sport was seen as a tool for social reform, a generator of community solidarity and an implement for reviving a republic imperiled by rapid modernization.

Sport became enmeshed in American political debates and in the struggles between socioeconomic classes, races, ethnic groups, and genders. Promoters of sport made claims about athletics' universal power to reinvigorate the republic. Sporting republicans insisted that sport could reconstitute popular representative government. They preached that sport could restore public virtue. They argued that sport could produce shared communal values. They believed that sport could increase the public good.

American sport, defined by a critical mass of thinkers as a moral equivalent for war, both reproduced existing social constructions and opened new terrain. Just as other technologies sometimes reproduced the status quo and other times dramatically changed social conditions, modern sport opened a variety of possibilities. Debates over the politics and the meanings of sport engaged an intellectual class that before World War I exercised considerable power in the United States. These intellectuals took sport seriously. They considered it to be a tool for social change. Then came the Great War. The war destroyed any chance that the Olympics would be held in Berlin in 1916. It also changed American understandings of sport. It gravely wounded the idea of a republic of sport.

Participation in World War I would quickly mute the growing belief within both popular and intellectual cultures that sport could serve as a moral equivalent for armed combat. Initially, when most Americans considered the war to be Europe's descent into lunacy, James's vision still held power. In 1914 Edward J. Ward pointed to the playgrounds, athletic fields, stadiums, and gymnasiums in which Americans enjoyed athletic competition as being bastions of reason and morality in a world in which national vitality had been turned away from progressive channels and toward the horrors of total war. "Out of the very soul of America these neighborhood buildings that belong to all of us have come," proclaimed Ward. "Like raised letters that even the blind can read, they stand out across this one unstricken land, declaring our common sincere will, our united devotion not to pride, nor force, nor selfishness, but to the deep and worthy ideals of humanity's true advance." Ward and many others believed that sport cemented a national feeling that opposed war.[1]

The ideal of using athletic endeavor to conserve human energy for peaceful uses, never fully accepted by the American intellectual class or the public in the first place, soon became a casualty of what Randolph Bourne called "a war made deliberately by the intellectuals."[2] Mustered into the "great crusade," athletic technology lost much of its previous meaning. Indeed, the easily made connection between sport and national power that even James endorsed undermined his vision of an equivalent discipline for war.

Sport, the Great War, and American Visions of a New World Order

Nationalism and war made a powerful martial combination. The gospel of fair play helped to shape American perceptions of the war. The English adroitly played on American prejudices and perceptions of sportsmanship to move American sentiment toward the Allied cause. French war correspondent Georges Lechartier captured the connection between sport and American entrance into the Great War in 1917: "Though this nation did enter the war in the service of a great ideal,—for the Yankees are incorrigible idealists,—another important motive, a controlling motive, was their love of sport." The French journalist recalled the way in which a San Francisco newspaperman had explained to him the pro-German sentiment in the United States. "When we see Germany, with all the world against her, holding her own and even driving back the Russians, we feel that she plays the game well and applaud her skill. If the man on the street is pro-German, it is because of his sporting instinct," Lechartier quoted the San Franciscan. "It was sporting sentiment, again, that made the American almost unanimous for war as soon as they saw Germany breaking the rules of the game with her submarines," Lechartier concluded.[3]

Athletic references often found their way into American commentaries on the war. *The Outlook* asserted that "the English are more dogged fighters than are the Germans because of British devotion to outdoor sports." The American weekly reported that British and American officers were encouraging athletics in the interests of "military efficiency."[4] In another wartime issue of *The Outlook,* the editors declared that "the same qualities that lead a man to ride at a high fence, to dive from full speed in a tackle, or to swap blows in a roped ring, are among the qualities which fit him for high deeds when he is called to charge across that greater gridiron, called 'No Man's Land,' which lies between the smoking trenches of Teutonic and Allied armies." Given the American devotion to the strenuous life, the editors predicted great success for the United States when it entered the war. "The young men of America, who lead all of the young men of the world in point of all-round distinction in athletics, can be counted on as a valuable asset to their country in time of war, and the zeal and spirit which they have shown in athletics will make a success of universal military training in this country when it comes," insisted *The Outlook.*[5] William James—who died in 1910, the year his "Moral Equivalent for War" was published—would have been disheartened.

American sporting ideology, which colored American views of the war, also tinged their perspectives of the peace. President Wilson's moralistic efforts to engineer a lasting world harmony owed much to the American gospel of strenuosity, which he imbibed during his formative years. As a boy Wilson had played football and baseball well enough to retain a lifelong interest in sport. He had been enrolled at an Ivy League college, Princeton, during the years in which the sporting republic was invented. He considered sport to be a key ingredient in the struggle to forge a modern republic, just as Theodore Roosevelt did. When he manned the "bully pulpit," homilies from the playing field came as easily to Wilson—though with less of a rough-and-tumble tone—as they did to Roosevelt.[6] In fact, Wilson proposed to institute the gospel of fair play as a standard of international behavior. He capped his plan with an international umpire—the League of Nations—that would ensure fair play for all. His plan, the logical conclusion of his definition of the war as a crusade to liberate all humanity, was premised on the notion that the world would come to understand American conceptions of equity.

Many Americans shared Wilson's convictions. "'Have we time, have we means, have we interest, to teach sportsmanship to the Boche?' Ask some of us here," wrote Katherine Mayo, a correspondent for *The Outlook* who covered the war in Europe. She theorized that "if the Boche had been taught fair play before 1914 he might not have crucified kittens that their wails should lure better men to their deaths, he might not have maimed women, or starved and beaten gallant British wounded that fell into his power." Mayo concluded that "if canniness is our motto, have we a cannier use to make of our time, means, and interest than to spread a knowledge of 'fair play' in the dark places of the world?

Darkness abroad has already cost us empty places by our own firesides, heavy taxes, hungry children, bread-lines for able men." She and Wilson wanted to teach the world how to play the game by American definitions of fairness.[7]

The Decline of the Sporting Republic

A year after the war ended in 1918, Europe remained devastated by the conflict. To resurrect the Old World the United States engineered a "remarkable exhibition of the sportsmanlike spirit" and reintroduced the old moral equivalent of war to civilization. According to the official American report, the so-called Inter-Allied Games of 1919 were motivated by the American love of fair play, a belief that athletics had helped to win the war, and a "wish to continue and strengthen the ties of comradeship developed on the battlefield."[8] Had the quest for athletic moral equivalents of war been resurrected?

In fact, in the new postwar cultural contexts, the connections between athletics and political visions of progressive civilization had been substantially weakened. The idea of sport as a regenerator of individual vigor continued to grow, but the concept of sport as a rejuvenator of the polity increasingly lost favor. Although James's ideal of a moral equivalent of war would continue to be mouthed as a platitude by athletic sentimentalists, Olympic patrons, and media commentators, the original power of the ideas that linked sport, the state, and national vitality had diminished substantially.

Three important changes in the way in which postwar culture interpreted sport accounted for sport's loss of political vigor. First, the vast majority of American intellectuals who had initially served as the engineers and popularizers of athletic technology abandoned their campaign to use sport as an agent of social change. From the 1920s to the present few American thinkers have taken the idea of sport as a political instrument seriously. Instead, they have consistently "exposed" sport as misguided amusement, wasted energy, or the mindless expression of mass culture.

Secondly, entrepreneurs and business elites found huge markets for athletic technology, a development that further increased the intellectuals' disdain for sport. The business of sport had deep roots in American history, but it exploded in the decades after the World War I. Commodifying sport helped to destroy any notion that athletics could serve as a moral equivalent for war.

Finally, the evolution of sport as a cultural innovation reduced its impact. For the generation that invented modern sport, athletic technology seemed pregnant with power. It had not prevented war, however, nor had it totally restructured society. For the generation that inherited the new athletic techniques, sport had become a part of the landscape of given consciousness.[9] Taken for granted, it was not understood as an important political tool, especially after it had been abandoned by the intellectual class and fiercely appropriated by business interests. After 1920 sport no longer seemed such a powerful tool for social change.

Still, to properly understand the idea of a moral equivalent for war, scholars need to recall the historical context in which modern sport developed. In its original version sport played a far more powerful role in shaping American ideas about the state and national vitality than current commentary indicates. Between the end of the celebration of the nation's centennial and the end of the Great War, American thinkers crafted a new organization of sport that they understood as promising civic renewal, national vitality, and the prospect of a republic forged by strenuous challenges and yet free from the scourge of war. As James himself imagined in 1910, following the insights of H. G. Wells, sport would create a world where "the conceptions of order and discipline, the tradition of service and devotion, of physical fitness, unstinted exertion, and universal responsibility, which universal military duty is now teaching European nations, will remain a permanent acquisition, when the last ammunition has been used in the fireworks that celebrate the final peace."[10]

For at least one generation American intellectuals dreamed that playing fields might replace battlefields, that a moral equivalent of war might spring from new understandings of sport. They asserted that an athletic technology could both replace military science and prevent the physical and moral degradation of their nation. They proposed, in typical and paradoxical American fashion, a technological solution for problems associated with technological change.

Athletic technology constituted a special category of technics. James recoiled from the fantastic visions of scientific prophets and technocrats who dreamed of a future in which technology would replace all human muscle and transmute *Homo sapiens* into a species of beings with gigantic cranial domes whose sole exertion of energy would be "floods of learned and ingenious talk." A world without sport, without strenuous endeavor, repelled James. "I am sure your flesh creeps at this apocalyptic vision," he wrote. "Mine certainly did so; and I cannot believe that our muscular vigor will ever be a superfluity."[11]

James and his fellow intellectuals would have been shocked by any social or political theory that considered sport to be a superfluous activity—as many contemporary American intellectuals do. For a generation searching after moral equivalents of war, sport was an essentially political institution.

An Olympic Epilogue

In 1918, during the November in which the warring world finally agreed to an armistice, *Everybody's Magazine* published a gloomy reminiscence about American glory at the Stockholm games in 1912 and the life and times of the late James Edward Sullivan. William G. Shepherd, a sportswriter who had covered the Stockholm Olympics, had returned to Sweden to cover a benefit for war orphans. As he sat in the stadium in which during 1912 the games of the Fifth Olympiad had been held, surrounded by the sounds and colors of gay festivities designed to raise money for the orphans, he was "overwhelmed by the ghosts" of the Olympic past. On that bright day in 1918 Shepherd saw not the scene in front him but visions of athletes from bygone days, particularly of American champions humiliating their haughty German adversaries. "Out there, in the center of the field, are the ghosts of those trimly clad German teams, marching shoulder to shoulder, . . . each man looking like all the others, each man walking, striding, jumping, spreading legs like everybody else— massed formation in sport, with no individuality, no personal responsibility, except to see that you do your best to win the coveted cup by crushing your individuality and doing everything as everybody else does it." Shepherd remembered that in 1912 the world had laughed at the "machine-like movements" of the Germans. "The day was to come when we would shudder at what we laughed at then."

All the specters in the stadium moved Shepherd to reflect on the most important lesson he had learned in Stockholm. He had panicked when his editors in the United States cabled him requesting a story on past American Olympic victories and predictions of success in 1912. He confessed that he was not an expert in athletics and hurriedly begged an audience with AOC leader James Sullivan to acquire the "inside dope." Over a summer evening dinner in a Swedish garden, the leader of the American Olympic movement explained to the young reporter the secrets of the sporting republic. When Shepherd confessed to Sullivan what his editors wanted, the AOC chief wondered what the problem was. "I'm no sporting editor. This is all new to me," replied Shepherd, admitting his ignorance of athletic history. "But sport hasn't anything to do with it," claimed Sullivan. "This isn't a study in athletics. It's a problem in Americanism." Sullivan then proceeded to lecture the young reporter on the true nature of "America's athletic missionaries."

Sullivan explained to Shepherd that American Olympians were products of the melting pot who were shaped by the American institutions into champions who could beat anyone from their former homelands. The American champions represented the adventuresome souls who had escaped the tyranny and repression of the Old World to participate in the great republican experiment of America, insisted Sullivan. "That's why we'll win these Olympic games, this time and every time, until we cease to attract the pick of the folk from Europe," Sullivan assured Shepherd. Of course, Sullivan added, given the good work of

"America's athletic missionaries" and the attraction of the "city on a hill," such a day would never come to pass.

"The games, that were to have been held in that great stadium on the outskirts of Berlin, in 1916, are being held in French and Flemish fields and in Italian mountains," intoned a solemn Shepherd, returned to the present from his visits with ghosts. "Our Olympic team has gone to Europe, and Jim Sullivan's dope is good and sure," Shepherd continued, referring to the American Expeditionary Force engaged in combat on the Continent. The result of the war, like the result of the Stockholm games, had been decided even before the contest began, he declared. "By Jim Sullivan's dope we *can* do the job; all we have to do is to go ahead and *do* it."[12] When *Spalding's Athletic Almanac* reprinted Shepherd's tale in 1919, the editors added a postscript. "'Jim Sullivan's Dope,' was true to form," wrote the compilers of the athletic journal that Sullivan himself had founded.[13]

As the Great War ended, the Olympic Games were once again revived and scheduled for Antwerp, Belgium, in 1920. The IOC had chosen Antwerp as the host of the games of the Seventh Olympiad before the war had forced a cancellation of the games of the Sixth Olympiad at Berlin. In spite of the war-ravaged condition of the "city of Rubens," the IOC elected to honor its pledge to Antwerp to symbolize the spirit of the brave Belgian defense against the overwhelming onslaught of the German army in World War I.[14] Baron Pierre de Coubertin spent the war years in a self-imposed exile in Lausanne, Switzerland, writing letters and addresses in a desperate attempt to keep the Olympic idea alive. After the war Coubertin kept the IOC in Switzerland as a gesture to the spirit of internationalism and because he had tired of the ceaseless political wrangles in France. As soon as the war ended, Coubertin and the Belgian representative to the IOC, Count Henri Baillet-Latour, moved to ensure that despite the distressed condition of Belgium, the seventh Olympics would be held in Antwerp.[15]

Americans hoped that the Antwerp Games would yield the same confirmations and celebrations of national values that a well-established Olympic mythology claimed for past celebrations of the Olympics. Perhaps the Olympics could rekindle the practical idealism that had guided the nation in the years before the war. The nation once again looked to its Olympic athletes for proof that they were still a "chosen people." "Another American Expeditionary Force is soon to take ship for Europe, and is expected to return as liberally covered with glory and so widely held in renown as those contingents who a year ago looked with gladdened eyes on the shores of home," *The Literary Digest* predicted of the 1920 U.S. Olympic team. The magazine recalled "the bloodless fields of Stockholm," where the United States had performed magnificently and thrilled to the chant of "Rah, rah, ray! U.S.A. A-M-E-R-I-C-A."[16]

Sport and Republicanism in American History

The nostalgic longing for the glorious experiences Americans remembered from Stockholm, London, St. Louis, Paris, and Athens masked the reality that the relationships between sport, politics, and culture had changed radically by the 1920s. The sporting republic, as the people who invented it and defined its constitutional principles understood it, reached its apogee at Stockholm in 1912. Sport would play new roles in the politics and culture of the rest of the twentieth century. Working forces in human societies evolve. Common consciousness does not remain static.

A photograph appeared in the picture section of the *Sunday New York Times*. It shows several suit-clad American athletes cavorting on the deck of the steamer carrying them to London for the 1908 Olympics. They laugh and egg on a teammate as he performs a jig for the photographer. "Tewanima the Indian Competitor in the Marathon leads the fourth of July War Dance," reads the caption.[17] The picture symbolizes the way in which the Olympics animated American conceptions of a sporting republic. For believers in the sporting republic, the Hopi Indian from Arizona and Carlisle Indian School doing a war dance on the Fourth of July surrounded by his giggling, good-natured teammates illustrated the democracy of American sport, which recognized no class or color distinctions. It highlighted the patriotism of the American Olympic expedition. Some Americans believed their Olympic teams had since 1896 quadrennially proved that the United States was the world's most vigorous nation. The picture was a photographic ode to the power of sport in making republican citizens. It paid homage to the melting pot, the supposed crucible of American athletic success, which always allowed the best man, or at least the best American, to win. Truly they were "America's athletic missionaries" who witnessed for the power of their republican culture.

Read in such a way, however, the photograph also obscured social realities. The picture actually offers more insights into the categories of the excluded and included in American sporting culture. Very few Native Americans in the late nineteenth and early twentieth centuries ever had opportunities to compete in athletics, let alone to make an Olympic team. Sport had not made most of Tewanima's fellow Native Americans into willing citizens of the republic, nor did it provide them with equal opportunities in turn-of-the-century American society. The sporting republic excluded most non-Europeans and limited women's access. At best the photograph illustrates the ideal that everyone someday might be welcome in the sporting republic. At worst it represents a cynical attempt to pretend that the ideals of the sporting republic matched social practices.

Clearly modern sport belongs to political and civic life rather than to some separate sphere of its own. Since 1896 Olympic sport has played an important role in American political culture. Through essays, polemics, and exposes about the experiences of "America's athletic missionaries," American thinkers generated a new national language that allowed communication between intellectual and popular cultures. No one was really sure how many Americans read the political editorials, philosophical treatises, or compendiums of social criticism produced by the "thinking classes." Cynics thought the readers to be few and quite inbred. Even optimists worried that so few of their fellow citizens bothered with political ideas that a public virtue based on a shared cultural literacy was no longer sustainable. Seemingly everyone perused the sports pages, however. That meant a much wider audience for republicans who learned the language of sport. Theodore Roosevelt understood that. So did "Mr. Dooley."

The sporting republicans thought they had invented a tool and a language for making national standards of their ideas about republican forms of government, their beliefs in constitutionalism and rule by law, their conceptions of public virtue, and their definitions of community. Whether their ideas really increased the commonweal, encouraged public virtue, solved social conflicts, influenced government, or created a national commitment to fair play, they knew that if they failed to discover an arena in which to debate the issues, then the republic was indeed doomed. Republics require debate about ideals. Republics also require debate about social practices. American stories about the Olympic Games sometimes provided opportunities for both.

Notes

Introduction

1. Harrison Rainie, "Such Good Friends, at Work and Play," *U.S. News and World Report,* June 21, 1993, p. 6.

2. William James, "The Moral Equivalent of War," in *William James: The Essential Writings,* ed. Bruce C. Wilshire (Albany: State University of New York Press, 1984), 349–61. "The Moral Equivalent of War" originally appeared in the popular press in *McClure's* 35 (Aug. 1910): 463–68; and in *Popular Science Monthly* 77 (Oct. 1910): 400–410.

Chapter 1: Inventing the Sporting Republic

1. Michael Oriard's *Reading Football: How the Popular Press Created an American Spectacle* (Chapel Hill: University of North Carolina Press, 1993) examines the literature of football as an expression of that national language. Indeed, the language has even generated its own dictionary; see Tim Considine, *The Language of Sport* (New York: Facts on File, 1982).

2. The imagery of ideas as working forces in the common consciences of cultures is developed by Clifford Geertz; see Clifford Geertz, *Local Knowledge: Further Essays in Interpretive Anthropology* (New York: Basic, 1984), 47.

3. The translation of *republic* as "a thing belonging to the people" comes from *The Encyclopedia Americana,* s.v. "Republics, History of" (New York: Encyclopedia Americana, 1919).

4. Louis Kronenberger, *The Republic of Letters: Essays on Various Writers* (New York: Knopf, 1955); Grant Webster, *The Republic of Letters: Postwar American Literary Opinion* (Baltimore: Johns Hopkins University Press, 1979); Dave Morley and Ken Warpole, eds., *The Republic of Letters: Working Class Writing and Local Publishing* (London: Comedia, 1982); Dena Goodman, *The Republic of Letters: A Cultural History of the French Enlightenment* (Ithaca, N.Y.: Cornell University Press, 1994); James Morton Smith, ed., *The Republic of Letters: The Correspondence between Thomas Jefferson and James Madison, 1776–1826* (New York: Norton, 1995); Michael Polanyi, "The Republic of Science: Its Political and Economic Theory," *Minerva* 1 (Autumn 1952): 54–73.

5. George Ripley and Charles A. Dana, eds., *The New American Cyclopaedia: A Pop-

ular Dictionary of General Knowledge, s.v. "Republic" (New York: D. Appleton, 1870); Frederick Converse Beach, ed., *The Encylcopedia Americana*, s.v. "Republic" (New York: Americana, 1904); *The Encyclopedia Americana*, s.vv. "Republic," "Republics, Duration of," and "Republics, History of" (New York: Encyclopedia Americana, 1919); Charles Morris, ed., *The Great Republic: By the Master Historians*, 4 vols. (New York: Great Republic, 1913 [1897]). In an opening statement the editors proclaimed that if *The New Republic* "could bring sufficient enlightenment to the problems of the nation and sufficient sympathy to its complexities, it would serve all those who feel the challenge of our time" (*The New Republic* 1 [Nov. 7, 1914]: 3).

6. As Daniel T. Rodgers has discovered, republicanism is in some ways a vague and murky concept used by a wide variety of both historians and historical actors to argue about a multitude of issues. Originally a paradigmatic device constructed to explain late eighteenth- and early nineteenth-century American developments, republicanism has been employed across the chronological spectrum of American history. Nevertheless, as Rodgers indicates, republicanism remains maddeningly difficult to define. See Daniel T. Rodgers, "Republicanism: The Career of a Concept," *Journal of American History* 79 (June 1992): 11–38.

7. Price Collier, "Sport's Place in the Nation's Well-Being," *Outing* 32 (July 1898): 382–88.

8. *Scribner's* magazine serialized Connolly's fictional account of the first Olympics, "An Olympic Victor," in 1908. See "An Olympic Victor," *Scribner's* 44 (July 1908): 18–31; 44 (Aug. 1908): 204–17; and 44 (Sept. 1908): 357–70. Connolly's other works on the Olympics include "The Shepherd's Bush Greeks," *Collier's* 41 (Sept. 5, 1908): 12–13; "The Spirit of the Olympian Games," *Outing* 48 (Apr. 1906): 101–4; and "The Also Ran," *Collier's* 82 (July 14, 1908): 8, 41.

9. Connolly, "An Olympic Victor," 210.

10. Ibid.

11. William James, *Pragmatism*, ed. Bruce Kuklick (Indianapolis: Hackett, 1981 [1907]), 52–53.

12. Richard Lipsky, "Toward a Theory of American Sports Symbolism," in *Games and Sports in Cultural Context*, ed. Janet C. Harris and Roberta J. Park (Champaign, Ill.: Human Kinetics, 1983), 83.

13. [Caspar Whitney], "The Minister and Athletics: Mr. Caspar Whitney's Views," *The Outlook* 55 (Jan. 9, 1897): 181–83.

14. James Madison, "Federalist Number 10," in *The Papers of James Madison*, ed. Robert A. Rutland, Charles F. Hobson, William M. E. Rochal, and Fredrika J. Teute, 17 vols. (Chicago: University of Chicago Press, 1977), 10:263–70.

15. Woodrow Wilson, *The New Freedom: A Call for the Emancipation of the Generous Energies of a People*, comp. William Bayard Hale (New York: Doubleday, Page, 1914), 170.

16. John Corbin, "A Harvard Man at Oxford," *Harper's Weekly* 42 (Feb. 26, 1896): 212.

17. George Hibbard, "The Sporting Spirit: Ancient and Modern," *Outing* 36 (Sept. 1900): 601–2.

18. Richard Holt, *Sport and the British: A Modern History* (New York: Oxford University Press, 1989).

19. For example, see Josiah Strong, "The Problem of the Twentieth Century City," *The North American Review* 165 (Sept. 1897): 343–49.

20. "City Athletics," *Harper's* 68 (Jan. 1884): 297.

21. "Editor's Open Window," *Outing* 7 (Dec. 1885): 338–41.

22. H. H. M., "Greek vs. Modern Physical Culture," *Outing* 3 (Dec. 1883): 216.

23. J. R. Dodge, "Rural Recreations," *Outing* 7 (Dec. 1885): 307.

24. The idea of culture came into fashion during the 1870s. Intellectuals used the term to describe the human-created systems that bound people together. Culture stood for a sense of civic engagement and national identity that united the people who shared it, regardless of class, ethnic, or other differences. Culture was synonymous with the idea of virtue in the older tradition of republican political theory. American political thinkers who articulated modern forms of republicanism argued that a common culture was a basic ingredient in the creation of stable nations. See Lewis Perry, *Intellectual Life in America* (New York: Franklin Watts, 1984), 261–75.

25. C. Turner, "The Progress of Athletism," *Outing* 13 (Nov. 1888): 109.

26. "Play for the People," *The Independent* 62 (Feb. 28, 1907): 514.

27. John J. MacAloon has made some provocative insights into the structure of games and sports as communication systems and argued that sport performs as an important semiotic "code" in modernizing societies. See his "Olympic Games and the Theory of Spectacle in Modern Societies," in *Rite, Drama, Festival, Spectacle: Rehearsals Toward a Theory of Cultural Performance,* ed. John MacAloon (Philadelphia: Institute for the Study of Human Issues, 1984), 241–80.

28. Turner, "The Progress of Athletism," 109.

29. Douglas Tallack, *Twentieth-Century America in Intellectual and Cultural Context* (New York: Longman, 1991), 1–34.

30. See William J. Lampton, "The Fascination of Fast Motion," *Cosmopolitan* 33 (June 1902): 136.

31. Martin Heidegger, "The Question Concerning Technology," in *Martin Heidegger: Basic Writings,* ed. David Farrell Krell (New York: Harper and Row, 1977), 287–317.

32. Turner, "The Progress of Athletism," 109.

33. Frederic L. Paxson, "The Rise of Sport," *Mississippi Valley Historical Review* 4 (Sept. 1917): 145.

34. See Lloyd Bryce, "A Plea for Sport," *The North American Review* 128 (May 1879): 518–19; "Editor's Open Window," *Outing* 7 (Oct. 1885): 96.

35. Richard Henry Edwards, *Popular Amusements* (New York: Arno, 1976 [1915]), 23–24.

36. Elting E. Morison, "Gunfire at Sea: A Case Study in Innovation," in *Men, Machines and Modern Times* (Cambridge, Mass.: MIT Press, 1966), 17–43.

37. Benjamin Rader, "The Quest for Subcommunities and the Rise of American Sport," *American Quarterly* 29 (Fall 1977): 355–69.

38. Hibbard, "The Sporting Spirit," 601.

39. James T. Kloppenberg, *Uncertain Victory: Social Democracy and Progressivism in European and American Thought, 1870–1920* (New York: Oxford University Press, 1986).

Kloppenberg ties "progressive" thought to the construction of modernity. *Progressivism* is a useful label for describing the thought and discourse of certain reformers, even if it is not an accurate label for describing a singular political movement. See Robert M. Crunden, *Ministers of Reform: The Progressives' Achievement in American Civilization, 1889–1920* (Urbana: University of Illinois Press, 1984); Daniel T. Rodgers, "In Search of Progressivism," *Reviews in American History* 10 (Dec. 1982): 113–32.

40. The distinction between older and newer middle classes has been employed to chart a shift that is as much cultural as it is economic. Descriptions and explanations of the shift appear in most of the fundamental critiques of the modern social order, ranging from the work of Karl Marx and Friedrich Engels to that of Max Weber and Hannah Arendt, and even of Alvin Toffler. In American social science, Thorstein Veblen's *Theory of the Leisure Class* (New York: Macmillan, 1899) and C. Wright Mills's *White Collar: The American Middle Classes* (New York: Oxford University Press, 1953) greatly influenced the basic paradigm. For an interesting survey of the idea of class between the Civil War and the end of World War I, see Glenn C. Altschuler, *Race, Ethnicity, and Class in American Social Thought, 1865–1919* (Arlington Heights, Ill.: Harlan Davidson, 1982); and Robert Wiebe, *The Search for Order, 1877–1920* (New York: Hill and Wang, 1967). Efforts to forge a middle-class national culture are explored in T. J. Lears's *No Place of Grace: Antimodernism and the Transformation of American Culture, 1880–1920* (New York: Pantheon, 1981) and Alan Trachtenberg's *Incorporation of America: Culture and Society in the Gilded Age* (New York: Hill and Wang, 1982). H. Wayne Morgan, in *Unity and Culture: The United States, 1877–1900* (Baltimore: Penguin, 1971), examined desires to create national standards in American high-brow culture. Studies on the "search for order" in mass culture remain scarce. Randolph Bourne's Progressive Era essay "The Puritan's Will to Power," *The Seven Arts* 1 (Apr. 1917): 631–37, remains an insightful critique of middle-class efforts to construct cultural hegemony in the United States. See also Eric Hobsbawm, *Nations and Nationalism since 1780: Programme, Myth, Reality* (New York: Cambridge University Press, 1990); and Eric Hobsbawm and Terence Ranger, eds., *The Invention of Tradition* (New York: Cambridge University Press, 1983).

41. For a brief biography of Connolly, see "Chronicle and Comment," *The Bookman* 28 (Oct. 1908): 107.

42. Allen Johnson and Dumas Malone, eds., *Dictionary of American Biography,* s.v. "Collier, Price" (New York: Scribner's, 1930).

43. Gertrude Dudley and Frances A. Kellor, *Athletic Games in the Education of Women* (New York: Henry Holt, 1909), title page.

44. John A. Garraty, ed., *Dictionary of American Biography,* Supplement 5, 1951–55, s.v. "Kellor, Frances" (New York: Scribner's, 1977).

45. John A. Garraty and Edward T. James, eds., *Dictionary of American Biography,* Supplement 4, 1946–50, s.v. "Shaw, Albert" (New York: Scribner's, 1974).

46. Benjamin G. Rader, *American Sports: From the Age of Folk Games to the Age of Spectators* (Englewood Cliffs, N.J.: Prentice-Hall, 1983), 152–57; Donald Mrozek, *Sport and American Mentality, 1880–1910* (Knoxville: University of Tennessee Press, 1983), 204–5.

47. *National Cyclopaedia of American Biography*, s.v. "Sullivan, James Edward" (New York: James T. White, 1916).

48. "Chronicle and Comment: Some Writers on Sports," *The Bookman* 33 (Aug. 1911): 563–64; John Lucas, *The Modern Olympic Games* (New York: A. S. Barnes, 1980), 64–73; Allen Guttmann, *The Games Must Go On: Avery Brundage and the Olympic Movement* (New York: Columbia University Press, 1984), 12–22.

49. Thorstein Veblen, *The Theory of the Leisure Class* (New York: Modern Library, 1934 [1899]). See also Maurice Thompson, "The Limit of Athletics for Brain Workers," *The Chautauquan* 19 (May 1894): 148–52; Arlo Bates, "The Negative Side of Modern Athletics," *Forum* 31 (May 1901): 287–97; and Oliver S. Jones, "Morality in College Athletics," *The North American Review* 160 (June 1895): 638–40.

50. "The Athletic Craze," *The Nation* 57 (Dec. 7, 1893): 422–23. Other representative critical editorials include "Sports in and out of College," *The Nation* 36 (Mar. 29, 1883): 268–69; "Athletics and Health," *The Nation* 59 (Dec. 20, 1894): 457–58; "Capitalizing the Outdoor Life," *The Nation* 89 (Nov. 11, 1909): 451–52; "Democratic and Aristocratic Sport," *The Nation* 90 (Apr. 14, 1910): 309; "The Standardization of Sport," *The Nation* 75 (Dec. 4, 1902): 439; and "'Strenuous' Excitement," *The Nation* 69 (Dec. 14, 1899): 440–41.

51. John Corbin, "Outing Monthly Record," *Outing* 24 (Apr. 1894): 2.

52. Lears, *No Place of Grace*.

53. Anthony Giddens, *The Class Structure of Advanced Societies* (New York: Harper and Row, 1974), 23–40; Loren Baritz, *The Good Life: The Meaning of Success for the American Middle Class* (New York: Harper and Row, 1989).

54. Peter Levine, *A. G. Spalding and the Rise of Baseball* (New York: Oxford University Press, 1985).

55. Donald Kyle, "E. Norman Gardiner and the Decline of Greek Sport," in *Essays in Sport History and Sport Mythology*, ed. Donald G. Kyle and Gary D. Stark (College Station: Texas A&M University Press, 1990), 7–44. See also Bryce, "A Plea for Sport"; Robert Raymond Williams, "Physical Prowess," *Munsey's* 8 (Nov. 1892): 169–77; J. William White, "A Physician's View of Exercise and Athletics," *Lippincott's* 39 (June 1887): 1008–9.

56. Bryce, "A Plea for Sport," 517, 525.

57. John P. Foley, "Outdoor Life of the Presidents—George Washington," *Outing* 13 (Nov. 1888): 99–108; idem, "Outdoor Life of the Presidents—Andrew Jackson," *Outing* 13 (Feb. 1889): 437–44.

58. Levine, *A. G. Spalding*, 112–21.

59. Theodore Roosevelt, *The Winning of the West*, 6 vols. (New York: Putnam, 1889–96).

60. Theodore Roosevelt, "The American Boy," in *The Strenuous Life: Essays and Addresses* (New York: Century, 1902), 155–64.

61. The vast majority of the American intellectual class was not about to abandon altogether either individualism or many of the familiar axioms of liberal republicanism. Instead, they practiced adaptation and conservation, blending new methods and traditional values in a process that the historian Robert Crunden has identified as "in-

novative nostalgia," as they marked a path toward a middle ground amid the flux of change. See Robert M. Crunden, *Ministers of Reform: The Progressives' Achievement in American Civilization* (Urbana: University of Illinois Press, 1984).

62. In defining the relation of the new middle classes to the dominant modes of production, ideas, attitudes, and beliefs—or cultural folklore—can be as important as occupation and income. See Thurman Arnold, *The Folklore of Capitalism* (New Haven, Conn.: Yale University Press, 1937). Sport served as an important part of their folklore. It became one of what the historian Eric Hobsbawm has identified as the invented traditions of middle-class historical experience; see Hobsbawm and Ranger, eds., *The Invention of Tradition*.

63. Thomas Jefferson, *Notes on the State of Virginia*, in *The American Intellectual Tradition*, 2d ed., ed. David Hollinger and Charles Capper, 2 vols. (New York: Oxford University Press, 1993), 1:174.

64. "Glances at Our Letter File," *Outing* 32 (Aug. 1898): 543; "Glances at Our Letter File," *Outing* 32 (Sept. 1898): 647.

65. Price Collier, "The Ethics of Ancient and Modern Athletics," *Forum* 32 (Nov. 1901): 317–18.

66. See, for instance, H. Addington Bruce, "Baseball and the National Life," *The Outlook* 104 (May 17, 1913): 105; "The Building of Muscle," *Harper's* 69 (Aug. 1884): 385.

67. Luther Halsey Gulick, "The New Athletics," *The Outlook* 98 (July 15, 1911), 597–600.

68. Francis Tabor, "Directed Sport as a Factor in Education," *Forum* 42 (Feb. 12, 1898): 321.

69. Theodore Roosevelt, "The Strenuous Life," speech before the Hamilton Club, Chicago, Apr. 10, 1899; cited in *The Works of Theodore Roosevelt*, 24 vols., ed. Hermann Hagerdorn, vol. 13, *American Ideals, The Strenuous Life, Realizable Ideals* (New York: Scribner's, 1926), 331.

70. "A Letter from *President Roosevelt* in Favor of Public Playgrounds," *The Playground* 1 (Apr. 1907): 5.

71. George Edwin Rines, "Recent Political History of the Nation," in *The Great Republic,* ed. Charles Morris, 4:363; George E. Johnson, "Catching up with Athens," *The Survey* 22 (May 1, 1909): 165–66.

72. Cultural conservatism shaped some of Theodore Roosevelt's gospel of the strenuous life. True, Roosevelt recoiled from what he perceived as the effeminate sterility of contemporary American Victorianism, but he aimed at reinvigoration rather than rejection. He certainly did not want the strenuous life to undermine the beliefs in elite leadership, capitalist progress, or cultural unity that animated Victorian thought. See George Cotkin, *Reluctant Modernism: American Thought and Culture, 1880–1900* (New York: Twayne, 1992), 123–25.

73. "Roosevelt on Rural Recreation," *The Playground* 8 (Feb. 1915): 407–8.

74. Theodore Roosevelt, "American Ideals," *Forum* 18 (Feb. 1895): 743–50.

75. Elliot Gorn and Warren Goldstein, *A Brief History of American Sport* (New York: Hill and Wang, 1993), 138–49.

76. C. S. Loch, "Good Citizenship and Athletics," *International Journal of Ethics* 9 (July 1899): 451–52.

77. "Good Citizenship and Athletics," *The American Review of Reviews* 20 (Aug. 1899): 196.

78. Allen Johnson and Dumas Malone, eds., *Dictionary of American Biography*, s.v. "Bryce, Lloyd" (New York: Scribner's, 1929).

79. Bryce, "A Plea for Sport," 519–23.

80. Ibid., 523.

Chapter 2: Athens, 1896

1. The October 1968 issue of *Quote* had Lombardi asserting, "Winning is not the important thing; it's everything." Lombardi himself later claimed: "I have been quoted as saying, 'Winning is the only thing.' That's a little out of context. What I said is that 'Winning is not everything—but making the effort to win is'" (cited in George Flynn, ed., *Vince Lombardi on Football* [New York: Van Nostrand Rheinhold, 1981], 14). The quotation seems to have originated with Vanderbilt University football coach Red Sanders in 1940; see Thomas Tutko and William Burns, *Winning Is Everything and Other American Myths* (New York: Macmillan, 1976), 4.

2. The designation "America's Athletic Missionaries" comes from the title of Edward Bayard Moss's piece on the 1912 U.S. Olympic team in *Harper's Weekly* 56 (July 27, 1912): 8–9.

3. John J. MacAloon, "Olympic Games and the Theory of Spectacle in Modern Societies," in *Rite, Drama, Festival, Spectacle,* ed. John J. MacAloon (Philadelphia: Institute for the Study of Human Issues, 1984), 241–80.

4. Clifford Geertz, "Notes on a Balinese Cockfight," in *The Interpretation of Cultures* (New York: Basic, 1973), 448.

5. Lloyd Bryce, "A Plea for Sport," *The North American Review* 128 (May 1879): 524.

6. Baron Pierre de Coubertin, *Une Campagne de 21 Ans* (Paris: Librairie de l'Education Physique, 1908), 5, as quoted in John J. MacAloon, *This Great Symbol: Pierre de Coubertin and the Origins of the Modern Olympic Games* (Chicago: University of Chicago Press, 1981), 59.

7. Baron Pierre de Coubertin, "Athletics in the Modern World," in *The Olympic Idea: Discourses and Essays,* ed. Carl-Diem-Insitut and the Deutschen Sporthochschule, Koln, Rev. Liselot Diem and O. Anderson, trans. John G. Dixon (Stuttgart: Hofmann, 1967), 7–10, as quoted in MacAloon, *This Great Symbol,* 188–89.

8. "Athletic Sports as a Factor in European Life," *The American Review of Reviews* 10 (Aug. 1894): 208.

9. Clive Gammon, "Still Carrying the Torch," *Sports Illustrated,* July 16, 1984, p. 57.

10. Henry Wysham Lanier, "In the Field of International Sport," *The American Review of Reviews* 12 (Nov. 1895): 575–78.

11. W. S. Bansemer, "The Olympian Games," *New England Magazine* 14 (May 1896): 261.

12. Rufus B. Richardson, "The New Olympian Games," *Scribner's* 20 (Sept. 1896): 267.

13. "Princeton at Athens: What the Sportsman Should Know before He Goes to Greece," *New York Times,* Mar. 29, 1896, p. 3.

14. Paul Shorey, "Can We Revive the Olympic Games," *Forum* 19 (May 1895): 323.

15. Connolly was readmitted and graduated in 1899. Richard D. Mandell, *The First Modern Olympics* (Berkeley: University of California Press, 1976), 116, 185.

16. Andrew Carnegie, *The Empire of Business* (New York: Doubleday, 1902), 147.

17. Eugene L. Richards, "College Athletics," *Popular Science Monthly* 24 (Feb. 1884): 451.

18. Walter Camp, "Some Abuses in Athletics," *The Independent* 52 (Mar. 22, 1900): 714–17.

19. Albert Shaw, "The Re-establishment of Olympic Games: How International Sports May Promote Peace among the Nations," *The American Review of Reviews* 10 (Dec. 1894): 643–44.

20. E. Digby Baltzell, *The Protestant Establishment* (New York: Random House, 1964); G. Edward White, *The Eastern Establishment and the Western Experience: The West of Frederic Remington, Theodore Roosevelt and Owen Wister* (New Haven, Conn.: Yale University Press, 1968); C. Wright Mills, *The Power Elite* (New York: Oxford University Press, 1956); Laurence Veysey, *The Emergence of the American University* (Chicago: University of Chicago Press, 1965); Daniel Walker Howe, ed., *Victorian America* (Philadelphia: University of Pennsylvania Press, 1976); Louise L. Stevenson, *The Victorian Homefront: American Thought and Culture, 1860–1880* (New York: Twayne, 1991); George Cotkin, *Reluctuant Modernism: American Thought and Culture, 1880–1900* (New York: Twayne, 1992); Robert Wiebe, *The Search for Order, 1877–1920* (New York: Hill and Wang, 1967).

21. Owen Johnson, *Stover at Yale* (New York: Collier, 1968), 10.

22. William A. Elliot, "The New Olympic Games," *The Chautauquan* 23 (Apr. 1896): 50.

23. Baron Pierre de Coubertin, "The Re-establishment of the Olympic Games," *The Chautauquan* 19 (Sept. 1894): 700.

24. Charles Waldstein, "The Olympic Games at Athens," *Harper's Weekly* 40 (Apr. 18, 1896): 391.

25. Elliot, "The New Olympic Games," 47–51.

26. Coubertin, "The Re-establishment of the Olympic Games," 700.

27. Mandell, *The First Modern Olympics,* 116–17.

28. Charles J. P. Lucas, *The Olympic Games: 1904* (St. Louis: Woodward and Tiernan, 1905), 11.

29. "For the Olympian Games," *New York Times,* Mar. 22, 1896, p. 12.

30. Mandell, *The First Modern Olympics,* 117.

31. "For the Olympian Games," 12.

32. Ibid.

33. "The New Olympic Games," *The Chautauquan* 23 (July 1896): 363.

34. "Princeton Will Send Team to Athens," *New York Times,* Mar. 17, 1896, p. 6.

35. James B. Connolly, "The Spirit of the Olympian Games," *Outing* 48 (Apr. 1906): 104.

36. "Outing Monthly Record: The New Olympian Games," *Outing* 28 (May 1896): 161; Mandell, *The First Modern Olympics,* 115–16.

37. "For the Olympic Games," *New York Times,* Mar. 18, 1896, p. 7.

38. "For the Olympian Games," 12.

39. Shaw, "The Re-establishment of Olympic Games," 646.

40. Ibid., 643.

41. Theodore Roosevelt, "American Ideals," *Forum* 18 (Feb. 1895): 743–50.

42. John Lucas, "The Influence of Anglo-American Sport on Pierre de Coubertin—Modern Olympic Games Founder," in *The Modern Olympics,* ed. Peter J. Graham and Horst Ueberhorst (Cornwall, N.Y.: Leisure, 1976), 17.

43. George Horton, "Revival of Olympian Games," *The North American Review* 162 (Mar. 1896): 273.

44. S. P. P. Lambros and N. G. Polites, *The Olympic Games: b.c. 776–a.d. 1896* (New York: American Olympic Committee, 1896), 60–61.

45. D. Karopothakes, "The Olympic Games at Athens in 1896," *The Nation* 61 (Oct. 3, 1895): 238.

46. Charles Waldstein, "The Olympian Games at Athens," *Harper's Weekly* 40 (May 16, 1896): 490.

47. Connolly, "The Spirit of the Olympian Games," 102.

48. Richardson, "The New Olympian Games," 269–69.

49. James B. Connolly, "An Olympic Victor," *Scribner's* 44 (Aug. 1908): 209.

50. "The 1896 Olympics," *The American Review of Reviews* 86 (Aug. 1932): 50.

51. Karopothakes, "The Olympic Games at Athens," 237.

52. Attendance figures were provided in "American Athletes Won: Princeton and Boston Boys Successful in Olympian Games," *New York Times,* Apr. 7, 1896, p. 1; and "The Americans Ahead: Progress of the Olympic Games at Athens," *New York Times,* Apr. 8, 1896, p. 3.

53. "Outing Monthly Record: The New Olympian Games," 162.

54. Richardson, "The New Olympian Games," 276–78.

55. "The 1896 Olympics," 50.

56. Waldstein, "The Olympian Games at Athens," 490.

57. "An Example from Olympia," *Scribner's* 19 (June 1896): 792.

58. "The Olympian Games," *New York Times,* Apr. 8, 1896, p. 4.

59. "Americans Win Olympian Laurels," *Scientific American* 74 (Apr. 18, 1896): 243.

60. Caspar Whitney, "Amateur Sport," *Harper's Weekly* 40 (Apr. 18, 1896): 406.

61. "The New Olympic Games: How They Impressed an Eyewitness," *New York Times,* Apr. 26, 1896, p. 16.

62. "The Olympic Games," *Scientific American* 74 (May 16, 1896): 313.

63. "The New Olympic Games," *The Chautauquan,* 363.

64. "The Americans Ahead," 3; "American Athletes Won," 1; "Honor for Americans: Sustained Their Reputations at the Olympic Games," *New York Times,* Apr. 11, 1896, p. 8.

65. Mandell, *The First Modern Olympics,* 143.

66. "The Olympian Games," 4.

67. Whitney, "Amateur Sport," 406.

68. "Outing Monthly Record: The New Olympian Games," 161–63.

69. Richardson, "The New Olympian Games, 281.

70. Paul Gallico, *The Golden People* (Garden City, N.Y.: Doubleday, 1965), 21–29. In

Sports in the Western World (Totowa, N.J.: Rowman and Littlefield, 1982), William J. Baker
has perceptively stressed the importance of the media in the creation of modern sporting culture.

71. Quoted in Maynard Butler, "The New Olympic Games," *The Outlook* 53 (May 30,
1896), 994.

72. Richardson, "The New Olympic Games," 284.

73. Butler, "The New Olympic Games," 995.

74. James B. Connolly, "An Olympic Victor," *Scribner's* 44 (Sept. 1908): 361. A reviewer
in the "Chronicle and Comment" section of *The Bookman* called Connolly's description of the race "one of the best bits of writing that we have seen for a long time" (*The
Bookman* 28 [Oct. 1908]: 107).

75. Baron Pierre de Coubertin, "The Olympic Games of 1896," *Century* 53 (Nov.
1896): 53.

76. Waldstein, "The Olympic Games at Athens," 391.

77. Coubertin, "The Olympic Games of 1896," 53.

78. "Outing Monthly Record: The Olympian Victors," *Outing* 28 (June 1896): 41.

79. "Boston Athletes Arrive," *New York Times*, May 7, 1896, p. 3.

80. Associated Press and Grolier, *Pursuit of Excellence: The Olympic Story* (Danbury,
Conn.: Grolier, 1979), 13.

81. Lambros and Polites, *The Olympic Games*, 69.

82. Charles Waldstein, "A Last Word on the Olympian Games," *Harper's Weekly* 40
(May 23, 1896): 515.

83. William Milligan Sloane, "The Greek Olympiads," in *Report of the American Olympic Committee, 1920* (Greenwich, Conn.: Conde Nast, 1920), 59.

84. William Milligan Sloane, "Modern Olympic Games," in *Report of the American
Olympic Committee, 1920*, 83.

Chapter 3: Paris, 1900

1. Caspar Whitney, "Athletic Development in France," *Outing* 36 (May 1900): 178–81.

2. Price Collier, "Sport's Place in the Nation's Well-Being," *Outing* 32 (July 1898):
382–88.

3. Caspar Whitney, "Non-Athletic China," *Harper's Weekly* 42 (Feb. 19, 1898): 189–90.

4. Caspar Whitney, "Athletic Awakening of the Japanese," *Harper's Weekly* 42 (Feb. 12,
1898): 165–66.

5. Lloyd Bryce, "A Plea for Sport," *The North American Review* 128 (May 1879): 524.

6. Baron Pierre de Coubertin, "The Meeting of the Olympian Games," *The North
American Review* 170 (June 1900): 802–10.

7. Henry Adams's famous essay penned at the exposition, "The Dynamo and the
Virgin," captured the perception of change from traditional to modern society fostered
by the Paris world's fair. See Henry Adams, *The Education of Henry Adams: An Autobi-
ography* (Boston: Houghton Mifflin, 1961 [1918]), 379–90.

8. John Brisben Walker, "Preface—Why and How," *Cosmopolitan* 37 (Sept. 1904): 483.

9. John Brisben Walker, "What the Louisiana Purchase Exposition Is," *Cosmopolitan* 37 (Sept. 1904): 485.

10. Robert Rydell, *All the World's a Fair: Visions of Empire at American International Expositions, 1876–1916* (Chicago: University of Chicago Press, 1984).

11. Coubertin, "Meeting of the Olympian Games," 802.

12. Jacques Barzun, *Classic, Romantic and Modern* (Boston: Little, Brown, 1961).

13. Baron Pierre de Coubertin, "The Re-establishment of the Olympic Games," *The Chautauquan* 19 (Sept. 1894), 696–700.

14. William L. Shirer, *The Collapse of the Third Republic: An Inquiry into the Fall of France in 1940* (New York: Simon and Schuster, 1969), 35–112.

15. John J. MacAloon, *This Great Symbol: Pierre de Coubertin and the Origins of the Modern Olympics* (Chicago: University of Chicago, 1981), 106–12.

16. *National Cyclopaedia of American Biography,* s.v. "Sullivan, James Edward" (New York: James T. White, 1916).

17. John Lucas, *The Modern Olympic Games* (New York: A. S. Barnes, 1980), 64–73; Allen Guttmann, *The Games Must Go On: Avery Brundage and the Olympic Movement* (New York: Columbia University Press, 1984), 12–22.

18. *National Cyclopaedia of American Biography,* s.v., "Curtiss, Julian W." (New York: James T. White, 1947).

19. Burton J. Bledstein, *The Culture of Professionalism: The Middle Class and the Development of Higher Education in America* (New York: Norton, 1976).

20. American Olympic Committee, *Report of the American Olympic Committee: Seventh Olympic Games* (Greenwich, Conn.: Conde Nast, 1920), 2–3.

21. James E. Sullivan, ed., *Spalding's Official Athletic Almanac for 1904* (New York: American Sports, 1903), 187.

22. Whitney, "Outdoor Sports—What They Are Doing for Us," *Harper's Weekly* 52 (June 7, 1900): 1362.

23. Shirer, *Collapse of the Third Republic,* 48–84.

24. MacAloon, *This Great Symbol,* 256–75; Lucas, *The Modern Olympic Games,* 45–63.

25. Whitney, "Outdoor Sports," 1362.

26. Lucas, *The Modern Olympic Games,* 50.

27. Coubertin, "Meeting of the Olympic Games," 802–11.

28. Caspar Whitney, "The Way of the Sportsman: American Athletes at Paris," *Outing* 36 (July 1900): 423.

29. "American Athletes Abroad," *New York Times,* June 24, 1900, p. 8.

30. William B. Curtis, "A Peaceful Invasion," *Harper's Weekly* 44 (July 7, 1900): 632.

31. "American Athletes Abroad," 8.

32. Curtis, "A Peaceful Invasion," 6. For a eulogy to Curtis, see James E. Sullivan, ed., *Spalding's Official Athletic Almanac for 1901* (New York: American Sports, 1901), 4; "The Sportsman's View-Point: The Death of 'Father Bill' Curtis," *Outing* 36 (Aug. 1900): 557. Curtis perished in a "severe storm" while climbing Mt. Washington between July 1 and 3. One of the founders of the New York Athletic Club, he was an ardent sportsman and proselytizer for athletics.

33. "Eight out of Thirteen," *Chicago Tribune*, July 8, 1900, p. 17.

34. Whitney, "The Way of the Sportsman: No Sunday Athletic Meetings," 424.

35. William Oscar Johnson, "The Taking Part," *Sports Illustrated*, July 10, 1972, p. 38.

36. George Orton, "The Paris Athletic Games," *Outing* 36 (Sept. 1900): 690–91.

37. Caspar Whitney, "The Sportsman's View-Point: Broken Faith at the Paris Games," *Outing* 36 (Sept. 1900): 678.

38. "Our Athletes in Paris," *New York Times*, July 12, 1900, p. 5.

39. "Clean Sweep for Americans," *Chicago Tribune*, July 15, 1900, p. 17.

40. "American Athletes Win," *New York Times*, July 15, 1900, p. 4.

41. Orton, "The Paris Athletic Games," 691.

42. "Clean Sweep for Americans," 18.

43. Sullivan, *Spalding's Almanac for 1901*, 88.

44. "American Athletes Win," 4.

45. "Seven More Victories," *Chicago Tribune*, July 17, 1900, p. 9.

46. "American Athletes Win," 4; "Clean Sweep for Americans," 18.

47. Orton, "The Paris Athletic Games," 690–91.

48. "Yankee Athletes Barred," *New York Times*, July 16, 1900, p. 5; "Americans Win at Paris," *Chicago Tribune*, July 16, 1900, p. 8.

49. "Yankee Athletes Barred," 5; "Americans Win at Paris," 8.

50. "Americans Again Lead," *New York Times*, July 17, 1900, p. 5.

51. "Yankee Athletes Barred," 1.

52. Caspar Whitney, "The Sportsman's View-Point: Mug Hunters and Disregarded Agreements at Paris Games," *Outing* 36 (Aug. 1900): 566–67. Whitney's list of "mug hunters" included "Kraenzlein, Baxter, Colket, Tewkesbury and Orton, Penn; Holland and Monahan, Georgetown; Long, Columbia; Sheldon, N.Y.A.C.; Hall, Brown; Bray, Williams."

53. Whitney, "The Sportsman's View-Point: Broken Faith," 678–79; idem, "Mug Hunters," 566–67.

54. Orton, "The Paris Athletic Games," 691–92.

55. "Americans Win at Paris," 8. Prinstein and Kraenzlein were longtime rivals. The sports columnist for the *New York Mail and Express*, Malcolm Ford, reported that Prinstein wrote him to claim that Kraenzlein "broke faith with him *personally*" in the Olympic long jump incident. See Bernard Postal, Jesse Silver, and Roy Silver, *Encyclopedia of Jews in Sport* (New York: Bloch, 1965), 480–82.

56. "Seven More Victories," 9.

57. "Americans Win at Paris," 8.

58. "Yankee Athletes Barred," 1.

59. "Americans Again Lead," 5.

60. "Paris Games Terminate," *New York Times*, July 23, 1900, p. 7.

61. Bill Henry and Patricia Yeomans, *An Approved History of the Olympic Games* (Sherman Oaks, Calif.: Alfred, 1983), 47–48.

62. Caspar Whitney, "The Sportsman's View-Point: Record of American Athletes Abroad," *Outing* (Sept. 1900): 677.

63. Caspar Whitney, "The Sportsman's View-Point: England's Athletic Somnolence and Why America Defeats England," *Outing* 36 (Sept. 1900): 677–78.

64. "Americans Again Lead," 5.

65. Most American commentators thought that Kraenzlein was the better of the two athletes. Malcolm W. Ford wrote that "Kraenzlein is surely one of the best specimens of an athlete the world has yet produced" and thought that he would soon surpass Prinstein in the long jump (Malcolm W. Ford, "Remarkable Athletic Performances, *Outing* 35 [Mar. 1900]: 607–8). Caspar Whitney thought the two might divide honors at the Olympics but considered Kraenzlein a superior overall athlete (Whitney, "The Way of the Sportsman: American Athletes in Paris," 423).

66. "Yankee Athletes Barred," 1.

67. "Seven More Victories," 9.

68. Hjalmar Hjorth Boyesen, "The Most Athletic Nation in the World," *Cosmopolitan* 37 (May 1904): 83.

69. Orton, "The Paris Games," 691–95.

70. The Olympic maxim now reads, "The essential thing is not to have conquered but to have fought well." Coubertin actually proclaimed that "the importance of life is not the triumph, but the struggle." The bishop of Pennsylvania's 1908 sermon proclaiming that "the importance of the Olympiads lies not so much in winning as in taking part" inspired Coubertin. See Lucas, *The Modern Olympic Games,* 62–63, for the genesis of the quotation.

71. Charles J. P. Lucas, *The Olympic Games: 1904* (St. Louis: Woodward and Tiernan, 1905), 13–14.

72. Coubertin, "The Meeting of the Olympian Games," 811.

Chapter 4: St. Louis, 1904

1. Robert K. Barney, "Born from Dilemma: America Awakens to the Modern Olympic Games, 1901–1903," *Olympika* 1 (1992): 92–135.

2. "Olympic Games in America," *New York Times,* July 28, 1900, p. 5.

3. Barney, "Born from Dilemma," 94–96.

4. James E. Sullivan, "Athletics and the Stadium," *Cosmopolitan* 31 (Sept. 1901): 501–8.

5. Barney, "Born from Dilemma," 97.

6. John Lucas, *The Modern Olympic Games* (New York: A. S. Barnes, 1980), 67–71; Barney, "Born from Dilemma," 93–104.

7. Henry J. Furber Jr., "Modern Olympian Games Movement," *The Independent* 54 (Feb. 13, 1902): 384–86.

8. "The Olympic Games of the World's Fair," *World's Fair Bulletin* 5 (Oct. 1904): 16; *National Cyclopaedia of American Biography,* s.v. "Sullivan, James Edward" (New York: James T. White, 1916).

9. "May Play Olympian Games at the Fair," *St. Louis Republic,* July 11, 1902, in Louisiana Purchase Exposition Scrapbooks, vol. 31, Missouri Historical Society, St. Louis, Missouri.

10. A sampling of titles reveals the progression of the transfer process: "May Lose Olympian Games," *Chicago Chronicle,* Nov. 11, 1902; "May Lose Big Games," *Chicago Record Herald,* Nov. 11, 1902; "Problem of the Olympian Games," *Chicago Tribune,* Nov. 12, 1902; "Chicago Yields Games to St. Louis," *Chicago Inter-Ocean,* Nov. 13, 1902; "Olympian Games Tangle," *St. Louis Globe-Democrat,* Nov. 13, 1902; "Olympian Games Will Be Held in St. Louis," *St. Louis World,* Feb. 12, 1903; "St. Louis Gets Olympic Games," *St. Louis Globe-Democrat,* Feb. 2, 1903. All in Louisiana Purchase Exposition Scrapbooks, vol. 31, Missouri Historical Society.

11. A. G. Spalding to J. F. W. Skiff, Oct. 9, 1902, Executive Committee Minutes, Louisiana Purchase Committee Minutes, Louisiana Purchase Company Collection, series 11, subseries 3, folder 10 (typescript), Missouri Historical Society; James E. Sullivan, "Review of the Olympic Games of 1904," in *Spalding's Official Athletic Almanac for 1905,* ed. James E. Sullivan (New York: American Sports, 1905), 157; Edmund S. Hoch, "The Olympic Games," *World's Fair Bulletin* 4 (Mar. 1903): 10–15.

12. Baron Pierre de Coubertin to Sir, Feb. 10, 1902, Executive Committee Minutes, Louisiana Purchase Committee Minutes, Louisiana Purchase Company Collection, series 11, subseries 3, folder 10 (typescript), Missouri Historical Society.

13. Hoch, "The Olympic Games," 10–15.

14. Sullivan, "Review of the Olympic Games of 1904," 157.

15. Roosevelt quoted in John Wesley Hanson, *The Official History of the Fair, St. Louis, 1904, with the Assistance and Approval of the St. Louis Fair Officials* (St. Louis: J. W. Hanson, 1904), 49–58.

16. Lincoln Steffens, *The Shame of the Cities* (New York: McClure, Phillips, 1904).

17. "St. Louis Celebrates," *Bulletin of the Missouri Historical Society* 11 (Oct. 1954): 54–67.

18. John Patrick Diggins, "Republicanism and Progressivism," *American Quarterly* 37 (Fall 1985): 572–98; Dorothy Ross, *The Origins of American Social Science* (New York: Cambridge University Press, 1991); Sean Wilentz, *Chants Democratic: New York City and the Rise of the American Working Class, 1788–1850* (New York: Oxford University Press, 1984); Leon Fink, *Workingmen's Democracy: The Knights of Labor and American Politics* (Urbana: University of Illinois Press, 1983); Steven J. Ross, *Workers on the Edge: Work, Leisure, and Politics in Industrializing Cinncinati, 1788–1890* (New York: Columbia University Press, 1985).

19. "Athletics at the St. Louis Exposition," *Cleveland Leader,* Aug. 2, 1902, Louisiana Purchase Exposition Scrapbooks, vol. 31, Missouri Historical Society.

20. John Brisben Walker, "Athletics and Health," *Cosmopolitan* 37 (Sept. 1904): 593.

21. See articles in the *Cleveland Leader, Los Angeles Times, Rome* [Georgia] *Tribune, Salt Lake City Tribune, Spirit of the Times, Albany* [Oregon] *Herald,* and *Waukesha* [Wisconsin] *Herald* in the Louisiana Purchase Exposition Scrapbooks, vol. 31, Missouri Historical Society.

22. Sullivan text reproduced in David R. Francis, ed., *The Universal Exposition of 1904* (St. Louis: Louisiana Purchase Exposition Company, 1913), 536.

23. *Olympic Games Programme: Physical Training Section,* Department of Physical Culture, Louisiana Purchase Exposition, 1904, Missouri Historical Society; James E.

Sullivan, ed., *Spalding's Official Athletic Almanac for 1904* (New York: American Sports, 1903), 186–87; "American Physical Education Society," *St. Louis Globe-Democrat*, Aug. 26, 1904, p. 2.

24. Sullivan, *Spalding's Almanac for 1904*, 186–87; the scholastic Olympics were underwritten by William Randolph Hearst. See Luther Halsey Gulick, "St. Louis World's Fair," *New York American*, Apr. 17, 1904, Louisiana Purchase Exposition Scrapbooks, vol. 198, Missouri Historical Society.

25. Mark Bennitt, ed., *History of the Louisiana Purchase Exposition* (St. Louis: Universal Exposition, 1905; repr., New York: Arno, 1976), 568.

26. Francis, *The Universal Exposition of 1904*, 537.

27. The organizers hyped the scientific angle. Gulick gave talks entitled "Machinery Taking away Muscular Work" and "Clean Sport a Great Factor in the Moral Development of Boys" at the Catholic Summer School at Lake Champlain. See "Sullivan and Gulick on Physical Education," *Brooklyn Citizen*, Aug. 29, 1903. See articles in the *New York Herald, Chicago Inter Ocean, Brooklyn Citizen, Brooklyn Eagle*, and *Boston Transcript* in the Louisiana Purchase Exposition Scrapbooks, vol. 31, Missouri Historical Society.

28. Sullivan, *Spalding's Almanac for 1905*, 184.

29. Francis, *The Universal Exposition of 1904*, 539.

30. *National Cyclopaedia of American Biography*, s.v. "Francis, David R." (New York: James T. White, 1935).

31. Sullivan, *Spalding's Almanac for 1904*, 184–85; idem, *Spalding's Almanac for 1905*, 157–63; Francis, *The Universal Exposition of 1904*, 536–42. See articles on associated sports in the *New York Sun, Hartford Telegram, Kalamazoo Telegraph, New York American, New York News-Telegram, New York Commercial-Advertiser, Denver News, Louisville Courier-Journal*, and *Shreveport Journal* in the Louisiana Purchase Exposition Scrapbooks, vol. 31, Missouri Historical Society. The official programs can be found in the *Louisiana Purchase Exposition—Catalogue of Physical Culture Department and Olympic Games Program*, Missouri Historical Society.

32. WJ McGee, "Anthropology," *World's Fair Bulletin* 5 (Feb. 1904): 4–9; idem, "Strange Races of Men," *The World's Work: The St. Louis Exposition* 5 (Aug. 1904): 5185–88; Francis, *The International Exposition of 1904*, 522–29.

33. Sullivan, *Spalding's Almanac for 1905*, 249.

34. "Moros to Win Tribal Games," *St. Louis Globe-Democrat*, Aug. 11, 1904, p. 4.

35. "Moro Athlete Approaches World's Jumping Record," *St. Louis Globe-Democrat*, Aug. 11, 1904, p. 4.

36. Bennitt, *Louisiana Purchase Exposition*, 567.

37. "Indians Show Excellent Form in Intertribal Athletic Meet," *St. Louis Globe-Democrat*, Aug. 12, 1904, p. 4.

38. "Indians First; Filipinos, Second; Patagonians, Third," *St. Louis Star*, Aug. 13, 1904, p. 4.

39. Ibid.; "Pygmies Indulge in Mud Fight," *St. Louis Republic*, Aug. 13, 1904, p. 5; "Barbarians Meet in Athletic Games," *St. Louis Post-Dispatch*, Aug. 13, 1904, final page; "American Indians Capture Anthropology Athletic Meet," *St. Louis Globe-Democrat*, Aug. 13,

1904, p. 6; "At the Intertribal Games in the World's Fair Stadium," *St. Louis Star*, Aug. 14, 1904, sport sec., p. 4; "Pygmies Outdo Savage Athletes," *St. Louis Post-Dispatch*, Aug. 14, 1904, sec. 3.

40. "A Novel Athletic Contest," *World's Fair Bulletin* 5 (Sept. 1904): 50.

41. Bennit, *Louisiana Purchase Exposition*, 567. Bennitt compiled his "official" history using the reports written by the directors of every major division of the St. Louis fair. James E. Sullivan directed both the Physical Culture Exhibition and the Olympic Games. Sullivan wrote official reports on both events.

42. Ibid., 573.

43. "A Novel Athletic Contest," 50; Sullivan, *Spalding's Almanac for 1905*, 253–57.

44. "A Novel Athletic Contest," 50.

45. Baron Pierre de Coubertin, *Une Campagne de 21 Ans* (Paris: Librairie de l'Education Physique, 1908), 161, as quoted in Allen Guttmann, *The Games Must Go On: Avery Brundage and the Olympic Movement* (New York: Columbia University Press, 1984), 20.

46. "Disagrees with Russell Sage: Doctor McGee Praises Recreation as Builder of Mind, Body and Morals," *St. Louis Republic*, Aug. 27, 1904, sec. 2, p. 1.

47. "The Olympic Games," *St. Louis Post-Dispatch*, Aug. 28, 1904, Scrapbook 1904 B, United States Olympic Committee Archives, Colorado Springs, Colo.

48. "Olympic Games of 1904," *New York Times*, July 20, 1904, p. 3.

49. Barney's "Born from Dilemma" details the national press coverage of the St. Louis Olympics. In early August 1903, articles touting the games appeared in papers all over the country, including the *Columbus* [Ohio] *Press, Salt Lake City Tribune, Youngstown* [Ohio] *Telegram, Des Moines Leader, Brooklyn Eagle, Washington Star-Post, Chicago Journal, Detroit Free-Press, Pittsburgh Gazette, Baltimore Sun, Milwaukee Sentinel, Philadelphia Record, San Francisco Post, St. Louis Globe-Democrat, Cleveland Press, Los Angeles Express, Great Falls* [Montana] *Leader, Beloit* [Wisconsin] *Free-Press, Waterloo* [Iowa] *Reporter, Burlington* [Vermont] *Journal*, and *Minneapolis News*, all in the Louisiana Purchase Exposition Scrapbooks, vol. 31, Missouri Historical Society. See articles on the history of the Olympics in the *Buffalo Courier, New Haven Leader, Binghamton* [New York] *Herald, Baker City* [Oregon] *Democrat, Berkeley Gazette, Walla Walla Statesman, Kansas City World*, and *Akron Democrat*, all in the Louisiana Purchase Exposition Scrapbooks, vol. 32, Missouri Historical Society.

50. See articles in the *Brooklyn Times, Louisville Courier-Journal, New Haven Palladium*, and *Minneapolis Times* in the Louisiana Purchase Exposition Scrapbooks, vol. 31, Missouri Historical Society. See also the *St. Louis Globe-Democrat, St. Louis Post-Dispatch*, and *St. Louis Republic* for August 1904.

51. "Athletes of All Nations Will Battle in Olympic Games at Stadium Monday," *St. Louis Globe-Democrat*, Aug. 28, 1904, Scrapbook 1904 B, United States Olympic Committee Archives.

52. "Now for the Olympic Games, with the World's Greatest Athletes in Competition!" *St. Louis Post-Dispatch*, Sunday Magazine, Aug. 28, 1904.

53. Sullivan, *Spalding's Almanac for 1904*, 191.

54. "A Chance for Girl Athletes to Achieve Fame," *Colorado Springs Telegraph*, Sept. 6, 1903; Louisiana Purchase Exposition Scrapbooks, vol. 31, Missouri Historical Society.

55. Charles J. P. Lucas, *The Olympic Games: 1904* (St. Louis: Woodward and Tiernan, 1905), 15. Lucas held the world's record in an arcane event known as gathering potatoes—or at least he held the mark for gathering ten potatoes. On Aug. 18, 1903, the *Louisville Courier-Journal* reported that Lucas was set to defend his national title in a St. Louis AAU meet. "At St. Louis Lucas will attempt to break the record for gathering twelve potatoes, four feet apart, distance 208 yards. This record has stood since 1877, and is held by C.G. of Rochester, N.Y." The potato-gatherer's eyewitness account, *The Olympic Games: 1904*, provided the most extensive coverage of the St. Louis games. Apparently Lucas was an expert "gatherer." He held world records in a variety of "stone-gathering" events. In 1902 he gathered eight stones, two yards apart, with a five-yard finish, in thirty-one seconds. In 1904 at St. Louis he gathered ten stones separated by five-yard intervals from a course that measured 183⅓ yards and had nineteen "rightabout turns" in forty-two seconds. He also set another ten-stone record on a different course and held a twelve-stone record. See James E. Sullivan, ed., *Spalding's Official Athletic Almanac for 1910* (New York: American Sports, 1910), 29.

56. "Athletes of All Nations Will Battle in Olympic Games at Stadium Monday," Scrapbook 1904 B, United States Olympic Committee Archives.

57. "West against All the World," *Louisville Courier-Journal*, July 31, 1904, Scrapbook 1904 B, United States Olympic Committee Archives.

58. "Olympian Games Begin Today," *Chicago Tribune*, Aug. 29, 1904, p. 8.

59. "N.Y.A.C. Leads in Olympic Games," *Chicago Tribune*, Aug. 30, 1904, p. 6.

60. The *Chicago Tribune* and *St. Louis Post-Dispatch* counted 5,000. The *St. Louis Globe-Democrat* counted 10,000 and another 1,000 on a hillside. Charles Lucas remembered 3,000. See "N.Y.A.C. Leads in Olympic Games," *Chicago Tribune*, Aug. 30, 1904, p. 6; "New Olympic Records Made in Olympic Games," *St. Louis Post-Dispatch*, Aug. 30, 1904; and "American Athletes Smother Foreigners in Olympic Championship Contests," *St. Louis Globe-Democrat*, Aug. 30, 1904, all in Scrapbook 1904 B, United States Olympic Committee Archives; see also Lucas, *The Olympic Games: 1904*, 23.

61. "New Records Made in Olympic Games"; Lucas, *The Olympic Games: 1904*, 23–42.

62. "Olympian Games Begin Today," 8.

63. See coverage of record-breaking American victories in the August and September 1904 editions of the *St. Louis Republic, St. Louis Post-Dispatch, St. Louis Star,* and *St. Louis Globe-Democrat*.

64. Sullivan, *Spalding's Almanac for 1904*, 191.

65. Associated Press and Grolier, *Pursuit of Excellence: The Olympic Story* (Danbury, Conn.: Grolier, 1979), 53.

66. Sullivan, *Spalding's Almanac for 1905*, 167–71.

67. "How the Great Marathon Was Run and Won," *St. Louis Star*, Aug. 31, 1904, Scrapbook 1904 B, United States Olympic Committee Archives; "Americans Seeking to Seize Classic Honors in Marathon Today," *St. Louis Post-Dispatch*, Aug. 30, 1904.

68. Lucas, *The Olympic Games: 1904*, 48.

69. "Lentauw's Great Race over Stubble Field," *St. Louis Globe-Democrat,* Aug. 31, 1904, Scrapbook 1904 B, United States Olympic Committee Archives.

70. Lucas, *The Olympic Games: 1904,* 45–66; "Carvajal, Cuban Distance Runner, Lost Marathon Race Because of Hunger," *St. Louis Chronicle,* Aug. 31, 1904, in "Louisiana Purchase Exposition—Olympic Games," Missouri Historical Society Vertical File.

71. Lucas, *The Olympic Games: 1904,* 45–66.

72. "Big Crowd Cheers When Lorz Finishes," *St. Louis Globe-Democrat,* Aug. 31, 1904, Scrapbook 1904 B, United States Olympic Committee Archives.

73. Lucas, *The Olympic Games: 1904,* 45–66; "Hicks, an American, Winner and Hero of the Marathon Race," *St. Louis Post-Dispatch,* Aug. 31, 1904; "Thos. Hicks of Cambridge Won the Marathon Race," *St. Louis Chronicle,* Aug. 31, 1904; "New Englander Wins Marathon Race at the Fair," *St. Louis Republic,* Aug. 31, 1904, in "Louisiana Purchase Exposition—Olympic Games," Missouri Historical Society Vertical File; "How the Great Marathon Was Run and Won," 10.

74. "How the Great Marathon Was Run and Won," 10.

75. Lucas, *The Olympic Games: 1904,* 61; "How the Great Marathon Was Run and Won," 10.

76. "Olympic Games Officials Condemn Marathon Race," *St. Louis Globe-Democrat,* Sept. 4, 1904, Scrapbook 1904 B, United States Olympic Committee Archives.

77. "New York Athletes' Victory Protested, *New York Times,* Sept. 4, 1904, p. 10.

78. J. W. McConaughy, "Great Work Done by Athletes in the Stadium Events," *St. Louis Post-Dispatch,* Sept. 11, 1904, sec. 2, p. 6.

79. Lucas, *The Olympic Games: 1904,* 100–101; J. W. McConaughy, "Chicago Protests New York's Victory in Olympic Games," *St. Louis Post-Dispatch,* Sept. 4, 1904, p. 10; R. F. Baldwin, "Chicago A.C. Officials Say That DeWitt Is a 'Ringer,' " *St. Louis Star,* Sept. 4, 1904, sec. 3, p. 1; "Storm of Protests Mark N.Y.A.C.'s Victory by 1 Point in Olympic Games," *St. Louis Globe-Democrat,* Sept. 4, 1904, p. 15.

80. "Chicago Men Beat C.A.A.," *Chicago Tribune,* Sept. 5, 1904, p. 8.

81. "Great Olympic Games End at World's Fair," *Louisville Herald,* Sept. 4, 1904, Scrapbook 1904 B, United States Olympic Committee Archives.

82. "World's Championship Trophy for N.Y.A.C.," *New York Times,* Nov. 22, 1904, p. 7.

83. Francis, *The Universal Exposition of 1904,* 539.

84. Sullivan, *Spalding's Almanac for 1905,* 161.

85. Ibid., 157–65.

86. "Foreign Visitors to Fair Say Olympic Games Were without Athletic Parallel," *St. Louis Globe-Democrat,* Sept. 4, 1904, sec. 3, p. 10.

87. Francis, *The Universal Exposition of 1904,* 535.

88. "The Olympic Games of the World's Fair," *World's Fair Bulletin* 5 (Oct. 1904): 16–21.

89. "Small Crowds at Olympic Games," *St. Louis Star,* Sept. 4, 1904, sport sec., p. 2.

90. "Modern Sprinters Strive to Break the Records of Ancients," *St. Louis Republic,* Aug. 31, 1904, p. 5.

91. Owen Wister, *The Virginian* (New York: Grosset and Dunlap, 1904), 147.

92. McConaughy, "Great Work Done by Athletes," 6.

93. "The final results of the Olympic Games proved conclusively what has often been claimed, that the colleges of America will furnish the champion athletes of the future," affirmed Sullivan. He provided statistics to back his claim. Counting the twenty-four individual events (he excluded the tug-of-war and team race) in the "official" program, Sullivan tabulated fifteen victories for collegians (Sullivan, *Spalding's Almanac for 1905*, 165–71). In the version of his report that appeared in Francis's *Universal Exposition of 1904*, Sullivan claimed that college men won sixteen out of twenty-four events and had fifty-two of the top ninety-four places (540).

94. Lucas excepted Princeton, Chicago, Washington University of St. Louis, Stanford, the University of Oklahoma, St. Louis University, the University of Missouri, and the University of Colorado from his indictment of American colleges; see Lucas, *The Olympic Games: 1904*, 15–17.

95. Ibid., 45–47, 141.

96. "T. J. Hicks and A. J. Corey, Who Ran One-Two in the Great Marathon, Were Born in England and France, Respectively," *St. Louis Star*, Aug. 31, 1904, p. 10.

97. Ray Ginger, *Age of Excess: The United States from 1877 to 1914*, 2d ed. (New York: Macmillan, 1975), 242–49.

98. "Two Surprises at Last Week's Olympian Games at the St. Louis Fair," *Chicago Tribune*, Sept. 4, 1904, sporting sec., p. 8; Lucas, *The Olympic Games: 1904*, 25, 78. St. Louis's African American weekly, *The Palladium*, did not mention Poage or his accomplishments.

99. "Olympic Games Result in Feats," *Chicago Tribune*, Sept. 2, 1904, p. 8.; Lucas, *The Olympic Games: 1904*, 96–97.

100. Thomas I. Lee, "The Record Breakers," *Munsey's* 25 (July 1901): 472.

101. Arthur Ruhl, "The Men Who Set the Marks," *Outing* 52 (July 1908): 387.

102. "A Novel Athletic Contest," 50.

Chapter 5: The Limits of Universal Claims

1. Robert Haven Schauffler, "What Is Sportsmanship?" *The Outlook* 99 (Nov. 11, 1911): 626. Schauffler, an American expatriate living in Europe, played tennis for Italy in the 1906 "interim" Olympics in Athens.

2. "The Olympic Games," *The Outlook* 89 (July 25, 1908): 636.

3. "Race Questions at the Olympics," *The Independent* 73 (July 25, 1912): 214.

4. Davis Edwards, "Col. Thompson Praises America's Olympic Athletes," *New York Times*, Aug. 25, 1912, sec. 5, p. 10.

5. Edward Bayard Moss, "America's Olympic Argonauts," *Harper's Weekly* 56 (July 6, 1912): 11; Edward Bayard Moss, "America's Athletic Missionaries," *Harper's Weekly* 56 (July 27, 1912): 8.

6. Carl Crow, "America First in Athletics," *The World's Work* 27 (Dec. 1913): 194.

7. Edward Alsworth Ross, "Introduction," in Richard Henry Edwards, *Popular Amusements* (New York: Arno, 1976 [1915]), 5–6.

8. Lester F. Ward, *Applied Sociology: A Treatise on the Conscious Improvement of So-*

ciety by Society (Boston: Ginn, 1906); Herbert Croly, *The Promise of American Life* (New York: Macmillan, 1909).

9. Daniel T. Rodgers, "In Search of Progressivism," *Reviews in American History* 10 (Dec. 1982): 113–32; Don S. Kirschner, "The Ambiguous Legacy: Social Justice and Social Control in the Progressive Era," *Historical Reflections* 2 (Summer 1975): 69–88.

10. John Corbin, "The Modern Chivalry," *The Atlantic Monthly* 89 (Apr. 1902): 601–11.

11. Luther Halsey Gulick, "Popular Recreation and Public Morality," *Annals of the American Academy of Political and Social Science* 34 (July 1909): 33.

12. Thorstein Veblen, *The Vested Interests and the Common Man: The Modern Point of View and the New Order* (New York: Huebsch, 1919).

13. Gulick, "Popular Recreation and Public Morality," 33. See also Richard Cabot, "The Relation of Play to a Civilization of Power," *The Playground* 7 (Aug. 1913): 183–95; Henry S. Curtis, "The Man without the Hoe," *The Playground* 6 (Dec. 1912): 309–11; Gustavus T. Kirby, "The Recreation Movement; Its Possibilities and Limitations," *The Playground* 5 (Oct. 1911): 224; Joseph Lee, "American Play Tradition and Our Relation to It," *The Playground* 7 (July 1913): 148–59; idem, "Play the Life Saver," *The Playground* 8 (Mar. 1915): 417–27; F. G. Wallace, "The Cry of Our Brother," *The Playground* 7 (June 1913): 117–21.

14. Elliot Gorn, *The Manly Art: Bare-Knuckle Prize Fighting in America* (Ithaca, N.Y.: Cornell University Press, 1986).

15. Elliot Gorn and Warren Goldstein, *A Brief History of American Sport* (New York: Hill and Wang, 1993), 114–29.

16. John F. Kasson, *Amusing the Millions: Coney Island at the Turn of the Century* (New York: Hill and Wang, 1978).

17. Peter Levine, *A. G. Spalding and the Rise of Baseball* (New York: Oxford University Press, 1985); Allen Guttmann, *The Games Must Go On: Avery Brundage and the Olympic Movement* (New York: Columbia University Press, 1984), 12–22; John Lucas, *The Modern Olympic Games* (New York, A. S. Barnes, 1980), 64–73.

18. Joseph Lee, "Play as an Antidote to Civilization," *The Playground* 5 (July 1911): 120.

19. Melvin Adleman, *A Sporting Time: New York City and the Rise of Modern Sport, 1820–1870* (Urbana: University of Illinois Press, 1986), 269–96.

20. Edwards, *Popular Amusements,* 194–95; Dorothy Bocker, "Social Cleavage and the Playground," *The Playground* 9 (May 1915): 89–90.

21. Frederic L. Paxson, "The Rise of Sport," *Mississippi Valley Historical Review* 4 (Sept. 1917): 167–68.

22. Dudley Sargent, "Are Athletics Making Girls Masculine?" *Ladies Home Journal* 29 (Mar. 1912): 11, 71–73.

23. Carrol Smith-Rosenberg, *Disorderly Conduct: Visions of Gender in America* (New York: Oxford, 1985).

24. Patricia Vertinsky, "Feminist Charlotte Perkins Gilman's Pursuit of Health and Physical Fitness as a Strategy for Emancipation," *Journal of Sport History* 16 (Spring 1989): 5–26.

25. Charlotte Perkins Gilman, *Women and Economics: A Study of the Relation between*

Men and Women as a Factor in Social Evolution, ed. Carl N. Degler (New York: Harper Torchbooks, 1966 [1898]), 58–63.

26. Anne O'Hagan, "The Athletic Girl," *Munsey's* 25 (Aug. 1901): 729–30.

27. Price Collier, "Sport's Place in the Nation's Well-Being," *Outing* 32 (July 1898): 387.

28. For two interesting and opposing visions of the interconnections of republicanism and gender, see Linda Kerber, *Women in the Republic* (Chapel Hill: University of North Carolina Press, 1980); and Mary Beth Norton, "The Evolution of White Women's Experience in Early America," *American Historical Review* 89 (June 1984): 593–619.

29. Catharine Beecher, *A Treatise on Domestic Economy, for the Use of Young Ladies at Home, at School*, rev. ed. (New York: Harper and Brothers, 1841); Kathryn Kish Sklar, *Catharine Beecher: A Study in American Domesticity* (New York: Norton, 1976).

30. Mary Taylor Bissell, "Athletics for City Girls," *Popular Science Monthly* 46 (Dec. 1894): 147–48.

31. O'Hagan, "The Athletic Girl," 730.

32. Kirk Munroe, "Modern Canoeing," *The Wheelman* 3 (Dec. 1883): 217–24; Mary K. Browne, Mrs. R. H. Barlow, Annette Kellerman, Mrs. Emerson Hough, Gail Kane, and Ann Murdock, "The Girl and Her Sports," *Ladies Home Journal* 32 (July 1915): 9–11; J. N. Laurvik, "The American Girl Out-of-Doors," *Women's Home Companion* 39 (Aug. 1912): 17–18; B. D. Knobe, "Chicago's Women's Athletic Club," *Harper's Bazaar* 39 (June 1905): 538–46.

33. Gertrude Dudley and Frances A. Kellor, *Athletic Games in the Education of Women* (New York: Holt, 1909), 3–10.

34. Dudley and Kellor's arguments match those made for men's sport by Luther Halsey Gulick in "The New Athletics," *The Outlook* 98 (July 15, 1911): 597–600.

35. Dudley and Kellor, *Athletic Games in the Education of Women*, 3–10.

36. As cited in Anna de Koven, "The Athletic Woman," *Good Housekeeping* 55 (Aug. 1912): 150.

37. Dudley and Kellor, *Athletic Games in the Education of Women*, 25–38.

38. Robert Crunden, *Ministers of Reform: The Progressives' Achievement in American Civilization* (Urbana: University of Illinois Press, 1984).

39. Jane Addams, *The Spirit of Youth and the City Streets* (New York: Macmillan, 1909), 6, 95–98.

40. Jane Addams, "Some Reflections on the Failure of the Modern City to Provide Recreation for Young Girls," *Charities and the Commons* 21 (Dec. 5, 1908): 365–68. On the extension of the playground movement to rural women, see Marie Turner Harvey, "Recreation of the Farm Woman," *The Playground* 6 (Oct. 1912): 248–55; Martha Van Rensselaer, "Recreation of the Farmer's Wife," *The Playground* 6 (Oct. 1912): 255–59. See also Mrs. Charles Frederick Wheeler, "Life for Girls," *The Playground* 7 (Aug. 1913): 201–9.

41. Dudley and Kellor, *Athletic Games in the Education of Women*, 3–10.

42. Ibid., 10–18.

43. O'Hagan, "The Athletic Girl," 733; Bissell, "Athletics for City Girls," 146–48; Alice Katharine Fallows, "Athletics for College Girls," *Century* 66 (May 1903): 60–65.

44. Christine Terhune Herrick, "Women in Athletics: The Athletic Girl Not Unfeminine," *Outing* 40 (Sept. 1902): 713–21.

45. Dudley and Kellor, *Athletic Games in the Education of Women,* 24–25.

46. De Koven, "The Athletic Woman," 151.

47. Robert Tyson, "The Bicycle and the Canoe," *Wheelman* 3 (Dec. 1883): 227.

48. F. G. Aflalo, "Women in Sport," *The Living Age* 269 (May 6, 1911): 382.

49. O'Hagan, "The Athletic Girl," 738.

50. Dudley and Kellor, *Athletic Games in the Education of Women,* 26.

51. Sargent, "Are Athletics Making Girls Masculine?"

52. Bissell, "Athletics for City Girls," 145.

53. John Garraty and Edward T. James, eds., *Dictionary of American Biography,* Supplement 4, 1946–50, s.v. "Lewis, William Henry" (New York: Scribner's, 1974); Rayford W. Logan and Michael R. Winston, *Dictionary of American Negro Biography,* s.v. "Lewis, William, Henry" (New York: Norton, 1982).

54. Editorial reprinted, with commentary, in "What's the Matter with White Men?" *The Crisis* 4 (July 1912): 123–24.

55. George Cotkin, *Reluctant Modernism: American Thought and Culture, 1880–1920* (New York: Twayne, 1992), 51–73.

56. David K. Wiggins, " 'Great Speed but Little Stamina': The Historic Debate over Black Athletic Superiority," *Journal of Sport History* 16 (Summer 1989): 158–61; Randy Roberts, *Papa Jack* (New York: Free Press, 1983).

57. Edwin B. Henderson, "The Colored College Athlete," *The Crisis* 2 (July 1911): 115–19.

58. Annie McCary, "Breaking the Color-Line," *The Crisis* 9 (Feb. 1915): 193–95.

59. See the covers featuring 1912 Olympian and University of Southern California sprinter Howard P. Drew (*The Crisis* 10 [July 1915]) and the University of Pennsylvania's great quarter-miler, John P. Taylor (*The Crisis* 2 [July 1911]), or C. H. Tobias's ode "The Colored Y.M.C.A." (*The Crisis* 9 [Nov. 1914]: 32–36).

60. John Henry Adams, "The National Pastime," *The Crisis* 1 (Jan. 1911): 18.

61. Collier, "Sport's Place," 382–88.

62. Franklin H. Giddings, "The American Idea," *Harper's Weekly* 48 (Nov. 5, 1904): 1713.

63. Ward, *Applied Sociology,* 110.

64. Schauffler, "What Is Sportsmanship?" 626.

65. Arthur Mann, *The One and the Many: Reflections on the American Identity* (Chicago: University of Chicago Press, 1979), 125–35; Sidney Mead, *The Lively Experiment: The Shaping of American Christianity* (New York: Harper and Row, 1963), 153; Ralph Henry Gabriel, *The Course of American Democratic Thought,* 2d ed. (New York: Ronald, 1956), 367–86.

66. Schauffler, "What Is Sportsmanship?" 627.

67. Ibid., 628.

68. Alan Trachtenberg, *The Incorporation of America: Culture and Society in the Gilded Age* (New York: Hill and Wang, 1982), 140–81.

69. Schauffler, "What Is Sportsmanship?" 622–23.

70. Clayton Sedgewick Cooper, *American Ideals* (Garden City, N.Y.: Doubleday, Page, 1915).

71. Addams, *The Spirit of Youth.*

72. William D. P. Bliss, editor-in-chief, *The New Encyclopedia of Social Reform,* s.vv. "Recreation Centers" and "Playgrounds" (New York: Funk and Wagnalls, 1908).

73. Joseph Lee, "American Play Tradition and Our Relation to It," *The Playground* 7 (July 1913): 148–59.

74. Henry S. Curtis, "Public Provision and Responsibility for Playgrounds," *Annals of the American Academy* 35 (July 1910): 337.

75. Otto T. Mallery, "The Social Significance of Play," *Annals of the American Academy of Political and Social Science* 35 (July 1910): 368.

76. Steven Riess, *City Games: The Evolution of American Urban Society and the Rise of Sports* (Urbana: University of Illinois Press, 1989), 93–123.

77. Sherman C. Kingsley, "Improper Recreations," *The Playground* 8 (Mar. 1915): 424–27.

78. J. P. Casey, "Our Great American Game," *The Independent* 61 (Aug. 16, 1906): 375; Francis Tabor, "Directed Sport as a Factor in Education," *Forum* 42 (Feb. 12, 1898): 321; Allen Guttmann, *From Ritual to Record: The Nature of Modern Sport* (New York: Columbia University Press, 1978), 87–89; Donald Mrozek, *Sport and American Mentality, 1880–1910* (Knoxville: University of Tennessee Press, 1983), 161–88.

79. Gustavus T. Kirby, "The Recreation Movement; Its Possibilities and Limitations," *The Playground* 5 (Oct. 1911): 217–24. See also F. G. Wallace, "The Cry of Our Brother," *The Playground* 7 (June 1913): 117–21; Edward T. Devine, "How Fundamental Is the Play Movement?" *The Playground* 8 (Mar. 1915): 422–23; Joseph Lee, "Play as Medicine," *The Playground* 5 (Dec. 1911): 289–302; Beulah Kennard, "Pittsburgh's Playgrounds," *The Survey* 22 (May 11, 1909): 184–96; Everett B. Mero, "How Public Gymnasiums and Baths Help to Make Good Citizens," *The American City* 1 (Oct. 1909): 69–76; Henry S. Curtis, "The Need of a Comprehensive Playground Plan," *The American City* 5 (Dec. 1911): 338–40; idem, "The Neighborhood Center," *The American City* 7 (July 1912): 14–17 and (Aug. 1912): 133–37.

80. Bocker, "Social Cleavage and the Playground," 87–90.

81. Amalie Hofer Jerome, "The Playground as a Social Center," *Annals of the American Academy* 35 (July 1910): 347.

82. Ernest Poole, "Chicago's Public Playgrounds," *The Outlook* 87 (Dec. 7, 1907): 776–77.

83. Mallery, "The Social Significance of Play," 372.

84. Poole, "Chicago's Public Playgrounds," 776–77; Mallery, "The Social Significance of Play," 372.

85. Trachtenberg, *The Incorporation of America,* 70–100.

86. Poole, "Chicago's Public Playgrounds," 781.

87. *The Playground* 1 (Mar. 1908): front cover.

88. Jacob A. Riis, "The Old Order Changeth," *The Playground* 8 (Mar. 1915): 415.

89. Jacob A. Riis, "Fighting the Gang with Athletics," *Collier's* 46 (Feb. 11, 1911): 17.

90. Victor Von Borosini, "Our Recreation Facilities and the Immigrant," *Annals of the American Academy of Political and Social Science* 35 (July 1910): 357–67.

91. Jane Addams, "Recreation as a Public Function in Urban Communities," *The American Journal of Sociology* 17 (Mar. 1912): 615–19.

92. Lewis Perry, *Intellectual Life in America* (New York: Franklin Watts, 1984), 263–76.

93. Dudley Allen Sargent, "Competition and Culture," *American Physical Education Review* 15 (Nov. 1910): 581–85.

94. Alan M. Kraut, *The Huddled Masses: The Immigrant in American Society, 1880–1920* (Arlington Heights, Ill.: Harlan Davidson, 1982), 136.

95. As cited in H. Perry Robinson, *The Twentieth Century American* (New York: Putnam's, 1908), 426.

96. "The Higher Athletics," *The Nation* 85 (Dec. 5, 1907): 510.

97. "Race Questions at the Olympics," *The Independent* 73 (July 25, 1912): 214–15. The Italian from Paterson, New Jersey, who killed a king was Gaetano Bresci (1869–1901). Bresci was an Italian anarchist and silk weaver who immigrated to the United States in December 1897 and joined the Italian American anarchist conclave in Paterson. Bresci belonged to the "direct action" wing of the anarchist movement. Loyal to his philosophy, he returned to Italy in 1900 and on July 29 of that year shot King Humbert I to death at Monza, near Milan. Bresci committed suicide in 1901 after being sentenced to life in prison for his crime. "The struggle between reactionaries and liberals ended grievously with the assassination, on 29 July at Monza, of the noble and chivalrous King Humbert by an anarchist recently arrived from America," lamented Benedetto Croce in identifying the assassin as American in origin (Benedetto Croce, *A History of Italy, 1871–1915*, trans. Cecilia M. Ady [Oxford: Clarendon, 1929], 212). For information on Bresci see Christopher Seton-Watson, *Italy from Liberalism to Fascism, 1870–1925* (London: Metheun, 1967), 167; Frank J. Coppa, ed., *Dictionary of Modern Italian History* (Westport, Conn.: Greenwood, 1985), 52–53.

The Italian from Paterson who "won" a race actually finished third. Gaston Strobino, an Italian American distance runner from the South Paterson Athletic Club, won the bronze medal in the marathon—the highest American finish—at the Stockholm Olympics in 1912. Two South Africans, K. K. MacArthur and C. W. Gitsham, beat Strobino's time of 2 hours, 38 minutes, and 42.2 seconds (James Edward Sullivan, ed., *The Olympic Games: Stockholm, 1912*, Spalding "Red Cover" Series of Athletic Handbooks No. 17R [New York: American Sports, 1912], 73, 221).

98. Mann, *The One and the Many*, 178.

99. Schauffler, "What Is Sportsmanship?" 626.

Chapter 6: Athens, 1906, and London, 1908

1. Vincent Van Marter Beede, "Greek Games Old and New," *The Chautauquan* 43 (May 1906): 243–52.

2. Curtiss, the AOC treasurer, had long been active in New York City sporting circles. Weeks, a former president of the AAU, was president of the AAU's Metropolitan Association. Rubien was the vice-president of the Metropolitan chapter. Thompson and Gulick had been instrumental in the creation of the PSAL and active in New York's play-

ground movement. See James E. Sullivan, ed., *Spalding's Athletic Almanac for 1907* (New York: American Sports, 1907), 24–38.

3. D. Karopothakes, "The Olympic Games," *The Nation* 82 (June 7, 1906): 466.

4. James B. Connolly, "The Spirit of the Olympian Games," *Outing* 48 (Apr. 1906): 104.

5. James E. Sullivan, *The Olympic Games at Athens, 1906,* Spalding's Athletic Library No. 275 (New York: American Sports, 1906), 129–30.

6. James E. Sullivan, "American Athletes in Ancient Athens," *The American Review of Reviews* 34 (July 1906): 44.

7. Sullivan, *Spalding's Almanac for 1907,* 211–28; Sullivan, "American Athletes in Ancient Athens," 43–48.

8. Sullivan, *Spalding's Almanac for 1907,* 211–28; Sullivan, *The Olympic Games at Athens,* 9.

9. James E. Sullivan, "American Athletes Champions of the World," *Outing* 48 (Aug. 1906): 625.

10. Karopothakes, "The Olympic Games," 466.

11. Sullivan, "American Athletes in Ancient Athens," 43–48; Sullivan, "American Athletes Champions of the World," 625–27.

12. Sullivan, "American Athletes in Ancient Athens," 43.

13. Karopothakes, "The Olympic Games," 466.

14. William N. Bates, "The Olympic Games of 1906," *The Independent* 60 (May 23, 1906): 1209–10.

15. Sullivan, "American Athletes Champions of the World," 625–27.

16. Sullivan, "American Athletes in Ancient Athens," 44–48.

17. Sullivan, *Spalding's Almanac for 1907,* 218 (Roosevelt); Sullivan, *The Olympic Games at Athens,* 43–47 (Roosevelt, Spalding, and editorial). For an explanation of the role of the olive trees of Altis in Greek mythology, see Manolis Andronicos, *Olympia* (Athens: Ekdotike, 1990), 5.

18. Sullivan, *The Olympic Games at Athens,* 139–43; Sullivan, *Spalding's Almanac for 1907,* 216–17.

19. Karopothakes, "The Olympic Games," 467.

20. Sullivan, "American Athletes in Ancient Athens," 48.

21. John Lucas, *The Modern Olympic Games* (New York: A. S. Barnes, 1980), 45–63.

22. "American Competitors for the Olympic Games," *Collier's* 41 (June 20, 1908): 13.

23. "American Olympic Committee Reportedly Receives Little Money from Source outside A.A.U.," *New York Times,* May 17, 1908, sec. 4, p. 2.

24. Caspar Whitney, "The View-Point: Still Talking—Excerpts from Official Reply of British Olympic Council to 'Certain Criticisms,'" *Outing* 53 (Feb. 1909): 643.

25. "The Olympic Games," *The Outlook* 89 (July 25, 1908): 636.

26. "American Competitors at the Olympic Games," 13.

27. Caspar Whitney, "The View-Point: America at the Olympic Games," *Outing* 52 (July 1908): 497.

28. Edward G. Hawke, "The Olympic Games in London," *The American Review of Reviews* 38 (July 1908): 81.

29. Reproduced in James E. Sullivan, ed., *Spalding's Official Athletic Almanac, 1909* (New York: American Sports, 1909), 118.

30. "The Athletes of the Nation," *The Living Age* 257 (June 13, 1908): 697.

31. "Musings without Method," *Blackwood's* 184 (Aug. 1908): 272.

32. "The Modern Olympic Games," *New York Times*, July 15, 1908, p. 1.

33. Hawke, "The Olympic Games in London," 80.

34. "The Fourth Olympiad," *Current Literature* 45 (July 1908): 20–24; Hawke, "The Olympic Games in London," 78–79.

35. James B. Connolly, "The Shepherd's Bush Greeks," *Collier's* 41 (Sept. 5, 1908): 12.

36. "The Athletes of the Nations," 699.

37. William Oscar Johnson, "The Taking Part," *Sports Illustrated*, July 10, 1972, p. 40. In *All That Glitters Is Not Gold: The Olympic Games* (New York: Putnam's, 1972), 128, Johnson identified Martin Sheridan, an Irish American New York City police officer and discus thrower, as the flag bearer and grumbler, but Johnson's *Sport's Illustrated* article and all the other sources agree that Rose bore the flag and uttered the famous line. Both Rose and Sheridan were proud sons of Ireland, irked by the English refusal to allow Irish athletes to compete as a separate team.

38. "Musings without Method," 272.

39. Caspar Whitney, "The View-Point: Olympic Games American Committee Report," *Outing* 53 (Nov. 1908): 244.

40. "Chronicle and Comment: The Olympic Muddle," *The Bookman* 28 (Oct. 1908): 104–5.

41. Ibid.

42. Reproduced in "The Olympic Contests," *Current Literature* 45 (Sept. 1908): 247.

43. Reproduced in Whitney, "The View-Point: American Committee Report," 248.

44. "Sullivan Scores British," *New York Times*, July 26, 1908, sec. 4, pp. 1–2.

45. Whitney, "The View-Point: Still Talking," 646.

46. "A Bitter Wrangle over Olympic Race," *New York Times*, July 24, 1908, p. 6.

47. Connolly, "The Shepherd's Bush Greeks," 13.

48. Kirby quoted in Whitney, "The View-Point: American Committee Report," 245.

49. Whitney, "The View-Point: Still Talking," 646.

50. Whitney, "The View-Point: American Committee Report," 246.

51. Caspar Whitney, "The View-Point: Reflections," *Outing* 52 (Sept. 1908): 765–66.

52. Ruhl, "The Men Who Set the Marks," 389.

53. Connolly, "The Shepherd's Bush Greeks," 12.

54. Ibid., 13. Pietri's exploits inspired Irving Berlin to write a song called "Dorando," the first piece for which he created both the lyrics and the music. See Johnson, "The Taking Part," 41.

55. Reproduced in "The Olympic Contests," 245.

56. Whitney, "The View-Point: American Committee Report," 246–47.

57. Connolly, "The Shepherd's Bush Greeks," 13.

58. "The Olympic Contests," 245.

59. Finley Peter Dunne, "'Mr. Dooley' on the Olympic Games," *American Magazine*

66 (Oct. 1908): 617. In 1902 Dunne married Margaret Abbott. She was the first American woman to win an Olympic gold medal, taking the honors in the women's golf tournament at Paris in 1900 (David Wallechinsky, *The Complete Book of the Olympics* [New York: Penguin, 1984], 544).

60. Kirby quoted in Whitney, "The View-Point: American Committee Report," 247.

61. Ibid., 248.

62. See Michael Oriard, *Reading Football: How the Popular Press Created an American Spectacle* (Chapel Hill: University of North Carolina Press, 1993), 148–62.

63. Whitney, "The View-Point: Reflections," 766.

64. "Queen Presents Medals to Athletes," *New York Times*, July 26, 1908, sec. 4, p. 2; "Sullivan Scores British," sec. 4, p. 2.

65. Whitney, "The View-Point: Reflections," 763.

66. Whitney, "The View-Point: American Committee Report," 247.

67. "Big Welcome for Yankee Athletes," *New York Times*, July 19, 1908, sec. 5, p. 12.

68. "The Olympic Squabbles," *Collier's* 41 (Sept. 12, 1908): 10.

69. "American Athletes Abroad," *The Outlook* 89 (Aug. 1, 1908): 739.

70. Whitney, "The View-Point: Reflections," 761.

71. "The Olympic Muddle," 103–6.

72. "Englishmen Unfair, Says Gus Kirby," *New York Times*, Sept. 12, 1908, p. 8.

73. Whitney, "The View-Point: American Committee Report," 244–49.

74. Ibid., 244.

75. Whitney, "The View-Point: Reflections," 764.

76. Whitney, "The View-Point: American Committee Report," 245.

77. Quoted in Whitney, "The View Point: Still Talking," 643–46.

78. H. J. Whigham, "American Sport from an English Point of View," *The Outlook* 93 (Nov. 27, 1909): 738–44.

79. "America First at Olympia," *Harper's Weekly* 52 (Aug. 1, 1908): 7.

80. Associated Press and Grolier, *Pursuit of Excellence: The Olympic Story* (Danbury, Conn.: Grolier, 1979), 64.

81. Walter Camp, "The Olympic Games," *Collier's* 41 (Sept. 5, 1908): 22.

82. Whitney, "The View-Point: Reflections," 762.

83. "The Olympic Games," 636.

84. Camp, "The Olympic Games," 22.

85. "Roosevelt Cables Congratulations to Olympic Athletes," *New York Times*, July 28, 1908, sec. 2, p. 8.

86. "The Olympic Results," *New York Times*, July 26, 1908, sec. 2, p. 6.

87. Connolly, "The Shepherd's Bush Greeks," 12.

88. Ibid.

89. Johnson, *All That Glitters,* 129.

90. Sullivan, *Spalding's Almanac for 1909,* 48. None of the contemporary accounts mentions Smithson running with a Bible; see, for instance, "America's Triumph in Olympic Games," *New York Times*, July 26, 1908, sec. 4, p. 2.

91. Connolly, "The Shepherd's Bush Greeks," 12.

92. "The Olympic Muddle," 105.

93. Whitney, "The View-Point: Reflections," 762.

94. Connolly, "The Shepherd's Bush Greeks," 13.

95. Charles E. Woodruff, "The Failure of Americans as Athletes," *The North American Review* 186 (Oct. 1907): 200–204; idem, "Why the Native American Does So Badly at the Olympic Games," *Current Literature* 53 (Aug. 1912): 182–84.

96. Dunne, "'Mr. Dooley' on the Olympic Games," 615.

97. Ibid., 615–17.

98. "When Greek Meets Greek," *New York Times*, July 19, 1908, sec. 5, p. 12.

99. "Big Welcome for Yankee Athletes," 2.

100. "Mr. Roosevelt and the Athletes," *New York Times*, Sept. 2, 1908, p. 6.

101. "Welcoming the Olympians," *New York Times*, Aug. 30, 1908, p. 6.

102. Whitney, "The View-Point: Reflections," 761.

103. Ibid., 766.

104. Ibid., 763–64.

105. Whitney, "The View-Point: American Committee Report," 247.

106. "Musings without Method," 270–72.

107. Connolly, "The Spirit of the Olympic Games," 104.

Chapter 7: Stockholm, 1912

1. "The Olympic Games at Stockholm," *Current Literature* 53 (July 1912): 15.

2. William Milligan Sloane, "The Olympic Idea: Its Origin, Foundation and Progress," *Century* 84 (July 1912): 408–9.

3. Edward Bayard Moss, "America's Olympic Argonauts," *Harper's Weekly* 56 (July 6, 1912): 11.

4. Sloane, "The Olympic Idea," 414.

5. James E. Sullivan, ed., *The Olympic Games: Stockholm 1912*, Spalding "Red Cover" Series of Athletic Handbooks No. 17R (New York: American Sports, 1912), 29–35.

6. Davis Edwards, "Col. Thompson Praises America's Olympic Athletes," *New York Times*, Aug. 25, 1912, sec. 5, p. 10; Sullivan, *The Olympic Games*, 33–35.

7. "The Fifth Olympic Games," *New York Times*, June 11, 1912, p. 8.

8. Sullivan, *The Olympic Games*, 246.

9. "Rockefeller Gives $500 to Fund," *New York Times*, Apr. 14, 1912, sec. 4, p. 9; "Carnegie Gives $500," *New York Times*, Feb. 14, 1912, p. 9; "Gould Gives $500 to Olympic Fund," *New York Times*, June 8, 1912, p. 14; Sullivan, *The Olympic Games*, 247.

10. Sullivan, *The Olympic Games*, 246–48.

11. Sullivan quoted in Moss, "America's Olympic Argonauts," 11–12.

12. Ibid. Colonel Thompson noted that about 65 percent of the team came from the collegiate ranks (Edwards, "Col. Thompson Praises America's Olympic Athletes," sec. 5, p. 10).

13. "Race Questions at the Olympics," *The Independent* 73 (July 25, 1912): 214.

14. Moss, "America's Olympic Argonauts," 11; Edward Bayard Moss, "America's Athletic Missionaries," *Harper's Weekly* 56 (July 27, 1912): 8.

15. Edward Lyell Fox, "Our Olympic Flyers," *Outing* 60 (July 1912): 395–96.

16. Moss, "America's Athletic Missionaries," 9. Sockalexis was identified as an Onondaga even though Old Town, Maine, was in the Penobscot Indian reservation.

17. "Personal," *The Crisis* 4 (July 1912): 115.

18. Moss, "America's Athletic Missionaries," 9.

19. Durkin's article reproduced in "Memories of the Last Olympic Games," *The Literary Digest* 66 (July 3, 1920): 96.

20. Moss, "America's Olympic Argonauts," 11.

21. Fox, "Our Olympic Flyers," 397.

22. "Athletics Abroad," *The Nation* 94 (Apr. 5, 1912): 408. By 1912 both E. L. Godkin and Wendell Phillips Garrison had retired from *The Nation*'s staff. Perhaps their absence softened the magazine's perspective on sport. See Frank Luther Mott, *A History of American Magazines*, 5 vols. (Cambridge, Mass.: Harvard University Press, 1938), 3:331–56.

23. "The Fifth Olympiad," *The Outlook* 101 (June 29, 1912): 460–61.

24. Moss, "America's Olympic Argonauts," 11; Sullivan, *The Olympic Games*, 41–43.

25. Edwards, "Col. Thompson Praises Athletes," sec. 5, p. 10; Sullivan, *The Olympic Games*, 237–39.

26. William Simons, "Abel Kiviat Interview," *Journal of Sport History* 13 (Winter 1986): 247.

27. Sullivan, *The Olympic Games*, 55–89.

28. Will T. Irwin, "The Olympic Games," *Collier's* 50 (Aug. 10, 1912): 9. Irwin was a prominent journalist during the Progressive Era. He became a famous war correspondent during World War I and wrote one of the best biographies of Herbert Hoover, a classmate of his at Stanford University (*The National Cyclopaedia of American Biography*, s.v. "Irwin, Will T." [New York: James T. White, 1949]).

29. Will Irwin, *The Making of a Reporter* (New York: Putnam's, 1942), 182.

30. Edwards, "Col. Thompson Praises Athletes," sec. 5, p. 10.

31. Irwin, "The Olympic Games," 9.

32. Sullivan, *The Olympic Games*, 57–59.

33. Edwards, "Col. Thompson Praises Athletes," sec. 5, p. 10.

34. Sullivan, *The Olympic Games*, 220.

35. Erik Bergvall, ed., *The Fifth Olympiad: Official Report of the Olympic Games Committee of Stockholm, 1912*, trans. Edward Adams-Ray (Stockholm: Wahlstrom and Widstrand, 1913), 865.

36. Sullivan, *The Olympic Games*, 75.

37. "The Olympic Games," *The Outlook* 101 (July 27, 1912): 655–56.

38. Moss, "America's Athletic Missionaries," 8–9.

39. "The Stars and Stripes at the Olympic Games," *Current Literature* 53 (Aug. 1912): 131.

40. Reproduced in "Our Olympic Laurels," *The Literary Digest* 45 (July 27, 1912): 131–32.

41. James E. Sullivan, "What Happened at Stockholm," *Outing* 61 (Oct. 1912): 22–31.

42. "America at the Olympic Games," *The Outlook* 101 (July 20, 1912): 603.

43. "Our Olympic Laurels," 132.

44. "More Remarks on Our Athletic Supremacy," *The Literary Digest* 45 (Aug. 10, 1912): 213.

45. "Race Questions at the Olympics," 214.

46. "Ill Training and Snobbery in British Athletics," *The Literary Digest* 45 (Aug. 31, 1912): 30; Philip J. Baker, "Olympiads and Liars," *The Outlook* 102 (Oct. 19, 1912): 355–60.

47. "The Folly of International Sport," *Blackwood's* 192 (Aug. 1912): 252–53.

48. "Games versus Athletics," *The Spectator* 109 (July 20, 1912): 85.

49. "The Olympic Games," *The Spectator* 109 (Aug. 10, 1912): 198.

50. Among the signees were Lord Grey, Lord Harris, Lord Roberts, Lord Rothschild, Lord Strathcona, and the duke of Westminster ("The British Athletic Slump," *The Literary Digest* 47 [Sept. 20, 1913]: 464). The notables who signed the appeal were ardent imperialists who had played major roles in constructing the British Empire. Lord Grey, the governor general of Canada from 1904 to 1911, had served Britain with distinction in Africa and was a great admirer and friend of Cecil Rhodes. Lord Roberts came from a distinguished colonial family and had a successful military career in the empire, culminating in a position as the supreme commander of British forces in South Africa during the early years of the Boer War. Lord Strathcona was a Canadian financier who, after a long apprenticeship in the Hudson Bay Company, helped James J. Hill to build the Great Northern Railroad and led a successful takeover of the Canadian Pacific. Known as the "Cecil Rhodes of Canada," Lord Strathcona exerted enormous power in English financial circles. Another financier among the signers, Lord Rothschild, was descended from the famous Austrian banking family and became the first professing Jew to enter the House of Lords. He was a leader of the Jewish community in England, a powerful banker, and a major philanthropist. Lord Harris, descended from a family that had been instrumental in the creation of British India, had introduced cricket on the Indian subcontinent and pushed for its spread throughout the Empire. See H. W. C. Davis and J. R. H. Weaver, eds., *Dictionary of National Biography, 1912–1921*, s.vv. "Grey, Albert Henry George," "Roberts, Frederick Sleigh," "Rothschild, Sir Nathan Meyer," and "Smith, Donald Alexander" (London: Oxford University Press, 1927); L. G. Wickham Legg, ed., *Dictionary of National Biography, 1931–1940*, s.v. "Harris, George Robert Canning" (London: Oxford University Press, 1949).

51. "The British Athletic Slump," 464.

52. Some Americans predicted that the British would give up their notions of amateurism and adopt the American athletic ethic. See "Two Athletic Standards," *The Nation* 95 (Aug. 22, 1912): 163–64.

53. "The British Athletic Slump," 464.

54. "Sullivan Defends American Athletes," *New York Times*, Aug. 31, 1912, p. 4.

55. Sullivan, *The Olympic Games*, 71–73.

56. "Our Olympic Laurels," 131. In the final years of his life, Thorpe told friends that he had replied, "thanks King," to the Swedish monarch's accolade (Dick Schaap, *An Illustrated History of the Olympics*, 3d ed. [New York: Knopf, 1975], 134–35).

57. "The Amateur," *The Outlook* 103 (Feb. 8, 1913): 294.

58. Sullivan, *The Olympic Games*, 81–89.

59. "Race Questions at the Olympics," 214.

60. Carl Crow, "America First in Athletics," *The World's Work* 27 (Dec. 1913): 191.

61. "The Moral of the Games," *New York Times,* July 15, 1908, p. 8.

62. See, for example, "American Results and Methods," *New York Times,* July 16, 1912, p. 8.

63. Rozet quoted in "Call Our Sporting Morals Very Lax," *New York Times,* Sept. 29, 1912, sec. 3, p. 4.

64. "Race Questions at the Olympics," 215.

65. Crow, "America First in Athletics," 192–93.

66. "Personal," *The Crisis* 4 (Aug. 1912): 166.

67. "Race Questions at the Olympics," 214–15.

68. "Ill Training and Snobbery in British Athletics," 330.

69. "Crow, "America First in Athletics," 193–94 (includes the Reichnau quotation).

70. Finley Peter Dunne, "Dooley on Supremacy of the English in Athletics," *New York Times,* July 28, 1912, sec. 5, p. 9.

71. Sullivan, *The Olympic Games,* 233–34.

72. "Olympic Champions Cheered and Dined," *New York Times,* Aug. 25, 1912, p. 4.

73. "Team Honored at a Dinner," *New York Times,* Aug. 25, 1912, p. 4. The offerings included "Grape Fruit, fresh from *Craig's* farm, Chicken consommé à la *Babcock,* potatoes à la *McGrath,* Sauce *Meredith,* Potato Croquettes, *Kelly* style, *Reidpath* Asparagus, Sauce *Strobino, Jim Thorpe* Spring chicken in casserole from '*Babe' MacDonald's* Hennery, Salad à la *Lippincott,* and Lampote *Sheppard,*" Apollinaris. Ralph Craig won the 100- and 200-meter dashes. Henry Babcock won the pole vault. Matt McGrath triumphed in the hammer throw. James Meredith won the 800-meter run. Fred Kelly finished first in the 110-meter hurdles. Charles Reidpath won the 400-meter race. Gaston Strobino finished third in the marathon. Jim Thorpe triumphed in the pentathlon and decathlon. Pat "Babe" MacDonald won the shot put. Donald Lippincott finished third in the 100-meter race and second in the 200-meter contest. Melvin Sheppard placed second in the 800-meter run.

74. Allen Guttmann, *The Games Must Go On: Avery Brundage and the Olympic Movement* (New York: Columbia University Press, 1984), 27.

75. "The Amateur," 293–94.

76. "Thorpe's Disqualification," *The Literary Digest* 46 (Feb. 8, 1913): 301–4.

77. "The Amateur," 293–95.

78. "Amateur Athletics: A Poll of the Press," *The Outlook* 103 (Feb. 15, 1913): 344.

79. Will Irwin, "The Problem of the 'Semi-Pro,'" *Collier's* 50 (Mar. 1, 1913): 20.

80. "Amateur Athletics," 344–45.

81. "Thorpe's Disqualification," 302.

82. "Amateur Athletics," 345.

83. "Snobbery of Sport," *The Independent* 74 (Feb. 16, 1913): 277–78.

84. "Amateur Athletics," 346.

85. "The Amateur," 293.

86. "Thorpe's Disqualification," 305–6.

87. "Amateur Athletics," 346.

88. "Thorpe's Disqualification," 305.

89. "Amateur Athletics," 346.

90. "Thorpe's Disqualification," 301.

91. Dunne, "Dooley on Supremacy of the English in Athletics," 9.

92. Henry F. May, *The End of American Innocence* (New York: Knopf, 1959); Christopher Lasch, *The New Radicalism in America, 1889–1963: The Intellectual as a Social Type* (New York: Vintage, 1965).

93. Sullivan, *The Olympic Games*, 101.

94. Crone quoted in Elwood S. Brown, "Athletics in the Philippine Islands and the Far Eastern Olympic Games," *American Physical Education Review* 18 (Oct. 1913): 479–82.

95. Sullivan, *The Olympic Games*, 246.

96. Edwards, "Col. Thompson Praises Athletes," sec. 5, p. 10.

97. Ibid.

98. "Sees 1916 Olympic Triumph," *New York Times*, Aug. 3, 1912, p. 4.

99. Bartow Weeks suggested the creation of a permanent American Olympic Association with a $5 membership fee to fund future teams. Sullivan believed that thousands of Americans "would gladly enroll in such an organization for the furtherance of the Olympic Idea" (Sullivan, *The Olympic Games*, 245).

100. "Sees 1916 Olympic Triumph," 4.

101. Mack Whelan, "How Europe Is Learning to Play the Game," *Outing* 63 (Jan. 1914): 485–86.

102. Irwin, *The Making of a Reporter*, 180.

Chapter 8: The Idea of a Sporting Republic

1. "The Olympic Games at Stockholm," *Current Literature* 53 (July 1912): 15.

2. James Edward Sullivan, ed., *The Olympic Games: Stockholm, 1912*, Spalding "Red Cover" Series of Athletic Handbooks No. 17R (New York: American Sports, 1912), 233–34.

3. Rick Telander, *Heaven Is a Playground* (New York: Simon and Shuster, 1976).

4. H. G. Bissinger, *Friday Night Lights: A Town, a Team, and a Dream* (Reading, Mass.: Addison-Wesley, 1990).

5. Theodore Roosevelt, "The Strenuous Life," a speech before the Hamilton Club, Chicago, Apr. 10, 1899, in *The Works of Theodore Roosevelt*, 24 vols., ed. Hermann Hagerdorn, vol. 13, *American Ideals, The Strenuous Life, Realizable Ideals* (New York: Scribner's, 1926), 331.

6. "Sport: Trials & Tryouts," *Time*, July 20, 1936, p. 52.

7. "Mr. Roosevelt and the Athletes," *New York Times*, Sept. 2, 1908, p. 6.

8. "The President's Ideas about Sports," *Ladies Home Journal* 23 (Aug. 1906): 17.

9. Gustavus T. Kirby, "The Recreation Movement; Its Possibilities and Limitations," *The Playground* 5 (Oct. 1911): 217; G. W. Harris, "The Playground City," *The American Review of Reviews* 32 (Nov. 5, 1905): 574–80.

10. Caspar Whitney, "The Sportsman's View-Point," *Outing* 45 (Jan. 1905): 493.

11. William Allen White, "Taft, A Hewer of Wood," *American Magazine* 66 (May 1908): 19–32.

12. Ralph D. Paine, "Taft at Yale," *Outing* 53 (Nov. 1908): 135–50.

13. Reinhold Niebuhr, *The Children of Light and the Children of Darkness: A Vindication of Democracy and a Critique of Its Traditional Defense* (New York: Scribner's, 1944); see also Hannah Arendt's chapter entitled "The Political Emancipation of the Bourgeoisie" in *The Origins of Totalitarianism* (New York: Harcourt, Brace and World, 1966), 123–57.

14. Woodrow Wilson, "The Social Center," *Bulletin of the University of Wisconsin Extension Division,* no. 470 (1911): 3–15.

15. Charles Beard, *An Economic Interpretation of the Constitution of the United States* (New York: Macmillan, 1913).

16. Ray Stannard Baker, *Woodrow Wilson: Life and Letters,* 6 vols. (New York: Scribner's, 1946), 1:305–6.

17. Woodrow Wilson, *The New Freedom: A Call for the Emancipation of the Generous Energies of a People,* comp. William Bayard Hale (New York: Doubleday, Page, 1914), 170.

18. Owen Wister, *The Virginian* (New York: Grosset and Dunlap, 1904), 147; Edward A. Ross, *Social Control: A Survey of the Foundations of Order* (New York: Macmillan, 1916), 34–35.

19. Wilson, *The New Freedom,* 45, 105–6, 114, 131, 153.

20. James T. Kloppenberg, *Uncertain Victory: Social Democracy and Progressivism in European and American Thought, 1877–1920* (New York: Oxford University Press, 1986), 298–300.

21. Ross, *Social Control.*

22. George E. Howard, "Social Psychology of the Spectator," *The American Journal of Sociology* 18 (July 1912): 47.

23. G. Stanley Hall, *Life and Confessions of a Psychologist* (New York: D. Appleton, 1923); Luther Halsey Gulick, *A Philosophy of Play,* foreword by Joseph Lee (New York: Scribner's, 1920; Joseph Lee, *Play and Education* (New York: Macmillan, 1915); Dorothy Ross, *G. Stanley Hall: The Psychologist as Prophet* (Chicago: University of Chicago Press, 1972).

24. Henry S. Curtis, "The Neighborhood Center," *The American City* 7 (July 1912): 14–17 and (Aug. 1912): 133–37; idem, "The Need of a Comprehensive Playground Plan," *The American City* 5 (Dec. 1911): 338–40.

25. Everett B. Mero, "How Public Gymnasiums and Baths Help to Make Good Citizens," *The American City* 1 (Oct. 1909): 73.

26. Jacob Riis, "The Old Order Changeth," *The Playground* 8 (Mar. 1915): 415–17.

27. William James, "The Energies of Men," in *Essays on Faith and Morals,* ed. Ralph Barton Perry (New York: Longmans, Green, 1947), 216–37.

28. "In any game that fascinates, wrote Royce, "one loves victory and shuns defeat, and yet as a loyal supporter of the game scorns anything that makes victory certain in advance; thus a lover of fair play preferring to risk the defeat that he all the while shuns, and partly thwarting the very love of victory that from moment to moment fires his hopes" (Josiah Royce, "The Problem of Evil," as cited in David Hollinger and Charles Capper, eds., *The American Intellectual Tradition,* 2 vols. [New York: Oxford University Press, 1989], 2:75).

29. "Play tends to reproduce and affirm the crudities, as well as the excellencies, of surrounding adult life," wrote Dewey in his typically obtuse manner. "It is the business of the school to set up an environment in which play and work shall be conducted with reference to facilitating desirable mental and moral growth," he continued. "It is not enough just to introduce plays and games, hand work and manual exercises. Everything depends up the way in they are employed" (*Democracy and Education: An Introduction to the Philosophy of Education* [New York: Macmillan, 1916], 230). See also the chapter entitled "Play," in John and Evelyn Dewey, *Schools of To-Morrow* (New York: Dutton, 1915), 103–31.

30. Simon Nelson Patten, *Product and Climax* (New York: B. W. Huebsch, 1909); "Amusement as a Factor in Man's Spiritual Uplift," *Current Literature* 47 (Aug. 1909): 185–88; Donald Mrozek, *Sport and American Mentality, 1880–1910* (Knoxville: University of Tennessee Press, 1983), 28–66.

31. Richard T. Ely, *Studies in the Evolution of Industrial Society* (New York: Macmillan, 1903), 147; idem, *Outline of Economics,* 5th rev. ed. (New York: Macmillan, 1931).

32. "The Attitude of the Press toward Neighborhood Play Centers," *The Playground* 9 (Sept. 1915): 189–97.

33. Richard Henry Edwards, *Popular Amusements* (New York: Arno, 1976 [1915]); Julia Schoenfeld, "Commercial Recreation Legislation," *The Playground* 7 (Mar. 1914): 461–81.

34. "Self-Government in Public Recreation," *The Survey* 30 (Aug. 23, 1913): 638–39.

35. William Harmon, "The Commercial Value of Playgrounds," *The Survey* 23 (Dec. 11, 1909): 359–61.

36. Beulah Kennard, "Pittsburgh's Playgrounds," *The Survey* 22 (May 11, 1909): 184–96.

37. Edwards, *Popular Amusements;* Howard S. Braucher, "The Reason Why," *The Playground* 7 (July 1913): 160–63.

38. Charles Frederick Weller, "What Is Happening in America?" *The Playground* 7 (June 1913): 106.

39. Arthur B. Reeve, "What America Spends for Sport," *Outing* 57 (Dec. 1910): 300–308.

40. Starting in 1876, with an $800 capital investment garnered from their mother, the Spalding brothers began business. In 1892 their athletic "trust" incorporated in New Jersey, capitalized at $4 million; see Peter Levine, *A. G. Spalding and the Rise of Baseball* (New York: Oxford University Press, 1985), 71–81.

41. W. M. Dean Pulvermacher, ed., *Official Handbook of the Public School Athletic League,* Spalding's Athletic Library No. 313 (New York: American Sports, 1910), unnumbered advertising section at the end.

42. Ibid.; James Edward Sullivan, *The Olympic Games at Athens, 1906,* Spalding's Athletic Library No. 275 (New York: American Sports, 1906), unnumbered advertising section at the end.

43. Mark Dyreson, "The Emergence of Consumer Culture and the Transformation of Physical Culture: American Sport in the 1920s," *Journal of Sport History* 16 (Winter 1989): 261–81.

44. Samuel P. Hays, *Conservation and the Gospel of Efficiency: The Progressive Conservation Movement, 1880–1920* (Cambridge, Mass.: Harvard University Press, 1959).

45. William James, "The Moral Equivalent of War," in *William James: The Essential Writings,* ed. Bruce C. Wilshire (Albany: State University of New York Press, 1984), 349–61. "The Moral Equivalent of War" had quite a run in the popular press, appearing in *McClure's* 35 (Aug. 1910): 463–68 and in *Popular Science Monthly* 77 (Oct. 1910): 400–410.

46. Mrozek, *Sport and American Mentality, 1880–1910.*

47. James T. Kloppenberg, *Uncertain Victory: Social Democracy and Progressivism in European and American Thought, 1870–1920* (New York: Oxford University Press, 1989).

48. Paul A. Carter, *Revolt against Destiny: An Intellectual History of the United States* (New York: Columbia University Press, 1989).

49. James, "The Moral Equivalent of War," 359.

50. "Athletics and Morals," *The Atlantic Monthly* 113 (Feb. 1914): 147.

51. William James, *The Will to Believe and Other Essays* (New York: Dover, 1956).

52. Caspar Whitney, "Outdoor Sports—What They Are Doing for Us," *The Independent* 52 (June 7, 1900); R. P. Davis, "Athletics at the U.S. Military Academy," *Outing* 39 (Jan. 1902): 436–41; A. R. Chafee, "Athletics in the Army," *Outing* 43 (Mar. 1904): 707; E. L. Butts, "Soldierly Bearing, Health and Athletics," *Outing* 43 (Mar. 1904): 707–11; F. G. Aflalo, "Statesmen and Sportsmen," *The Living Age* 241 (June 11, 1904): 667–79; D. A. Willey, "The Spirit of Sport in the Army," *Harper's Weekly* 50 (Aug. 1906): 1100–1101; Palmer E. Pierce, "Athletics in the Army," *Collier's* 46 (May 11, 1911): 16; George E. Johnson, "Play as a Moral Equivalent of War," *The Playground* 6 (July 1912): 111–23.

53. Henry S. Curtis, *Education through Play* (New York: Macmillan, 1915).

54. Howard, "Social Psychology of the Spectator," 47.

55. Dorothy Bocker, "Social Cleavage and the Playground," *The Playground* 9 (May 1915): 87–90.

56. Howard Braucher, "How to Aid the Cause of Public Recreation," *The American City* 8 (Apr. 1913): 367–71.

57. George L. McNutt, "Chicago's Ten-Million Dollar Experiment in Social Redemption," *The Independent* 57 (Sept. 1904): 612–17.

58. "The Higher Athletics," *The Nation* 85 (Dec. 5, 1907): 510.

59. Ely, *Outlines of Economics,* 14.

Chapter 9: The Decline of the Sporting Republic

1. Edward J. Ward, "America's Call to Colors," *The Playground* 8 (Nov. 1914): 287.

2. Randolph Bourne, "The War and the Intellectuals," *The Seven Arts* 2 (June 1917): 133.

3. Georges Lechartier, "Americans and Sport," *The Living Age* 310 (Sept. 10, 1921): 658.

4. "Athletics and the War," *The Outlook* 118 (Apr. 3, 1918): 523.

5. "Athletics and War," *The Outlook* 115 (Feb. 28, 1917): 350.

6. John Morton Blum, *Woodrow Wilson and the Politics of Morality* (Boston: Little, Brown, 1956).

7. Katherine Mayo, "Fair Play for the World," *The Outlook* 129 (Dec. 21, 1921): 650.

8. *The Inter-Allied Games of 1919* (New York: Games Committee, 1919), 46.

9. O. B. Hardison, *Disappearing through the Skylight: Culture and Technology in the Twentieth Century* (New York: Penguin, 1989), xii–xiii.

10. William James, "The Moral Equivalent of War," in *William James: The Essential Writings,* ed. Bruce C. Wilshire (Albany: State University of New York Press, 1984), 361.

11. James, "The Gospel of Relaxation," in *Essays on Faith and Morals,* ed. Ralph Barton Perry (New York: Longmans, Green, 1947), 243.

12. William G. Shepherd, "Jim Sullivan's Dope," *Everybody's Magazine* 39 (Nov. 1918): 48–50.

13. *Spalding's Official Athletic Almanac, 1919* (New York: American Sports, 1919), 15.

14. Baron Pierre de Coubertin, "The Seventh Olympic Games," in American Olympic Committee, *Report of the American Olympic Committee: Seventh Olympic Games* (Greenwich, Conn.: Conde Nast, 1920), 58.

15. John Lucas, "American Preparations for the First Post World War Olympic Games, 1919–1920," *Journal of Sport History,* 10 (Summer 1983): 30–32.

16. "Memories of the Last Olympic Games," *The Literary Digest* 65 (July 3, 1920): 94–95.

17. "Tewanima the Indian Competitor in the Marathon Leads the Fourth of July War Dance," *New York Times,* July 26, 1908, Sunday picture sec., p. 7.

Bibliographic Essay

The history of the United States from 1877 to 1919 has received extensive attention from scholars. Histories detailing most aspects of American civilization—ideas, politics, social structures, popular culture, race, economics, gender, and so on—illuminate the period. Since the 1970s historians have produced numerous studies of the republican tradition in American, European, and global contexts. During that same period the number of solid academic studies of the history of American sport has grown at exponential rates.

The Olympic Games and the Role of Sport in Modern Culture

Allen Guttmann, *The Olympics: A History of the Modern Games* (Urbana: University of Illinois Press, 1992), provides a good survey of the modern Olympics. Another important overview is John Lucas, *The Modern Olympic Games* (New York: A. S. Barnes, 1980). William Oscar Johnson, *All That Glitters Is Not Gold: The Olympic Games* (New York: Putnam's, 1972), is an entertaining and insightful source. John J. MacAloon, "Olympic Games and the Theory of Spectacle in Modern Societies," in *Rite, Drama, Festival, Spectacle: Rehearsals toward a Theory of Cultural Performance,* ed. John MacAloon (Philadelphia: Institute for the Study of Human Issues, 1984), 241–80, offers important clues into the meaning of the Olympics. Peter J. Graham and Horst Ueberhorst, eds., *The Modern Olympics* (West Point, N.Y.: Leisure, 1976); and Jeffery O. Segrave and Donald Chu, eds., *The Olympic Games in Transition* (Champaign, Ill.: Human Kinetics, 1988), contribute critical essays. John Hoberman produces a fascinating treatise on the Olympic movement in *The Olympic Crisis: Sport, Politics and the Moral Order* (New Rochelle, N.Y.: Aristide D. Caratzas, 1986).

On the history of the Olympics from 1896 to 1912, important sources include Allen Guttmann, *The Games Must Go On: Avery Brundage and the Olympic Movement* (New York: Columbia University Press, 1984); and Richard Mandell, *The First Modern Olympics* (Berkeley: University of California Press, 1976). Robert K. Barney chronicles the twists and turns of the battles over the 1904 Olympics in "Born from Dilemma: America Awakens to the Modern Olympic Games, 1901–1903," *Olympika* 1 (1992): 92–135.

John MacAloon's *This Great Symbol: Pierre de Coubertin and the Origins of the Modern Olympic Games* (Chicago: University of Chicago Press, 1981) is the best inquiry into the origins of the modern Olympics and provides a thorough biography of its founder. See also Horst Ueberhorst, "Return to Olympia and the Rebirth of the Games," and John Lucas, "The Influence of Anglo-American Sport on Pierre de Coubertin—Modern Olympic Games Founder," both in Graham and Ueberhorst, eds., *The Modern Olympics*. John Lucas details the return to the Olympics after World War I in "American Preparations for the First Post World War Olympic Games, 1919–1920," *Journal of Sport History* 10 (Summer 1983): 30–32. Scholarly articles on the Olympics appear frequently in *The Journal of Sport History, Olympika, The International Journal of Sport History,* and *The Canadian Journal of Sport History.*

Allen Guttmann's *Games and Empires: Modern Sports and Cultural Imperialism* (New York: Columbia University Press, 1994) traces the role of the Olympics and other athletic events as agents in the imperial drive of Western civilization. Guttmann's study provides a global context for understanding the power of sport in modern cultures. *Games and Empires* presents readers with a thought-provoking study of the diffusion of sporting practices throughout the world. It also explores the consequences of that diffusion.

Crucial works addressing the role of sport in culture theory include Johan Huizinga, *Homo Ludens* (Boston: Beacon, 1938); John M. Hoberman, *Sport and Political Ideology* (Austin: University of Texas Press, 1984); Lewis Mumford, "Sport and the 'Bitch Goddess,'" in *Technics and Civilization* (New York: Harcourt Brace Jovanovich, 1934), 303–7; José Ortega y Gasset, "The Sportive Origin of the State," in *Toward a Philosophy of History* (New York: Norton, 1941); David Sansone, *Greek Athletics and the Genesis of Sport* (Berkeley: University of California Press, 1988); and Stephen Hardy, "Entrepreneurs, Structures, and the Sportgeist: Old Tensions in a Modern Industry," in *Essays in Sport History and Sport Mythology,* ed. Donald G. Kyle and Gary D. Stark (College Station: Texas A&M University Press, 1990), 45–82. Addressing the conceptual power of sport are two thoughtful essays: Theodore Roszak, "Forbidden Games," in *Sport in the Socio-Cultural Process,* ed. M. Marie Hart (Dubuque, Iowa: W. C. Brown, 1972), 91–104; and Richard Lipsky, "Toward a Theory of American Sports Symbolism," in *Games and Sports in Cultural Context,* ed. Janet C. Harris and Roberta J. Park (Champaign, Ill.: Human Kinetics, 1983). Kendall Blanchard's "Basketball and Culture-Change Process: The Rimrock Navajo Case," *Council on Anthropology and Education Quarterly* 5 (1974): 8–13, presents a fascinating explanation of the ways in which cultures use sport to define, protect, and transform themselves.

Histories of American Sport

Scholarly approaches to sport have become increasingly sophisticated in the past twenty-five years. Elliot Gorn and Warren Goldstein's outstanding *Brief History of American Sports* (New York: Hill and Wang, 1993) assesses the major themes and trends in American sport history. Other first-rate surveys include Benjamin G. Rader, *American Sports:*

From the Age of Folk Games to the Age of Spectators (Englewood Cliffs, N.J.: Prentice-Hall, 1983); and William J. Baker, *Sports in the Western World* (Totowa, N.J.: Rowman and Littlefield, 1982).

The genesis of modern sport in the United States between the 1820s and 1920s has recently been explored using the "modernization" paradigm. Allen Guttmann's work on these issues has shaped American sport history. Guttmann proposes a sophisticated Weberian modernization scheme in *From Ritual to Record: The Nature of Modern Sport* (New York: Columbia University Press, 1978). He amplifies his theoretical arguments and applies them directly to the history of American sport in *A Whole New Ball Game: An Interpretation of Modern Sport* (Chapel Hill: University of North Carolina Press, 1988).

The modernization paradigm has dominated recent approaches to American sport. In *A Sporting Time: New York City and the Rise of Modern Athletics, 1820–1870* (Urbana: University of Illinois Press, 1986), Melvin Adelman uses modernization theory to explain the structures of modern sport in New York City. Adleman's pioneering work successfully pushed back the origin of modern sport into the 1820s. In "The Promise of Sport in Antebellum America," *Journal of American Culture* 2 (Winter 1980): 623–34, Peter Levine links sport to antebellum reform campaigns aimed at modernizing American society. Studies of the development of particular modern sports include Warren Goldstein, *Playing for Keeps: A History of Early Baseball* (Ithaca, N.Y.: Cornell University Press, 1989); and George B. Kirsch, *The Creation of American Team Sports: Baseball and Cricket, 1838–1872* (Urbana: University of Illinois Press, 1979).

A number of excellent monographs and journal articles explore the patterns of American sport in the late nineteenth and early twentieth centuries. In "The Quest for Subcommunities and the Rise of American Sport," *American Quarterly* 29 (Fall 1977): 355–69, Benjamin Rader details the ways in which sport was used to delineate class, status, and ethnic boundaries. Two outstanding books chart the class dimensions that shaped the development of urban sport recreation: Stephen Hardy, *How Boston Played: Sport, Recreation and Community, 1865–1915* (Boston: Northeastern University Press, 1982); and Roy Rosenzweig, *Eight Hours for What We Will: Workers and Leisure in an Industrial City, 1870–1920* (Cambridge: Cambridge University Press, 1983).

Two important books explore American attitudes toward sport from very different angles. Elliot J. Gorn, *The Manly Art: Bare-Knuckle Prize Fighting in America* (Ithaca, N.Y.: Cornell University Press, 1986), details the importance of violent rituals celebrating manliness in working-class culture. Peter Levine's *A. G. Spalding and the Rise of Baseball* (New York: Oxford University Press, 1985) recounts the evolution of baseball as a consumer product aimed at middle-class culture. Steven Riess examines the connections between sport and Progressivism in *Touching Base: Professional Baseball and American Culture in the Progressive Era* (Westport, Conn.: Greenwood, 1980). He also connects sport to urban history in *City Games: The Evolution of American Urban Society and the Rise of Sports* (Urbana: University of Illinois Press, 1989).

S. W. Pope's recent *Patriotic Pastimes: Sporting Traditions in the American Imagination, 1876–1926* (New York: Oxford University Press, 1997) is a major new work that artfully analyzes the role of sport in American culture. The finest study of sport and American thought in the Progressive Era is Donald Mrozek, *Sport and American Mentality, 1880–1910* (Knoxville: University of Tennessee Press, 1983). Other valuable works that investigate the role of sport in Gilded Age and Progressive Era American cultures include Steven Pope, "Negotiating the 'Folk Highway' of the Nation: Sport, Public Culture and American Identity, 1870–1940," *Journal of Social History* 27 (1993): 183–85; Don S. Kirschner, "The Perils of Pleasure: Commercial Recreation, Social Disorder and Moral Reform in the Progressive Era," *American Studies* 21 (Fall 1980): 27–42; Michael Isenberg, *John L. Sullivan and His America* (Urbana: University of Illinois Press, 1988); and Dominick Cavallo, *Muscles and Morals: Organized Playgrounds and Urban Reform, 1880–1920* (Philadelphia: University of Pennsylvania Press, 1981).

The press played a crucial role in making sport into a cultural institution. In *Sports in the Western World* William J. Baker perceptively stresses the importance of the media in the creation of modern sporting culture. Melvin Adelman details the power of American journalists in shaping attitudes toward sport in his chapter "The Press and the Ideology of Modern Sport," in *A Sporting Time*. A very fine recent work on the issue, Michael Oriard's *Reading Football: How the Popular Press Created an American Spectacle* (Chapel Hill: University of North Carolina Press, 1993), should be read by everyone interested in American sport. Allen Guttmann has written an intriguing history of public responses to athletic spectacles entitled *Sports Spectators* (New York: Columbia University Press, 1986).

Several scholars have noted the importance of new technologies in shaping sport. A good survey of the impact of industrial technology on American sport can be found in Richard Mandell's chapter entitled "American Sport to the 1920s," in *Sport: A Cultural History* (New York: Columbia University Press, 1984). Other helpful sources include John Rickard Betts, "The Technological Revolution and the Rise of Sports, 1850–1900," *Mississippi Valley Historical Review* 40 (Sept. 1953): 231–56; and Benjamin Rader, *American Sports*.

Gender issues and definitions of masculine and feminine are embedded in attitudes about sport. Allen Guttmann stresses that culture rather than biology accounts for most, if not all, of the differences between men's and women's sports in his excellent survey *Women's Sports: A History* (New York: Columbia University Press, 1991). Important works on gender, physical culture, and sport include J. A. Mangan and Roberta Park, eds., *From "Fair Sex" to Feminism: Sport and the Socialization of Women in Industrial and Post-Industrial Eras* (London: Frank Cass, 1987); Roberta Park, "Physiology and Anatomy Are Destiny!?" *Journal of Sport History* 18 (Spring 1991): 31–63; idem, "Physiologists, Physicians and Physical Educators: Nineteenth Century Biology and Exercise—Hygienic and Educative," *Journal of Sport History* 14 (Spring 1987): 28–60; Gwendolyn Captain, "Enter Ladies and Gentlemen of Color: Gender, Sport, and the Ideal of African American Manhood and Womanhood during the Late Nineteenth and Early Twentieth Centuries," *Journal of Sport History* (Spring 1991): 81–102; and Donald Mrozek, *Sport and American Mentality*. Other provocative studies of sport and gender include J. A. Mangan and James Walvin, eds., *Manliness and Morality: Middle-Class Masculinity in Britain and America, 1800–1940* (New York: St. Martin's, 1987); Cynthia Eagle Russett, *Sexual Science: The*

Victorian Construction of Womanhood (Cambridge, Mass.: Harvard University Press, 1989); and Patricia Vertinsky, *The Eternally Wounded Woman: Women, Doctors and Exercise in the Late Nineteenth Century* (Manchester: Manchester University Press, 1990).

The racial dimensions of the American sporting experience have been explored in most of the major surveys of sport in the United States, such as Gorn and Goldstein's *Brief History of American Sports* and Rader's *American Sports*. Allen Guttmann's chapter "Black Athletes" in *A Whole New Ball Game* explores the contradictions between nationalism and racism fostered by American sporting practices. For insightful commentary on the complexities of race and athletic life in the United States, see, in particular, Randy Roberts, *Papa Jack: Jack Johnson and the Era of White Hopes* (New York: Free Press, 1983); William J. Baker, *Jesse Owens: An American Life* (New York: Free Press, 1986); and Jules Tygiel *Baseball's Great Experiment* (New York: Oxford University Press, 1983).

American Thought and Culture, 1877–1919

The United States underwent tremendous social, economic, and political changes between 1877 and 1919. A voluminous literature exists on the crises of the late nineteenth-century American society and programs for cultural regeneration. Especially helpful are two general surveys, Robert Wiebe's classic synthesis *The Search for Order, 1877–1920* (New York: Hill and Wang, 1967) and Ray Ginger's *Age of Excess: The United States from 1877–1919*, 2d ed. (Prospect Heights, Ill.: Waveland, 1975).

A variety of approaches have been applied to late nineteenth- and early twentieth-century American thought. Morton White, *The Revolt against Formalism* (New York: Oxford University Press, 1976), illuminates the pragmatists' assaults on tradition by focusing on major figures such as William James, John Dewey, and Oliver Wendell Holmes Jr. David Noble, in *The Paradox of Progressive Thought* (Minneapolis: University of Minnesota Press, 1958) and *The Progressive Mind* (Chicago: Rand McNally, 1970), charts the broader popular trends of American thought as well as the ruminations of the "thinking classes." Glenn C. Altschuler, *Race, Ethnicity, and Class in American Social Thought, 1865–1914* (Arlington Heights, Ill.: Harlan Davidson, 1982), focuses on the specific categories of race and class.

For the impact of this discourse on broader patterns of American thought, see the appropriate sections in Paul A. Carter, *Revolt against Destiny: An Intellectual History of the United States* (New York: Columbia University Press, 1989); and Ralph Henry Gabriel, *The Course of American Democratic Thought*, 2d ed. (New York: Ronald, 1956).

Jean Quandt, *From the Small Town to the Great Community: The Social Thought of Progressive Intellectuals* (New Brunswick, N.J.: Rutgers University Press, 1970), traces the powerful desire among progressive intellectuals for consensus and community. In *Ministers of Reform: The Progressives' Achievement in American Civilization* (Urbana: University of Illinois Press, 1984), Robert Crunden offers a brilliant explanation of the progressive worldview. Crunden claims that American thinkers sought to find a way to preserve traditional cultural norms while embracing innovative strategies.

The changes in patterns of thought occasioned by the development of corporate capitalism have been the subject of intense scrutiny. On the historical development of a "culture of professionalism," see Burton J. Bledstein, *The Culture of Professionalism: The Middle Class and the Development of Higher Education in America* (New York: Norton, 1976). Alan Trachtenberg's provocative *Incorporation of America: Culture and Society in the Gilded Age* (New York: Hill and Wang, 1982) details the impact of modernism on American psyches and society. T. J. Jackson Lears thinks that reluctant embraces of modernism shaped American thought and culture, which he charts in *No Place of Grace: Antimodernism and the Transformation of American Culture, 1880–1920* (New York: Pantheon, 1981). George Cotkin concurs in *Reluctant Modernism: American Thought and Culture, 1880–1900* (New York: Twayne, 1992).

Lears and Cotkin raise important questions about the meaning of "Progressivism" for American thinkers that other historians have engaged. The most insightful study of the building of a *via media* between traditional and modern societies is James T. Kloppenberg's *Uncertain Victory: Social Democracy and Progressivism in European and American Thought, 1870–1920* (New York: Oxford University Press, 1989). Kloppenberg ties "progressive" thought to the construction of modernity.

Peter Filene, "An Obituary for 'The Progressive Movement,'" *American Quarterly* 22 (Spring 1970): 20–34, consigns Progressivism to the boneyard of outmoded historical labels. He argues that the progressive movement lacked intellectual and political coherency. Still, perhaps because early twentieth-century thinkers and politicians described themselves as progressives, the concept has clung to life in historical scholarship. Progressivism is a useful label for describing the thought and discourse of certain reformers, even if it is not an accurate label for describing a singular political movement. See Robert M. Crunden, *Ministers of Reform;* and Daniel T. Rodgers, "In Search of Progressivism," *Reviews in American History* 10 (December 1982): 113–32.

The progressives sought to create a vital and vigorous national culture. The term *culture,* popularized in intellectual discourse beginning in the 1870s, provided a broad explanatory term for describing the cognitively imposed "order" that provided coherency in human social systems. Synonymous with the notion of virtue in older republican theorizing, the idea of culture came to signify the sense of civic duty and national identity transcending any class, ethnic, or special interest that many American political thinkers considered to be the absolutely crucial component in the modern state. The "politics of culture" is explored in Lewis Perry, *Intellectual Life in America* (New York: Franklin Watts, 1984). The drive to construct a nationalized culture is hinted at in many of the works concerned with the American thought, particularly in Lears's *No Place of Grace,* Trachtenberg's *Incorporation of America,* Altschuler's *Race, Ethnicity, and Class in American Thought,* Kloppenberg's *Uncertain Victory,* and Crunden's *Ministers of Reform.*

H. Wayne Morgan, in *Unity and Culture: The United States, 1877–1900* (Baltimore: Penguin, 1971), offers a provocative essay on the effort to construct a national style in high culture. Less work has been done on the "search for order" in mass culture. One can gain a strong appreciation for the pervasiveness of the bourgeois effort to inculcate its standards from the writings of critics of middle-class efforts at constructing some sort of hegemony. See Randolph Bourne's provocative article "The Puritan's Will to

Power," *The Seven Arts* 1 (Apr. 1917): 631–37. Important theoretical models are developed in Eric Hobsbawm and Terence Ranger, eds., *The Invention of Tradition* (New York: Cambridge University Press, 1983). For progressive blueprints on constructing a national culture, see Herbert Croly, *The Promise of American Life* (New York: Macmillan, 1909); Walter Lippmann, *A Preface to Politics* (New York: Macmillan, 1914); and Walter E. Weyl, *The New Democracy: An Essay on Certain Political and Economic Tendencies in the United States* (New York: Macmillan, 1912).

Theodore Roosevelt occupies a crucial place in the invention of the sporting republic. Perhaps more than any other person he popularized the fusion of sport and politics. Howard Mumford Jones identifies Roosevelt as the strenuous leader of the middle-class rise to power in *The Age of Energy: The Varieties of American Experience, 1865–1915* (New York: Viking, 1971). Other insightful sources on Roosevelt's strenuous politics include John Milton Cooper Jr., *The Warrior and the Priest: Theodore Roosevelt and Woodrow Wilson* (Cambridge, Mass.: Harvard University Press, 1983); John M. Blum, *The Republican Roosevelt* (Cambridge, Mass.: Harvard University Press, 1954); George E. Mowry, *Theodore Roosevelt and the Birth of Modern America* (New York: Harper and Row, 1958); and David McCullough, *Mornings on Horseback* (New York: Simon and Schuster, 1981). Donald Mrozek's *Sport and American Mentality* offers the best explanations of Roosevelt's ideas about sport and the rejuvenation of American civilization. Mrozek argues persuasively that in a culture profoundly disturbed by the artificiality of modern life, many Americans sought individual regeneration through sport. His work adds important insights to the understanding of fin de siècle American thought and culture.

Many turn-of-the-century thinkers became enamored with the idea of an athletic technology. One of the most interesting explanations of the role of technology in modern thought and culture can be found in O. B. Hardison Jr.'s *Disappearing through the Skylight: Culture and Technology in the Twentieth Century* (New York: Penguin, 1989). Another useful source is Thomas P. Hughes, *American Genesis: A Century of Invention and Technological Enthusiasm, 1870–1970* (New York: Viking, 1989). Two important studies, Leo Marx, *The Machine and the Garden: Technology and the Pastoral Ideal in America* (New York: Oxford University Press, 1964); and John Kasson, *Civilizing the Machine: Technology and Republican Values in America, 1877–1900* (New York: Grossman, 1976), investigate the relationship between technological processes and republican political philosophy.

American Republicanism and Theories of Culture

Clifford Geertz's ruminations on the philosophy and methodology of cultural interpretation continue to spur new discoveries; see his *Local Knowledge: Further Essays in Interpretive Anthropology* (New York: Basic, 1984) and *The Interpretation of Cultures* (New York: Basic, 1973). His "Deep Play: Notes on a Balinese Cockfight," in *The Interpretation of Cultures,* has greatly influenced recent scholarship on sport.

Cultural practices such as sports reveal crucial outlines of civic identity and public consciousness. To paraphrase the American historian of ideas David Hollinger, the behavior of sportswriters, athletes, fans, politicians, culture critics, and public moralists is at least partly to be understood in terms of ideas common to the publics of which they were members. Hollinger proposes a model of intellectual and cultural history organized around "communities of discourse" and defines intellectuals not as professional thinkers but as any population that uses symbols, values, beliefs, and concepts to organize reality—in short, all human beings. See David Hollinger, *In the American Province: Studies in the History and Historiography of Ideas* (Baltimore: Johns Hopkins University Press, 1989).

In the United States between 1877 and 1919, sport served a variety of different communities in discourses concerning the nature and practice of republican political culture. Debates over the meanings of liberal and republican ideas continue to rage in American historiography. Proponents of each school seek to champion liberalism or republicanism as the most important ingredient in American political thought. Other scholars, such as James T. Kloppenberg, insist that the relationship between liberalism and republicanism is far more complex and syncretic than is allowed by the story of newer liberal concepts supplanting older republican ideas at some vague moment after the creation of the United States. Kloppenberg details the efforts of progressive intellectuals to "resurrect the common good" in *Uncertain Victory*. On the enduring power of republicanism in shaping American thought, see Robert Kelley, "Ideology and Political Culture from Jefferson to Nixon," *American Historical Review* 80 (June 1977): 531–62; Robert Shalhope, "Toward a Republican Synthesis: The Emergence of an Understanding of Republicanism in American Historiography," *William and Mary Quarterly*, 3d ser., 29 (Jan. 1972): 49–80; and Paul A. Carter, *Revolt against Destiny*. Daniel T. Rodgers, "Republicanism: The Career of a Concept," *Journal of American History* 79 (June 1992): 11–38, critiques the republican schools of interpretation.

Index

Abbott, Margaret, 111

Academy, 138, 141

Acropolis, the, 56

Adams, John Henry, 115

Addams, Jane, 21, 109, 119, 122–23, 191. *See also* Progressivism; Settlement houses

Adelman, Melvin, 247–48

Adrian College (Michigan), 158

Affirmative action, 13

Aflalo, F. G., 111

African Americans: athletes, superiority of, 114; and basketball, 181; discrimination against, 93–95, 112–15, 177; disfranchised, 99–100; and integration through sport, 113–15, 188; Olympians of 1904, 95, 97–98, 112–13; Olympians of 1908, 101, 135; Olympians of 1912, 157–58, 160, 167–68, 177–78; political activists and sport, 1, 114–15, 188; and progressive reform, 123; and segregation in the sporting republic, 98, 112–15, 125, 177–78. *See also* Drew, Howard; Ethnicity; Poage, George; Racism; Taylor, J. B.

Africans: exhibited at Louisiana Purchase Exposition, 81; participating in Anthropology Days, 81–85; participating in Olympics of 1904, 82, 88–89

A. G. Spalding and Brothers, 79, 156, 192–93. *See also* Spalding, A. G.

Ainus, 81. *See also* Anthropology Days

Alcibiades, 37

Alexandra, queen of United Kingdom of Great Britain, 131

Allegheny College, 38–39

Altschuler, Glenn C., 249–50

Alverstone, Lord, 64

Amateur Athletic Union (AAU): connections to American Olympic Committee, 73–76, 80, 86, 90–92, 129–30, 135, 137, 143, 155–56; control of Olympic Games of 1904, 73–76, 80, 86, 90–92; control of Olympic team of 1900, 63; control of Olympic team of 1908, 135, 137, 143; control of Olympic team of 1912, 155–56; control of team for Panathenaic Games of 1906, 128–30; and the development of superior athletic equipment, 161; and leadership in the sporting republic, 21; and segregation in American sports, 177; and the Thorpe scandal, 171–74. *See also* American Olympic Committee

Amateurism, 39, 71, 141, 170–74

American Academy of Political and Social Science, 102, 122

American Bar Association, 113

American Expeditionary Force, 205

American Indians. *See* Native Americans

American League, 80

American Magazine, 149

American Olympic Committee: connection to A. G. Spalding and Brothers, 192; criticizes International Olympic Committee, 74, 131, 134, 152, 161; and Olympics of 1904, 73–74, 80; and Olympic team of 1900, 63; and Olympic team of 1908, 135, 137–39, 141–47, 151–53; and Olympic team of 1912, 155–57, 161, 165–66, 170, 176–79; organization and leadership of, 22, 40–41, 60–61, 155, 184, 204, 232–33 n. 2; and the Panathenaic Games of 1906, 128–32; responds to the Thorpe scandal, 171, 173; seeks to control Olympic movement, 152; supports permanent Olympic site in Athens, 133; U.S. presidents serve as honorary presidents of, 187. *See also* Am-

Spalding, J. Walter, 60, 155
Spalding's Official Athletic Almanac, 73, 205
Spalding trophy, 91
Spanish-American War, 70
Spectator, 143, 164
Sport: as the American civic language, 5, 7–8, 17–20, 31, 127, 194, 207; as a common language, origins of, 15; as a common language and Great Britain's effort to craft universal rules for athletics, 136; as a common language for debating political and social issues, 1–4, 199; as a common language for the Olympic movement, 34–35, 211 n. 27; as a common language for the progressive polity, 180–94; as a common language in the national media, 23–24; as a common language promoted by sporting republicans, 22; and the frontier thesis, 19, 26, 76–77; as invented tradition, 26–28, 214 n. 62; opposition to, 22, 37; and origins of modern athletics in United States, 22–23; as a technology for building nations, 5–6, 99, 122–24, 166, 173, 175; as a technology for constructing community, 2, 5, 17–18, 24–26, 29, 38, 121, 180–81; as a technology for designing modern civilizations, 2–4, 73, 119–20; as a technology for engineering a modern republic, 7, 16, 29–31; as a technology for implementing social reforms, 16, 27, 57–58, 78–79, 109, 119–22, 188–91, 199; as a technology for imposing American culture on the world, 70; as a technology for organizing human energy, 17–20, 145, 178–79, 187, 194, 202–3; as a technology for replacing war, 195–96, 199–201, 203; as a technology in modern cultures, 2–4, 17–20. *See also* Ancient Greek sport; Sporting republic; Strenuous life; War, moral equivalent of
Sporting clubs, 16, 20, 24, 90–91, 156
Sporting goods manufacturing and sales: and A. G. Spalding and Brothers empire, 21, 23, 79, 192–93; as big business, 4, 23, 103–4, 202
Sporting Life, 139
Sporting republic: African American intellectuals' interpretations of, 114–15; and alternative athletic ideologies, 103–5; and American political culture, 8–9, 14–16, 27, 98–99, 122, 126–27, 154–55, 180–87, 193–94, 196–99; as antidote to socialism, 29–30; and assimilation of immigrants, 115–26; and class, 30, 101–3; and commercialism, 190–93; and conflict between American ideals and social

realities, 206–7; decline of, 202–5; definitions of, 2–3, 7–8; demand for government funding and extension of, 196–97; and ethnicity, 115–26; eulogy for, 204–5; and gender, 105–12, 125; historical context for development of, 4; ideas about, 11, 17, 199, 203; and the inculcation of civic virtue, 15–16, 25–28, 100–105, 110, 120–24; as invented tradition, 26–28; inventors of, 20–22; limits on participation in, 100–101, 124–26; Mr. Dooley as voice of, 174–75; and national well-being, 8–10; and Olympic Games of 1896, 36, 50; and Olympic Games of 1900, 71; and Olympic Games of 1904, 80, 93; and Olympic Games of 1908, 135, 139, 151; and Olympic Games of 1912, 157–58, 160, 164–70, 174–79; and Olympic movement, 98, 180, 194; organization and popularization of, 22–26; and Panatheniac Games of 1906, 133–34; and Progressivism, 103–5, 185, 190–93; and segregation of African Americans, 112–15, 125; as symbolic of American ideals, 36, 50, 71, 93, 100–101, 124–26, 127, 157–58, 168, 174–79, 180, 196–98, 199–207; and Theodore Roosevelt as personification of, 28–30, 181–83, 207; and William Howard Taft as personification of, 183–85; and Woodrow Wilson as personification of, 185–87; and World War I, 199–202
Square Deal, 13
Stagg, Amos Alonzo, 65, 67, 74
Stark, Gary D., 246
St. Louis Globe-Democrat, 83, 86–87, 89, 90
St. Louis Post-Dispatch, 85, 91
St. Louis Republic, 76
St. Louis Star, 83
Strenuous life: and American nationalism, 158–59; and American Olympic victory, 163; and American political culture, 28–30, 99, 175, 193, 214 n. 72; as antidote to commercialism, 191; calls for commitment to, 167, 179; class, gender, and ethnicity as limiting participation in, 100–101; and gender, 109; *Outing* as chronicle of, 183; as preparation for World War I, 201–2; and the presidency, 181–87; and the sporting republic, 197; and westward expansion, 76–80; William James's version of, 194–96. *See also* Roosevelt, Theodore; Sporting republic
Strobino, Gaston, 232 n. 97
Strong, Josiah, 118
Suffolk Athletic Club (Boston), 40
Sullivan, James Edward: as assistant director

MARK DYRESON is an associate professor at Weber State University. He has published essays on American culture and sport in *The New American Sport History* (University of Illinois Press, 1997), the *Journal of Sport History,* the *International Journal of Sport History, Olympika,* and several other journals. He is currently working on a book on modern culture and sport in the 1920s, 1930s, and 1940s.

Books in the Series Sport and Society

Reprint Editions